# 500 Great Books for Teens

## Books by Anita Silvey

CHILDREN'S BOOKS AND THEIR CREATORS

THE ESSENTIAL GUIDE TO
CHILDREN'S BOOKS AND THEIR CREATORS

100 BEST BOOKS FOR CHILDREN

500 GREAT BOOKS FOR TEENS

Anita Silvey

# 500 Great Books
## *for* *Teens*

A FRANCES TENENBAUM BOOK

Houghton Mifflin Company • Boston • New York

2006

Visit our Web site: www.houghtonmifflinbooks.com.

*Library of Congress Cataloging-in-Publication Data*
Silvey, Anita.
500 great books for teens / Anita Silvey.
p.   cm.
Includes bibliographical references and index.
ISBN-13: 978-0-618-61296-3
ISBN-10: 0-618-61296-3
1. Teenagers—Books and reading—United States.  2. Young
adult literature—Stories, plots, etc.  3. Young adult
literature—Bibliography.  4. Best books—United States.
I. Title: Five hundred great books for teens.  II. Title.
Z1037.S577  2006
028.5'5—dc22    2006003350

Book design by Melissa Lotfy

PRINTED IN THE UNITED STATES OF AMERICA

EUS  10  9  8  7  6  5  4  3  2  1

# Contents

*For my father, John Silvey, with love.*

———

Because he worked in the coal mines as a teenager,
I have been free to devote my life to books.

# Acknowledgments

IN THE FINAL STAGES of this book, Patty Campbell and Michael Cart, veteran young adult book critics, looked over my list of titles. They definitely led me to some better choices in many of the categories. I value both of them for their insight, passion, and years of devoted service to the cause of young adult books.

Over the past few years, some of my students in the Simmons Graduate School of Library and Information Science have applied their superb research abilities to many of the books in this volume and found material that I incorporated. Thanks to Georgia Alexander, Michelle Angell, Eileen Barrett, Heather Dubnick, Carrie Eastman, David Flynn, Jacqueline Gaston, Senele Gonzalez, Jackie Hockett, Danielle Kimerer, Sarah Mason, Suzanne McGowan, Nell Mone, Sam Musher, Sarah Paquet, Michael Sapiroto, Vijay Shah, Rosanne Sheridan, and Anne-Marie Taylor.

Some professional groups agreed to listen to early stages of my research and gave me invaluable feedback. With great thanks to the Loudoun (Virginia) County school system, particularly W. David Jones, supervisor of the Library Media Services, and librarians Connie Niccolls, Beth Jespersen, Karen Farzin, Willa Kiser, Esther Kim, and Janice Smith for their spirited defense of titles I had not previously considered. To members of the Ohio Library Association in general and to Rollie Welch of the Cleveland Public Library, in particular, for their recommendations of new sports titles and books that appeal to male teens. To Anne Scott MacLeod of the University of Maryland for her insights into early-twentieth-century literature and its similarities to early-twenty-first-century literature.

I particularly want to thank the entire staff of the Westwood (Massachusetts) Public Library for their willingness to share their opinions with me. The glorious Minuteman Library Network allowed me to examine several thousand titles for this book.

As I worked on different sections, certain specialists and critics helped me decide on the contents. Young adult enthusiast and author Susan Cappetta guided me through the thorny paths of edgy, trend-setting fiction; Ruth Lynn, the author of *Fantasy Literature for Children and Young Adults,* scrutinized the final titles in the fantasy section. GLIS students David Flynn and Sam Musher not only educated me about the art form of the graphic novel but helped me choose some of the best examples of the genre. Maria Salvadore aided me in selecting titles in "Historical Fiction," "Humor," "Many Cultures, Many Realities," and "War and Conflict." Maria and I have worked together on projects for almost three decades, and she gets smarter every year!

The research assistant for the volume, Peter Sieruta, pulled together material for most of the essays. He also worked on choosing titles in "Plays," "Poetry and Poetic Novels," and "Short Stories." Peter's enthusiasm for work that others would find daunting always amazes me. We've collaborated on every book that I have published, and I always benefit from his fine counsel and advice. He also keeps me going when the going gets tough.

Leda Schubert — the most widely read individual I know in young adult and adult literature — spent long hours with me discussing these books. Her patient husband, Bob Rosenfeld, listened, amused, through many of these sessions. Unfortunately, I could not include his favorite title, *Terry and Bunky Play Football.*

Many others made helpful suggestions along the way. But I'm especially indebted to Ellen Myrick, who wanted me to include the best audio titles. With Tracy Taylor and Jeannine Wiese, Ellen actually listened to the available audios of these 500 books and pulled together the recommendations at the back of the book.

Several people conducted reality tests with teenage readers. My deep appreciation goes to Erica and Molly Wilder of Rhode Island; Emma Pancoast of New Hampshire; Dr. Charlotte Bennett and the staff of St. John School in Newburgh, Indiana; Christi Showman and young readers at the Flint Memorial Library in North Reading, Massachusetts; and Teresa Gallo-Toth, librarian at the Martin Sleeper Library, and the amazing readers of the seventh and eighth grades at the John D. Runkle School in Brookline, Massachusetts.

Some individuals provided insights and personal support. With thanks to Marge Berube, Susan Bloom, Bindy Fleischman, Vicky Hallett, Anne Marie Kennedy of Barnes and Noble, Joanne Lee, Stephanie Loer, Karen MacPherson, Harold T. Miller, Neal Porter, Dave Richardson of the Blue Marble Bookshop, Ann Rider, Hannah Rodgers of Curious George Goes to WordsWorth, Terri Schmitz of the Children's Book Shop, Carol Stoltz of the Porter Square Bookshop, Duncan Todd, and Laura Williams McCaffrey.

For all of those who participated in "adbooks," a YA discussion group, a thousand thanks. I eavesdropped in cyberspace every day, and you led me to a lot of superb titles. Although I wasn't able to include everyone's favorites, I tried to mirror the enthusiasm and commitment of this group.

Laura Wollett, a fine editor in her own right, agreed to give the manuscript a final read to check facts. Any errors are still mine, but she saved me numerous times.

No book of this complexity and scope exists without a very dedicated publishing team behind it. Without the enthusiasm and good cheer of my agent, Doe Coover, I might never have embarked on the project. Frances Tenenbaum, Houghton's legendary editor still working in her eighties, enthusiastically tackled a book about adolescent reading. In the early stages of the project, Dave Thomas shared his ideas about what would be helpful to parents. For the last four years, Megan Wilson has never failed to provide publicity for all my books, and on this one Carla Gray stepped in with valuable marketing assistance. The Houghton Mifflin sales representatives, one of the finest groups ever assembled, did the rest. I loved them when I worked on staff with them; as an author, I appreciate them even more.

# Introduction

WE LIVE IN A GOLDEN AGE of young adult publishing. A decade ago, critics proclaimed the death of the young adult novel, but this amazingly resilient group of books has surprised everyone and taken on new life. The range of titles published, their excellence, and their variety have never been more exciting, not even in the last heyday of young adult publishing, in the 1970s. New population demographics have brought eighty million young readers into the teenage category, the echo boomers of the baby boomers. Bookstores have increased space and visibility for teen books, causing more enthusiasm and more exposure. Harry Potter swept on the scene and then became an adolescent with a huge teen following. At the same time, revived by the movies, J.R.R. Tolkien captured his next devoted adolescent audience. Several titles that first appeared on adult lists — *The Curious Incident of the Dog in the Night-Time, Life of Pi,* and *The Secret Life of Bees* — were picked up and embraced by teens. Publishers started to hunt, frantically, for crossover books, books like *Curious Incident* that have wide appeal. Now, any consumer — in schools or libraries or bookstores — has many superb choices. In 2006 several thousand new titles will be published for readers twelve to eighteen.

But how can anyone analyze all the young adult titles available? How can a concerned parent, teacher, grandparent, or teen find the best of this genre? How can adults select books that they feel comfortable giving? With these questions in mind, I set out to provide a guide for those perplexed about young adult books.

# The Nature and History
# of Young Adult Books

I have over the last thirty-five years read thousands of young adult books, trying to understand the literature, what it can do at its best, and why it engenders such controversy. When I entered the publishing field in 1970, young adult books had just emerged as a distinct form. A year later, as the youngest person on the *Horn Book* review staff, I read these titles for authenticity; did they truly reflect teenagers of the 1960s and 1970s? As editor of *The Horn Book Magazine*, I watched young adult books mature in the 1980s and stagnate in the 1990s. Authors relied too much on formulas and assumptions about what teens wanted to read, and the literature lost its vitality. Then, around 2000, young adult literature gained a new passion, new focus, and new purpose.

Great teenage literature has always addressed the fundamental questions of the teenage years: Who am I? Do I matter? How do I relate to others? In that literature, teens get blown off course by their hormones, just as they do in the real world. Teenage angst and ennui shape many of the characters. All young adult literature explores the problems of separation and empowerment. Sometimes that process can have terrible results — as Robert Cormier demonstrated in *The Chocolate War* — but usually in coming-of-age stories the movement from childhood to adulthood is inevitable and necessary. Through their angst, the protagonists become adults, separate from parents, and exercise independent judgment from the adults around them.

Hence the very content of this literature sometimes threatens adults; young adult books are the most challenged and censored books in the United States. Adults want to keep their children young and protected; teens want to strike out on their own. The literature that talks about this separation makes everyone nervous.

# This Book's Organization and Scope

I have tried to address the needs of both teenagers and their parents. Teens need honest, open literature that talks about their problems. Adults want to know what teens are reading. Hence my essays reveal the contents of each of the 500 books. Too often for this literature, only a two- or three-sentence annotation sums up the plot. I wanted to make sure that everyone understood the major focus of each title.

*500 Great Books for Teens* will help adults find books appropriate in age and content, given the parameters set. If a teen likes edgy, controversial books—and you support this—you'll be able to find the best ones. If you want to avoid these books altogether, you'll know which ones to skip. Adults who read *500 Great Books for Teens* will find a multitude of books that they can share with their teenagers. Teens can find books to read alone.

I divided the 500 books into twenty-one sections representing different reading tastes and genres. In each section I included several books that have set the standard for the literature. Then I tried to balance each section for the age of readers, reading skills, and backgrounds. I searched not only for some of our older gems but worked to find the best titles of the twenty-first century. At the beginning of each section, I wrote about the standard-bearers in that genre, the reasons this literature is popular, and some of the qualities of these particular books.

Since teens have the reading skills necessary for all literature, they read from all of it. They still cling to series they began as children; they read books specifically written for them; and they also choose some of the best that the adult world has to offer. Hence I selected titles originally published for children, young adults, and adults. I wanted the selections to reflect the way teenagers actually read—not the ghettos we sometimes create for books. Having spent half my life in publishing, I also know that a certain degree of whimsy determines which department publishes a book; in the end, the only question that matters is who reads it.

In each essay, I included author and title, recommended ages, original publisher, publishing year, and page count. I also indicated if the book was recognized by the Newbery or Michael L. Printz Award committees of the American Library Association or was selected as a Pulitzer or National Book Award winner or finalist. Sometimes other awards get mentioned in the discussion of the book. Each essay presents the basic plot or story line and some of the issues raised by the book; on occasion, I mention the controversies surrounding the book, its publishing history, or a sense of the ideal use for the title.

# Criteria for Inclusion

Beginning in the year 2000 the Young Adult Library Services Association of the American Library Association has honored several books for teens under the Michael L. Printz Award. Chosen annually for their literary merit by a committee of YALSA, the Printz winner and honor books naturally cause a lot of discussion among young adult book experts. Rather than engage in a debate about these awards, I wanted to honor the work of all YALSA members who have attempted to give the award its definition and meaning. Therefore all of the Printz winners and honor books chosen in 2000–2005 have been included in *500 Great Books for Teens*.

For the rest of the books, I worked with a variety of criteria. First and foremost, I am always hunting for books that demonstrate the highest quality of writing. I looked for writers who had a story to tell and could do so; I evaluated voice and style, the development of the character and setting, the accuracy, themes, and even the design and format of the book. I also hunted for books that have found a devoted readership over time, favoring those with a wide audience of teens, teachers, parents, librarians, booksellers, and young adult experts. Many of the classics need no introduction, and I have put them in their own section in "Beyond the 500."

Since I was pulling together a book of this magnitude, I talked to and polled hundreds of people, including teens, to see what books they favor. I am always hunting for books that create a passionate response in readers.

We often burden young adults with worthy books, ones we believe they should know. At the 2005 meeting of ALA's Best Books for Young Adults committee, a young reader said, "This book should come with a fork so you can stick yourself while you read it, because it is so dull." Often in our well-meaning ways we give teens books that need a fork. I have tried, whenever possible, to stay away from the "fork" books.

I present these 500 books in a sincere desire to provide a useful and inspiring volume that leads to many wonderful titles. I know that I could have described other books in these pages, but I believe these 500 will excite even the most hesitant readers. "The only bad part was when it ended," one teen wrote about a book I included. In *500 Great Books for Teens*, I have searched for, described, and celebrated titles that will keep readers turning the pages — only regretting that they have come to the end of the story.

# 500 Great Books for Teens

# Adventure and Survival

**N**EVER OUT OF FASHION, adventure and true survival accounts have attracted teenagers ever since Daniel Defoe wrote *Robinson Crusoe*. Readers with enough heat, light, and food encounter peers who are starving and struggling. Then they can tuck themselves into a comfortable bed with a bit more appreciation of their own lives.

One of the most frequent fears, and fantasies, of adolescents concerns survival. How could they survive without their family? What if they didn't have the comforts of civilization? How could they handle living in the wilderness if they suddenly found themselves there?

These and other issues lie at the heart of our best survival and adventure novels. These books most frequently pit man or woman against nature. But they can also put a family, such as the Tillermans in *Homecoming*, in an urban landscape, attempting to survive without adults.

Survival tests our character, our strengths, and our weaknesses. For those attempting to find out who they are — the issues of self-identity central to the teenage years — adventure fiction allows them a chance to do so against a background that might literally kill them.

MARIAN CALABRO

## *The Perilous Journey of the Donner Party*

12–14 • Clarion • 1999 • 192 pp.

In 1846 George and Jacob Donner, James Reed, and their families left Illinois for the unsettled territory of California. Of the ninety travelers, teenagers and children made up half the party. Using memoirs, diaries, and letters, the author of this nonfiction account shows the joy at the beginning of the journey, then the rancor and cruelty that surfaced as mishaps began to occur. Much of the experience is conveyed through the eyes of Virginia Reed, who turned thirteen on the trek; Virginia's powerful letter at the end of the ordeal appears in its entirety. Marian Calabro discusses many of the bad decisions that the party made and how the survivors ended up resorting to "the last taboo," cannibalism, which made these settlers an object of horror in their own time. Illustrated with maps, drawings, and etchings, the skillful narrative unfolds a tragic episode in the history of the West.

BROCK COLE

## *The Goats*

12–14 • Farrar, Straus • 1987 • 184 pp.

In the middle of the night, a thirteen-year-old boy and girl are stripped of all their clothing by their campmates and left stranded on an island. In this yearly ritual, considered a harmless prank, the camp always punishes two social misfits, or goats. These two nameless individuals start to invent their own rules, however. They escape from the island and break into a summer cabin to find food and clothing. They also start a journey away from the camp that ultimately provides healing and some self-esteem.

Brock Cole drew his inspiration from lines by Yeats: "The ceremony of innocence is drowned; / The best lack all conviction, while the worst / Are full of passionate intensity." Raw in its emotion, showing the brutality of the young toward the young, *The Goats* has been frequently challenged and censored since its publication. But it speaks to all who have felt themselves outcasts, alienated from their peers. In the end, the story affirms the human spirit and the ability of the individual to rise above adversity, no matter how emotionally painful.

JEAN CRAIGHEAD GEORGE

## My Side of the Mountain

12–14 • Dutton • 1959 • 177 pp.

↪ *NEWBERY HONOR*

For almost half a century, Jean Craighead George's *My Side of the Mountain* has fired the imagination of young readers wondering if they could survive in the wilderness. Sam Gribley leaves his New York City home with a penknife, a cord, an ax, a flint and steel, and some money to try to live on his family's property in the Catskill Mountains. Relying on his research in the New York Public Library, Sam has to hunt desperately for food and shelter. But he learns to live in a tree, find wild strawberries, produce a fire, and acquire a companion, Frightful, a young falcon. Although the book contains references to civilization, the narrative basically stays in the heart of the wilderness — its scents, its sounds, its events.

George, who grew up in a family of scientists, spent a lot of time with her father exploring nature; they also raised and trained falcons. But she was a wife and mother when she wrote this book, and it allowed her to fantasize about running away, at least on paper.

Although the premise strains credulity in the modern age — that parents would allow a young man to stay alone in the wilderness for a year — the story sweeps readers along and leaves them savoring Sam's cuisine, which includes acorn pancakes. When the book was first reviewed, the editor of *Horn Book* wrote: "I believe it will be read year after year, linking together many generations in a chain." It has done just that, enticing new readers with each coming year. *My Side of the Mountain* — along with its sequels, *On the Far Side of the Mountain* and *Frightful's Mountain* — remains one of the books remembered most fondly by adults long after they have experienced its joys.

WILL HOBBS

## Downriver

12–14 • Atheneum • 1991 • 204 pp.

One summer a group of problem teenagers find themselves in an outdoor education program, Discovery Unlimited, under the guidance of an adult they don't appreciate. So one day they take the situation in hand, borrow the necessary equipment, and head downriver into the Grand Canyon, enjoying the caves and waterfalls and the thrills of whitewater rafting.

Told by fifteen-year-old Jessie, who is angry at her father for re-marrying, the story shows her growth and development as well as that of the rest of her group. Eventually pursued by park rangers and helicopters, the teens emerge battered and wounded from their wilderness experience. But Jessie and her friends have learned a great deal in the process about themselves and nature — and the reader has been taken along for a ride packed with thrills and adventure.

SEBASTIAN JUNGER

## The Perfect Storm:
## A True Story of Men Against the Sea

14–18 • Norton • 1997 • 256 pp.

A perfect storm" can be defined as one unsurpassed in ferocity and duration, in which various meteorological events converge to create an overwhelming outcome. But before readers of this true story actually experience that storm, they learn about the town of Gloucester, Massachusetts, which is sliding downhill economically because of the decline of the North Atlantic fishing industry. In October of 1991 the captain and the five-man crew of the *Andrea Gail,* a swordfishing vessel, set out from Gloucester and eventually headed into a perfect storm, with winds over 100 miles an hour and waves that topped 110 feet. Although the National Guard attempted to rescue the boat, the mission failed. When the ship disappeared, the people of Gloucester had to deal with this devastating loss: six members of the community simply vanished into the ocean.

Readers experience what those on the boat felt and saw. Armchair adventure at its best, *The Perfect Storm* can make readers simply grateful for the solid ground underneath their feet. Made into an exciting survival film in 2000, the book contains extensive background and scientific detail but still keeps readers breathlessly turning the pages.

JON KRAKAUER

## *Into Thin Air*

14–18 • Villard • 1997 • 368 pp.

I n March of 1996 the veteran journalist and mountain climber Jon Krakauer joined an expedition hoping to reach the summit of Mount Everest. Writing for *Outside* magazine, he planned to analyze the problems created by the ever-increasing commercialization of Everest. Wealthy clients, with little experience or skill, would hire expensive guide operations, like Adventure Consultants and Mountain Madness, who made it possible for these "trophy climbers" to get to the top. During the climb, however, Krakauer began to understand that no safety exists in the mountain; Everest continues to kill about a fourth of those who actually summit the mountain. When the group's ascent turned tragic and a dozen people died on Everest that year, Krakauer looked unflinchingly at all the contributing factors, including his own sense of guilt as a survivor.

Incorporating a great deal of Everest history and lore, information about high altitude climbs, and the drama and suspense involved, Krakauer has written one of the most compelling climbing books to date, a nonfiction title that reads like a fiction thriller.

ALFRED LANSING

## *Endurance: Shackleton's Incredible Voyage*

14–18 • McGraw-Hill • 1959 • 282 pp.

W hen the wooden ship *Endurance* was crushed by ice in the Weddell Sea in 1915, Sir Ernest Shackleton and his twenty-seven-member crew faced an incredible ordeal. For over five months they camped on the Antarctic ice floes; they drifted in open boats and eventually reached land. Shackleton and a small crew then sailed to South Georgia Island, eight hundred miles away, where they walked over sawtoothed mountains to a whaling station. Because of their desire to survive and Shackleton's amazing leadership, all the members of the ill-fated expedition were saved.

A harrowing reading experience that makes one shiver with cold and feel weak from hunger, Lansing's nonfiction account, written more than forty years after the event, relies on diaries and interviews with these survivors, no longer young. Over the years, it has enticed others to travel across Antarctica and has even served as the basis for leadership seminars. In 2000 a lavishly illustrated edition of the book, presenting numerous photographs by Frank Hurley from the expedition, has enticed even more readers to pick up this classic survival story.

IAIN LAWRENCE

## The Wreckers

12–14 • Delacorte • 1998 • 191 pp.

On the barren coast of Cornwall, England, a community of people prayed for shipwrecks because they could feed and clothe themselves from the items salvaged from the vessels. In church they sang hymns: "If sailors there are, / And wrecks there must be, / I beseech You / To send them to me." Then they began to lure the ships in with lights and kill all those aboard.

In 1799, on his first trip with his father sailing on the *Isle of Skye*, fourteen-year-old John Spencer survives the demise of the ship only to face a more sinister threat, the wreckers. In this community gone awry, he doesn't know whom to trust — the lovely Mary, her guardian Simon, the parson, or Eli, the man with his tongue cut out. When John finds his father still alive but chained with rats surrounding him, John needs to take action.

In a swashbuckling, edge-of-the-chair thriller, Iain Lawrence combines just the right amount of action with moral dilemmas that keep readers riveted until the final pages. Even his chapter titles intrigue viewers — "The Legless Man," "Across the Moor," "A Dead Man Rises." Yet the story actually presents a historical period and time quite different from those found in history texts. Cornwall, English history, the sailing trade, and even dead men come alive in the hands of one of Canada's most brilliant storytellers; he has created a novel worthy of Robert Louis Stevenson himself.

NORMAN MACLEAN

## Young Men and Fire

14–18 • University of Chicago • 1992 • 316 pp.

On August 5, 1949, sixteen members of the elite U.S. Forest Service Smoke jumpers landed in Mann Gulch, Montana. Within an hour, thirteen were dead or mortally burned, having been caught in a rare explosion of flames and wind. In the first half of this nonfiction account, Norman Maclean records these events. In the second half, he and two survivors return to the gulch to piece together what actually happened.

For some twenty-five years, the incident haunted Maclean, the author of *A River Runs Through It and Other Stories*. A native of the area, he worked for the Forest Service in his youth. For *Young Men and Fire*, his last book, he conducted exhaustive research, interviewing survivors, friends in the service, and fire experts so that he might understand this tragedy.

Maclean not only recreates the rolling rocks, exploding trees, and flames of the fire but also explores the tragedy and loss of this terrible accident.

YANN MARTEL

## Life of Pi

14–18 • Harcourt • 2001 • 401 pp.

An earnest young man, Pi Patel grows up as the son of a zookeeper in Pondicherry, India. Embracing three religions (Hinduism, Christianity, and Islam), at sixteen Pi leaves India for Canada on a ship containing the animals from his family's zoo, which are being transported all over the world. But when the vessel sinks, he finds himself cast adrift in a lifeboat with a zebra, hyena, an orangutan, and the huge Bengal tiger, Richard Parker. Eventually, only Pi and Richard Parker share the lifeboat for 227 days at sea. In constant terror of Richard, Pi supplies him with fish, turtles, and fresh water. But on this truly amazing journey Pi has ample time to relate a story suffused with wonder. Winner of the Booker Prize, this tale of adventure and terror also explores a great deal of folklore and information about animals, zoos, and religions.

Some readers have great difficulty with Martel's ending, believing it creates confusion. Others, however, love the shifting point of view and the mystery of what really happens. Younger adolescents love the character of Richard Parker; older ones enjoy the novel's discussion of ideas — life, death, human consciousness, and the nature of faith.

"I write for someone who is intelligent or curious. . . . A mind connected to a heart. My reader is me," Yann Martel has written. Thousands of adolescents have become his ideal reader, and many declare that this adventure story, spiced with wit and wisdom, emerges as their favorite novel encountered in the teenage years. As some have said, it makes their "soul sing."

VICTORIA MCKERNAN

## Shackleton's Stowaway

12–14 • Knopf • 2005 • 319 pp.

This fictional account of the 1914–1916 Antarctic expedition focuses on eighteen-year-old Perce Blackborow, who hid on Shackleton's *Endurance* so that he could sail with a friend. With Perce as the protagonist, readers share the point of view of those who served as the crew rather than the officers. Pulling readers into the heart of the action immediately, the story begins with Perce's enduring the amputation of his frostbitten toes and then swings back to present a chronological narrative.

Conducting interviews with the Blackborow family and studying published and unpublished journals, Victoria McKernan has crafted an exciting, highly absorbing story that can be used in conjunction with nonfiction accounts such as Lansing's *Endurance* and Jennifer Armstrong's *Shipwreck at the Bottom of the World*.

KENNETH OPPEL

## Airborn

12–14 • HarperCollins/Eos • 2004 • 355 pp.
⮞ *PRINTZ HONOR*

## Skybreaker

12–14 • HarperCollins/Eos • 2005 • 369 pp.

Fifteen-year-old Matt Cruse, a cabin boy on the airship *Aurora*, spies a hot-air balloon sinking slowly against the night sky. Although Matt saves the elderly balloonist, the adventurer dies the next day mumbling about "beautiful creatures." A year later, his granddaughter Kate travels on the luxury airship, hoping to learn more about her grandfather's last venture. Much like the ocean liners of the early twentieth century, the *Aurora* ferries wealthy passengers from city to city, providing elaborate meals and group activities. But after pirates attacks, the crew and passengers find themselves shipwrecked on an island, and Kate and Matt discover an unrecorded life form, a beautiful "cloud cat" that can fly.

Matt and Kate's proclivity for high-wire adventure continues in the sequel, *Skybreaker*. They team up with a flying entrepreneur and the daughter of a pirate in order to salvage the *Hyperion,* the airship of a wealthy and idiosyncratic inventor that disappeared forty years earlier.

Although basically fantasies, since the world of airship travel has been completely invented by the author, the swashbuckling adventures recall the tales of Jules Verne and Robert Louis Stevenson. These sophisticated survival stories, appealing to both males and females, adults and young adults, contain adventure, danger, intrigue, and even romance.

GARY PAULSEN

## *Hatchet*

12–14 • Bradbury • 1987 • 189 pp.

↩ *NEWBERY HONOR*

A lifelong outdoorsman with a love of nature, Gary Paulsen wanted to create a book like *Hatchet* all his life. His visit to the Hershey, Pennsylvania, middle school inspired the book. While talking to students about their passions, Paulsen realized that he should write the survival tale that had been brewing in his mind, and he dedicated the book to those children.

In *Hatchet* a troubled city boy, thirteen-year-old Brian Robeson, manages to stay alive for two months in the Canadian wilderness, with only a hatchet to aid him. Remarkable for its fast-paced action and harrowing escapes, the book evokes the sights, sounds, and feeling of the wilderness.

According to Paulsen, "I was concerned that everything that happened to Brian should be based on reality. . . . I did not want him to do things that wouldn't or couldn't really happen in his situation. Consequently, I decided to write only of things that had happened to me or things I purposely did to make certain they would work for Brian."

Paulsen, who had run the Iditarod, drew on his own experiences. He himself had been attacked by a moose and by mosquitoes. But he decided to spare Brian the black flies, horseflies, and deerflies that Paulsen had also encountered. One of his hardest tasks was to start a fire with a hatchet and a rock, but eventually he accomplished this feat in four hours. He then tried eating snapping turtle's eggs, which he describes as tasting like "old motor oil or tired Vaseline." Although he was not successful at getting them down, he decided that Brian, being much hungrier, would be able to do so.

Paulsen's varied experiences ultimately shaped a book that leaves readers feeling as if they have been living alone in the wilderness. Consequently, *Hatchet*, the best modern survival story for young readers, proves to be far more exciting and believable than anything seen on television or in the movies.

NATHANIEL PHILBRICK

## Revenge of the Whale:
## The True Story of the Whaleship Essex

12–14 • Putnam • 2002 • 164 pp.

Adapting and abridging his National Book Award winner, *In the Heart of the Sea*, for adolescents, Nathaniel Philbrick immediately takes readers into the harrowing nonfiction account of the *Essex* in 1820. Hailing from Nantucket, the *Essex*, like other Quaker whalers, set out for the whaling grounds off the coast of Chile. With a captain and crew of twenty, including six Black sailors, the ship experienced difficulties along its route. Then the unthinkable happened: when the *Essex* is rammed and sunk by an enraged sperm whale, the hunters became the hunted. Piling into three leaky whale boats, the men are rescued after three months at sea; dehydration, despair, and ultimately cannibalism marked those terrible days.

To create this grueling account, Philbrick relied heavily on the recently discovered account of the youngest member of that crew and one of the eight survivors, fourteen-year-old Thomas Nickerson. Hence the excitement of whaling and the plight of the crew seem quite true to the way an adolescent would experience them. Philbrick never loses sight of telling a good tale or yarn, and by the end of this true story, readers understand completely how the story of the *Essex* inspired the greatest whaling novel of all time, Herman Melville's *Moby Dick*.

## LOUIS SACHAR

### *Holes*

12–14 • Farrar, Straus • 1998 • 233 pp.

↬ *NEWBERY MEDAL*

Although this book can be appreciated by children, it has found a devoted audience in the younger teen set. Hot Texas summers inspired Louis Sachar to write *Holes*: "Anyone who has ever tried to do yard work in Texas in July can easily imagine Hell to be a place where you are required to dig a hole five feet deep and five feet across day after day under the brutal Texas sun."

As he wrote, Sachar envisioned the place first, Camp Green Lake, with no lake and hardly anything green, and then the characters and plot grew out of this setting. In the process, buried treasure, a famous outlaw named Kissin' Kate Barlow, Stanley Yelnats (whose name reads the same way forward and backward), and yellow-spotted lizards emerged from Sachar's heat-infected brain. In *Holes* the hero, Stanley, finds himself unfairly incarcerated in a boot camp for juvenile delinquents. Here the inmates have to dig holes five feet deep by five feet wide, spurred on by a villainous Warden with venom-tipped nails.

*Holes* captivated reviewers and critics by its inventiveness, structure, pacing, and reader appeal. With a screenplay by the author, it was also transformed into an entertaining movie in 2003. If there is any moral or lesson in the book, Sachar believes it to be a simple one: "Reading is fun." It would be difficult to find a fan of *Holes* who doesn't agree with him.

## JOE SIMPSON

### *Touching the Void: The Harrowing First-Person Account of One Man's Miraculous Survival*

14–18 • Harper • 1988 • 174 pp.

In 1985, while climbing in the Peruvian Andes with his partner, Simon Yates, Joe Simpson shattered his leg and fell 150 feet. Although at first the two worked in tandem as Yates tried to get Simpson down the mountain, eventually Yates cut his partner loose rather than perish. Surviving for four days without food or water, battered, exhausted, and dehydrated, Simpson manages to get back to the base camp.

A true survival story, now a classic in the genre, *Touching the Void* begins with a line from T. E. Lawrence: "All men dream: but not equally." For any climbing enthusiast or a couch potato who enjoys learning about extreme sports, *Touching the Void* reveals the dreams and accomplishments of two amazing mountaineers as it explores the issues of bravery, friendship, physical endurance, and the code of the mountains.

CYNTHIA VOIGT

## Homecoming

12–14 • Atheneum • 1981 • 312 pp.

One day the four Tillerman children are abandoned by their mentally ill mother in a car at a shopping mall in Connecticut. Thirteen-year-old Dicey, practical and responsible, an adult before her years, takes over the care of James, Maybeth, and Sammy. With limited funds, the four children set out on a dangerous journey walking down U.S. Route 1 to Crisfield, Maryland, where their grandmother lives. They must use their wits, strength, and resourcefulness, and make moral choices in order to reach their destination. Although their grandmother welcomes them reluctantly, she tentatively agrees to share her life with these four needy children.

Voigt wrote six other books about the Tillermans, including *Dicey's Song,* which won the Newbery Award. Readers of that book will still want to begin with *Homecoming* — a book with vivid descriptions, a strong sense of place, memorable characters, and a rhythm and cadence to the language.

Although the fast-paced plot has a great deal of suspense, the book deals with the pain of death, separation, and poverty. But it ultimately tells the story of the survival — and resilience — of four memorable children and their grandmother. Cynthia Voigt always said that Dicey was the young person she would liked to have been — and readers of the Tillerman saga often feel the same way.

ROBB WHITE

## *Deathwatch*

12–14 • Doubleday • 1972 • 220 pp.

Ben, a twenty-two-year-old geology student, agrees to serve as a guide for Madec, a cynical business tycoon with a permit to shoot a bighorn sheep. But when Madec accidentally kills an old man, he decides not to report the crime. Instead, he leaves Ben in the desert to die, without food, clothing, or water. Outwitting and outmaneuvering his adversary, Ben survives his ordeal, only to face the evidence of a murder that has been piled up against him. Written in a straightforward, reportorial style, the book grabs the reader's attention on the first page; it appeals to those who like suspense and a struggle between two very different but well-matched opponents.

# Autobiography and Memoir

A T THE BEGINNING OF A LIFE, reading about the whole arc of someone else's experiences can be beneficial. Teenagers struggle with those perennial questions: What will my life be about? What choices should I make? Often the autobiographies picked up by teenagers or selected for them show lives that were difficult or hard; books such as Augusten Burroughs's *Running with Scissors* may make an adolescent's own life seem easy in comparison.

Written for adults, Tobias Wolff's *This Boy's Life* has long been the standard-bearer for an autobiography with great artistic quality that appeals to an adolescent audience; almost all of the memoirs read by teenagers, in fact, first appeared as books for adults. More recently Jack Gantos, a writer for young readers, has crafted in *Hole in My Life* an honest and unforgettable book written with an adolescent reader in mind. Both books help define what can be accomplished in this category.

These autobiographies show the ability of the human being to triumph over adversity. In many cases written by those who became professional writers, they are worth reading simply for their creators' ability to describe their experience and for their literary style. All of them provide answers to a young person searching for a roadmap for life.

MAYA ANGELOU

## *I Know Why the Caged Bird Sings*

14–18 • Random House • 1969 • 281 pp.

Dancer, actress, cook, streetcar conductor, brothel madam, and writer, Maya Angelou created an autobiography that describes her slow and painful growth toward identity. In a chronological first-person narrative, told in dialect, she brings her characters and settings so vividly to life that readers feel as if they can touch them. They seem more real than the people one meets on the street.

Raised by her grandmother in Stamps, Arkansas, Maya and her brother also lived with their mother in St. Louis, and in one particularly powerful scene she recounts how she was raped by her mother's boyfriend. In this memoir she focuses on segregated life in the South, social injustice, economic hardship, and racism. But ultimately the book chronicles the triumph of a young girl over all these obstacles to become her own person. The book, like its author, is sassy, vibrant, intelligent, and full of laughter and love.

Angelou originally turned down the offer of Robert D. Loomis, an editor at Random House, to write an autobiography. But several months later he posed the idea to her again, saying, "Autobiography as literature is the most difficult thing anyone can do." Angelou, always up for a challenge, produced this powerful piece of literature at the age of forty-one, taking her title from Sir Paul Lawrence Dunbar's poem "Sympathy."

The resulting book has become part of the American literary canon, a story that lingers with readers for decades after they have encountered it.

AUGUSTEN BURROUGHS

## *Running with Scissors*

14–18 • St. Martin's • 2002 • 304 pp.

In this memoir, Burroughs recounts the horrifying, grotesque story of his childhood in Northampton, Massachusetts, in the late 1970s. When his manic-depressive mother, a poet, and his cold, alcoholic father separated, his mother put him under the care of her lunatic psychiatrist. Hence at the age of twelve Burroughs landed in the home of Dr. Finch with a few of his other patients. Unnerved by their squalid household, the boy became friends with the Finches' daughters, joining them in substance abuse and wrecking the family's Victorian home. The doctor encouraged Burroughs to become involved sexually with an "adopted" son; then Finch helped Burroughs stage a suicide attempt in order to avoid school. Through all the insanity, the boy soldiers on with humor and unflagging optimism.

Although this story of one of the most dysfunctional families and childhoods ever recorded should not be read by the squeamish, it has attracted a wide audience of adolescents. Their own homes don't seem quite so awful after living in the Finch household for a few hundred pages.

ROALD DAHL

## Boy: Tales of Childhood

12–14 • Farrar, Straus • 1984 • 160 pp.

Although Roald Dahl's fiction has always been embraced by his readers — children or young adults — adults have often been troubled by the elements of sadism inherent in many of his plots. In this autobiography, written a few years before he died, Dahl revealed why he wrote the kinds of books he did — because he experienced physical punishment, frequently and often, as a youth. From the age of nine to eighteen, he endured English boarding schools, in which adults wielded terrible power over the innocent students. The horror of these sadistic and ritual beatings by masters and prefects remained: "I couldn't get over it. I never have gotten over it."

More a collection of episodic and remembered incidents than an extensive autobiography, *Boy* still reveals an enormous amount about the author; he continued his story in *Going Solo*.

DAVE EGGERS

## A Heartbreaking Work of Staggering Genius: Based on a True Story

14–18 • Simon & Schuster • 2000 • 375 pp.

Eggers, the editor of the literary journal *McSweeney's*, has created a powerful commentary on life and work at the start of the twenty-first century. After the death of both parents within weeks of each other, Eggers, then in his early twenties, and his eight-year-old brother, Toph (short for Christopher), "inherit each other." The two leave their suburban Chicago home to live closer to his only slightly older sister in California. His parents' deaths are described in painful detail, but the tone changes, as do the situations in which Eggers becomes involved and explores.

The form of this memoir-novel is extraordinary. Not only is it well paced, it is stylistically varied — making it difficult to separate fact from fiction, propagandizing from satire. Even the copyright page contains several jokes: "Published in the United States by Simon & Schuster, a division of a larger and more powerful company called Viacom Inc., which is wealthier and more populous than eighteen of the fifty states of America, all of Central America, and all of the former Soviet Republics combined and tripled." Marked by brilliant storytelling, this work of fiction happens to be heartbreaking and hysterically funny at the same time.

PAULA FOX

## *Borrowed Finery: A Memoir*

14–18 • Holt • 2001 • 213 pp.

Dropped off at an orphanage shortly after her birth, Paula Fox was rescued by a clergyman — to whom she paid tribute in *One-Eyed Cat* — and passed along to various relatives or her parents' drinking buddies. For brief periods she returned to her parents, but her alcoholic father could not really care for her, and her mother openly rejected her.

Now a brilliant novelist, Fox excels in the telling detail and striking images; in this account of her first twenty years she never engages in self-pity or whining. Ultimately she survives these years, transcends her past, and becomes both an adult writer of *Desperate Characters* and the Newbery Medal–winning author of *The Slave Dancer*. This compelling memoir reveals how she developed her extraordinary sensibility.

ANNE FRANK

## *The Diary of a Young Girl: The Definitive Edition*

12–14 • Doubleday • 1995 • 335 pp.

Edited by Otto H. Frank and Mirjam Pressler; translated by Susan Massotty. Born into an upper-class Jewish family in Frankfurt,

Germany, Anne Frank moved with her family to Amsterdam in 1933. But in 1941, when the Nazis began rounding up Amsterdam's Jews, Otto Frank and his business partners prepared a secret hiding place in their office building on Prinsegracht Canal.

In June of 1942 Anne celebrated her thirteenth birthday and received a clothbound diary, in which she recorded her feelings and thoughts from June 12, 1942, to August 1, 1944. Through her words, we learn about life in the annex as a group of eight remained hidden and virtually imprisoned for two years. In August of 1944, the Nazis discovered their hiding place; the following March Anne died of typhoid fever in the Bergen-Belsen concentration camp.

Motivated by a strong desire to write, Frank named her diary Kitty and structured her entries as letters. This book serves as a candid self-portrait, a picture of domestic life, an account of people threatened with death, a depiction of the problems common to young adults, and an examination of moral issues. The writing also shows the triumph of the human spirit in terrible times.

Of the inhabitants of the annex, only Otto Frank survived. When he returned to Amsterdam, Anne's writings came into his hands. He typed a copy, which at first circulated among friends, then was published in Germany in 1947. Five years later, the English and American editions appeared.

Although critics at first were chary, afraid the book might be too difficult in its emotional content, by the end of the year young readers had convinced them of the diary's power. That 1952 edition did not include a great deal of material that Otto Frank considered inappropriate. After his death, the Anne Frank Foundation decided to make the entire diary available. With about 30 percent more material than in the original version, the definitive edition gives a better sense of Anne's growing sexual awareness and of her observations about people.

For over fifty years, *The Diary of a Young Girl* has described the horror of the war as seen through the eyes of a young woman. With more than fifteen million readers worldwide, in the end this book has fulfilled one of Anne Frank's greatest dreams: "I want to go on living even after my death!"

JACK GANTOS

## *Hole in My Life*

14–18 • Farrar, Straus • 2002 • 200 pp.

⌐ *PRINTZ HONOR*

A well-loved and respected author of children's and young adult books, Jack Gantos moves in this extraordinary book into territory not often explored by such writers. At twenty, he helped smuggle a ton of hashish from St. Croix to New York City. He takes readers along on the voyage — the insanity of his fellow smuggler Hamilton, the near misses with law enforcement officers, and the fear and paranoia of the drug dealer's life. But rather than telling a story of a youthful misdemeanor, Gantos relates how he paid for his crime — fifteen months in the Ashland, Kentucky, federal prison. There he experiences all the vulnerability of a young man in a horrible situation, frightened by everything around him. To keep his sanity, he gives up drugs and writes; although he can't obtain a journal, he scribbles between the lines of *The Brothers Karamazov*. By applying to college, he escapes prison for a writing program. In time he leaves Ashland to become what he always wanted to be — a writer.

Gantos always believed that his life story might be written but thought that it would be crafted with an adult audience in mind. After he read Walter Dean Myers's *Monster*, he felt that his own personal prison saga could, if presented in the right way, help teenagers explore what happens when an individual makes a bad choice. With the book's publication, Gantos began speaking in prisons and with those tough readers not necessarily attracted to other titles. One teen told him that *Hole in My Life* was the "only book I've ever finished."

In the spare, lean language of Raymond Carver, brutally honest, without a trace of self-pity or self-justification, the memoir keeps readers at the edge of their seats. At times the breathless pace brings to mind one of Gantos's own favorite titles, Jack Kerouac's *On the Road*. Gantos has said that not only does this book cover the details of his life, "it covers nearly every important theme in my life — my dedication to reading, my desire to write, my love of what is humanly artful and naturally beautiful, and my strong belief that life tumbles forward from violation to redemption."

Successfully used as an all-community-reads title, *Hole in My Life* shows how a bad beginning to a life does not always lead to a bad life story.

HOMER HICKAM

## Rocket Boys/October Sky

14–18 • Delacorte • 1998 • 428 pp.

In 1957 the Russians launched Sputnik, and fourteen-year-old Homer Hickam of Coalwood, West Virginia, discovered his mission: to become a rocket scientist like Dr. Werner von Braun, work for NASA, and beat the Soviets. But since he was only a sophomore in high school, he resorted to building rockets in Coalwood, a company mining town that was slowly dying. With the help of some other boys in the community, Homer launched a series of homemade rockets. At first they went awry, sometimes causing damage to his home and the town, but Homer pressed on, unwilling to sacrifice his dream just because he lived in a small West Virginia town. Eventually almost everyone in the area pitched in with help, advice, books, equipment, and manufacturing parts — including the preacher and some rather remarkable teachers. In the end, Homer won a gold medal at the National Science Fair and became a NASA engineer.

The bare outline of this memoir only scratches the surface of the material included. The book explores the age-old conflict of father and son, younger and older brothers, and the pain of unrequited first love. But it also embraces communal and global issues — the plight of families in West Virginia, the life of coal miners, the space race, and the 1960 election of John F. Kennedy. For science enthusiasts, it provides specific details about how the rockets got built and launched.

For those who like to read about triumph over adversity, few books present that theme as magnificently; this stunning tour de force brings to life the concepts of passion, hope, confidence, self-realization, and following and living a dream. Not only superb for independent reading, it has been used quite successfully in classrooms — in English, math, and science — even providing strength and hope for students at Columbine High School.

JEANNE WAKATSUKI HOUSTON AND JAMES D. HOUSTON

## *Farewell to Manzanar*

14–18 • Houghton Mifflin • 1973 • 188 pp.

On December 7, 1941, Jeanne Wakatsuki and her family learned of the bombing of Pearl Harbor. Although her father burned his Japanese flag at that moment, all the family was arrested by the FBI and moved from one Japanese ghetto to another. Then President Roosevelt signed Executive Order 9066, and the Wakatsuki family moved to Manzanar Relocation Center, 225 miles northeast of Los Angeles. With cramped living conditions, badly prepared food, swilling dust, and camp toilets with no privacy, the family began to disintegrate. Seven-year-old Jeanne had to deal with fear, confusion, and bewilderment, and her father, once a samurai warrior, became a violent drunk.

In 1944 the Supreme Court ruled such internment illegal, and the camps started closing. Young Jeanne adjusted to a more normal school life, but still encountered enormous prejudice against Japanese-Americans. Some thirty years later, she returned to Manzanar, realizing the tremendous impact the camp had had on her life and on the lives of other Japanese-Americans.

In the early 1970s, the writer James Houston interviewed his wife in a series of audiotapes about her experience during World War II. At first they believed the tapes would be shared only with family members, many born at the Manzanar camp, who knew little of the family history. However, they ultimately turned this personal history into one of the first, and most moving, books about the experience of Japanese-Americans during the war. Long a staple of school curriculums, this true and heartbreaking story has taken on even greater significance since the terrorist attacks in 2001; it forces readers to think about how Americans deal with "the enemy" in wartime.

FRANCISCO JIMÉNEZ

## *The Circuit: Stories from the Life of a Migrant Child*

12–16 • University of New Mexico • 1997 • 116 pp.

A professor of modern language today, Francisco Jiménez grew up as the son of migrant farmworkers who came to the United States illegally when he was four. Although his own family was illiterate, Jiménez describes his own fascination with books and how he learned to read. At six he began working in the fields, moving from place to place. As he writes poignantly in the book, his education was interrupted again and again because the family had to move with the crops. His parents and their eight children lived in one-room shacks and tents; when Jiménez was in junior high, they all were caught by the INS and sent back to Mexico. However, in time they acquired visas and returned legally.

The Circuit, originally called "Harvest of Hope: Life of a Migrant Child," presents in a dozen stories a chronicle of the 1940s. It has often been compared to The Grapes of Wrath but has been told from the Mexican-American point of view. Jiménez read Steinbeck's work in college and felt it was the first book he could actually relate to: "For the first time, I realized the power of the written work, that an artist can write creatively and make a difference in people's lives."

In The Circuit, told powerfully in the first person, readers feel the pain and confusion of a young boy. They experience his excitement about learning to read. But they also see how the family stays together with a strong work ethic, perseverance, pride in their Mexican heritage, and strong religious faith. Jiménez continued his memoirs in a second book about high school, Breaking Through.

"I wanted readers to hear the child's voice, to see through his eyes, and to feel through his heart," Jiménez wrote. He accomplished this and more in this slim volume. For the right readers at the right moment, The Circuit can alter the way they view migrant workers. A perfect book to use with students studying English as a second language, it also appeals to those who like uplifting stories about Americans who work for their dreams and achieve a better life.

FRANK MCCOURT

## Angela's Ashes: A Memoir

14–18 • Scribner • 1996 • 368 pp.

↶ PULITZER PRIZE

Worse than the ordinary miserable childhood is the miserable Irish childhood, and worse yet is the miserable Irish Catholic childhood." Born in Brooklyn in 1930 to Irish immigrants Malachy and Angela, Frank McCourt grew up in the slums of Limerick when they returned to Ireland. Since Frank's father remained chronically drunk and unemployed, the family had to live on the dole, charity, the Catholic Church, and the support of unsympathetic relatives. Were McCourt not such a gifted storyteller, the material would be too bleak even for Dickens. But in his hands, the sights, smells, and realities of this impoverished childhood have been rendered with black humor and grace. As child after child in the McCourt family dies from typhoid or consumption, Frank survives and lives to tell his story with exuberance and eloquence. As he tries out his wings as an adolescent post office delivery boy, every teen ever involved in a dead-end job will be able to identify with him. After many doors have been shut in his face, the young Frank finally earns his passage to America, intent on a better life.

A dazzling, literary recreation of McCourt's childhood and adolescent years, *Angela's Ashes* was followed by *'Tis: A Memoir* and *Teacher Man: A Memoir*.

WILLIE MORRIS

## *My Dog Skip*

12–14 • Random House • 1995 • 128 pp.

In 1943, nine-year-old Willie Morris fell in love with Skip, a smooth-haired fox terrier. "I was an only child, and he now was an only dog." Until Morris went to college, the two remained inseparable. Skip had tremendous talents. He could play football, drive a car (with a little help from his friend Willie), and run errands, wearing a small leather pouch. As the book tells stories about Skip, it also recounts Morris's boyhood in the sleepy town of Yazoo, Mississippi.

Morris once said, "Skip . . . was not my dog. He was my brother and I still miss him." Morris admitted that the only time he ever cried while writing came when he wrote the first two pages, describing Skip as a puppy, and when he wrote the ending of the book. Many have cried with him over this ultimate dog book, savoring his description of a boy's love affair with his dog.

WALTER DEAN MYERS

## Bad Boy: A Memoir

12–14 • HarperCollins • 2001 • 214 pp.

Having grown up in Harlem in the 1940s, Walter Dean Myers shows in his autobiography how he slowly and painfully found his own identity, despite a quick and violent temper that kept him in constant trouble. Gifted as both an athlete and an intellect, Myers received help from teachers who recognized his talents. His high school English teacher, ultimately, gave him the best advice: "Whatever happens, don't stop writing."

In *Bad Boy*, Myers honestly examines the issues of being black in America, from his first exposure to the history of slavery to his realization that his best friend, who is white, has social opportunities that he himself does not. He also confronts gang violence and a serious speech impediment; as he struggles to speak, he finds that he can write what he can't say.

Ultimately, the book attests to the power of reading and writing, no matter what the cultural background of the individual. As in all his work, Myers exhibits honesty, humor, and hope for individuals to bring about their own salvation. Certainly, his multitude of fans have benefited from his transformation from a bad boy to a fine writer who can honestly examine his own past — in this book and in his poetry and fiction.

SYLVIA PLATH

## The Bell Jar

14–18 • Harper • 1971 • 264 pp.

Although written as a work of fiction, *The Bell Jar* presents only a lightly disguised account of Sylvia Plath's first suicide attempt at the age of twenty. In the book Esther Greenwood, brilliant, beautiful, and talented, spends a month in New York as one of twelve interns working for a women's magazine. In the city, she can barely cope with her life, and when she returns home, everything starts to spiral out of control. A psychiatrist and shock treatments only worsen the problem; she keeps planning her suicide and almost succeeds. Finally, after spending time in an institution, Esther returns to college. The bell jar that has trapped her has been lifted, although she doesn't know if she'll be caught in it again.

With its treatment of depression and suicide when these topics were seldom discussed, the book first appeared in England under a pseudonym, Victoria Lucas, because Plath did not want to scandalize her American family. A serious poet, she felt that the book might be considered substandard, and it did receive lukewarm reviews in England. But a few weeks after its publication, Plath killed herself, and the book took on a life of its own. Fans of her poetry read it to find reasons for her suicide; but many, then and later, began to appreciate its accurate and precise description of an adolescent's descent into depression and mental illness.

Many bootleg copies of the book arrived in America before it finally appeared in 1971 and became an immediate bestseller. American critics thought it a much better book than Plath had herself, and the book established itself as a staple of high school and college reading lists. This serious exploration of a woman's attempt to deal with mental illness has spoken to millions of readers. Although the book clearly reflects the attitudes of the 1950s, adolescents still deal with its core issues — how to sort out a life and be true to yourself.

DAVID SEDARIS

## Me Talk Pretty One Day

14–18 • Little, Brown • 2000 • 272 pp.

A zany satirist with heart, David Sedaris has a genius for turning autobiography into hilarious comedy. Material that might have been maudlin or sentimental in other hands emerges from his pen as amusing and absurd. Ranging from his troubled childhood in North Carolina to the years with his lover in France, the book's twenty-seven essays can be read independently as short stories. Sedaris thwarts his speech therapist by cleverly avoiding words with the s sound; he and his classmates in France try to explain the concept of Easter to a Moroccan Muslim; his sister Amy wears a fat suit to upset their weight-conscious father.

Turning self-deprecation into an art form, Sedaris has a slightly twisted sense of humor that often appeals to adolescents, who admit to reading the book with frequent belly laughs.

ELIE WIESEL

## *Night*

14–18 • Hill & Wang • 1960 • 128 pp.

In this powerful first-person account, Eliezer, a Jewish teenager, and his family begin their journey in Sighet, Transylvania, in 1941. Elie studies the Old Testament and Cabbala, but his instruction ends when the Germans deport his teacher. Eventually the German and Hungarian police set up ghettos for the Jews. Elie and his family arrive at Birkenau, where the boy finds himself separated from his mother and sister. Like other arrivals, he immediately begins to witness the horrors of the concentration camp, with open-pit fires that consume people and babies. Elie gets stripped, disinfected, and subjected to unimaginable cruelty. Treated as slave labor, beaten, and humiliated, he begins to lose his humanity and faith in God and those around him. Sent on to Auschwitz, Buna, Gleiwitz, and Buchenwald, Elie becomes one of only three members of his family to survive.

Often read as part of a Holocaust unit, *Night* was first published in Argentina in 1956. Some consider it a memoir; others, a novel based on the author's experience. In 1986 Elie Wiesel received a Nobel Peace Prize for his efforts as "author, teacher and storyteller to defend human rights and peace throughout the world." As someone who emerged from the kingdom of the night, he transformed those experiences into a story that continues to convey the horrors of the Holocaust to adolescent readers.

TOBIAS WOLFF

## *This Boy's Life*

14–18 • Atlantic • 1989 • 288 pp.

For his fourth book, Tobias Wolff wrote an autobiography, a coming-of-age story told in the first person. In 1955, moving with his divorced mother to Utah, Toby changes his name to Jack, in honor of Jack London. Jack's father, living in Connecticut, has married a millionairess. But his much poorer mother keeps moving with Jack, usually to avoid violent men; in Seattle she meets and marries Dwight, who turns out to be quite cruel to them both. Because the writer never pities the boy, Wolff shows the people he encounters with amazing objectivity. Readers move from watching *The Mickey Mouse Club* with him to seeing him forge letters of praise for his applications to private boarding schools. Although Jack attempts to run away many times, all his plans are foiled.

Eventually his luck turns, and an alumnus of the prestigious Hill School recommends Jack to the school, serves as his mentor, and provides a new wardrobe to send him off. Wolff describes the years at this elite prep school in a subsequent volume, *Old School*. Unfortunately, Jack cannot totally reform. He gets expelled his senior year and goes to fight in Vietnam.

A remarkable account of a seemingly unremarkable life, *This Boy's Life* has set the standard for other writers' memoirs and has inspired titles such as Rick Bragg's *All Over But the Shoutin'* and Dave Eggers's *A Heartbreaking Work of Staggering Genius*. At the time of its publication, many questioned whether anyone would want to read the story of a not-quite-famous author, but the success of the book surprised both Wolff and his publisher. Although it tells the particular saga of one young man, *This Boy's Life* also relates a universal story — of rebelling but still loving a mother, breaking away from a family, and hoping for a different, better life.

# Edgy, Trendsetting Novels

I N THIS SECTION THE SELECTIONS "push at the acceptable boundaries of subject content for teen fiction." Sometimes called "grit-lit," these titles define the genre of young adult fiction and over the years have expanded its boundaries to include sex, violence, abuse, and death. Although sometimes praised by the critics, edgy novels often make adults uncomfortable. They become our most challenged — or censored — books and in the process gain the notoriety that causes teens to seek them out. Generally these titles stay alive because of the teens themselves. After all, liking what your parents hate happens to be a cornerstone of young adult behavior.

Much of young adult publishing for about forty years was influenced by three books for adults in the 1950s — *The Catcher in the Rye*, *A Separate Peace*, and *Lord of the Flies*. In the 1960s and 1970s, a group of writers who were specifically interested in young adults began to give them the books they deserved — titles such as S. E. Hinton's *The Outsiders* and Robert Cormier's *The Chocolate War*. As we have moved through the decades, new voices — such as those of Francesca Lia Block, Laurie Halse Anderson, and David Klass — have played with the boundaries of fiction again, creating powerful novels that represent the best of young adult writing.

Edgy and trendsetting books do not always age well. They hold up best when crafted by seasoned writers such as J. D. Salinger, William Golding, and Robert Cormier. Some of the books that defined the field seem ludicrous today. *Go Ask Alice* and Judy Blume's *Forever* read more like manuals of clinical prescription than novels. *The Outsiders,* while still powerful in its portrayal of gang warfare, might be classified today as historical fiction. Consequently, I have divided this section into classic and contemporary books so that the casual browser can see what was once considered edgy and what today might be viewed as controversial.

## Classic

ANONYMOUS (BEATRICE SPARKS)

### Go Ask Alice

12–14 • Prentice-Hall • 1971 • 185 pp.

A troubled fifteen-year-old records in her diary a series of adolescent woes: what a boy might think of her, her weight gain, her problems at school and with her parents. Moving with her family to a new town, Alice attends a party where LSD gets slipped into her soft drink. She begins experimenting with drugs and loses her virginity; she moves from doctor-prescribed tranquilizers to heroin. Abandoning her family, going from place to place, at times Alice tries to kick the drug habit, but she always goes back; she is sexually abused and becomes a drug dealer and prostitute to support her habit. Three weeks after the diary ends, she dies of a drug overdose — whether premeditated or accidental remains unclear.

Although *Go Ask Alice* often gets assigned as nonfiction and is still being presented as a true story, it appears to be almost entirely a fabrication by the editor Beatrice Sparks, who was in her fifties when she concocted the diary. Overly didactic, the book presents a highly unrealistic treatment of drugs and adolescents — ten days after Alice gets slipped LSD, she's shooting speed intravenously. No proof of the actual diarist has ever been provided in three decades, and it is now widely believed that Sparks simply invented a story that parents and teachers would like to hear.

Whatever its flaws, the book has definitely been read with great interest by adolescents and was the first popular book to address the issue of teenagers and drugs. Since its publication, *Go Ask Alice* has sold over four million copies. Translated into sixteen languages, it has become one of the most challenged books in the country; it may even be the best-selling hoax of all time.

JUDY BLUME

## Forever

12–14 • Bradbury • 1975 • 224 pp.

If Judy Blume's *Forever* gets read these days, it will most often be by giggling twelve-year-olds rather than older teens. But in the development of young adult literature, it is impossible to ignore this seminal title. *Forever* tells of a high school senior, Katherine, who falls in love with Michael. They become sexually involved, a process presented in clinical detail. Because her parents disapprove of the relationship, over the summer they send Katherine to be a counselor at a tennis camp, where she finds herself attracted to another boy. Various subplots include characters like Sybil, who sleeps around and gets pregnant with a baby she cannot keep.

Exploring first love, sexual involvement, and teen infatuation honestly and graphically, the novel quickly became one of the most censored books in America as well as one that teenagers claimed passionately for their own. Critics often disliked the clinical approach — some sections read more like a sex manual than a novel. The text covers far too many issues — drinking, sex, drug use, sexually transmitted diseases, teen pregnancy, and suicide — for a focused narrative. But *Forever* presents a different world to adolescents than the rest of the literature of the era — a teenager who willingly has sex, uses birth control, does not get pregnant, and does not die.

There is no question that Blume courageously waded into shark-filled and unexplored waters when she wrote the book — published as an adult title so that it might be considered less shocking. As a consequence of this book and her others, Blume has spent the last three decades fighting for intellectual freedom and the right of adolescents to have honest books about topics that concern them. *Forever,* therefore, is not nearly as important a novel as it is a cause. Because of her brilliant defense of that cause, Blume has been frequently honored for her lifetime achievement and remains a heroine of many teens, now adults, who found in her someone who truly understood their issues and was willing to address their questions sympathetically.

ROBERT CORMIER

### *The Chocolate War*

12–14 • Pantheon • 1974 • 191 pp.

"They murdered him." So begins Robert Cormier's first book for teenagers, and the line might well describe what happened when critics wrote about the book. Before *The Chocolate War*, Cormier spent his entire life in Leominster, Massachusetts, working as a reporter, editor, and columnist for the *Fitchburg Sentinel*. He had written for adults, but an experience with his son encouraged him to write a different kind of book. When his son Peter refused to sell chocolates for his own school, Cormier created a saga of a similar school and used his anxiety about his son's decision to propel the story forward. Many publishers rejected the manuscript because of its unrelenting force; even after its publication, reviewers reacted with fury at Cormier's refusal to sugar-coat reality for young readers.

Incredibly honest about adolescent boys' fantasies, dreams, and fears, *The Chocolate War* presents a Catholic high school, where a gang, the Vigils, rules. To raise money, Brother Leon has devised a plan to sell 20,000 boxes of chocolates. But one boy, Jerry Renault, whose mother has recently died, decides not to participate. As he gazes at a poster with T. S. Eliot's words "Do I Dare Disturb the Universe," he refuses to bow to the pressure of his teacher or his peers. In a powerful ending, the bad guys win. But as the novelist Richard Peck wrote, "The young will understand the outcome. They won't like it, but they'll understand it."

Like his first famous protagonist, Jerry, Cormier refused to compromise, to alter the ending of the book. Over time, after observing the legions of fans that Cormier attracted, the critics grew to respect him. Young readers always adored him. A mild-mannered Clark Kent in real life, Cormier always seemed more like Superman to his readers — a man unafraid to face the darker side of truth; a writer who always kept faith with his readers.

WILLIAM GOLDING

## Lord of the Flies

14–18 • Coward • 1955 • 236 pp.

First written as a post–nuclear war novel called *Strangers from Within*, *The Lord of the Flies* was extensively revised, omitting the details of the war, before it appeared in England in 1954. William Golding focused instead on a group of boys between six and twelve, stranded on an island together, waiting for adults to rescue them. Strong individuals, the boys take on different roles, helping the group survive: Ralph, the civilized leader; Piggy, his intellectual sidekick; Jack, who represents wildness and anarchy; and Simon, the quasi mystic. In the process, the band of boys degenerate from being Englishmen, with a parliamentary government, to becoming savages.

Golding believed he was writing about the moral nature of civilization — that the defects in society mirror those in human nature. Reviewers and critics initially gave the book scant attention or dismissed it as completely "unpleasant." In the United States, the book sold only a few thousand copies and was out of print by 1957. Only when it was released in the new, experimental American paperback format, aimed at college students who could not afford hardcover books, did the novel begin to gain its current popularity and notoriety. These students recognized many of the boys they had encountered at summer camp — but in *Lord of the Flies* the counselors have all vanished.

Now considered a classic, the older, darker sibling of Salinger's *The Catcher in the Rye*, *The Lord of the Flies* has been studied in schools, written about, read and reread, and helped Golding win a Nobel Prize for Literature in 1983.

S. E. HINTON

## The Outsiders

12–14 • Viking • 1967 • 180 pp.

One of the handful of groundbreaking novels that defined the young adult genre, *The Outsiders* has shown signs of its age over the last decade; it seems much less shocking than it once did and reads a bit like historical fiction. Admittedly, even as historical fiction it demonstrates an edge, presenting a gritty place and time — Tulsa, Oklahoma, and the gangs (Socs and Greasers) who battle for turf. In this landscape, weighed down by poverty and shame, Ponyboy Curtis, age fourteen, engages in rumbles, gets involved in a killing, runs from the law, saves children from a burning church, and reunites with his brothers. Two of his buddies die, and this Robert Frost–quoting "hood" tries desperately to sort out his angst-ridden world. Focusing on the struggles between social classes, the book showcases Pony, an engaging and compelling hero. Although he smokes too many cigarettes (called "weed") and carries a knife, he often seems more tender than tough.

Susan Eloise Hinton began the novel when she was fifteen, basing the story on incidents in her school. She sent a "dog-eared, poorly spelt, chocolate cake smeared manuscript" to Marilyn Marlow of the Curtis Brown agency and received a contract from Viking on her graduation day from high school. When it appeared, the book shocked the literary world and set the groundwork for new realism in books for teens. Most young adult novels of the era dealt with the prom or gentle romance. Hinton believed that teenagers demanded books featuring contemporary figures, whom they could identify with and who experienced similar struggles and problems.

Even thirty years after its publication, the tension between the in and out groups — the haves and have-nots — seems familiar to most young readers today. Second in children's and young adult paperback sales only to E. B. White's *Charlotte's Web, The Outsiders* forcefully portrays the feeling of a teen who finds himself on the outside of society, looking in.

JOHN KNOWLES

## *A Separate Peace*

14–18 • Macmillan • 1959 • 205 pp.

Set in 1942–1943 at Devon, a New England prep school based on Exeter Academy, *A Separate Peace* develops an engaging cast of characters and shows their intense relationships with one another. A quiet intellectual student, the narrator Gene Forrester becomes close to his daredevil roommate, Finny, during the summer semester. A great athlete, Finny prods Gene to make dangerous jumps out from a tree in the river; in fact, they start a secret society based on this ritual. But one day Gene shakes the branch, and Finny falls and breaks his leg. The degree of Gene's guilt then becomes an issue — particularly when another break to Finny's leg causes his death during the operation. As these private school students worry about their responsibilities, World War II, always looming in the background, begins to claim class members as they enlist in the service.

With *The Catcher in the Rye, A Separate Peace* helped establish the field of young adult literature in the 1950s. Knowles based the book on his own years at Exeter; growing up in West Virginia coal country, he himself attended Exeter and Yale. His fellow writer Gore Vidal inspired the character of Brinker. A classic boarding school story, inspiring many others, *A Separate Peace* never attacks the institution by showing depraved students or sadistic teachers; consequently, it seems idyllic in comparison to much contemporary young adult literature.

## J. D. SALINGER

# *The Catcher in the Rye*

14–18 • Little, Brown • 1951 • 214 pp.

In a wry, flip, totally self-absorbed first-person narrative, Holden Caulfield tells readers how he landed in an institution in California. However, we learn quickly that Holden will prove an unreliable narrator; he warns us that he's the "most terrific liar you ever saw in your life."

Expelled from his prep school yet another time, at sixteen, Holden still believes himself superior to all teachers and phonies. Reluctant to face his parents, he heads to New York and has a variety of experiences — with taxi drivers, nuns, a prostitute, three girls from Seattle, and a former teacher. His running banter during these incidents never wavers; epitomizing teenage angst, Holden swears, uses slang, and discusses sex honestly. But his attempts to escape himself prove fruitless. Finally, saved by a meeting with his little sister, Phoebe, Holden gets the affection and true understanding he needs.

Although Salinger always insisted that he was not Holden Caulfield, their lives share some features. Unsuccessful at graduating from prep school, Salinger fought in World War II. Writing short stories, he published one called "Slight Rebellion Off Madison," featuring a young boy on Christmas break from prep school, Holden Caulfield. Salinger then developed Holden into the protagonist for a full-length novel. On the book's release, Salinger fled to Cornish, New Hampshire, refusing to participate in any kind of publicity and avoiding all contact with the public. He continues to live as a recluse, shunning the incredible fame or notoriety the book brought him — hence making himself even more famous. Although *The Catcher in the Rye* received mixed reviews, it headed up the *New York Times* bestseller list and quickly became the most censored book in the United States for the next twenty years.

Taking for his protagonist a boy who is bewildered, lonely, ludicrous, and pitiful, Salinger renders his mercurial change of mood, stubbornness, and disregard for reality in precise detail. Since his appearance, Holden has served as the prototypical cynical adolescent in rebellion and has spawned generations of descendants in books for young adults. Young readers find in him a kindred spirit, someone they understand and who would understand them. "I am Holden Caulfield," one young fan has written; for over fifty years, millions of adolescents have made the same claim.

PAUL ZINDEL

## The Pigman

12–14 • Harper • 1968 • 183 pp.

Two high school sophomores — John and Lorraine — enjoy playing pranks on unsuspecting people. Then a game on the telephone brings them into contact with an elderly widower, Angelo Pignati. Invited to Mr. Pignati's home, the teens discover that he collects statues of pigs. When the Pigman has a heart attack, John and Lorraine help him. But while he is in the hospital, they hold a party at his house and their friends destroy his pig collection. He banishes them, then dies suddenly, causing the teens to come to terms with how they have trespassed on his life. They also gain insight into their own lives. Deciding to go to acting school, John says, "I just don't want to wear a suit every day and carry an attaché case and ride a subway. I want to be me."

Paul Zindel had written one play, *The Effect of Gamma Rays on Man-in-the-Moon Marigolds,* when the editor Charlotte Zolotow contacted him about writing a book for young adults because he understood how they felt. A high school science teacher and would-be writer, Zindel based his two young characters on two teens he knew; the Pigman was inspired by an eccentric man he had met as a child. Zindel liked writing the party scene the best, because he could thinly disguise his friends and enemies as guests.

Over the years, school classes have actually staged funerals for Mr. Pignati, writing a eulogy and picking out music. One of the first of the new realistic young adult novels in the 1960s, *The Pigman* does not present a happy ending; instead, it describes what can happen when teenagers make the wrong decisions.

# Contemporary

LAURIE HALSE ANDERSON

## *Speak*

12–14 • Farrar, Straus • 1999 • 198 pp.

✑ *PRINTZ HONOR/NATIONAL BOOK AWARD FINALIST*

For Melinda Sordino, a freshman in high school, the social scene boils down to the predators and their prey. Unfortunately, she fits in with the prey and hides herself in a janitor's closet to be safe from IT, Andy Evans, a dangerous jock who torments her. "I am Outcast," she realizes on the first day of school. A social leper, she has been ostracized by everyone, including her best friends, because she called the police from an end-of-the-summer party. So Melinda decides not to speak; she literally loses her voice.

In *Speak,* the reader spends most of the book harbored in Melinda's mind. Although an unreliable narrator because she stands on the outside, Melinda has apt observations about all the cliques in the school — Jocks, Cheerleaders, Eurotrash, Future Fascists of America, Suffering Artists, and Goths. She provides lists of the lies students hear in high school. Aided by the art teacher and some other students, however, Melinda slowly heals and finally explains the reason for her silence: drunk at the party, she was raped by Andy Evans. Although he comes to attack her again, she manages to save herself and finds her own voice in a very satisfying ending.

Drawing on her own memories of being a freshman in a new school system, Laurie Halse Anderson captures the raw emotion and pain of teenage life. A powerful book for discussion, in mother-daughter book groups or in class, *Speak* appeals to both young readers and adults because of its honest portrayal of high school life.

FRANCESCA LIA BLOCK
## *Weetzie Bat*
14–18 • Harper • 1989 • 128 pp.

Although she hates high school in Hollywood, Weetzie Bat, a blond pixie, loves Marilyn Monroe and Chaplin and roller-skating waitresses. Dressing in her own style, including Harlequin sunglasses and 1950s taffeta dresses, she finds few who really understand her until she meets Dirk, who is gay. Together they find their mates: Dirk, a blond surfer, and Weetzie, Secret Agent Lover Man. When they all live together, the four of them make movies and a baby, Cherokee. Another child, Witch Baby, is left on their doorstep.

Reading like a fantasy or dream and containing dialogue loaded with slang, Francesca Lia Block's novel embraces pop culture and alternate life styles. Her heroines and heroes rarely spend time in school. They're far too engaged in singing in rock bands, surfing, communing with ghosts, and driving around Los Angeles in vintage convertibles. Using a limited third-person voice, Block does not judge her characters or their world.

Inspired by Gabriel García Márquez and Isabel Allende and written while Block was in college, the book brings together magical realism and Hollywood culture. Some believe it to be pure fantasy; others think it captures Los Angeles teen culture realistically, "Shangri-L.A." Five of Block's books — *Weetzie Bat, Witch Baby, Cherokee Bat and the Goat Guys, Missing Angel Juan,* and *Baby Be-Bop* — have appeared in a single volume, *Dangerous Angels.* These titles, books like *Girl Goddess #9,* and her unconventional love song to Los Angeles, *Weetzie Bat,* made Block the most heralded new writer of the 1990s.

MELVIN BURGESS

## *Doing It*

14–18 • Holt • 2004 • 326 pp.

Told from the point of view of three hormone-sodden high school boys, *Doing It* begins with their fantasizing about having sex with a variety of women — a bag lady, teachers, classmates, and even the queen of England. Readers then learn about their actual sexual experiences in precise detail. Dino tries desperately to get his gorgeous girlfriend to do more; Jonathan fancies a girl he can't admit liking because she's plump; and Ben has an affair with a lusty teacher.

Melvin Burgess wrote this book because he believes novels about love and sexuality usually get told from a woman's point of view. Dedicating the book to his penis, using British slang for sexual acts and body parts, he remains blunt and even raunchy through the entire novel.

Because of the perspective, many female readers dislike the book intensely, feeling that it minimizes women or reduces them to sexual objects. Fortunately, the first chapter will tell them whether they want to shut the book or not. For those who keep reading and enjoy the humor, *Doing It* has helped some boys understand that they are not alone in this world after all.


STEPHEN CHBOSKY

## *The Perks of Being a Wallflower*

14–18 • Simon & Schuster/MTV • 1999 • 213 pp.

In an epistolary novel, the narrator, Charlie, conjures up his freshman year in high school. Although schoolwork presents few problems for this very sensitive protagonist, Charlie has difficulty relating to his fellow students. Then he starts hanging around with two seniors, Samantha (Sam) and Patrick, and tries to cope with an overwhelming number of problems — drugs, suicide, sex, homosexuality, and abortion. Shy and introspective, Charlie finds himself watching life rather than taking part. In the final pages, readers learn that as a child, Charlie had been sexually molested by his aunt. In this uplifting coming-of-age tale, told in language quite plain and blunt, Charlie finally starts to participate in his life.

Because of the authenticity of the author's voice, nonreaders who have bought Cliff Notes often find themselves swept up in the novel. Although wildly popular with teenage readers, the book has also been extremely controversial because of the many issues it raises. But for its many enthusiastic readers, Charlie emerges not as a depressed teen who criticizes the world but as a thoughtful optimist, looking for an honest world in which he can live.

BROCK COLE

## The Facts Speak for Themselves

14–18 • Front Street • 1997 • 184 pp.

↬ *NATIONAL BOOK AWARD FINALIST*

In an absolutely flat, unemotional voice, thirteen-year-old Linda relates a horrific story. As the narrative begins in a police station, she tells officers how she watched Frank Perry shoot Jack Green. Then Frank committed suicide. Without wasting energy, without feeling, without trying to make sense of anything that happens, Linda simply survives in the most trying of circumstances. When her mother stops caring for the other children, Linda takes over. When her mother starts having a series of live-in boyfriends, Linda becomes sexually precocious. Then she carries on an affair with her mother's employer, Jack Green, again accepting it as part of the landscape. At the end, living in a Catholic Charities center, Linda does what seems expected of her in the same resigned, unthinking way.

The deceptively straightforward narrative almost makes the events seem normal, because they appear to be reasonable to Linda. No other voice intrudes; that role has been left entirely to the reader in this powerful and shocking novel.

SONYA HARTNETT

## Sleeping Dogs

14–18 • Viking • 1995 • 133 pp.

The Australian author of *Thursday's Child* and *What the Birds See* explores how a father emotionally and physically isolates and abuses his family. Griffin, a violent alcoholic Vietnam veteran, lives on a rundown Australian farm with his wife and five children. The crumbling farmhouse serves as a metaphor for the strangled lives inside. Gradually Griffin drives his wife into madness, and he regularly beats his son Jordan, a talented artist, who is involved in an incestuous relationship with his sister. In the end, learning the truth about his children, Griffin murders his son.

Told in the third-person present-tense voice, which brings readers right into the horror, the novel could have come from the pen of William Faulkner or Tennessee Williams. *Sleeping Dogs* explores in gritty detail how morality can be twisted by obsessive family loyalty.

DAVID KLASS

## *You Don't Know Me*

14–18 • Farrar, Straus/Foster • 2001 • 344 pp.

At fourteen, John has developed an unusual way of describing his world. He attends "anti-school," takes "anti-math," and lives with "the man who is not my father," an often-drunk petty criminal. In a unique second-person present-tense narrative, John, who says he was named after a toilet, reveals to readers what he survives on a daily basis. His soon-to-be-stepfather brutalizes him, and John believes that if he tells his mother, she will reject him. At school, he attempts to seem normal and plays in the school orchestra, saying: "My tuba is actually not a tuba, because it has never produced a musical sound. It is actually a giant frog pretending to be a tuba." John manages to get a date with his dream girl, the beautiful yet shallow Gloria, but that evening becomes a teenager's worst nightmare. Suspended from school, beaten senseless by his father, John begins to connect with those around him — including his mother and his music teacher — and get help.

The plot sounds depressing and deals with serious subject matter. But John's rapid-fire delivery, his dark, sarcastic humor, his detachment and irony, his painful honesty, and the upbeat ending actually make the story enjoyable. Fans of the book delight in the unique voice, which takes them into the mind of the character. In the end, they laugh and cry; they feel they know John very well and have grown to care deeply for him.

CHRIS LYNCH

## *Freewill*

14–18 • Harper • 2001 • 148 pp.

↬ *PRINTZ HONOR*

In a second-person, stream-of-consciousness narrative, the reader encounters a teenager, Will, who has lost his father and stepmother in an accident and has had trouble dealing with their deaths. As Will talks to himself, he reveals how disturbed and lonely he really is. Eventually, wood sculptures or totems that Will has made start to show up near the dead bodies of teenagers.

This dark and murky novel, with a teenager on the fringe of his peer group, takes place mainly inside Will's head. It focuses on the perennial adolescent concern of autonomy and choice. Can individuals determine their own fate or do they play out preordained roles?

PATRICIA MCCORMICK

## *Cut*

14–18 • Front Street • 2000 • 151 pp.

Silent to others for most of the narrative, Callie lives in a residential treatment facility, a hospital for teens with a variety of psychiatric disorders. Through her internal dialogue, she reveals how she cuts herself and the dynamics of her dysfunctional family. The other girls, suffering from anorexia, overeating, and substance abuse, also examine their families — "It's like we're invisible." As Laurie Halse Anderson does in *Speak,* McCormick creates a believable, sometimes even admirable, character who must find her own voice and outgrow her sense of powerlessness.

Those who appreciate the book often tend themselves to engage in self-mutilation or self-destruction, or have friends who do. Those who dislike it think that it makes cutting alluring or interesting. This powerful, spare, emotional novel examines a taboo subject in a story that pulls no punches.

JOHN MARSDEN

## *Letters from the Inside*

12–14 • Houghton Mifflin • 1994 • 160 pp.

After Tracey places an ad in a teenage magazine, she becomes pen pals with Mandy, another Australian teenager. The letters start innocently enough, but Mandy admits that she is struggling with an abusive older brother. Subsequently she discovers that Tracey lives in an institution for juvenile criminals and will be transferred to a women's prison when she is eighteen. Although readers never learn the nature of her crime, they do hear about her brutal life behind bars. In the meantime, Mandy's brother becomes increasingly violent, even cleaning guns in his room. In the end, Tracey's letters to Mandy come back, marked "Return to Sender." Neither Tracey nor the reader learns what has happened.

Told in alternating letters, the novel explores the violence and victimization of the two girls. Drawing material from real accounts and his own experience in prison, Marsden never trivializes their experience in this frightening and thought-provoking novel, which is ideal for group discussion.

JESS MOWRY

## *Babylon Boyz*

12–14 • Simon & Schuster • 1997 • 192 pp.

Thirteen-year-old Dante, an African-American boy, and his friends Pook, who is gay, and Wyatt, overweight, form an alternate family in a section of Oakland, California, called Babylon. In this landscape of gang violence and drugs, Dante's crack-addicted mother died when he was born, leaving him with a bad heart. His gay friend Pook wants desperately to get out of Babylon and go to medical school, but he lacks money. One night Dante and Pook witness a drug dealer throw a suitcase from his car while being pursued by the police. Retrieving the case, they discover that it contains enough cocaine to allow both Pook his dreams and Dante the operation he needs. But selling the drugs would contribute further to the problems of their community.

With realistic, gritty dialogue — and a story that includes several murders, a rape, and sex scenes — Babylon and its characters come vividly to life, and readers find themselves walking the mean streets of Oakland with Dante. Ultimately these young men, victims of poverty and drugs, struggle to make the right choices for their lives.

WALTER DEAN MYERS

## Monster

14–18 • Harper • 1999 • 281 pp.

↪ *PRINTZ AWARD/NATIONAL BOOK AWARD FINALIST*

A sixteen-year-old African American, Steve Harmon stands trial for a felony. Accused of acting as a lookout for a robbery that left a drugstore owner dead — and called "a Monster" by the prosecution — Steve faces a possible sentence of twenty-five years in prison. Throughout the narrative Steve's level of involvement in the crime remains unclear, and readers must determine the truthfulness of the defendants, witnesses, lawyers, and Steve himself. Steve tells his story in a first-person journal and a third-person screenplay. His photographs, actually artwork by Christopher Myers, help establish the character and setting. The author, in his typical manner, confronts the material in a realistic and graphic way, including a prison rape scene; he refuses to be anything less than honest with his readers.

To write the book, Myers visited Greenhaven Prison in New York, compiling 600 pages of interview notes. He wanted to understand why someone would become involved in criminal activity that would lead to imprisonment. He noticed that the people took steps along the way, bending rules and ignoring laws. Sitting in a courtroom, where a seventeen-year-old black male was on trial for armed robbery, Myers heard the laughter of schoolchildren outside the window. That juxtaposition of innocence and guilt formed the subject matter of *Monster*. With everyone writing and talking about stopping crime, Myers wanted to explore it from a teenager's point of view.

Type sizes change for the different formats, which, because of a great deal of white space on the page, remain quite readable and dynamic. "I've read this book twenty times and I don't specifically plan to stop," one teenager reader has written, and fans of the book admit they have read it over and over. One of the high-water marks of young adult literature, the book combines an innovative format, complex moral issues, and a sympathetic if flawed narrator. Ideal for reading aloud, *Monster* can be interpreted in many different ways and naturally generates discussion.

LAUREN MYRACLE

## *ttyl*

12–14 • Abrams/Amulet • 2004 • 209 pp.

Some books seem edgy because of their content and some because of their format. Lauren Myracle's *ttyl* ("talk to you later") has been executed entirely in the form of Internet instant messaging among three sophomore friends; they exchange comments as "mad maddie," "SnowAngel," and "zoegirl." As they chat from September to November in this modern epistolary novel, they reveal information about classes, boys, clothes, getting drunk, sex, the popular crowd, and difficulties with "rents" (parents). Frank in their language, as teens might be in IM, they manage to get into some serious trouble: "zoegirl" develops an inappropriate, potentially disastrous relationship with a teacher.

Very true to teenage language, social customs, and contemporary communication, *ttyl* has become wildly popular with its audience but has met resistance from many adults, who find the lingo and the format (fifteen to twenty IMs on each page) difficult to read. However, after decoding the text, the reader can enjoy eavesdropping on three friends who sound just like their high school friends. Although it may give "rents" headaches, *ttyl* keeps teens reading breathlessly through thousands of juicy snippets of gossip.

ADAM RAPP

## *Under the Wolf, Under the Dog*

14–18 • Candlewick • 2004 • 310 pp.

If Holden Caulfield ventured into the twenty-first century, he might sound just like sixteen-year-old Steve Nugent, who writes an autobiography, "A Pretty Depressing Time in My Life." In a recovery home for teens, Steve's relates a saga filled with trauma. His mother dies from cancer, his brother commits suicide, his father descends into depression, and he himself acts out — smashing items, stealing, taking drugs, shaving his head, and going on the road. Like Holden, he finds some refuge with a child, a young girl named June. But he ultimately abandons her on a bus headed to Florida, as he returns home and into treatment. Adam Rapp excels in turn of phrase and poetic language: "it started raining and all the pedestrians pulled out umbrellas and they sort of bloomed like these giant flowers." In the narrative, Steve cries out for help, and the optimistic ending makes readers feel that he may well be on his way to healing.

ROB THOMAS

## *Rats Saw God*

14–18 • Simon & Schuster • 1996 • 219 pp.

The son of a famous astronaut, Steve York arrives in his school counselor's office high on drugs. Since he may not graduate with his class, the counselor gives Steve an opportunity to make up his missing credits by writing a hundred-page paper. The narrative shifts between Steve's current life in California and the saga of his life in Houston, Texas, when he lived with his father. There, Steve became part of a club called Grace Order of Dadaists (GOD) and helped create Dada-inspired art projects with the group. He also fell in love, then discovered his girlfriend having sex with one of the high school teachers late at night.

Since it has been published, teens have embraced the book and consider Rob Thomas a genius as a writer, adept at capturing their life as it is, not as their parents want it to be. But the frank description of Steve's first sexual encounter and the consensual sex between a teacher and student have continued to make the book controversial.

For those who admire the book, Steve's funny, self-deprecating, sarcastic voice carries the narrative along. Off-beat and quirky, *Rats Saw God* brings a group of highly individual, very amusing individuals to life as it depicts Steve's journey as an adolescent — from sinking into the depths of despair to finally pulling his life together and heading to college.

# *Fantasy*

T O SOME DEGREE, all fantasy literature serves as the literary equivalent of a good vacation. We can withdraw from the real world for the length of the novel, then return with a deeper appreciation of our world or a sense of what it might be. We know we can't attend Harry Potter's school, Hogwarts, or teach there, but after being there for several hundred pages, it may help us go back to our own school or teach our own students. As one young reader wrote, "I like authors who make their characters real enough to relate to but magical enough to get you away from ordinary life."

The fantasy novels that follow show two major influences. Since the 1950s, J.R.R. Tolkien has served as the standard-bearer for this genre; so much of what has been written after him contains echoes of him or is written in response to him. But King Arthur, over the years, has served as the protagonist for some of the best and most enduring fantasies. He and his sidekick, Merlin, seem to provide endless possibilities for writers.

Fantasy books for young adults have burgeoned over the past few years, thanks to J. K. Rowling and the successful movie adaptations of Tolkien's books. Certainly a genre that goes in and out of fashion, well-crafted fantasy endures better than other genres — it does not depend on current slang or fashion. New writers make their bid for fame, fortune, and immortality every day, but many of the books in this section have long been favorites and only improve with age. All of these books take their readers on an exciting vacation, and they return not only refreshed but better able to handle their own lives as well.

RICHARD ADAMS

## Watership Down

12–14 • Macmillan • 1974 • 496 pp.

In an epic novel, Richard Adams glorifies the adventures of Hazel and his band of young male rabbits. Warned by his clairvoyant brother, Hazel believes they must leave their warren in the Berkshire, England, countryside. In a leisurely narrative they set out from home, cross rivers, avoid railroad trains, and ultimately find a new domicile on Watership Down. There the warren prospers before Hazel dies. Each rabbit has a distinct character; all have the power of speech; and they have their own mythology and language — a lapine glossary has been included.

As Adams told his daughters an extended rabbit tale, they urged him to write it down. A civil servant, he had never published anything. Eventually, after many rejections and much revision, the work appeared on a children's book list in England with a small print run of 2,500. Ecstatic reviews compared the author to Kenneth Grahame, George Orwell, and Tolkien. When the children's book editor Susan Hirschman acquired the U.S. rights to the book, she decided to place it on the adult list to give it extra marketing and publicity attention. That move proved prescient: the book sold close to 300,000 copies in its first weeks and remained on the bestseller list for over a year. Subsequently translated into twenty languages, *Watership Down* became a bestseller in Germany, Japan, and Italy.

Still unusual in its sprawling saga of rabbit life, its amazing cast of animal characters, and its feeling for the countryside and land, the novel continues to attract adolescent fantasy readers; it remains one of those books they remember with pleasure long after they have become adults.

T. A. BARRON

## The Lost Years of Merlin

12–14 • Philomel • 1996 • 304 pp.

In T. A. Barron's Merlin quintet, Emrys, a young boy at the beginning, ages to become the legendary figure of Merlin. Asking "What was the great Merlin like as a child?" Barron created a world rich in character and setting, from which Merlin began his journey to great power. In the first volume, *The Lost Years of Merlin,* Emrys discovers his magical powers; using them wrongly, with hate, he himself suffers and loses his eyesight. His second sight, however, allows him to see the world in a different way. In *The Fires of Merlin,* Merlin encounters Ector, the boy destined to become King Arthur. The epic reveals the discoveries, challenges, gains, and losses that ultimately prepare Merlin to take center stage as a great wizard; he emerges in these books as a human being, with joys and aspirations, struggles and sorrows.

A detailed and gripping plot, with many twists and turns, makes *The Lost Years of Merlin* and the other four books in the quintet excellent choices for reading aloud in class or at home.

## TERRY BROOKS
### *Magic Kingdom for Sale — Sold!*
14–18 • Ballantine • 1986 • 374 pp.

A widowed lawyer from Chicago, Ben Holiday pays a million dollars to purchase the magical kingdom of Landover. But when he becomes king, he joins a long line of people who have failed at the job. Ben sets about restoring the kingdom, now in ruin. He has a plethora of problems: barons refusing to recognize him, peasants without hope, and a dragon laying waste to the countryside.

*Magic Kingdom for Sale — Sold!* and its sequels — *The Black Unicorn, Wizard at Large, The Tangle Box,* and *Witches' Brew* — have been immensely popular with high school students ever since they were first published.

## KEVIN CROSSLEY-HOLLAND
### *The Seeing Stone: Arthur Trilogy, Book One*
12–14 • Scholastic/Levine • 2001 • 340 pp.

At thirteen, Arthur spends much of his time alone, recording his feelings, insights, observations, and desires. He wants to become a squire, not a schoolman. Then his friend Merlin gives him a strange stone; when Arthur looks into the polished obsidian, he glimpses visions of another Arthur, whose life parallels his own. A convincing and attractive narrator, Arthur continues his adventures in *At the*

*Crossing Places* and *King of the Middle March;* the trilogy covers the years 1199–1203, ending when Arthur is eighteen.

With short chapters, lean and spare language, and a clipped rhythm to the prose, the book provides another view of the young Arthur and has found an enthusiastic reception with those readers eager to learn more about the most popular hero of all, King Arthur.

PETER DICKINSON

## The Ropemaker

12–14 • Delacorte • 2001 • 376 pp.

<> *PRINTZ HONOR*

The magical protection — which has secured the Valley from marauders for nineteen generations — has started to break down; two elders and two young people, Tilja and Tahl, set out on a quest to find the mysterious man who may be able to help them restore it. As they move through hostile, unfamiliar terrain, Tilja gains confidence in her ability to neutralize magic, rending it impotent. After many dangerous, exciting adventures, the travelers eventually meet the Ropemaker, the mightiest magician in the Empire, and must return home.

Skillfully blending fantasy with Tilja's coming-of-age story, Peter Dickinson weaves a thoughtful and compelling story. A master at plot and setting, he also renders a wide number of believable characters, including a bad-tempered horse.

NANCY FARMER

## The Sea of Trolls

12–14 • Atheneum/Jackson • 2004 • 459 pp.

In a highly original saga set in A.D. 793, Jack, an eleven-year-old Saxon boy, and Lucy, age five, get kidnapped by a crew of Viking berserkers led by Olaf One-Brow. They travel across the sea to the kingdom of Ivar the Boneless, wed to the half-troll Queen Frith. The Bard selects Jack as an apprentice, teaching him some magic and the history of the Northmen and their enemies. To save his sister, Jack eventually undertakes a quest to drink "song-mead" from Mimir's

Well in the heart of troll country, a Middle Earth run by the matriarchy.

Combing Norse mythology, *Beowulf,* troll and dragon lore, the nursery rhyme "Jack and Jill," and medieval history in a story of epic proportion, *The Sea of Trolls* appeals to those who enjoy adventure novels, the Vikings, and Tolkien — or just being taken on an exciting journey.

CORNELIA FUNKE, AUTHOR-ILLUSTRATOR

## *Inkheart*

12–14 • Scholastic/Chicken House • 2003 • 536 pp.

Ever since her mother disappeared, twelve-year-old Meggie and her father, Mo, have focused their lives on books and reading. Mo repairs books in his workshop, and Meggie often falls asleep with a book under her pillow. But she has never heard her father read aloud, because when he does everything comes alive, literally. Characters emerge from the book with form and substance, and in a swap, a person from the real world becomes part of the book. At one reading, Mo sent his wife into a book called *Inkheart* and brought several villainous characters, like Capricorn and his henchmen, to life.

With this intriguing premise, Cornelia Funke has created a page-turning thriller, set in an Italian town with both medieval and modern elements. In a book-lover's book that works equally well for both young readers and adults, she skillfully develops plot and character. Each chapter begins with a favorite quotation of Funke's from the canon of literature. Sonorous character names — Dustfinger, Silvertongue — pepper the text, as well as some highly inventive scenes when some of the favorite characters of all times — like Tinkerbell — come to life in Meggie's presence.

Currently Germany's best-selling writer for young readers, Funke speaks and writes English and has overseen the translation to keep it in line with the original. This multitalented author, who began her life as an illustrator, has also contributed spot art to the text. She has combined all her talents to create a book — followed by *Inkspell* and *Inkblood* — that young readers find hard to put down and impossible to forget.

CORNELIA FUNKE, AUTHOR-ILLUSTRATOR

## *The Thief Lord*

12–14 • Scholastic/Chicken House • 2002 • 351 pp.

One of the few translated books for young readers ever to become a *New York Times* bestseller, *The Thief Lord* takes place in the magical city of Venice, with moonlit waters, a labyrinth of canals and streets, and magnificent palaces. In this spellbinding story — part fantasy, part mystery, part adventure — two orphan brothers, Prosper and Bo, run away from their aunt because she plans to split them up. Escaping to Venice, they join a desperate band of ruffians, who live in an abandoned and crumbling movie theater and follow the direction of the Thief Lord. A petty criminal, he steals jewels from homes to help the band get the clothing and food they need. While inhabiting this Dickensian world, Prosper and Bo find themselves pursued by a detective, who has been hired to take them back to their aunt.

The lush setting, quick-paced adventure, idiosyncratic plot, and lively characters have helped establish this book as a favorite of young readers.

WILLIAM GOLDMAN

## *The Princess Bride: S. Morgenstern's Classic Tale of True Love and High Adventure (The "Good Parts" Version), Abridged by William Goldman*

14–18 • Harcourt • 1973 • 283 pp.

Toying with the reader from the first sentence, William Goldman spins a fanciful tale about Buttercup, one of the twenty most beautiful women in the world. When she professes her love for the farm boy Westley, he leaves to seek his fortune and reportedly gets murdered by the Dread Pirate Roberts. While Buttercup prepares to wed Prince Humperdinck, she gets kidnapped by a criminal band. Westley saves her and takes her through a Fireswamp to avoid the Prince — but they are captured, and he gets tortured. Eventually they all live happily, if not perfectly, ever after.

This outrageously funny fairy tale, adventure, romance spoof —

based on the premise that Goldman is abridging another book, which doesn't really exist — contains some amazing author asides and dialogue: "Hello. My name is Inigo Montoya. You killed my father. Prepare to die." Adapted for a movie directed by Rob Reiner, the book and movie have remained cult favorites for several decades.

BRIAN JACQUES

## *Redwall*

12–14 • Philomel • 1986 • 333 pp.

G rowing up in the rough neighborhood around the docks of Liverpool, England, Brian Jacques attended an inner-city school that produced other international stars — Paul McCartney and George Harrison of the Beatles. While in school, Jacques wrote a story that turned out to be so expert that a teacher accused him of plagiarism. At that point, Jacques realized he might have a talent for writing.

Not encouraged to stay in school, at fifteen Jacques set out to find adventure as a merchant seaman and become a student of "the University of Life." Returning to Liverpool, he worked as a railway fireman, a longshoreman, a long-distance truck driver, a bus driver, a boxer, a police officer, a postmaster, and a stand-up comic. Then he began writing a story for the children at the Royal Wavertree School for the Blind, where he had delivered milk. He wanted to write something very descriptive, painting pictures with words so that the children could "see" the scenes in their imagination.

The residents of handsome Redwall Abbey, a place of serenity and peace, suddenly find their tranquility interrupted by Cluny the Scourge, an insane rat with hordes of villainous followers. Matthias, a novice at the Abbey who has been inspired by the legendary mouse hero Martin, mobilizes the defense of Redwall. A cast of distinctive characters — Constance the badger, Basil Stag Hare, Warbeak the sparrow, and the Abbot Mortimer — join forces to defeat Cluny and his hordes. *Redwall* provides readers with action, adventure, derringdo, truly evil villains, a clear sense of right and wrong — all the elements of great adventure fiction. It also contains standard fantasy conventions: the quest for the legendary sword, an awkward hero who discovers his true heritage, and the war between good and evil. But in *Redwall* rats serve as villains and mice as heroes.

As each book in the Redwall series has been released, Jacques has traveled extensively in the United States. He can imitate characters, set scenes, and help the audience imagine the landscape. He personally conveys the enthusiasm that millions of teenagers now feel for these adventures. All the titles in this lengthy series have proven popular, especially *Mattimeo, Marlfox,* and *Taggerung.*

DIANA WYNNE JONES

## Charmed Life

12–14 • Greenwillow • 1977 • 218 pp.

Long before J. K. Rowling invented the world of Harry Potter, Diana Wynne Jones envisioned a magical Great Britain, one in which the government licenses and supervises magic. In that world Gwendolen Chant shows potential to be a great witch. When her parents drown, Gwendolen and her brother, Cat, with no perceived magical talent, become the charges of Mrs. Sharp, a certified witch. While being tutored as well by a local necromancer, Gwendolen writes to Chrestomanci, a master who had corresponded with her parents. To be apprenticed to him, she and Cat go to live at Chrestomanci Castle. When she feels that Chrestomanci is not paying enough attention to her, Gwendolyn starts working forbidden spells. Cat discovers some magic happening in his own presence and begins to uncover the truth about himself, his sister, Chrestomanci, and his cousin Christopher Chant.

This highly original story has delighted serious fantasy readers for several decades; its advocates always argue its literary superiority to the Harry Potter saga. *Charmed Life* led to the other books in the Chrestomanci Cycle: *The Lives of Christopher Chant, The Magicians of Caprona, Witch Week,* and *Mixed Magics.*

DIANA WYNNE JONES

## Howl's Moving Castle

12–14 • Greenwillow • 1986 • 336 pp.

Sophie Hatter, a young girl who makes her living as a hatter, finds her fortunes immediately changed when the Wicked Witch of the Waste turns her into an old woman. Sophie seeks a haven inside a bizarre moving castle; owned by the wizard Howl and inhabited by the fire demon Calcifer, this strange home lurches around the country-side. Howl lives a madcap life, tries to escape the curse the witch has placed on him, and eventually finds in Sophie the girl of his dreams. Against her best judgment, Sophie falls in love with him too. But that outline simplifies a plot that at times becomes so complex that many readers need to diagram it. Diana Wynne Jones excels in humor and invention, and she manages to tie up all the loose ends of this rich and complex saga, bringing it to a satisfying conclusion.

MADELEINE L'ENGLE

## A Wrinkle in Time

12–14 • Farrar, Straus • 1962 • 211 pp.

⊹ *NEWBERY MEDAL*

A science fiction story, a coming-of-age story, and a philosophical novel, *A Wrinkle in Time* weaves these complex strands into a compelling plot line. Awkward and intense, Meg Murry and her pre-cocious little brother, Charles Wallace, join forces with three beings — Mrs. Whatsit, Mrs. Who, and Mrs. Which. They all try to save Meg's father, a physicist, from IT, a giant, pulsing brain and the embodiment of evil. Ultimately, what saves the Murry family and Charles Wallace turns out to be Meg's ability to love rather than hate.

The strength of *A Wrinkle in Time* lies in the general scope of the novel, which gives young readers room for discussion. Madeleine L'Engle's engaging, action-packed story has captured the imaginations of millions. Although some read the book as children, the combina-tion of philosophy and science — and its sequels *A Wind in the Door, A Swiftly Tilting Planet,* and *Many Waters* — often attracts young teenag-ers as well.

URSULA K. LE GUIN

## A Wizard of Earthsea

12–14 • Parnassus • 1968 • 183 pp.

An author of adult science fiction novels, Ursula Le Guin never ex-pected to write for another audience. But in 1967 the publisher of a small house wrote to Le Guin, asking if she would create a book for younger readers. The resulting title, *A Wizard of Earthsea,* gave her a chance to explore a coming-of-age story in a fantasy framework.

Taking place in an island community set back in time several hundred years, the book presents a society that views magic very seriously and protects it. The young goatherd Ged undertakes a journey to become a wizard through formal education at the wizards' academy and his experiences in the world. But his pride and ambition prove far more dangerous than dragons or evil sorcerers. These character defects cause him to summon from the darkness a shadow that almost destroys him. In a satisfying ending, Ged must ultimately turn to face this shadow, name it — and merge with it.

Le Guin decided to go against all fantasy convention when she gave her villains white skin and her heroes black or brown. Although she meant this device to be a strike against racial bigotry, she also wanted to subvert the entire European heroic tradition of fantasy. Ged remains an outsider to that tradition.

Le Guin crafted other books in the Earthsea saga, other novels such as *The Left Hand of Darkness,* and she won countless prizes. But *A Wizard of Earthsea* remains one of the standard-bearers of contemporary fantasy. It combines a superb quest or journey with a psychological reality — learning to face the darkness inside.

C. S. LEWIS

## *The Lion, the Witch and the Wardrobe*

12–14 • Macmillan • 1950 • 189 pp.

When he was sixteen, C. S. Lewis saw a vivid image: a faun carrying an umbrella in a snowy wood. In 1939 he tried creating a book from this image and failed. Nine years later, a lion leapt into a story, and he began working on a book called "The Lion."

Intensely unhappy and physically depleted, Lewis turned to the realm of his childhood reading, images, and thinking. Although he originally thought the book would stand alone, he got swept up in the characters and the concepts and produced the five books of the Narnia series in two years; eventually he wrote seven. In March 1949 Lewis read the first story, "Lion," to his old friend Roger Lancelyn Green. Green helped him revise the manuscript, and soon the book was accepted for publication.

In *The Lion, the Witch and the Wardrobe,* four children have been evacuated during the London blitz to stay with an elderly professor. They find a wardrobe that leads to another world, Narnia. There, because of the spell of the evil White Witch, it is "always winter and never Christmas." The true ruler of Narnia, Aslan the Lion, has come to free the world from the spell of the White Witch. Aslan dies for the sins of the children and rises again from the dead. Through this book, Lewis presented Christianity and Christian concepts to young readers. The Lion, Aslan, served as his image for Christ.

Many who encounter these books have no sense of their Christian underpinnings; they simply want to enter the magical world of Narnia, again and again.

## RAFE MARTIN
### *Birdwing*
12–14 · Scholastic/Levine · 2005 · 359 pp.

In the Brothers Grimm story "The Six Swans," a wicked queen turns her stepsons into wild swans; their little sister can free them only by staying silent for six years and weaving them shirts of nettles. In this novel, which basically starts where the fairy tale ends, all the brothers regain human form, but the youngest, Ardwin, returns from the wild with one human arm and one swan wing. That wing can seem both a blessing and a curse to this teenager, often targeted as a freak. But when Ardwin learns that the king may surgically remove the wing and replace it with a mechanical arm, he runs away from the palace and searches for the wild swans he once knew.

In a haunting, extraordinary novel, Ardwin communicates with animals; his quest leads him on a picaresque journey that sweeps readers along with him. A magical, funny, vital reinterpretation of a fairy tale, *Birdwing* appeals to those who love intelligent fantasy.

## ANNE MCCAFFREY
### *Dragonflight*
14–18 · Ballantine · 1968 · 309 pp.

First published for adults but now a staple for teens, *Dragonflight* is the first volume of an extraordinarily popular series about the

Dragons of Pern and their riders. A distant star, colonized by humans and then forgotten, Pern gets attacked by the Red Star, a planet with an erratic elliptical orbit that comes close enough to Pern to drop the deadly Thread. To fight Thread, Pern's scientists develop winged, tailed, and fire-breathing dragons who are trained so that empathetic humans can ride them and defend the skies.

Over the centuries, some of this knowledge has been forgotten, becoming the stuff of legend. F'lar, one of the Dragonmen, senses that the Red Star will be attacked again and goes in search of a strong-willed woman to bond with a soon-to-be-hatched Dragon Queen. Lessa of Ruatha, the only surviving member of a ruling family, goes with him, impresses the newborn golden dragon, and becomes its life-long companion. Then, after a long period of peace, Tread begins to fall on Pern, and the struggle begins. Both F'lar and Lessa emerge as passionate, heroic individuals, searching for solutions to problems rather than succumbing to despair.

For this novel, Anne McCaffrey took mythical archetypes and combined them with the technology of the far future. In her portrait of the dragons, she has found the perfect fantasy companion for every adolescent — these fascinating beasts breathe fire, teleport themselves between places, and serve as intelligent and caring best friends. One day she asked herself: "What if dragons were the good guys?" Then these magnificent, multicolored creatures and their riders became the basis for a short story in *Analog Magazine,* which won McCaffrey a Hugo Award, the first given to a woman. From a humble beginning, the dragons of Pern became the stars of a series of books published from 1968 to 2003. One of the most popular fantasy–science fiction series of all time, it explores how to rediscover and preserve the past while maintaining flexibility and incorporating new ideas.

PATRICIA MCKILLIP

## *The Riddle-Master of Hed*

12–14 • Atheneum • 1976 • 228 pp.

Written and published when fantasy trilogies were rarer than they are today, the first of the Riddle-Master volumes focuses on an unlikely hero, Prince Morgon. The prince would prefer to be a farmer on his small island, but a series of events and several attacks on his life send him on a quest. A brilliant student at the College of Riddle-Masters, affectionate, and stubborn, Prince Morgon and his companion, Deth, Harpist of the High One, trek across the winter fields to seek help from the High One. On the way, Prince Morgon receives gifts of a harp and sword with three stars, identical to his birthmark. In his land, the dead come back again and again from their graves to form a spectral army that fights.

Like most high fantasists, Patricia McKillip borrows from Tolkien but adds her own strengths and also develops strong female characters; she became a fantasy writer because of her awe for Tolkien's accomplishment. Followed by *Heir of Sea and Fire* and *Harpist in the Wind*, *The Riddle-Master of Hed* — although negatively reviewed when it appeared — has established itself as a fantasy classic, one of those books long remembered and loved into adult years. All three novels have been combined in a single volume, *Riddle-Master*.

ROBIN MCKINLEY

## *The Hero and the Crown*

12–14 • Greenwillow • 1984 • 246 pp.

✧ *NEWBERY MEDAL*

In the mythical kingdom of Damar, Aerin, an only child, cannot succeed her father the king because the court believes that her mother bewitched him. Tall, with orange hair and a bit clumsy, at eighteen Aerin does not exhibit any psychic powers, the usual gift of Damar nobility. Sensitive about her failings but devoted to her father, she trains to slay the small dragons that plague the outlying villages of the kingdom. But her role actually proves to be far greater than she could have imagined. Ultimately she slays the Black Dragon, overcomes an evil mage, and restores the lost Hero's Crown to the rulers of Damar.

In this medieval fantasy landscape — where Robin McKinley's *The Blue Sword* occurs five hundred years later — the author creates a determined, vibrant, and spirited heroine. From adolescence a devoted reader of Tolkien, McKinley decried the lack of women central to the plot in *The Lord of the Rings*. Here she fashioned a worthy heroine, a girl who takes action and saves the kingdom.

GARTH NIX

## *Sabriel*

12–14 • Harper • 1996 • 491 pp.

An eighteen-year-old apprentice necromancer at Wyverley College, Sabriel must enter the realm of the dead to save her trapped father and defeat the evil spirit who took him there. She therefore leaves the modern world and goes on a long journey through the Old Kingdom, a magical medieval world with strange characters like the Mogget, a natural force contained in the form of a cat. Desperate to find her father, determined to help save the Old Kingdom from destruction, Sabriel endures violent confrontations, extreme exhaustion, and challenges to her supernatural abilities.

Using many of the traditional fantasy elements — necromancy, magical creatures, swords, ancient lands, and magical spells — the Australian novelist Garth Nix has added his own inventions and created a compelling female hero quest, which he continues in *Lirael: Daughter of the Clayr* and *Abhorsen.*

CHRISTOPHER PAOLINI

## *Eragon*

12–14 • Knopf • 2003 • 544 pp.

Fifteen-year-old Eragon, a farmboy, discovers a blue stone in a mystical mountain hiding place. When the stone hatches a sapphire-blue dragon, Saphira, Eragon bonds with the dragon and becomes the last of the Dragon Riders. They have an important part to play in the war against the cruel and oppressive King Galbatorix; after the king's servants murder the boy's family, Eragon embarks on a quest for vengeance. More suited to devoted rather than casual fantasy fans, the novel contains sixty-five characters; maps and glossaries help sort them out as well as explain the phrases in various invented languages.

As much a phenomenon as the book itself, Christopher Paolini began writing *Eragon* when he was fifteen. Educated at home, Paolini set out to write a novel for his own entertainment rather than going to college. Since his parents owned a small publishing company, they released the book, and the teenager appeared in schools and bookstores in the Northwest, decked out in a billowy red swordsman's shirt, black pantaloons, and black lace-up suede boots. Discovered by the writer Carl Hiaasen, who passed the book along to his editor at Knopf, Paolini was given a contract for his "Inheritance Trilogy."

A media darling because of his age and story, Paolini, however, ultimately needed the respect of young readers, who are not often fooled by the press. They have responded enthusiastically to his writing in *Eragon* and *Eldest* in part because the characters, Eragon and Saphira, appeal to them. Although much indebted to Tolkien, McCaffrey, and other fantasy writers, Paolini has crafted his own world of dragons, elves, dwarves, and magic and has certainly attracted his own devoted base of fans.

TAMORA PIERCE

## *Alanna: The First Adventure*

12–14 • Atheneum • 1983 • 240 pp.

In a generic medieval world, a twin brother and sister decide to trade places for their schooling. Consequently, Thom trains to become a sorcerer. Alanna disguises herself as a boy and becomes a royal page, so as Alan of Trebond she begins her journey to knighthood. Finding the journey difficult, she must master the skills necessary for battle, but she also needs to learn to distinguish her enemies from her allies.

Tamora Pierce began her "Song of the Lioness" quartet as a single 732-page novel for adults. But her agent suggested she break it into four books for adolescents. Pierce discovered that she loved writing for this audience, and *Alanna* was followed by the three other volumes: *In the Hand of the Goddess, The Woman Who Rides Like a Man,* and *Lioness Rampant.* In *Trickster's Choice,* Pierce began a series about Alanna's daughter, Aly, who wants to become a spy despite her parents' disapproval.

An author absolutely beloved by young readers, Pierce often proves to be a better storyteller than writer. But her books keep readers turning the pages breathlessly and have gained her a devoted, enthusiastic audience that loves to read about girls who do important things.

PHILIP PULLMAN

## *The Golden Compass*

12–14 • Knopf • 1996 • 399 pp.

In a world parallel to earth, Victorian in its details, all humans possess daemons, an integral part of their being that takes the form of an animal. Tied together by an emotional bond, the human and daemon cannot be separated without indescribable suffering or death. In the human's youth, the daemon can take many forms, but in adulthood it has one distinct shape. Orphaned Lyra Belacqua and her daemon, Pantalaimon, live in Jordan College, Oxford, in the care of the Master. Eleven-year-old Lyra has been given a rare and unusual alethiometer; it looks like a compass but can answer questions of all kinds, even about the future. When her best friend, Roger, disappears along with many other children, Lyra and her friends the "gyptians," who live on canal boats, set off to Lapland to find the missing children. On the way Lyra helps free an armored bear, who becomes a powerful ally. They locate the children at an experimental station, where a terrible operation separates the child from its daemon.

Since Pullman himself didn't like fantasy, he intentionally wanted to write a book that would appeal to those who usually wouldn't read the genre. Hating C. S. Lewis's Christian allegorical fantasies, he wanted his Dark Materials series to provide an antidote; he uses them to promote an anticlerical theme. Not surprisingly, this aspect of the books has created the most controversy.

With constant plot twists, escalating tension, beautifully descriptive language, and brilliant invention, *The Golden Compass* set the stage for two superb sequels, *The Subtle Knife* and *The Amber Spyglass*. Certainly the most celebrated fantasy novels of the 1990s, Pullman's books have not only garnered millions of fans but have been taught from grade school through college. Like the Harry Potter books, the Dark Materials trilogy has attracted a young adult audience and a large adult one as well.

J. K. ROWLING

## *Harry Potter and the Sorcerer's Stone*

12–18 • Scholastic/Levine • 1998 • 312 pp.

As a way to entice the young into reading, few stories surpass the Harry Potter novels. In *Harry Potter and the Sorcerer's Stone,* Harry and his new friends, Hermione Granger and Ron Weasley, enter Hogwarts School of Witchcraft and Wizardry. Although the book takes place in the 1990s, the story feels old-fashioned: the children get letters delivered by owls rather than e-mail. At school Harry finds that he possesses a particular talent for the school game of quidditch — a game of immense skill that combines flying, goalkeeping, and broomsticks. With the help of his friends, Hagrid, a giant, and Albus Dumbledore, the headmaster, Harry unearths an old enemy camped beneath the school, the evil Voldemort. With each volume of the series, Harry grows a year older, and the sense of darkness increases. As he matures into a teenager and gains skills — from a variety of teachers, including the short-lived Defense Against the Dark Arts instructors — the evil that he must combat also grows in strength.

The Harry Potter books contain a number of stock ingredients: a school story, an orphan story, a friendship chronicle, and the struggle between good and evil. Although games like quidditch have been invented for the saga, Rowling tends to mine old, established forms but develops them masterfully. The books also depend on a class struggle — between those born to parents with magic blood and those born to Muggles, nonmagic parents. Like Oliver Twist and David Copperfield, Harry Potter experiences early tragedy and lives with cruel surrogate parents. An apparently ordinary child, he turns out to be extraordinary.

No matter how much anyone appreciated these books, no one anticipated the Harry Potter phenomenon. The books climbed to the top of the *New York Times* bestsellers' list; J. K. Rowling, once poverty-stricken, became wealthier than the queen of England; scores of young people, many who had remained oblivious to the charms of reading, found themselves beguiled by Harry; movie adaptations set box-office records. In its first twenty-four hours, the sixth book sold over ten million copies, a record unsurpassed by any other book.

Any book or series this popular will naturally find its detractors.

Although the struggle between good and evil underscores most fantasies, some groups took umbrage with Harry Potter, destroying copies in public and attempting to get the book banned from schools and libraries. For the last several years, the Harry Potter books have been the most challenged books in America.

With Rowling and her rags-to-riches personal story and with a series of books so quickly becoming part of the American culture, nothing like Harry Potter has ever been seen in the book world. Like its protagonist, a seemingly ordinary book became extraordinary.

ANTOINE DE SAINT-EXUPÉRY
## The Little Prince (Le Petit Prince)
12–18 • Harcourt • 1943 • 96 pp.

After crashing his plane into a desert, a pilot attempts to repair it when a child appears before him, the Little Prince. Born on another planet and now visiting Earth, the child tells the pilot about his planet. He must dig up baobab sprouts every day lest they take over the landscape; he passionately loves his special rose, the only one of its kind. The Little Prince describes his journey through different asteroids, where he meets some very strange grownups — a king, a businessman, and a drunkard. And he asks the pilot to draw him a picture of a sheep wearing a muzzle, so it won't eat his rose. When the plane gets repaired, the Little Prince departs for his planet, but both the pilot and the readers have been changed by their exposure to this incredible being.

Delighting both adult and young adult readers for more than sixty years, this fable about love and loneliness explores the issues of growing up, perception, and what is truly important in life. Consequently, it can be used quite effectively in teen-adult discussion groups.

LEMONY SNICKET, AUTHOR
BRETT HELQUIST, ILLUSTRATOR
## The Bad Beginning
12–14 • HarperCollins • 1999 • 176 pp.

Although younger readers have embraced Lemony Snicket's thirteen-volume Series of Unfortunate Events, many reluctant teen readers also find themselves engaged by the books. In a mock-serious tone, Lemony Snicket, the narrator, warns readers: "People who hate stories in which terrible things happen to small children should put this book down immediately."

The three Baudelaire children — Violet, Klaus, and Sunny — lose their parents in a fire and become wards of the terrible Count Olaf. He tries to murder them, wed Violet for her fortune, and dispose of the adults who try to help them. The orphans have to use their skills at invention, reading, and in the case of Sunny, the youngest, biting to save themselves time and time again. Ultimately, the orphans triumph — dealing with what comes their way, supporting one another, and creating a family that stays together.

Fast-paced and action-driven, the books are filled with word play and funny asides. Although many adults don't enjoy them, young readers find them humorous and sly.

MARY STEWART

## *The Crystal Cave*

14–18 • Morrow • 1970 • 529 pp.

Merlin and King Arthur have long provided fodder for creative minds. In a modern rendition of these legends, Mary Stewart envisions a very human Merlin, at first a young boy in Wales. The son of a king's daughter, Merlin gets rough treatment as a bastard; his mother will not reveal his father's name. To escape being killed by his uncle, Merlin sets fire to his room and then flees. On his journey, he discovers not only his father's identity but also his own purpose in life — as a wizard and confidant to British kings. Merlin emerges as a sympathetic and believable human being rather than a shadowy magician; his magical powers, which at first he cannot control, develop in an understandable way.

In an easy, accessible style, Stewart transforms the stuff of legend into fiction. Set in fifth-century Britain, the complex story pays careful attention to historical detail. Stewart continued her saga in three other popular titles: *The Hollow Hills, The Last Enchantment,* and *The Wicked Day.*

JONATHAN STROUD

## *The Amulet of Samarkand*

12–14 • Miramax • 2003 • 462 pp.

In a fantasy with echoes of many other works, Jonathan Stroud still weaves an enthralling tale. The magicians who rule England derive their power from demons — afrits, djinn, and imps. Although these characters often execute the magicians' commands, they also hunt for a loophole. Bartimaeus, a smart-mouthed djinni, gets summoned by a young magician, Nathaniel, to steal the Amulet of Samarkand. At first Bartimaeus tries to wiggle out of his assignments from Nathaniel. But in the end, because of an ingenious spell, Bartimaeus works with Nathaniel to defeat the evil mastermind Simon Lovelace.

Filled with Bartimaeus's diatribes, often in the form of lengthy footnotes, the book and its sequels in the trilogy exude humor and adventure and keep young readers turning the pages. These books often satisfy the request, "What do I read after Harry Potter and Philip Pullman?"

J.R.R. TOLKIEN

## *The Hobbit*

12–18 • Houghton Mifflin • 1938 • 330 pp.

In 1917 J.R.R. Tolkien, a professor at Oxford, began chronicling the legends of the First Age of Middle-earth, a mythological epic eventually called *The Silmarillion*. He returned to the saga again and again; for Middle-earth he even invented elvish languages.

One day, as Tolkien graded exam papers, he found a blank page. He took up his pen and wrote: "In a hole in the ground there lived a hobbit." At that point he decided he'd better figure out what hobbits were. As he played with the idea, he envisioned them as creatures of small imagination but great courage — the kind of courage he had seen in the trenches in World War I. Around 1930 he began writing the story of one such hobbit, Bilbo Baggins, and told tales about hobbits at night to his three sons. Although the saga began as personal entertainment, eventually Bilbo strayed into the rich history of Middle-earth that Tolkien had already created in *The Silmarillion*.

In *The Hobbit* Bilbo Baggins, a comfort-loving, ordinary, and unlikely hero, joins a band of dwarfs gathered with the aid of the wizard Gandalf. They set out from Baggins's home to seek the treasure horded by Smaug, the dragon. As they go through various adventures and escape spiders, goblins, and the dragon itself, Bilbo grows in courage, strength, and wisdom. Along the way, he retrieves from the Gollum a magic ring, which makes him invisible

At the end of the book, Gandalf tells Bilbo: "'You are a very fine person, Mr. Baggins, and I am very fond of you; but you are only quite a little fellow in a wide world after all.'" But as many millions of readers have found Bilbo and his nephew, Frodo Baggins, the world of the hobbit has continued to expand. This little fellow, Bilbo Baggins, has played a major role in the canon of world literature.

J.R.R. TOLKIEN

## The Lord of the Rings (The Fellowship of the Ring, The Two Towers, The Return of the King)

14–18 · Houghton Mifflin · 1954, 1955 · 1,137 pp.

One Ring to rule them all, One Ring to find them, One Ring to bring them all and in the Darkness bind them." So the Oxford don J.R.R. Tolkien begins the trilogy now viewed as one of the most powerful pieces of literature ever written by a human being. At the beginning Bilbo Baggins, the hero of *The Hobbit*, gives his nephew Frodo the Ring of Invisibility he acquired on his journey. From the lush and green hobbit shire, Frodo starts out on his own quest, which takes him to Mordor, devoid of life, and ultimately to Mount Doom, to destroy this ring. In the process, Frodo and the reader meet an incredible cast of characters: Gandalf; Sauron (the antagonist); the hobbits Sam, Merry, and Pippin; the mysterious Strider; Tom Bombadil; Elrond and Legolas, elves; and Gimli, a dwarf — not to mention orcs, goblins, evil wizards, Treebeard, the guardian of the forest, and one of fiction's greatest tragic figures, the Gollum, who is obsessed by the ring. As the designated ring-bearer, Frodo becomes increasingly corrupted by its power; he must battle himself at every turn. Essentially, the protagonists take on nearly impossible odds to defeat evil in this amazingly rich story that draws on mythology, legend, and world literature.

With the great success of *The Hobbit*, Tolkien's British publisher asked for yet more stories. A perfectionist and constant reviser, Tolkien took some twelve years to deliver the sequel, which ran over a thousand pages and was infinitely darker and more complex. At first no one knew what to do with the manuscript; eventually the firm decided to publish it as three separate volumes. The editorial report of Anne Barrett, who acquired the American rights for *The Fellowship of the Rings,* presents the general issues: "A rich book and a deadly serious one. I think it is wonderful, but it has its drawbacks. Who will read 423 pages about an unfinished journey undertaken by mythical creatures with confusing names? Probably no one, but I still say it is wonderful and — with my heart in my mouth — *to publish.*"

Although immediately accepted by a small coterie of fans, the trilogy slowly gained a wider audience. In 2003 the British public voted the book their best-loved novel. Recently, a series of movies directed by Peter Jackson brought the books to cult status with teenage readers.

T. H. WHITE
## The Once and Future King
14–18 • Putnam • 1965 • 639 pp.

A medieval scholar fascinated with the Arthurian legends, T. H. White crafted the penultimate book on the subject in the course of twenty years. First published as three individual titles (*The Sword in the Stone* appeared in England in 1938), White pulled them together in the late 1950s and added a final section to produce *The Once and Future King.*

The first section, "The Sword in the Stone," introduces readers to Wart, a young boy growing up in the castle of Sir Ector, his foster father. Wart and his friend Kay, the heir to the title, spend their days together while Kay gets trained for knighthood. Wandering in the forest, Wart meets Merlyn, who becomes the boys' tutor. The magician can see into the future, so he often gets confused about what has and what has not happened. He always brings anachronisms into events, wearing clothing not yet invented, for instance. However, he proves a masterful tutor for Wart and transforms him into all kinds of animals so that he can learn the universe from different perspectives. Robin Wood (now known as Hood) and some of his band meet Wart as well. At the end of the first section, Kay, now a knight, participates in a tournament to pull the sword from the stone and become England's rightful king. On an errand for Kay, Wart removes the sword — becoming King Arthur, the next king of England.

Through the next sections Arthur fights to keep his crown, creates the Knights of the Round Table, goes in search of the Holy Grail, establishes Camelot, marries, and is betrayed by Guinevere.

In this rich saga, White brings the ancient legends of England to life, giving the people form and substance. The humor, emotion, drama, and action keep readers mesmerized, but in the end all grow to love and understand these multidimensional characters. Used as the basis of the hit musical *Camelot*, adapted for the Disney movie *The Sword in the Stone*, and read and reread by devotees, *The Once and Future King* still stands as the one book about King Arthur that no reader should miss.

PATRICIA C. WREDE AND CAROLINE STEVERMER

## *Sorcery & Cecelia, or, The Enchanted Chocolate Pot*

12–14 • Harcourt • 1988 • 316 pp.

Take a little bit of Jane Austen, stir in some Georgette Heyer, add a spell or two from J. K. Rowling, and you have nothing nearly as delicious as the plot for *Sorcery & Cecelia*. In letters two cousins, Kate and Cecelia, talk about their respective seasons in London and the country in 1817. Kate almost gets poisoned at the Royal College of Wizards; Cecelia attempts to figure out who placed the charm bag under her brother's bed — and then how to make more of them. Then the goose-witted young man ends up being turned into a tree and disappears. Dresses and parties and picnics and mysterious men keep both girls immensely busy as they get involved with some battling wizards. In the end, they quickly plan a double wedding.

Out of print for several years, the book was reissued in 2003 to great fanfare. *Sorcery & Cecelia* had been written as a Letter Game by the two authors; neither knew where the plot was going and responded only to the last letter. The book thus reads like a literary tennis match; readers learn what is happening at the same time the writers do.

With twists and turns of plot, humor, panache, and great charm, *Sorcery & Cecelia* has gained cult status. Readers will want to continue the saga, perfect for mother-daughter discussion groups, in *The Grand Tour;* they may also want to pick up Wrede's Enchanted Forest Chronicles, another favorite in middle school.

# Graphic Novels

IN ALMOST ANY CHAIN BOOKSTORE, you are likely to see teenage boys and girls reading manga, thick black-and-white comic books imported from Japan. The sale of these books in the United States alone has doubled since 2002.

Recently, the Del Rey imprint, under Random House, and Scholastic books have both launched their own graphic novel lines, importing or adding color to existing work. Upton Sinclair's *The Jungle* and Kafka's books have already been adapted for this form, and publishers are releasing everything from Harlequin romances to *The Babysitter's Club* as graphic novels.

Often disliked by adults for their sex and violence, graphic novels have been embraced by teens to some degree because adults dismiss them or can't read them. But adolescents also enjoy the form for what it can accomplish; the immediacy and power of the best graphic work conjures up movies or music videos.

In their infancy as an artistic form, graphic novels are still developing as a genre. With their current popularity and their appeal to young artists, they hold infinite possibilities.

NEIL GAIMAN

## *The Sandman*

16–18 • DC Comics • 1990–1997 • approximately 1,450 pp.

Illustrated by various artists. One of the first comics to be popular enough to be collected for a trade paperback, *The Sandman,* a dark and complex saga, was first published in seventy-five single issues between 1988 and 1996. Dream, otherwise known as the Sandman, and his siblings — Death, Delirium, Desire, Destiny, Destruction, and Despair — are collectively known as Endless. Their story ranges through a number of settings, including our waking world, dreaming, and hell. Each volume contains a distinct plot; in *Preludes & Nocturnes,* Dream must escape from prison and reclaim his realm, The Dreaming, as well as his helmet, pouch, and amulet. In creating this epic, Neil Gaiman drew on various human mythologies, religion, and the culture of the last three thousand years.

Over time, the story has gained a devoted adolescent following. Gaiman once wrote: "What I enjoy most is when people say to me, 'When I was sixteen I didn't know what I was going to do with my life and then I read *Sandman* and now I'm at University studying mythology.'"

DEREK KIRK KIM, AUTHOR-ILLUSTRATOR

## *Same Difference and Other Stories*

14–18 • Top Shelf Productions • 2004 • 143 pp.

Different offerings in this collection of a novella and short stories feature a young man in his twenties and another in his teens. The novella focuses on two friends and the consequences of dishonesty in romantic relationships, creating a tale of longing, regret, and forgiveness. Derek Kirk Kim's Korean background and his perspective of moving to the United States and living in an integrated family — with a white father — inform this graphic novel, particularly the story "Hurdles."

Kim originally serialized these stories on his Web site; then he received a Xeric Grant (established by Peter Laird of "Teenage Mutant Ninja Turtle" fame) and self-published the book in 2003. He continues to serialize his stories on his Web site, smallstoriesonline.com.

KAZUO KOIKE, AUTHOR

GOSEKI KOJIMA, ILLUSTRATOR

## Lone Wolf and Cub: The Assassin's Road

16–18 • Dark Horse Comics • 2000 • 303 pp.

Nine stories set in feudal Japan present the story of Ogami Itto the Lone Wolf, a masterless samurai, and Daigoro the Cub, his infant son. Although Itto still clings to the samurai code of conduct, he has become a ronin, a wandering sword for hire. Itto travels with his infant son, who becomes more than a prop as the series progresses. The violence of the Ittos' life and the frank sexual content make the volumes more appropriate for older teens.

Koike has become famous for this meticulously researched and fascinating epic set in the Edo period of Japan. Often hailed as cinematic, Kojima's artwork captures the motion of the swordplay and conveys a sense of the pastoral setting. He frequently develops the story by means of wordless panels, creating a tense and brooding atmosphere. Constituting 8,000 pages and twenty-eight volumes when originally published in Japan, the last volume was released in the United States in 2002.

SCOTT MCCLOUD, AUTHOR-ILLUSTRATOR

## Understanding Comics: The Invisible Art

14–18 • Kitchen Sink Press • 1993 • 216 pp.

Narrated by the author, the book begins in his studio. In nine simply drawn chapters, Scott McCloud sets out to define comics as an art form, to explore their history, and to show how they affect readers. *Understanding Comics* demonstrates that like television and the movies, comics have emerged as a powerful and valid form of art.

Frustrated because people didn't give comics their due, McCloud wanted to show readers how they work aesthetically. In this volume he created the perfect title for any reader to gain an appreciation of comics, including those adults who want to understand why adolescents are reading graphic novels rather than *Moby Dick*.

FRANK MILLER, AUTHOR-ILLUSTRATOR

## Batman: The Dark Knight Returns

14–18 · DC Comics · 2002 · 224 pp.

S tory cycles of superheroes rarely treat them as they age or die. In 1986 Frank Miller focused on Batman in his fifties. In the morally, spiritually, and financially bankrupt Gotham City, Bruce Wayne finds himself bored and restless in his retirement. With Batman long forgotten, violent gangs rule the streets. Deciding to don his cape once again, Batman returns to battle some of his most famous foes and some of his closest friends. Much like Alan Moore's *Watchmen*, the book explores morality, the use of power, and the legitimacy of superheroes. It also tackles the issue of motivation — why a multimillionaire like Wayne would fight crime as Batman. Ultimately, the novel shows the power of a hero to inspire others; in a sprawling, ugly city, one human being can truly make a difference.

With a series of scenes that happen only a fraction of a second apart, the images work like a high-speed camera or strobe light. The panels are often juxtaposed with the reactions on a character's face for dramatic effect. Although created twenty years ago, *The Dark Knight* still feels fresh, vibrant, and contemporary.

HAYAO MIYAZAKI, AUTHOR-ILLUSTRATOR

## Nausicaä of the Valley of Wind

12–14 · Viz Communications · 2004 · approximately 1,200 pp.

T his seven-volume saga takes place a thousand years after a final war in which Earth's industrial society has destroyed itself and left the planet a wasteland. A gifted teenage princess, Nausicaä, lives in the Valley of Wind, a small place being threatened by a growing poisonous forest, the Sea of Corruption. There giant insects and plants emit spores that kill humans if breathed for even a moment. Nausicaä's complex ecological and adventure epic has been illustrated with lush, detailed art in an oversized format.

For a graphic novel that took thirteen years to complete, Hayao Miyazaki took the name of Nausicaä from *The Odyssey*, in which she is a girl who saves Odysseus, and combined her with the Japanese heroine of *The Tales of the Past and Present*, a young woman who loves nature. In the United States, Miyazaki has become best known for his movies — *Spirited Away, Princess Mononoke,* and most recently *Howl's Moving Castle.* But this graphic novel is considered a manga classic and a superb example of the form, particularly in a story with a heroine at its core.

ALAN MOORE, AUTHOR
DAVE GIBBONS, ILLUSTRATOR

## *Watchmen*

16–18 • DC Comics • 1986–1987 • 400 pp.

The only graphic novel to date to win the Hugo Award for the best science fiction work, *Watchmen* was first issued as a series of twelve individual volumes. It takes place in the United States around 1985, with flashbacks to the 1940s, 1960s, and 1970s. Some of the events also occur on Antarctica and Mars.

After the murder of Edward Blake, the superhero known as "The Comedian," it gradually becomes clear that a plot exists to discredit or destroy the remaining former members of the Minutemen and Crimebusters, two superhero teams disbanded by the government in 1977. Rorschach persuades his former partner, Nite Owl, to come out of retirement; however, in the process of following leads, they uncover a plan far more chilling in magnitude and scope than they could have imagined.

A legendary eccentric and self-professed anarchist, Moore explores the impact that superheroes would have on a society, both domestically and internationally. Are they righteous individuals or simply sadists, who use their opportunity to abuse others? In a text that contains excerpts from a variety of sources (novels, government documents, psychological evaluations, interviews, and memos), the artist juxtaposes panels from these different narratives for a powerful — even shocking — graphic effect. Sometimes called the *Citizen Kane* of comics, *Watchmen* has inspired graphic novel creators, musicians, and filmmakers for the past twenty years.

KATSUHIRO OTOMO, AUTHOR-ILLUSTRATOR
## *Akira*
16–18 • Dark Horse Comics • 2000 • approximately 2,000 pp.

Otomo's science fiction epic takes place in Neo-Toyoko City in 2030, thirty-eight years after World War III. Once appearing as a monthly comic book, *Akira* has been reissued in six volumes. In the first one Kaneda, the male teenage leader of a biker gang, encounters a strange child with the features of an old man who possesses extraordinary powers. The story includes a lot of action: motorcycle chases, gunfights, and gigantic machinery. Kaneda finds himself enmeshed in a conflict between two agencies, fighting to save the world over something unnamed and terrifying, locked away, and frozen to absolute zero.

With drawings that explode across the page, the book has been successfully adapted into an animated film, which has developed a large cult following in the United States.

MARJANE SATRAPI, AUTHOR-ILLUSTRATOR
## *Persepolis*
14–18 • Pantheon • 2003 • 154 pp.

An Iranian girl, Marji Satrapi tells the story of her life from the age of ten until she was fourteen, in 1984, when the Iran-Iraq war caused her parents to send her to Europe for safety. Although her family favors overthrowing the shah, they soon realize that the new regime is proving to be much more restrictive than the last.

As an Iranian, Satrapi felt "that an entire nation should not be judged by the wrongdoings of a few extremists." She did not want the "Iranians who lost their lives in prisons defending freedom . . . or who were forced to leave their families and flee their homeland to be forgotten."

Believing that if you have the talent to draw and write you should do both, Satrapi chose to put her political concerns into the form of a graphic novel. With bold lines and deceptively simple scenes, she presents a compelling portrait of a society in this *New York Times* bestseller that has been embraced by adolescents. The sequel, *Persepolis II,* has been equally popular.

JEFF SMITH, AUTHOR-ILLUSTRATOR

## Bone

12–14 • Cartoon Books • 2004 • 1,300 pp.

Originally published as a series of comic books from 1991 to 2004, *Bone* has been gathered into both a one-volume collection and nine individual titles, which Scholastic Books is republishing in color. Winner of every conceivable comic industry award, the series takes place in "The Valley," a kingdom that stretches from the dragons' land in the north to the capital city in the south. Fone Bone, a Pogo-esque young creature, and his cousins, Phoney Bone and Smiley Bone, come from Boneville, a place much discussed but never visited. The Bone family gets swept up in an epic conflict, in which dragons, monsters, an exiled princess, and evil forces try to conquer the world. Exciting, funny, and still scary, this series failed to attract a single publisher. Jeff Smith then started his own publishing house, living off his wife's salary. The gamble paid off, and by the sixth installment *Bone* was on its way to its position as a classic. Although deceptively simple, it grows darker and more complex with each chapter; the color editions from Scholastic have been produced with great care, allowing fans to see the subtleties of the art, printed with soft color on beautiful paper.

ART SPIEGELMAN, AUTHOR-ILLUSTRATOR

## Maus I: A Survivor's Tale: My Father Bleeds History

14–18 • Pantheon • 1986 • 160 pp.

Beginning with a quotation from Hitler — "The Jews are undoubtedly a race, but they are not human" — Art Spiegelman presents the Holocaust in graphic novel form as he relates the experiences of his father, Vladek, in Nazi-occupied Poland. Portrayed as cats, the Nazis gradually increase the repressive measures until the Jews, shown as mice, get systematically hunted down and sent to the Final Solution. By a combination of luck and wits, Vladek saves himself and his wife and settles in Rego Park, New York, but his experiences haunt him and affect his son's adjustment to life as well.

Spiegelman had created comics since 1960, so when he decided to tell his father's story, comics seemed a natural avenue of expression. As he tried to make sense out of his own history, the graphic form allowed him to approach horrible events with the metaphor of the cat and mouse. A few years later, Spiegelman published *Maus II: A Survivor's Tale: And Here My Troubles Began,* the first graphic novel to win a Pulitzer Prize.

Such a powerful and troubling work often gets included in Holocaust units, but it also is picked up every year by devotees, who appreciate Spiegelman's genius and the importance of his message.

BRYAN TALBOT, AUTHOR-ILLUSTRATOR

## The Tale of One Bad Rat

12–14 • Dark Horse Comics • 1995 • 136 pp.

Teenaged Helen Potter has run away from a sexually abusive father, and her journey to recovery takes her from London to an inn in the British countryside. Along the way she meets characters and situations derived from the work of her namesake, Beatrix Potter. In the end, she can confront her father about his actions and move toward healing. In brilliant full color, Bryan Talbot crafts a work often used as a resource in child abuse centers in both the United States and Britain.

CRAIG THOMPSON, AUTHOR-ILLUSTRATOR

## Blankets

16–18 • Top Shelf Productions • 2003 • 590 pp.

The author uses himself as a senior in high school as the protagonist in this realistic story of a young boy growing up in snowy Wisconsin in a Christian fundamentalist family. The story, told when Craig is twenty-something and looking back, includes images of his boyhood, when he and his brother, Phil, engage in boyhood pranks such as urinating on each other. But in high school Craig grows up, falls in love, gets sexually involved, and begins to understand the moral complications of his relationship as well as the limits of his faith.

This large, sprawling, realistic graphic novel is often appreciated by those with little exposure to the form.

CRAIG THOMPSON, AUTHOR-ILLUSTRATOR

## *Good-bye, Chunky Rice*

12–14 • Top Shelf Productions • 1999 • 128 pp.

Feeling like a turtle that has outgrown its shell, Chunky Rice decides to move away from his home and his best friend, Dandel, a bug-eyed mouse. With this simple, ambiguous plot, the story moves between heartbreak and triumph. This meditation on loss reminds readers that leaving something precious allows something new to be discovered. In order to have beginnings, one must first have endings.

Fluid lines and dramatic brushstrokes characterize Craig Thompson's art. In this book he uses black in a dramatic fashion — as the color of the sea, between panels, and surrounding each page. His own move from Wisconsin to Portland, Oregon, before writing the book clearly influenced the action and tone of the story. Popular with inveterate graphic novel readers, the book also works particularly well for those new to the literature. Its universal themes and its execution allow parents, teachers, or grandparents to understand the appeal and charm of this genre.

# Historical Fiction

RECENTLY AT A GRADUATION PARTY, I was talking to a high school junior about *500 Great Books for Teens*. "Oh," she said anxiously, "I hope you're going to include the best book that I've read?" "And what would it be?" I asked. "*To Kill a Mockingbird*," she said breathlessly. "I really love it; do you know about it?" I had to smile; some great books really do stand the test of time. Like all of us, this young reader believed she had made a discovery — books are new to us when we find them.

When it comes to adolescent literature, two genres fare the best over time — fantasy, already in some other realm, and historical fiction, which occurs in the past. If writers of historical fiction work to make their book universal, rather than just representing contemporary concerns, their novels can stand for decades, even centuries. Teens have been known to read the nineteenth-century classics — such as Jane Austen's *Pride and Prejudice* or Mark Twain's *The Adventures of Huckleberry Finn* — with incredible passion.

Because so much excellent historical fiction works with teen readers, I could be extremely selective in this section, which also includes some Westerns. For a historical novel to stand as one of the best, it must re-create a place and time, believably and fully. The picky details of how people did and said things in another era must be observed. But in the best historical fiction, the research does not overwhelm the story.

Without a doubt the favorite genre of the classroom teacher — because of the many ways these books tie into the curriculum — the best historical fiction often finds its way to the top of teens' favorite book lists as well. I myself loved this genre as a teenager; I appreciate its possibilities even more as an adult.

---

LAURIE HALSE ANDERSON

## Fever 1793

12–14 • Simon & Schuster • 2000 • 252 pp.

In August of 1793, fourteen-year-old Mattie Cook finds her life suddenly overturned. A vague rumor of some disease down by the Philadelphia docks quickly leads to news of the sudden death of one of Mattie's childhood friends. With church bells ringing all day, yellow fever swiftly claims the citizens of Philadelphia; the death toll eventually reaches 10 percent of the population. At first Mattie and her family try to keep their coffeehouse running. When Mattie's mother becomes ill, Mattie attempts to escape from the city, but she is turned back and ends up in Bush Hill, the city hospital set up to cope with the epidemic.

The plot tends to be episodic, moving Mattie from one place to another. Easily paired with Jim Murphy's *An American Plague,* the two books explore a period of history not often described but made extremely relevant by contemporary concerns about pandemics.

---

ADAM BAGDASARIAN

## Forgotten Fire

14–18 • DK/Kroupa • 2000 • 273 pp.
↔ NATIONAL BOOK AWARD FINALIST

Told in a series of flashbacks, the experiences of a twelve-year-old boy during the mass genocide of the Armenians in Turkey (from 1915 to about 1918) are presented in a nonstop, grisly, and unnerving manner. Watching his father escorted out of their lives by the Turkish police, his brothers shot, his grandmother murdered, and his sister take poison rather than be raped, Vahan begins to understand what his father meant when he said, "This is how steel is made. Steel is made strong by fire."

The ferocity brought on by blind hatred is conveyed brilliantly. The language is rich and seems to flow effortlessly, making it hard for readers to turn away from the intense prose even when they want to. This riveting and unforgettable account has been based on a little-known piece of history and the experiences of Adam Bagdasarian's great-uncle.

GARY BLACKWOOD

## The Shakespeare Stealer

12–14 • Dutton • 1998 • 216 pp.

England is a paradise for women, a prison for servants, and a hell for horses. Prentices were too lowly to even deserve mention." But Widge, a fourteen-year-old apprentice under the direction of a new master, embarks on an amazing adventure. In 1601 he arrives in London, guarded by the evil Falconer, to attend the Globe Theatre's new production of *Hamlet*. Since Widge knows a form of shorthand, he attends the play to transcribe its dialogue; his master will then adapt it for his own theater productions. But Widge ends up as part of the cast, an apprentice in training for the theater. There he works with Shakespeare and Burbage and even performs the role of Ophelia before the Queen.

With a plot as fast-paced, exciting, and bold as those created by Shakespeare himself, the book takes readers behind the curtain in the Elizabethan theater. Fighting, dueling, tension between cast members, the constant threat of Falconer's kidnapping Widge, all keep readers turning the pages until a neat twist at the end. Along with its sequels, *Shakespeare's Scribe* and *Shakespeare's Spy*, schools sometimes choose *The Shakespeare Stealer* for all members of an incoming class to read. It has something for all tastes — drama, history, swordplay, a character faced with a moral dilemma, and the triumph of an appealing orphan.

MICHAEL CHABON

## The Amazing Adventures of Kavalier & Clay

14–18 • Random House • 2000 • 639 pp.

↝ *PULITZER PRIZE*

Even the outline of the plot of this sprawling, funny, rambunctious novel gives some idea of its complexity. In Prague a young Jewish boy, Josef Kavalier, apprentices himself to an escape artist; then his mentor smuggles Josef out of Nazi territory in a coffin. In 1939 he arrives in Brooklyn, New York, to live with his aunt Ethel and becomes part of a team with his cousin Sam Klayman. Driven by an urgent need for money, the two young men pour their talents — Josef as an artist, Sam as a writer — into creating comic books. Out of their own fantasies, fears, and dreams, they concoct the legend of their first success, a character called the Escapist. As their adventures continue, they take part in the nascent, crazed world of comic books. In a saga where the heroes often pull off escapes, Joe falls in love with a bohemian artist, Rosa; Sam begins to understand, and then reject, his own attraction to men. They meet Orson Welles and Salvador Dalí and get completely swept up in the New York art scene of the 1940s. Never, however, does Joe forget about rescuing the rest of his family in Prague — fanatical hatred of Hitler and fascism informs every comic spread he creates.

Spinning an elaborate web of words that ensnares the reader, the novel creates a vast panorama of the American Depression, isolationism, sexual repression, the Holocaust, Jewish mysticism, World War II, and the paranoia of the 1950s. Although a work of fiction, it parallels closely the development of the comic book industry. Chapters read like comic book narratives — with thrills, action, and superb timing. Readers get treated to Superman, Batman, media tycoons, U-boats, radio plays, pulp fiction, big bands, bar mitzvahs, baseball games, and the 1939 World's Fair.

This stunning tour de force won Michael Chabon a Pulitzer Prize and a place in the canon of twenty-first-century fiction; it captures perfectly the bravado of the young and reckless. Although the novel runs over 600 pages, it truly makes readers say, "The only bad part came when it ended."

AIDAN CHAMBERS

## Postcards from No Man's Land

14–18 • Dutton • 2002 • 312 pp.

⇨ *PRINTZ AWARD*

In the late 1990s, seventeen-year-old Jacob Todd travels from England to Amsterdam to attend a ceremony honoring his grandfather, who died as a soldier in World War II. There he visits the Dutch family that cared for his grandfather during the Allied invasion to liberate the Netherlands. Sexually ambivalent, unsure of whether he prefers boys or girls, Jacob moodily explores the streets and canals of this new city, paying particular attention to the location of his favorite book, *The Diary of Anne Frank.*

The novel also presents a parallel story. Young Geertrui, who lives in Oosterbeek, rescues and conceals a wounded English soldier during the Battle of Arnhem, and they fall in love. Although readers will quickly deduce that Geertrui's patient was Jacob's grandfather, the novel explores not only the history of the period and the choices people made but controversial topics as well, such as sexual identity and euthanasia. For those who willingly stay with its leisurely pace, *Postcards from No Man's Land* is a thought-provoking, rich, and complex novel about love, sexuality, friendship, and the long-term effects of the past on the present.

TRACY CHEVALIER

## Girl with a Pearl Earring

14–18 • Dutton • 1999 • 240 pp.

Sixteen-year-old Griet, the daughter of a Protestant Delft tilemaker who lost his sight, must help support her family by serving as a maid. Hired by the Catholic family of Johannes Vermeer, the painter, Griet joins a household filled with tension and conflicts, for Vermeer's wife and daughter resent the young maid. A slow painter — he produces only thirty-five known canvases — Vermeer often finds himself in debt. But as Griet becomes fascinated with his method of painting, the artist takes an interest in her, allowing her to help create the colors for his pigments. She lovingly grinds bones, white lead, madder, and massicot, mixing them with linseed oil to make sparkling paint. Because of her sense of color and composition, Vermeer even asks for her thoughts about his work. Eventually, Griet serves as the model for his famous painting *Girl with a Pearl Earring,* which adorns the cover of the book. Griet also becomes involved with a young man, Pieter, who later becomes her husband.

This sensual, first-person narrative gives readers a fascinating glimpse into another world. Not only do they learn in detail about Vermeer's paintings, they also absorb information about Dutch life in the seventeenth century. Often taught in high school and made more popular by a movie in 2003, *Girl with a Pearl Earring* appeals to adults and teens alike, making it ideal for parent-teen groups.

GENNIFER CHOLDENKO

## *Al Capone Does My Shirts*

12–14 • Putnam • 2004 • 228 pp.

↪ *NEWBERY HONOR*

In 1935, twelve-year-old Moose Flanagan moves with his family to Alcatraz Island, where twenty-three other children also live. Unlike the warden's daughter, Piper, who revels in talking about the convicts with her classmates, Moose simply longs to return to his former neighborhood in Santa Monica. But with jobs scarce during the Depression, his father now works as a guard for a prison filled with the most dangerous criminals of all time. And, as if living next to these inmates isn't enough of a problem, Moose increasingly has to take over the care of his older, severely autistic sister Natalie.

With humor, insight, and great compassion, Gennifer Choldenko presents a portrait of two very appealing children, Moose and Natalie. Although the prisoners of Alcatraz serve as a backdrop for the story, the most famous resident — Al Capone, who works in the laundry — always seems present in everyone's thoughts. In the end, deciding to take drastic action to help Natalie, Moose gets a message to Al Capone and asks for his aid.

A great title, a perfect ending, excellent historical notes, exciting dialogue, short chapters, and an unusual setting all make the book a great crowd-pleaser and an excellent choice for book talk or read-aloud. *Al Capone Does My Shirts* not only entertains young readers but also teaches them about autism, the Great Depression, and prison life.

CHRISTOPHER PAUL CURTIS

## *Bud, Not Buddy*

12–14 • Delacorte • 1999 • 256 pp.

↪ *NEWBERY MEDAL*

This winner of both the Coretta Scott King Award and Newbery Medal features a ten-year-old African-American orphan — Bud, "not Buddy" — on the run from an abusive foster home. Living in the 1930s in Flint, Michigan, Bud believes that his father is Herman E. Calloway, a jazz bass player. In search of Calloway, Bud gets into his share of trouble as he heads to Grand Rapids, and the musician himself is none too pleased to encounter someone erroneously claiming to be his son.

*Bud, Not Buddy* demonstrates Christopher Paul Curtis's ability to capture the language and feel of a historical period, the Depression, and explore social issues such as homelessness and poverty. Extremely popular with the younger teen crowd, the book features an engaging hero whom readers grow to love.

CHRISTOPHER PAUL CURTIS

## The Watsons Go to Birmingham — 1963

12–14 • Delacorte • 1995 • 211 pp.

↦ *NEWBERY HONOR*

Curtis's novel, told from the point of view of ten-year-old Kenny Watson, initially revolves around his thirteen-year-old brother, Byron, "officially a teenage juvenile delinquent." Some of Byron's escapes seem hysterically funny, such as the time he gets his tongue stuck to the frozen car mirror. But the tone in this episodic narrative changes when the African-American family decides to leave Flint, Michigan, and visit their grandmother in Birmingham, Alabama. With "Yakkety Yak, Don't Talk Back" booming from the car radio, the family heads into the racial tension that marked the South during the 1960s. And when a cheerful Sunday morning worship turns into a day of horror, Kenny must deal with the events that electrified an entire nation.

Kenny proves to be just the kind of friend many readers would like to have, so they can feel empathy for his plight and the discrimination he faces. This compelling, original novel brings a family's everyday life and our nation's history together to captivate young readers. Many admit that it has changed the way they feel about a period of history and even reading in general.

KAREN CUSHMAN

## *Catherine, Called Birdy*

12–14 • Clarion • 1994 • 212 pp.

↬ *NEWBERY HONOR*

In a series of journal entries for the year 1290, Catherine — called Birdy because she keeps caged birds in her room — gives the reader a vivid sense of her life as the daughter of an impoverished knight. "My mother seeks to make me a fine lady — dumb, docile, and accomplished — so I must take lady-lessons and keep my mouth closed. . . . My father, the toad, conspires to sell me like a cheese to some lack-wit seeking a wife." An inventive fourteen-year-old, she attempts to find creative ways to avoid being married — such as blackening her teeth. Cushman immerses her readers completely in the setting; they experience the tastes, smell the odors, and hear the archaic swear words of the era.

Millions of readers have grown to appreciate Birdy — assertive, imaginative, stubborn, brave, funny, and determined to be her own person. Although she lived in medieval times, Birdy has not only enchanted contemporary young girls, boys have also found her much to their liking.

JENNIFER DONNELLY

## *A Northern Light*

12–14 • Harcourt • 2003 • 387 pp.

↬ *PRINTZ HONOR*

In 1906, sixteen-year-old Mattie Gorky waitresses at a lake resort while she dreams of going to college. Her mother's death has kept her chained to the family farm, where she attempts to raise her younger siblings. One afternoon, a guest at the resort, Grace Brown, dies from drowning. The young woman had handed Mattie a packet of letters, with instructions to burn them. But Mattie reads them, discovers that Grace was pregnant by her wealthy employer, and that the man brought Grace to the hotel to kill her. Eventually leaving the letters to be found by the police, Mattie boards a train for New York, taking her own future into her hands.

The narrative shifts between Matty's life on the farm, told in past tense, and her experiences at the hotel, related in present tense. Based on the actual death of Grace Brown, which occurred in the Adirondacks (the incident that inspired Theodore Dreiser's *An American Tragedy*), *A Northern Light* combines the details of true crime and a coming-of-age story.

LOUISE ERDRICH

## The Game of Silence

12–14 • HarperCollins • 2005 • 256 pp.

Set in the mid-nineteenth century on an island in Lake Superior, the novel continues the story of Omakayas, who was introduced in *The Birchbark House*. In the opening scene, the small Ojibwe community is shocked by the arrival of strangers, half-starved and naked — other native people who have been displaced by white settlers. Although the book explores major issues, it is also filled with the details of daily life, such as snowball fights, sledding, and fishing excursions. However, a continual threat — the whites want the Native American tribe to leave their island home — underscores the entire narrative.

Written by one of the preeminent Ojibwe novelists in America, the novel can be read without the first volume in the series, although it may well send readers back to it. Both volumes were written to provide a Native American perspective on the time period and locale of Laura Ingalls Wilder's Little House books.

CHARLES FRAZIER

## Cold Mountain

14–18 • Atlantic • 1997 • 438 pp.
↷ *NATIONAL BOOK AWARD*

In this Civil War novel, W. D. Inman, a Confederate soldier from the highlands of North Carolina, slowly walks home to be with his sweetheart, Ada. Shot in the neck during the battle of Petersburg, he eventually gains the strength to escape from his duties as a soldier. As he avoids federal raiders and the brutal Home Guard, he meets an eccentric and colorful cast of characters who aid or deter him on his journey. Back home, Ada herself must change from a pampered socialite to a self-reliant farmer. After her father dies, she ekes out an existence on a farm in Cold Mountain and seeks the help of a young drifter, Ruby. In a leisurely, lyrical narrative, the soldiers and civilians change during the course of the narrative. Sustaining the tension throughout, Charles Frazier moves the book brilliantly toward its devastating conclusion.

Frazier took several years to write his novel, basing it on a family story about a Civil War soldier who walked home. With only a few details to work with, he used *The Odyssey* as the framework for the story; like Homer, Frazier wanted to tell the story of a warrior who longed to return home and what had happened there in his absence.

Appearing on many high school reading lists, the novel has also been adapted for a movie. While it is certainly intriguing for its plot, the book demands to be picked up or read aloud for its prose alone; on almost any page the reader can literally savor the beauty of the writing.

ERNEST J. GAINES

## *A Lesson Before Dying*

14–18 • Knopf • 1993 • 256 pp.

In a small Cajun community, Bayonne, Louisiana, in the 1940s, Jefferson, a young black man, has been convicted of murder — a crime he did not commit. The narrator, Grant Wiggins, a well-educated black, has accepted a teaching job on his return to Bayonne, his hometown, and the lives of these two men come together in unexpected, powerful, and achingly affecting ways.

Because the reader comes to understand and respect these characters, watching how they are demeaned and held hostage to prejudice and malice is all the more powerful. In the course of the novel Grant changes, but he has a tremendous impact on others. The book brilliantly recreates time, place, and a feeling of the community, but it also stands as a testimony to the ability of one person to effect change — turning an otherwise dismal story into a hopeful one.

MOLLY GLOSS

## Wild Life

14–18 • Simon & Schuster • 2000 • 255 pp.

In the barely tamed wilderness of western Oregon, Charlotte Bridger Drummond supports her young sons without the help of a husband by writing pulp fiction. In her journal for 1905, she relates events with lively, slyly humorous, and sometimes caustic wit. When her housekeeper's granddaughter disappears from a logging camp, Charlotte sets out to join the hunting parties but gets lost herself. After days of hunger and despair, she finds herself rescued by a band of semihuman giants, "apes or erect bears of immense size" in the deep woods.

While Charlotte's take on life and relationships will resonate with many contemporary readers, she still seems firmly rooted in the 1900s. This highly original book requires patient readers, who will let the author lead them through her amazing landscape.

BETTE GREENE

## Summer of My German Soldier

12–14 • Dial • 1973 • 230 pp.

✑ *NATIONAL BOOK AWARD FINALIST*

In a small Arkansas town during World War II, a friendship develops when a lonely twelve-year-old Jewish girl, Patty, helps an escaped German prisoner-of-war hide from the authorities. When Anton is finally captured and killed, Patty must face the criticism of her parents, particularly her physically abusive father, and the townspeople. Ultimately because of her actions, Patty ends up in the Arkansas Reformatory for Girls.

Often read as part of history or World War II units, *Summer of My German Soldier* brings the war into a small American town, raising questions about intolerance, prejudice, and appropriate social action.

IRENE HUNT

## *No Promises in the Wind*

12–14 • Follett • 1970 • 224 pp.

A llowing young readers to appreciate what it must have felt like to grow up during the Depression, Newbery Award–winner Irene Hunt presents the hardships experienced by two boys, Josh and Joey Grondowski. Filled with anger against his father, fifteen-year-old Josh runs away from his home in Chicago, with his younger brother, Joey, tagging along.

Appealing to universal teen concerns such as independence and the need for autonomy, the book captures the pain, the suffering, and the problems of those who have decided to live on the road. In the second chapter Howie, a friend who joins the brothers, gets killed while trying to board a railroad car illegally. In the end, dramatically changed by their experiences, the boys return home to a tearful, two-handkerchief ending.

M. E. KERR

## *Gentlehands*

12–14 • Harper/Nordstrom • 1978 • 183 pp.

S ixteen-year-old Buddy Boyle, who lives in Seaville, New York, in the 1970s, comes from a lower-middle-class background. When he starts to date Skye, a wealthy, older Long Island summer resident, he knows his parents will disapprove. To impress Skye, Buddy takes her to visit Grandpa Trenker, whom he has seen only once because of a family feud but who lives in a huge house by the ocean. Although readers may feel that the author intends simply to write about a love affair between a have and a have-not, the story takes a decided twist. After Buddy moves in with his grandfather, who loves classical music and gardens, he must face the reality that this old man had been a brutal Nazi officer in a concentration camp in World War II and was responsible for the deaths of hundreds of prisoners.

In a concise novel (written in three weeks), M. E. Kerr explores class differences, the nature of good and evil, and the unreliability of outside appearances. This powerful book is often used in schools, where some classes put Grandpa Trenker on trial for war crimes. In *Gentlehands*, Kerr makes the events of World War II approachable for young adults.

## SUE MONK KIDD

### *The Secret Life of Bees*

14–18 • Viking • 2002 • 303 pp.

At the age of four, Lily Owens finds her life changed irrevocably when her mother dies. Ten years later, she secretly worries about her own guilt and part in the tragic death. She lives on a South Carolina peach farm with her harsh, punishing father, T. Ray, and with Rosaleen, Lily's black stand-in mother. A spunky character, Rosaleen sparkles with wisdom, and she has been practicing cursive writing so she can register to vote after the passage of the Civil Rights Act of 1964. Rosaleen sets out to do so but is beaten up and placed in jail, defending her rights. Lily decides to save her, and the two of them, fugitives from justice, place their fate in a relic from Lily's deceased mother, a small picture of a black Virgin Mary. The picture takes them to Tiburon, South Carolina, to the headquarters of Black Madonna Honey, a flourishing business in honey and candle wax. From the three enchanting black beekeepers, Lily also learns about her own past and finds the healing she seeks.

A *New York Times* bestseller for a year and a half, *The Secret Life of Bees* excels in a sense of place — the oppressive heat, the swarming bees, the smells, and the incipient racism. Exploring loss, family, blurring social lines, and unmerited kindness, Sue Monk Kidd encourages readers to "find a mother inside yourself. We all do. Even if we already have a mother." Great for book discussion groups, the novel has even inspired high school students to create artwork and sculpture. With its exploration of prejudice and racism at the time of the Civil Rights Act and its exultation in finding love and community, *The Secret Life of Bees* is a perfect book to share with adolescents.

HARPER LEE

## *To Kill a Mockingbird*

14–18 • Lippincott • 1960 • 281 pp.

↝ *PULITZER PRIZE*

*To Kill a Mockingbird* began as a Christmas present. An Alabama transplant in New York, Harper Lee was working for an airline's reservations department when two friends gave her enough money for Christmas to write for a year. Drawing on her own life — she based the character of Dill on her cousin and childhood friend, Truman Capote — Lee explored the issues of race, miscarriage of justice, and questions about the moral nature of human beings in a coming-of-age story.

Eight-year-old Scout Finch ranks with Anne of Green Gables as one of fiction's most appealing children; her father, the lawyer Atticus, as one of fiction's finest parents. Although he ignores his children's exuberant antics, he tries to instill in them a social conscience. Wise beyond her years, Scout grows up in a sleepy Alabama town of Maycomb during the Depression. With her brother, Jem, and her best friend, Dill, she plays childish games and tries to sneak into a house to catch a glimpse of Boo Radley, who never ventures outside his home. To the consternation of Maycomb's white community, Atticus agrees to act as the defense attorney for a black man, Tom Robinson, who has been accused of raping a white woman. At that point the story, along with the mood in the town, grows darker. Despite all the evidence pointing to Tom's innocence and Atticus's spirited defense, the all-white jury convicts Tom, and he is eventually shot trying to escape from prison. Then, one Halloween night, Scout and Jem find their own lives threatened.

In its first year, *To Kill a Mockingbird* sold over a half-million copies and was translated into ten languages; in its first two years, it spent one hundred weeks on the bestseller list. An Academy Award–winning film, starring Gregory Peck, increased its visibility. Today, the book has sold more than fifteen million copies in forty languages, earning it a rightful place in the canon of American literature. Some forty years after its publication, it still has the ability to electrify young readers: they find themselves both intrigued and repulsed by Scout's comfortable southern world. It remains one of the most remembered books of adolescent reading, lighting up adults' eyes when they talk about it years later. As the novel explores the moral nature of human beings, Atticus and Scout both remain committed to the goodness in people, but in the end they both fully understand the nature of evil.

BOBBIE ANN MASON

## In Country

14–18 • HarperCollins • 1985 • 245 pp.

When Sam graduates from school in Hopewell, Kentucky, she faces all the normal teenage challenges — where she will attend college, how she can support herself, and if she should break up with her high school boyfriend. The child of a soldier she never met who died in Vietnam, Sam sets out to learn about her father. Through his letters and diaries and conversations with her uncle Emmett, another vet who appears to be suffering from the effects of Agent Orange, Sam relentlessly pursues her phantom father; she spends a night in a swamp, the better to understand wartime conditions in Vietnam, and tries to develop a relationship with another vet. Finally, when Sam, Emmett, and her grandmother visit the Vietnam Memorial in Washington, D.C., they all experience some healing and closure.

A book that explores the turbulent 1960s and the reaction to Vietnam veterans in the 1980s, *In Country* presents a truly likable and vibrant protagonist, who slowly moves away from becoming another victim of the war.

GERALDINE MCCAUGHREAN

## Stop the Train!

12–14 • HarperCollins • 2003 • 291 pp.

During the Oklahoma Land Rush in 1893, a group of settlers decide not to sell their land to the greedy railroad moguls. When the president of the Red Rock Railroad Company refuses to let the train stop at the new town of Florence, the settlers do everything in their power — including tying a child to the tracks — to reverse that decision. Ultimately they save their town as well as their investment in a new life.

Fast and funny, the book recounts a little-known story of how the train forever changed the West — and how it nearly destroyed the town of Enid, Oklahoma. With nonstop action, the characters move the plot forward in this madcap historical novel.

CARSON MCCULLERS

## The Heart Is a Lonely Hunter

14–18 • Houghton Mifflin • 1940 • 359 pp.

With the Depression as a backdrop and an unnamed southern town as the setting, Carson McCullers in her first book features John Singer as her protagonist, a deaf-mute who works in a jewelry shop. Beginning "In the town there were two mutes, and they were always together," the novel at its core shows the various relationships between people in the community and Singer. Four alienated outcasts each gravitate toward the man, feeling that he alone understands them. Because he says nothing, people assume he knows everything. But when Singer's deaf friend dies in an insane asylum, Singer commits suicide, depriving the community of its sainted listener.

While living in Charlotte, North Carolina, McCullers began a detailed outline of a novel with the theme "of man's revolt against his own inner isolation and his urge to express himself as fully as is possible," and she submitted her work for the new Houghton Mifflin Fiction Fellowship. Believing that she would produce a book of literary distinction, Houghton Mifflin awarded McCullers the prize and a contract for a book called *The Mute*. Published when the author was in her early twenties, the book became a literary sensation and has been a staple of high school reading lists ever since. The unusual story, rich southern setting, and the author's ability to portray loneliness, death, insanity, fear, and mob violence help make the novel remembered by adolescents long into adulthood.

LARRY MCMURTRY

## Lonesome Dove

14–18 • Simon & Schuster • 1985 • 843 pp.

↪ *PULITZER PRIZE*

This epic novel of the West focuses on the people who live there and their influence on one another. With humor and sly twists of writing, Larry McMurtry tells the story of a pair of drunken and aging former Texas Rangers and horse rustlers who herd cattle from Texas to Montana. Providing a realistic picture of life on the American frontier, he juggles a variety of characters and different points of view. In this vast panorama, readers encounter prostitutes and horse thieves, outlaws, gamblers, sheriffs, runaway wives, sodbusters — a whole array of intriguing and complex characters.

In a deceptively simple style, the story excels in pacing, evocative language, and a sense of place, making it a tremendously satisfying literary Western and grand saga.

CAROLYN MEYER

## *Mary, Bloody Mary*

12–14 • Harcourt • 1999 • 227 pp.

Mary Tudor narrates her story, infusing it with a believable perspective about her father, Henry VIII, and his life. The daughter of Catherine of Aragon, Mary finds herself a pawn in Henry's hand, driven as he was to produce a male heir. Pampered as a princess for part of her life, she then becomes a servant for her half-sister Elizabeth, born when Henry wed Anne Boleyn.

The complicated relationships are neatly distilled and explained. It is easy for a reader to identify with the teenager who will be called "Bloody Mary" and to sympathize with the bad hand she's been dealt by her father's lust, greed, and arrogance — as well as the inferior status of women in that period. This accessible and interesting book is the first volume in Meyer's popular Young Royals series — *Beware, Princess Elizabeth; Doomed Queen Anne;* and *Patience, Princess Catherine.*

TONI MORRISON

## *Beloved*

14–18 • Knopf • 1987 • 275 pp.

⤳ *PULITZER PRIZE*

Before the Civil War, Sethe, a black slave on a Kentucky plantation, decides to escape her sadistic new owner. She sends her older children ahead of her, but when the slave hunters come to recapture her, she kills her own infant, Beloved, so the baby can never become a slave. After the war, Sethe devotes herself to her surviving daughter, Denver. But she is haunted by memories of her slave life and is literally pursued by a vindictive and abusive ghost, the spirit of Beloved, who sets out to destroy her mother's household.

In a complex, nonlinear plot, the story shifts between Cincinnati in 1873 and the Kentucky plantation in the 1850s, weaving the past and the present, the physical and the spiritual. Toni Morrison felt that *Beloved* revolved around a central question for black people: How can they let go of the pain of the past and redeem the sacrifices made in their struggle for freedom? For brilliant, multilayered novels like *Beloved* and for the body of her work, Morrison received the Nobel Prize for Literature in 1993.

RICHARD MOSHER

## Zazoo

12–14 • Clarion • 2001 • 266 pp.

While thirteen-year-old Zazoo punts on a canal one day, a bicyclist inquires about someone who resides in her French village. A Vietnamese child, Zazoo lives with her adopted grandfather, a lockkeeper on the canal. But the stranger's questions cause her to start asking some herself, and the responses help her uncover secrets from World War II and her Grand-Pierre's and his town's past.

This multifaceted romance — about war, love, sorrow, and time healing all wounds — works best with readers who enjoy a slow, leisurely novel. Like a boat trip down a meandering stream in the summer, the book contains many rewards in its sensual imagery and human insight for those who relax on the journey.

URI ORLEV

## The Man from the Other Side

12–14 • Houghton Mifflin • 1991 • 184 pp.

Marek, a fourteen-year-old Polish Catholic boy, helps his stepfather smuggle goods into the Jewish ghetto during World War II. Traveling through foul sewers, they engage in this business not to be altruistic but to make handsome profits. Although Marek has imbibed the local anti-Semitism, his mother reveals that his father, now long dead, was indeed Jewish and was killed in prison because of his Communist politics. So Marek decides to help a Jewish boy, which takes him into the ghetto during the height of the 1943 uprising.

A survivor of that ghetto and of the Bergen-Belsen concentration camp, the Israeli writer Uri Orlev presents an amazingly balanced picture, neither glorifying nor demonizing the different fighters and collaborators. He based the character of Marek on a childhood friend, a Polish journalist who requested that his story be kept quiet during his lifetime. Shortly after his death, Orlev wrote *The Man from the Other Side*.

Winner of the international Hans Christian Andersen Award for the body of his work, Orlev has created a subtle, beautifully crafted, complex, and altogether compelling novel, often included in Holocaust units in school.

JULIE OTSUKA

## When the Emperor Was Divine

14–18 • Knopf • 2002 • 144 pp.

In the spring of 1942 in Berkeley, California, a notice appears for Japanese Americans to prepare to evacuate their homes. An unnamed woman follows the instructions — and kills an old white dog, the family pet. As the family travels to a barren desert camp, her daughter and son narrate the story of their daily life and deprivation. In the end, reunited in their ransacked home, they face poverty as well as discrimination from their former neighbors.

Although other books have shown the terrible plight of the Japanese Americans during World War II — such as *Farewell to Manzanar* — this short, spare, understated, yet haunting text makes it possible for readers to experience how it may actually have felt. A magnificent tour de force.

LINDA SUE PARK

## When My Name Was Keoko

12–14 • Clarion • 2002 • 201 pp.

In alternating chapters covering the years between 1940 and 1945, two siblings, Sun-hee and Tae-yul, describe their lives in Korea during the Japanese occupation. Their uncle works for the resistance movement, printing newspapers. Sun-hee and her father rebel in quieter ways. As Japanese citizens, they must take Japanese names, so for this period of time Sun-hee becomes Keoko. But teenage Tae-yul takes drastic action, risking his life in the process.

Basing the novel on extensive research, Linda Sue Park, the first Asian-American winner of the Newbery Medal for *A Single Shard,* also incorporated stories she learned from her Korean-born parents. Consequently the novel gives Western readers a window on a seldom-told piece of Eastern history. A powerful and riveting story, *When My Name Was Keoko* features a proud Korean family as it faces life and death with courage.

KATHERINE PATERSON

## *Lyddie*

12–14 • Lodestar • 1991 • 184 pp.

Young Lyddie Worthen must support herself, and in 1843, after working in a tavern for a year, she flees to Lowell, Massachusetts, to look for a better job. Employed by a textile factory, Lyddie buries herself in books, seized by a desire to educate herself and attend college. While realistically portraying Lyddie's hardships, the book also provides a heart-warming, believable character who becomes concerned about the rights of workers. As is true of all Katherine Paterson's writing, the beautiful, graceful, rhythmic, and evocative language mesmerizes readers.

Before writing *Lyddie,* Patterson came across the letters of Vermont farm girls who had worked in the Lowell textile miles. Deeply moved, she began extensive research into nineteenth-century factory life. Immensely popular in schools, often used in language arts and history classes, *Lyddie* also makes a superb novel for independent reading or mother-daughter book groups.

RICHARD PECK

## *A Long Way from Chicago: A Novel in Stories*

12–14 • Dial • 1998 • 148 pp.

↪ *NEWBERY HONOR*

In hilarious episodes that span the years from 1929 to 1942, Joey looks back on the summers that he and his younger sister, Mary Alice, spent in a small Illinois town with their one-of-a-kind Grandma Dowdel, a woman as "old as the hills." Each chapter presents a slightly older narrator documenting the next summer vacation with a never-changing, consistently unique grandmother.

The appeal of these stories lies in the irreverent, sometimes surprising, and always plausible situations and the humor inherent in these events. The Great Depression is actually as much a character as are the people in this rollicking tale. Appealing to a broad range of tastes, the novel — and its sequel, *A Year Down Yonder*, which won the Newbery Medal in 2003 — makes the historical period seem real, as readers grow to understand and enjoy these people.

RICHARD PECK

## The River Between Us

12–14 • Dial • 2003 • 164 pp.

Howard Hutchings and his father travel in a Model T Ford to visit Howard's grandparents in Grand Tower, Illinois, in 1916. There Grandma Tilly becomes the narrator, relating events of 1861 in the small Mississippi River town divided between supporters of the North and the South. A steamboat delivers two glamorous and mysterious strangers to town, Delphine Duval and her companion, Calinda, from New Orleans. Wealthy and vain, Delphine brings with her many trunks, gowns, a French accent, and an attitude about Yankees. Taking them in, Tilly worries that Calinda may be Delphine's slave; the townspeople believe that these Southern girls may be spies. But Delphine's true character is revealed when Noah, Tilly's twin brother, joins the Union army and becomes quite ill at Camp Defiance. After Delphine and Tilly nurse him back to health, Noah fights in the battle of Belmont, Missouri.

In a narrative with several unexpected turns, *The River Between Us* examines both family and national history.

CHARLES PORTIS

## True Grit

14–18 • Simon & Schuster • 1968 • 215 pp.

In the 1870s, fourteen-year-old Mattie Ross from Arkansas, an opinionated and unsentimental heroine, sets out to avenge her father's murder and convinces a one-eyed U.S. marshal, "Rooster" Cogburn, to join her. They pursue a murderous gang of outlaws into dangerous

Indian Territory, where they have the misfortune of tangling with Mattie.

In a fast-paced, often funny story, the humor is created by an interesting range of characters and their responses to their situations. Mattie as a female narrator makes the book even more intriguing. *True Grit* presents an unusual spin on the Western and was the basis of one of the most popular of John Wayne's films.

GRAHAM SALISBURY

## Under the Blood-Red Sun

12–14 • Delacorte • 1994 • 256 pp.

The 1941 bombing of Pearl Harbor serves as the central event of this absorbing novel. Living in Hawaii, thirteen-year-old Tomi Nakaji and his best friend, Billy Davis, have paid little attention to World War II, focusing instead on school and baseball. But when the bombs begin to fall, everything changes. Although Tomi was born in Hawaii, his parents and grandparents came from Japan — their neighbors now assume that they're connected to the enemy. When the adults in his life are arrested and imprisoned, Tomi must decide whether to take action based on his anger.

The setting, the humorous and vivid characterization, the action, and the World War II time period come together in the hands of a brilliant writer to produce an unusual and unforgettable book.

JACK SCHAEFER

## Shane

14–18 • Houghton Mifflin • 1954 • 135 pp.

Although published for adults in 1949, *Shane* seemed so natural for a young adult audience that the author adapted it in 1954 for them. This version of *Shane* continues to flourish and was most recently given a new visual interpretation by Wendell Minor.

At the beginning of the novel, young Bob Starrett sees a mysterious figure riding into the Wyoming valley in 1889 — a man with worn but elegant clothing and an impressive demeanor, yet with "the easiness of a coiled spring, of a trap set." Since the Starretts are having a rough time on their farm, Shane stays to help as a hired hand. Fletcher, the cattle baron, attempts to drive Shane and the farmers away. Finally, he goads Shane into action when he hires a gunfighter. Although Shane had given up fighting, he faces the gunman, kills him, then rides away: "He was the man who rode into our little valley out of the heart of the great glowing West and when his work was done rode back whence he had come and he was Shane."

A personification of the romantic West, antisocial and alienated, a knight errant, Shane represents the old West, which was being changed by civilization on the last frontier. With *The Virginian* and *The Ox-Bow Incident, Shane* stands as one of the few Western classics that have stood the test of time and is the only one actually adapted with an adolescent reader in mind.

GARY D. SCHMIDT

## *Lizzie Bright and the Buckminster Boy*

12–14 • Clarion • 2004 • 219 pp.

↬ *NEWBERY HONOR/PRINTZ HONOR*

Turner Buckminster III, the son of a Congregational minister, believes the last segment of his name may signify being behind bars. In 1911 his father takes the family to the small community of Phippsburg, Maine, where Turner finds his every action observed and criticized. As a result, he can't help getting into trouble — fistfights, bloody noses, unpleasant exchanges, and conduct unbecoming a minister's son. Only the residents of the nearby Malaga Island, African Americans, Native Americans, and the foreign-born, seem to accept Turner as an individual. A young African-American girl, Lizzie Griffin Bright, becomes Turner's sole friend, someone with whom he can play baseball or dig for clams for long hours. In the racially charged environment, this friendship alone causes problems. The white landowners of Phippsburg have decided to expel the island's residents so they can build a tourist resort, and Turner and Lizzie get caught up in violence and cruelty. Pastor Buckminster and Lizzie lose their lives; Turner himself matures, learns to stand up for his principles, but also discovers something about loss and forgiveness.

Marked by lyrical prose and a beautiful cadence to the language, *Lizzie Bright and the Buckminster Boy* develops the appealing characters of Turner and Lizzie and highlights the classic struggle between the powerful and the powerless. The novel also examines something quite rare in young adult fiction — racism in the North after the Civil War.

DAI SIJIE

## *Balzac and the Little Chinese Seamstress*

14–18 • Knopf • 2001 • 208 pp.

In 1971, Mao's Cultural Revolution banished "reactionary" Chinese intellectuals to the countryside to be reeducated. Two teenage boys, the sons of professionals and "enemies of the people," find themselves in the unforgiving mountain terrain called "the Phoenix of the Sky." There they mine coal and carry buckets of excrement up the mountain to fertilize the fields. But they bargain their way to a trunk of forbidden books, and when they read Balzac, a new world awaits them. Having been exposed only to Community ideology and propaganda all their lives, the boys fall "headlong into a story of awakening, desire, passion, impulsive action, love." When one of the boys falls in love with the beautiful daughter of an itinerant tailor, he brings her not only all his passion but his new love of literature.

Fascinating in its details of the Cultural Revolution as seen by those who suffer under it, *Balzac and the Little Chinese Seamstress* quietly seduces readers into its world as it moves toward an unexpected ending. Ultimately, the book — part historical novel, part fable, part love story — stands as a testimony to the transforming power of literature. Written by a filmmaker who survived the Cultural Revolution, the novel can be effectively paired with Ray Bradbury's *Fahrenheit 451* for classroom or teen-adult discussions.

BETTY SMITH

## *A Tree Grows in Brooklyn*

14–18 • Harper • 1943 • 489 pp.

At the turn of the century, from 1902 to 1919, the Nolan family lives in the Williamsburg slums of Brooklyn, New York. The book begins in the summer of 1912, when Francie, age eleven, introduces readers to her family and neighborhood. She experiences one joyful day, a Saturday, when she goes about her weekend chores — bargaining with the junkman to get pennies and visiting the library, the butcher's, and the candy store. Because the Nolans have few material goods, Francie values anything she can acquire; a good soup bone sends her into raptures. She loves and feels loved by her mother, Katie, who works as a janitor, and her father, Johnny, who drinks too much and sometimes gets hired as a singing waiter.

Subsequently, readers learn how Francie's parents met, and how Katie decided she would endure any hardship to spend a life with Johnny. They have two children, and Johnny's drinking problem gets worse. As the story progresses, Francie begins to lose her innocence. She encounters a sex offender, whom her mother shoots. Johnny dies on Christmas Day, and Francie stops believing in God. After graduating from eighth grade, she must work in a factory, although she longs to attend high school. Finally Katie meets a good man who will help support them all, and Francie can return to school.

A story by Thomas Wolfe about Brooklyn inspired Betty Smith to write her own, more authentic one. Smith created a thousand-page manuscript and submitted it to a nonfiction contest at Harper's, but the publisher thought it would work better as a novel. Smith agreed to rewrite the book as fiction, cutting it considerably. Although she certainly presented material that was quite controversial at the time, Smith made many changes to avoid offending conservatives as well as the Catholic Church. Even today, however, this poignant, honest appraisal of the life of the poor shocks some readers. Published during World War II, the book met with immediate success; with wartime shortages, Harper could not get enough paper to keep up with the demand.

A true classic, the book has been used in eighth grade, although it works best in high school. With its candid assessment of the needy, its sense of innocence, and the loss of innocence, it seems amazingly contemporary — even though it presents the world at the turn of the twentieth century.

MILDRED D. TAYLOR

## *Roll of Thunder, Hear My Cry*

12–14 • Dial • 1976 • 276 pp.

✧ *NEWBERY MEDAL*

At a critical point in her life, Mildred Taylor heard the story of a black boy who had broken into a store and was saved from lynching. She began narrating this saga, one that she thought might be for adults, but it turned out to be a book many critics consider one of the most important historical novels in the latter half of the twentieth century. Like Laura Ingalls Wilder, Taylor wrote family history, but her story tells of the problems of segregation and of the triumph and determination of blacks to overcome their plight.

The Logans, a proud black family living on their own land in Mississippi, experience all the racial prejudice of the 1930s. The children use handed-down textbooks; they see the night riders, who come to burn homes and terrorize blacks. They have to fight to keep their land. But they clearly emerge as worthy protagonists, and readers find themselves on the side of the Logans, battling prejudice with them.

Taylor continued the Logan saga in several books: *Let the Circle Be Unbroken, The Friendship, The Road to Memphis, Mississippi Bridge, The Well,* and *The Land.* Readers who are intrigued by Cassie, Stacey, Little Man, and David can follow their stories in these volumes. In *The Land,* Taylor discusses her own obsession with buying a piece of land. She sacrificed and sold many items — her house, furniture, and jewelry — to keep that land. Eventually, she sold the typewriter on which she had written *Roll of Thunder, Hear My Cry.*

A classroom favorite, the book explores a period of history in a very accessible way. In the entire series, Taylor clearly shows racism from the viewpoint of a young person, making it possible for readers of all backgrounds to experience emotionally the horrors of racial prejudice.

MARGARET WALKER

## Jubilee

14–18 • Houghton Mifflin • 1966 • 416 pp.

In the opening scene of *Jubilee,* Sis Hetta, a slave on John Dutton's Georgia plantation, dies in childbirth with her two-year-old daughter, Vyry, by her bed. At seven Vyry, Dutton's offspring, goes to work in the Big House; she bears a great resemblance to his white daughter, Little Missy Lillian. As she grows up, Vyry has tremendous resilience; she marries the blacksmith Randall, who goes to fight for the Union. Just as the lash could not break her spirit in slavery, so Reconstruction — with floods, fires, and the KKK — cannot alter her determination to have peace in her own family and an education for her children.

Based on the oral history of Margaret Walker's great-grandmother, *Jubilee* presents plantation life from the point of view of the slaves. In this African-American *Gone With the Wind,* chapters often open with folk sayings, and the narrative is laced with songs and excerpts from spirituals. This novel, which took three decades for the author to write, emerged in the 1960s as one of the most enduring of the neo-slave narratives, and it still appears on high school reading lists.

### YOKO KAWASHIMA WATKINS

## So Far from the Bamboo Grove

12–14 • Lothrop • 1986 • 184 pp.

Eleven-year-old Yoko, whose family is Japanese, has been raised in North Korea. At the end of World War II, she and her family flee to the South to escape from the Korean Communists, who have been seizing control in the North. They hurry on foot at night, get jammed into railroad cars, and experience fear and hunger. Ultimately they arrive in war-ravaged Japan, where Yoko and her sister make a home for themselves after their mother's death.

This tough and touching novel, written in a straightforward style, makes these historical events accessible to readers; it pairs well with Linda Sue Park's *When My Name Was Keoko,* presenting different stories about the same period of time.

### LARRY WATSON

## Montana 1948

14–18 • Milkweed • 1993 • 175 pp.

A portrait of a child, his family, their biases, and their moral dilemmas creates a riveting, wholly plausible story. In clear, clean, unpretentious prose, twelve-year-old David Hayden relates the incidents of 1948: how he learned that his uncle Frank, a doctor, had been abusing Native American girls; Frank's murder of one of the Sioux girls, who spoke against him; the decision of his father, the sheriff, to incarcerate Frank in their home; and Frank's suicide.

This compelling story unfolds with graceful pacing; readers grow to understand the bigotry of the times, small town life, and the aristocracy of the towns on the plains. This examination of a place and its people combines with an unforgettable coming-of-age story. Ultimately, *Montana 1948* puts a new spin on the American Western novel by revealing the disturbing prejudices and domestic history behind the myths.

LAURENCE YEP

## Dragonwings

12–14 • Harper • 1975 • 317 pp.

⊸ *NEWBERY HONOR*

I n 1903 an eight-year-old Chinese immigrant, Moon Shadow, comes to San Francisco to join his father, Windrider, whom he has never met. At first they live in the Chinese section of town, but eventually Windrider leaves his work in a laundry to become a repairman and freelance mechanic. Intrigued by model gliders, both father and son study aeronautical books and even correspond with the Wright brothers. Finally, after three years of work, they manage to build and fly *Dragonwings*.

In an attempt to challenge stereotypes, Laurence Yep wanted to show Chinese Americans doing things that readers might not expect. He found a newspaper account of a Chinese boy who had a twenty-minute airplane flight in 1909 before the plane came down. Covering eight years of California history, Yep also weaves material about the San Francisco earthquake of 1906 into the story.

Adapted for the theater and performed at the Kennedy Center and Lincoln Center, taught in thousands of classrooms, *Dragonwings* makes the Chinese immigrant experience personal. Readers grow to understand and connect to Moon Shadow and Windrider, who emerge as sympathetic human beings with their own fears, hopes, sorrows, and dreams.

JANE YOLEN

## Briar Rose

14–18 • Tor • 1992 • 224 pp.

E ver since Rebecca Berlin was a child, she and her sisters have heard a unique version of "Sleeping Beauty" or "Briar Rose" from their grandmother Gemma. At her grandmother's deathbed, Becca makes a promise to find the castle in the sleeping woods, and she uses clippings and photos that turn up after her grandmother's death to help her. The journey takes Becca to Poland and the Nazi extermination camp of Chelmno; she meets Josef Potocki, who knew her grandmother and was sentenced to the death camp because of his homosexuality. In a smooth blending of history and romance, Jane Yolen has written a heartbreaking novel that is often used in classrooms as part of Holocaust units.

# Horror, Ghosts, Gothic

**W**HEN YOU ASK TEENS about their favorite books today, speculative fiction titles — fantasy, science fiction, and horror — almost always lead the list. Many of the most popular horror books were originally published for adults. Those old chestnuts *Dracula, Frankenstein,* and *Rebecca* frequently appear on lists of adolescents' favorite ten titles. Stephen King and Anne Rice have been staples of teenage reading for over thirty years.

Like the rest of this genre, horror novels written specifically for adolescents have increased in the past few years, in number if not in literary quality. As a type, horror probably suffers more than most from its formulaic approach and sometimes cheesy writing. But the past decade has brought not only better writers to the forefront — M. T. Anderson, Pete Hautman, and Doris Lessing — it has also brought more complex and intriguing works as well. No doubt the appearance of Elizabeth Kostova's *The Historian* as a *New York Times* bestseller in 2005 will encourage other writers to explore the possibilities of the horror novel.

Whatever its future, it currently holds great attraction for readers; through horror they can get dollops of terror, then close the book when they have had enough. The titles listed below provide both literature and shivers — in the appropriate doses.

M. T. ANDERSON

## Thirsty

12–14 • Candlewick • 1997 • 256 pp.

Chris experiences a lot of normal teenage problems — bickering parents, a domineering older brother, and estranged friends. But he has some added difficulties: While going through the normal adolescent hormonal changes, he appears to be turning into a vampire. Chet, an avatar of the Forces of Light, offers to reverse this condition if Chris will help keep the Vampire Lord imprisoned beneath the Massachusetts reservoir nearby. Chris agrees to infiltrate the vampire group, then wonders if he has done the right thing.

With a brilliant, inventive mind, M. T. Anderson wrote his first book while he worked as an editorial assistant at Candlewick; then his manager published the novel. Filled with plot turns, dark humor, and snappy dialogue with innuendo, this morality tale has found enthusiastic readers in the young horror set; often they ask for a book just as good as *Thirsty.*

RICHARD BACHMAN (STEPHEN KING)

## The Long Walk

14–18 • New American Library • 1979 • 370 pp.

Sometime in the future, Ray Garraty enters an annual event involving one hundred teenagers walking through the state of Maine. They continue putting one foot in front of the other until only one of them survives. Hosted by the Major, the brutal game forces them to walk four miles an hour. Fed through tubes, they must continue their pace, even when they want to go to the bathroom. They get warnings if they fall behind; with the fourth warning, the teen gets taken out of the race and shot in the head.

Bloody, brutal, and sarcastic, the novel contains many of Stephen King's nightmares about the future of the human race. Published under a pseudonym that freed King to write even darker novels than he did under his own name — "the vampire side" of his existence — *The Long Walk* keeps readers at the edge of their seats, frightened but turning the pages.

PETER S. BEAGLE

## Tamsin

12–14 • Roc • 1999 • 335 pp.

A thirteen-year-old New Yorker, Jennifer Gluckstein, moves kicking and screaming to Dorset, England, to live with her mother, her English stepfather, and two stepbrothers. With her stepfather restoring the ramshackle, cold, and damp Stourhead Farm, Jenny finds a kindred spirit in the unhappy Tamsin Willoughby. Tamsin, a ghost, has been haunting the farm for more than three hundred years because of a love gone wrong during Monmouth's Rebellion, at the time of King James II. While Tamsin introduces Jenny to a variety of spirits — a Black Dog, Boggart, and Pooka — Jenny helps her friend escape her earthly bonds.

This ghost story, a satisfying tale of good triumphing over evil, explores English folklore and history while it develops the character of a very lively and compelling heroine.

LIBBA BRAY

## A Great and Terrible Beauty

12–14 • Delacorte • 2003 • 403 pp.

In 1895 sixteen-year-old Gemma Doyle must leave India with her opium-addicted father after her mother has been murdered. Because her mother's death was surrounded by strange circumstances that hint of the occult, Gemma tells no one at her new London school about the murder. There she faces the typical school problems — fitting in, cliques, and secret societies. But Gemma has a talent others lack, for she can connect them to the spirit world. Gradually she and her friends learn about the Order, an ancient group of women, and how two students unleashed an evil being from that realm by killing a Gypsy.

With a jacket that might be found on an adult romance novel, showing the back of a beautiful woman in a corset, the book pulls readers in and keeps them engaged. For those who prefer their horror in light doses, with some fantasy, historical fiction, and romance thrown in, Gemma and her friends continue their saga in Rebel Angels.

## CALEB CARR

### *The Alienist*

14–18 • Random House • 1994 • 496 pp.

In 1896, with Theodore Roosevelt having just been appointed police commissioner of New York City, a serial killer murders a young male prostitute, mutilating his body. To help solve this crime and others like it, Roosevelt enlists the aid of John Schuyler Moore, a reporter for the *New York Times,* and Dr. Laszlo Kreizler. Kreizler, called an "Alienist" in this time period, studied with William James at Harvard and has devoted himself to the psychological study of children. Roosevelt gives his two friends the help of a police secretary, Sara Howard, and two policemen. Using early attempts at psychological profiling, they explore the seamy side of New York in the late nineteenth century. There, with gaslights and horse-drawn carriages, pigs roam streets covered with sewage, slime, and blood.

A combination of mystery, history, and horror, *The Alienist* appeals particularly to those who like dark, dense thrillers that feature a disturbing serial killer.

## JOSEPH DELANEY

### *The Last Apprentice: Revenge of the Witch*

12–14 • Greenwillow • 2005 • 356 pp.

Twelve-year-old Thomas Ward, the seventh son of a seventh son, becomes the apprentice of the tall, hooded man called the Spook some centuries ago in England. He starts learning how to protect farms and villages from "things that go bump in the night" — boggarts, witches, and those possessed (the damned, dizzy, and desperate). In a world where evil remains palpable and the witch Mother Malkin feasts on infants, Thomas still has trouble telling his friends from his enemies. But he confronts his fears, faces demons, and at least survives the early part of his apprenticeship. With a lot of gristly horror — such as hairy pigs eating a witch's heart — the story still presents a very normal, believable young hero, and is already popular because of its page-turning suspense. Young readers admit they can't put it down and can't wait for the sequel.

DAPHNE DU MAURIER

## Rebecca

14–18 • Doubleday • 1938 • 357 pp.

Presenting some living, breathing individuals — Maximilian de Winter, Mrs. Danvers (the sinister housekeeper), and Rebecca — this old chestnut still gets assigned for summer reading every year simply because it works so well. The narrator, an orphaned young woman working for an elderly American lady, becomes the second Mrs. de Winter in Monte Carlo. But after she enters Maxim's ancestral estate, she feels she cannot compete with his first wife and the mistress of Manderley, Rebecca, who haunts the new bride continually. Told after Manderley has been destroyed by fire, the novel glamorizes Rebecca before showing her true character, bringing all of the details together in a totally believable conclusion.

Made into a classic movie, one of Alfred Hitchcock's most accomplished and with one of the great opening lines in fiction — "Last night I dreamt I went to Manderley again" — *Rebecca* remains one of the standard-bearers for the gothic novel and a totally satisfying reading experience.

MARY DOWNING HAHN

## Look for Me by Moonlight

12–14 • Clarion • 1995 • 208 pp.

In a vampire story and gothic romance, Cynda visits her divorced father at an old inn on the deserted Maine coast. She learns that her new home may be haunted by the ghost of a former innkeeper's daughter. But one moonlit night, a mysterious, dark, and handsome stranger arrives at the inn driving a silver Porsche. Vincent charms everyone; but eventually the vampire attacks Cydna's half-brother, and she must fight to save him.

In a style crisply contemporary yet lushly romantic, Mary Downing Hahn weaves a vampire story with a happy ending — ideal for readers who like their horror novels eerie but not violent.

PETE HAUTMAN

## *Sweetblood*

12–14 • Simon & Schuster • 2003 • 180 pp.

Sixteen-year-old Lucy Szabo was diagnosed with diabetes when she was six; she has been managing her disease with insulin, exercise, and food. She considers herself one of the modern Undead, whose life has been extended by medical science. In a brilliant but edgy paper for school, Lucy theorizes that the vampires of folk legend may well have been untreated diabetics. This premise gets her in trouble with her teacher, who finds Lucy, always dressed in black, a bit too weird. Because Lucy has checked into the Transylvania chat room in cyberspace, she has attracted a true predator in her town, someone she encounters as Dracula on Halloween.

Certainly not a simple vampire novel — and probably a horror title enjoyed most by those who don't usually read the genre — *Sweetblood* presents a smart, savvy, attractive protagonist who is transformed into another person before the end of the novel. As Lucy discovers that she is not her disease, she also learns to accept the love of those around her who have always been there — through all of her exasperating stages.

SHIRLEY JACKSON

## *The Haunting of Hill House*

14–18 • Viking • 1959 • 256 pp.

A noted writer of supernatural short fiction, Shirley Jackson also created the best haunted house novel of the twentieth century. She spent months trying to find the perfect house to appear in her story; she studied so many factual accounts of ghosts and hauntings that she had to read a few chapters of *Little Women* each night to calm herself before bed. The resulting novel, *The Haunting of Hill House,* no doubt has caused many readers to lose sleep as well.

When a professor of the paranormal invites several strangers to spend the summer investigating a dark Victorian house with a tragic history, he is joined by a man whose family owns the property, a female Bohemian artist, and Eleanor, an inhibited young woman who has spent much of her life caring for her recently deceased mother. Dark and drafty, Hill House is built at odd angles, making it difficult for the group to find their way from room to room. Over time, they begin to experience blasts of icy air, loud knocking, ghostly writing on walls ("HELP ELEANOR COME HOME"), and an incessant babbling voice.

Written in subtle, hypnotic prose, the novel suggests that some — but not all — of the events may be imagined by the troubled Eleanor; her increasingly bizarre behavior leads to an unforgettable conclusion as Hill House claims yet another victim. Fans will find the book impossible to forget, no matter how hard they try.

STEPHEN KING

## *Carrie*

14–18 • Doubleday • 1974 • 272 pp.

Raised by a religious fanatic, Carrie White at sixteen began her first menstruation period in the gym shower. As she believes herself to be bleeding to death, her classmates taunt her. But the onset of puberty releases Carrie's latent powers: she can move objects and cause them to change by the force of her mind. Henceforth she will no longer be a loser, the socially inept victim of student pranks and her mother's cruelty; she's going to get even. She'll give them a prom no one will ever forget — that is, no one who lives through it.

While teaching English to high school students, Stephen King began working on a short story about an outcast student with telekinetic powers. But he had trouble with the story, particularly with the character of the girl, and threw away the manuscript. When he came home from school the next night, he found his wife engrossed in the story; she encouraged him to continue. When Doubleday accepted *Carrie* from the man who would dominate the bestseller lists for the next thirty years, they paid him an advance of $2,500. It was not, however, until the 1976 movie directed by Brian De Palma that *Carrie* established King as a perennial bestseller.

Although King's writing improved over the next thirty years — so much so that his name has become synonymous with the horror genre — *Carrie* contains a haunting and powerful story, well plotted and emotionally charged. King eerily builds the tension as he unfolds a story of vengeance, which allows readers to vicariously experience the idea of getting even with their own middle or high school classmates.

ANNETTE CURTIS KLAUSE

## Blood and Chocolate

12–14 • Delacorte • 1997 • 288 pp.

Sixteen-year-old Vivian Gandillon may not be one of fiction's most likable heroines, but she is certainly one of the most memorable. When her father dies in a fire, she moves from West Virginia to a sleepy Maryland suburb. Preoccupied with her body and viciously competitive with the other girls, Vivian nourishes a crush on a new schoolmate — a sensitive poet with a feeling for the supernatural. At times he looks so delicious, she wants to "bite the buttons off his shirt." But this romance faces severe obstacles: Vivian happens to be a werewolf. Throughout the book, readers struggle between fascination, empathy, and revulsion toward her werewolf culture. Since her pack needs to choose a new leader, the males engage in physical combat, and the females compete for the title of Queen Bitch.

This coming-of-age story of a young female werewolf — based on the idea that hormones make teenagers want to howl — provides a gripping, thrilling, and original plot line. Horror fans often find this steamy, sensual book as addictive as chocolate. Fans of horror and Annette Curtis Klause also love her *The Silver Kiss*.

ELIZABETH KOSTOVA

## The Historian

14–18 • Little, Brown • 2005 • 642 pp.

In a horror novel reminiscent of Dan Brown's *The Da Vinci Code*, a sixteen-year-old American girl finds a mysterious book and letters in her father's library in Amsterdam in 1972. A diplomat, her father has temporarily ceased his search for the location of the tomb of Vlad the Impaler, the historical figure who inspired Bram Stoker's *Dracula*. Her father knows that Vlad still stalks the earth and needs to be killed by a silver stake or bullet. As the girl learns about all Vlad's details — from letters, books, historical documents, and libraries — she and her father travel through a variety of geographic settings where he spins out the story. In this lengthy and discursive novel, Elizabeth Kostova provides a Baedeker's guide to many locations — Istanbul, Budapest, Oxford — and piles up a great deal of Dracula lore. Ultimately, the girl discovers details about her own mother, who is presumed dead, and her own heritage as a descendant of Vlad.

Few genealogists have ever taken such an amazing journey. Although filled with all the traditional Dracula horror elements, the book might best serve as beach reading on a bright summer's day. In Kostova's world, all Dracula really longs for, besides some blood to keep him alive, is a first-rate historian who can catalogue his impressive horror book collection. Few novels have ever featured so many vampire librarians! *The Historian* holds great appeal for horror fans but also for those who do not consider themselves aficionados of the genre.

DORIS LESSING

## The Fifth Child

14–18 • Knopf • 1988 • 135 pp.

In a continuous narrative unbroken by chapters, Doris Lessing conjures up her version of a modern gothic horror novel. Living in England in the 1960s–1980s, Harriet and David, decidedly old-fashioned, want a large family and buy a sprawling Victorian house beyond their means. They proceed to have four children, relying on help from their parents. With visiting relatives and friends, their life seems idyllic until the fifth child, Ben, comes along. Demanding and monstrous even inside the womb, violent and uncontrollable, Ben quickly learns to kill animals and becomes part of a motorcycle gang as a small boy. Although he seems a throwback to an earlier stage of human development — a troll, savage, or Neanderthal — no one can give Harriet the handle she needs on this child or monster that she has created. He goes on to destroy all that she and David have worked to build, and slowly the family starts to dissolve.

Lessing admits that she hated writing this book, her thirty-fifth: the reader can alternately dislike reading it and not want to put it down. Using the format of a classic horror story, Lessing also explores attitudes toward children, family, and society; this disturbing book begs to be discussed in a classroom or in parent-teen reading groups. However, since the horror genre in general suffers from a lack of good writing, this book and its sequel, *Ben, In the World,* deserve attention simply for the brilliance of Lessing's prose and the deftness of her characterization.

IRA LEVIN

## *Rosemary's Baby*

14–18 • Random House • 1967 • 320 pp.

Rosemary and her actor-husband, Guy, move into the gloomy Bramford apartment building on upper Seventh Avenue in New York City. Although the building's history reads like a Shirley Jackson horror story, the newlyweds love their high-ceilinged warren and soon make friends with the charming couple next door. Soon, the actor competing with Guy for a part gets stricken blind, and Guy's career gets a boost. Then Rosemary becomes pregnant; she remembers a vivid dream sequence that involves her husband and a circle of others. Later Guy says he made love to her, celebrating his new part, after she passed out one night. Rosemary's neighbors fuss over her, giving her special concoctions and charms. After a friend sends her a book on witchcraft, Rosemary, a former Catholic, begins to suspect she's become involved with a witches' coven.

Drawing from the newspaper headlines of 1965–1966, Ira Levin weaves everyday incidents seamlessly with the satanic. Made into a memorable Roman Polanski movie in 1968, *Rosemary's Baby* caught the attention of adolescents in the 1960s and continues to draw readers into the dark corridors of the Bramford apartment building.

LAUREN MYRACLE

## *Rhymes with Witches*

12–14 • Abrams/Amulet • 2005 • 211 pp.

What would any teenager be willing to do to be popular, really popular, someone whose every action gets idolized? With a father who has abandoned the family, Jane copes with her problems by trying to be invisible. But she gets picked as the freshman member of the Bitches, the elite group at school, made up of one member from each class. As Jane begins to learn, the source of their popularity may not be good looks, style, money, class, or smarts; they may be practicing witchcraft, wreaking havoc with lives. Soon Jane starts stealing objects from her classmates, who experience setbacks as her star rises.

In a riveting page-turner — a blend of horror, chick lit, fantasy, and comedy — Lauren Myracle captures the graphic language and social hierarchy of contemporary high schools and slowly builds her story to a creepy dénouement.

STEWART O'NAN

## The Night Country

14–18 • Farrar, Straus • 2003 • 240 pp.

Halloween in New England: few combinations of time and place conjure up such rich imagery. Yet *The Night Country* is very much a contemporary, suburban ghost story, so its Connecticut landscape is littered with smashed pumpkins in the streets, fast-food restaurants, and flashy strip malls. A year earlier, on Halloween night, five teenagers hit a tree in a speeding car, killing Toe, Danielle, and Marco and leaving one friend permanently brain-damaged and the other unhurt but suicidal. Now the three dead teens are back, their spirits revisiting parents, classmates, and the policeman whose high-speed chase contributed to the fatal accident. Narrated by Marco — with Danielle and Toe's occasional caustic comments — the story moves with a sense of dread and foreboding toward its inevitably tragic conclusion.

Stewart O'Nan was inspired to write this novel by a newspaper article about two teenagers who survived a car accident but returned to the same location a year later and deliberately crashed their car, killing themselves. Never sensational, the book develops its atmosphere; the characters are sympathetically limned; and the ghostly narrators are a brilliant touch. The author's intriguing, intentionally sketchy descriptions of how these spirits communicate, instantly travel from place to place, and participate in the lives of the living hint at an unsettling parallel existence that will both comfort and chill readers. This evocative and haunting novel is the perfect choice for anyone who thinks horror stories usually fail as literature.

MEREDITH ANN PIERCE

## The Darkangel

12–14 • Atlantic • 1982 • 281 pp.

In a novel set on the moon, a young servant girl, Aeriel, struggles to destroy the black-winged Darkangel, the handsome and compelling vampire who has kidnapped her mistress. He has reduced thirteen wives to wraiths; robbed of their blood, hearts, and souls, they live in lead vials hanging from his neck. From the wraiths Aeriel learns to spin, weave, and stitch her own feelings into garments; her "charity made a thread so fine and long that she had not yet reached the end of it." Embarking on a perilous journey, Aeriel sets out to restore the souls of the victims.

The story was inspired by a woman's dream of a vampire living on the moon, which is recorded in *Memories, Dreams, Reflections*, by the psychologist Carl Jung. She continued this inventive trilogy in *A Gathering of Gargoyles* and *The Pearl of the Soul of the World*.

ANNE RICE

## The Vampire Lestat

14–18 • Knopf • 1985 • 560 pp.

*Interview with the Vampire*, the first volume of the Vampire Chronicles, introduces the character of Lestat de Lioncourt, a charismatic and powerful vampire. In this fascinating sequel, Lestat narrates his history, beginning with his life as a bright, sensitive, and conflicted boy who wants to become an artist. Since his impoverished mother encourages such ideas, he leaves home to pursue his dream. In Paris a few decades before the Revolution, Lestat becomes an actor, falls in love, and gets chosen by an older vampire to become one of the living dead. Moving from pre-Revolutionary France to New Orleans in the 1980s, this chronicle of an engaging hero explores ancient Egyptian legends along with other vampire sociology and lore. In the 1980s Lestat, looking a lot like David Bowie, renames his fledgling rock band "The Vampire Lestat" and writes his own autobiography.

In a baroque, ornamented style, Anne Rice moves through a landscape that some adults find ridiculous but that has captured adolescent readers by the millions. Her Vampire Chronicles comprise many volumes, including *The Queen of the Damned*, *The Vampire Armand*, and most recently *Blood Canticle*.

VIVIAN VANDE VELDE

## Companions of the Night

12–14 • Harcourt • 1995 • 224 pp.

When Kerry Nowicki, sixteen, goes to the Laundromat late one night, she interrupts a vigilante committee in her town of

Brockport, New York. They believe they have found a vampire, one of the undead, a handsome boy named Ethan Byrne who is injured. Since Kerry decides to help the boy escape, her father and brother get kidnapped in retaliation. In the ensuing cat-and-mouse game, Ethan exhibits great cunning and duplicity, and Kerry wants desperately to believe in him.

For over a decade the book has been a favorite of young horror fans, who get their vampire lore mixed in with a touch of romance. The book also appeals to those who like stories about innocent girls falling in love with bad boys.

# Humor

**W**HAT MAKES SOMEONE LAUGH? Why is something funny to one person and not another? What people consider funny changes with both age and experience. Often, adults don't appreciate the books that teens enjoy because they themselves don't find them funny. And young people frequently laugh about topics that adults don't, such as sex and authority.

Laughter creates bonds between people, helps make a shared experience, or can divide people; there is an enormous difference between laughing with and laughing at someone. Laughter is created by incongruities, fear, joy, and other emotions. It allows tough topics to be discussed, softening harsh, even devastating, edges.

In any random survey of adolescents, when asked what they want to read, they almost always say "funny books." The writer Gordon Korman has provided one of the best descriptions of the joys of reading light, comic material: "Only a book can give a couple hours of light nothing, a sustained mood, wiping away for the moment all thought, all responsibilities, penances, or problems other than those of the other world opened to us by its author." The books listed here many not seem funny to everyone, but those willing to give themselves over to the sensibility of the author will find many hours of "light nothing" in these books.

M. T. ANDERSON

## Burger Wuss

12–14 • Candlewick • 1999 • 208 pp.

With acerbic humor and caustic wit, sixteen-year-old Anthony narrates how he sought revenge when he lost his girlfriend to another boy, Turner. Anthony takes a job at O'Dermott's, a fast-food restaurant where Turner also works. The restaurant employs a vegan cook, who also happens to be an anarchist; O'Dermott's carries on a rivalry with another chain, Burger Queen. Superb dialogue, humorous situations, and broad satire make these burger battles fresh and often quite funny. Anyone who has worked for a fast-food chain will relate to many elements of this amusing novel.

JOAN BAUER

## Rules of the Road

12–14 • Putnam • 1998 • 201 pp.

Very few books for teens show them working or searching for a career. Hence tall, red-haired, sixteen-year-old Jenna Boller is one of the most refreshing heroines in the annals of teen literature. Jenna loves to work — in her case, sell shoes. She enjoys taking care of customers, finding what they need, making them happy with her vast knowledge about shoes. And she particularly admires the fine shoes sold by Gladstone's Shoe Store, her employer. Jenna becomes the ideal assistant and driver for Madeline Gladstone, the crusty owner of the company, on a trip from Chicago to Texas in Madeline's Cadillac. As they stop at each franchise, as they try to thwart a takeover of the enterprise, Jenna and Mrs. Gladstone share their commitment to work, shoes, and business integrity. In the process of learning some of the rules of the road, Jenna ultimately faces her most difficult personal problem — her drunken father back in Chicago.

Unlike so many novelists writing about alcoholism, Joan Bauer truly understands the disease and gives sound advice to readers. Far from a thin problem novel, however, *Rules of the Road,* filled with humor and tragedy, shows the development of a memorable and likable heroine. With this book and its sequel, *Best Foot Forward,* teens have enjoyed the details about getting a job, learning to drive a car, and taking an exciting road trip. Adults appreciate the well-developed plot and characters, the treatment of alcoholism, and the life lessons woven into the text. A perfect book to teach, to share in adult-teen book groups, or to read independently.

JOAN BAUER

## Squashed

12–14 • Delacorte • 1992 • 194 pp.

Joan Bauer excels in creating likable, often driven, protagonists who interact in a meaningful way with their community. In the case of sixteen-year-old Ellie Morgan, the star of *Squashed*, Bauer's first novel, the young Iowa girl has a passion for growing ribbon-winning pumpkins. A bit too plump and always trying to diet, Ellie struggles to make her pumpkin Max grow — feeding him special food, talking to him about success, protecting him during rain and frost. Will Max win the Rock River Pumpkin Weigh-In? Or will Ellie's nemesis triumph? When you add some pumpkin thieves and a new boy in town as interested in agriculture as Ellie is, you have all the ingredients for an enjoyable and ultimately satisfying novel.

Bauer demonstrates in this book and many others — *Hope Was Here, Backwater* — that wholesome characters and plot-driven novels can be written, with humor and panache, about the everyday joys of selling shoes or raising pumpkins. These novels have especially endeared her to readers in the Midwest, often the setting for her books, or anyone who loves a well-crafted, engaging story.

ANN BRASHARES

## The Sisterhood of the Traveling Pants

12–14 • Delacorte • 2001 • 294 pp.

In the first book of an extremely popular series, four friends from childhood — Tibby, Carmen, Bridget, and Lena — find they must spend a summer apart. But before they leave for places as distant as Greece or a soccer camp in Baja, California, they find a dream-come-true, perfect pair of jeans that fits each of them. They share the pants during this summer and support one another by letters in this breezy narrative told in four different, interwoven voices. As one of their rules states, "Remember: Pants=love. Love your pals. Love yourself."

BILL BRYSON

## A Walk in the Woods

14–18 • Broadway • 1998 • 276 pp.

For hiking purists, Bill Bryson's account of his months on the Appalachian Trail lacks the verisimilitude of someone who actually walked the entire 2,100-plus miles from Springer Mountain in Georgia to Mount Katahdin in Maine. But for armchair or would-be hikers, or someone who loves a great stylist and a humorous nonfiction voice, the book contains ample information to have earned its spot on the bestseller list. After all, Bryson hiked 870 of those miles, more than most people will do in their lifetime.

Because Bryson happens to be an out-of-shape, pudgy, perceptive human — not an extreme sports fanatic — he maintains perspective and irony about his trip; readers can easily imagine themselves struggling on the trail, feeling the way he does, and experiencing his fears as he contemplates nature raw in tooth and claw. As he moves along the Appalachian Trail, Bryson spins stories about its history, geography, flora, fauna, and wildlife and brings to life the hikers he encounters on the way, including his partner, Stephen Katz. With the humor of Dave Barry and the fluid writing style of John McPhee, Bryson brings American history, the social sciences, and the natural world to life; readers truly enjoy joining him as he takes a very long walk in the woods.

MEG CABOT

## The Princess Diaries

12–14 • HarperCollins • 2000 • 283 pp.

Living with her single mother, a painter, in Greenwich Village, Mia Thermopolis seems like an average urban teenager. One day her father arrives to inform her that he has withheld some information from her. Since he is the crown prince of Genovia, she, therefore, is a princess. With her mother dating her algebra teacher and the paparazzi showing up for photos, Mia suddenly finds herself overwhelmed.

Bearing little resemblance to the Disney adaptation, the book may disappoint some moviegoers hoping for a duplicate. However, this classic makeover novel brings a charming protagonist to the front of the stage; Mia continues her adventures in a multitude of sequels.

ANDREW CLEMENTS

## *Frindle*

12–14 • Simon & Schuster • 1996 • 105 pp.

Fifth-grader Nicholas Allen — an independent thinker with a reputation for devising clever, time-wasting schemes — wants to sabotage his Language Arts class. After studying how new words get added to the dictionary, he coins a new name for *pen* — *frindle* — and battles with his teacher about it. Ultimately, their war escalates, and Nicholas appears on the *Late Show* and *Good Morning America* to explain his new word — which ends up in the dictionary! Witty, true to the behavior of the young, with delightful sparring between Nicholas and his teacher, *Frindle* has been extraordinarily popular with elementary school students. But with more reluctant readers, it has also developed a middle school following, proving once again that a good story can attract a wide age range of devotees.

PAULA DANZIGER

## *Remember Me to Harold Square*

12–14 • Delacorte • 1987 • 139 pp.

Kendra, who has just finished ninth grade, gets sentenced to a summer in New York City with her ten-year-old brother. Things start to look better, however, when her parents announce that the fifteen-year-old son of their friends — a Wisconsin farmboy, albeit one with a girlfriend — will spend the summer with them. The adults devise a scavenger hunt that allows the threesome to discover and delight in the city — and gives time for a friendship to develop between Kendra and Frank.

Kendra's present-tense narrative is fast and funny. Providing a glimpse of New York City, the book also gives readers a sense of the warm and wonderful humor of the late Paula Danziger, one of the funniest writers for children and adolescents of all time. She wrote many fabulous books, including the equally popular *The Cat Ate My Gymsuit*.

ANN FINE

## Flour Babies

12–14 • Little, Brown • 1992 • 178 pp.

Room 8 at St. Boniface School contains the largest number of boys-least-likely-to-succeed, including the troublemaker Simon Martin, a "clumsy young giant" and assumed to be unthinking. But Simon ends up having a lot more going for him than soccer. He shows his mettle once the class starts a science project in which each boy is responsible for the well-being of a six-pound sack of flour. The teacher, Mr. Cassidy, worries about the havoc that one hundred pounds of sifted white flour might cause, but Simon somehow manages to take care of his flour baby. As he becomes attached to "her," he realizes that he isn't responsible for his father's leaving and that parenthood is either a lifetime sentence or the most important job in the world.

This thought-provoking, poignant, and well-paced novel by Ann Fine, the author of *Alias Madame Doubtfire*, contains a great deal of humor and highly original characters who behave in unexpected ways.

PAUL FLEISCHMAN

## A Fate Totally Worse Than Death

12–14 • Candlewick • 1995 • 128 pp.

In this spoof on horror novels, the Huns, Cliffside High's ruling clique, live with their wealthy parents in the Hundred Palms Estates. When a girl outside the clique, Charity Chase, sets her sights on Drew (whom one of the Huns wants for herself), she falls to her death off a cliff. Helga, an exotic Norwegian student, also has designs on Drew, and strange things start happening. The three Huns age rapidly, gaining liver spots and gray hair. Could Charity's ghost have returned to avenge her death?

Satire and slapstick humor combine with comic characters to create a wickedly funny book. Those who do not belong to the in-group will appreciate how the girls get their comeuppance in this caustic but satisfying parody.

JACK GANTOS

## *Joey Pigza Swallowed the Key*

12–14 • Farrar, Straus • 1998 • 154 pp.

↩ *NATIONAL BOOK AWARD FINALIST*

Describing himself as "wired," Joey Pigza suffers from attention deficit hyperactivity disorder (ADHD). As he tells his story in a nonstop, breathless voice, this lovable but disaster-prone hero creates havoc wherever he goes. When teachers ask him questions, Joey replies, "Can I get back to you on that?" He not only swallows his house key, he loses a fingernail to a pencil sharpener and accidentally slices off the tip of a classmate's nose. Although basically a good kid who wants to do the right thing, Joey cannot keep still and cannot stay focused. Finally he gets some of the medical attention he desperately needs and takes medication that helps. Both his running narrative and his antics keep readers laughing with him — not at him. His hilarious and heartbreaking saga continues in *Joey Pigza Loses Control* and *What Would Joey Do?*

FRANK B. GILBRETH, JR., AND ERNESTINE GILBRETH CAREY

## *Cheaper by the Dozen*

12–18 • Crowell • 1948 • 224 pp.

In the early 1900s, roadsters are the rage, and an engineer in Montclair, New Jersey, raises a vibrant, eccentric family of twelve children. Frank Gilbreth originated the science of motion study to increase efficiency. He and his wife, Lillian, a psychologist, apply that study to their large family with mixed but always humorous results. Mr. Gilbreth takes an active role in his children's education — they paint constellations on the ceiling and learn foreign languages in their bathroom time. The strength of Mr. Gilbreth's character and convictions, his sense of humor, and his love of family form the basis of this narrative, which was written by two of the children as they looked back on their remarkable parents.

Though clothing, hairstyles, and dating have changed significantly, the ways young people get their parents to accept them probably haven't. The situations and characters have a timeless humor; made more popular by a 2005 movie adaptation featuring Steve Martin, the book has long been a staple for homeschoolers.

K. L. GOING

## Fat Kid Rules the World

14–18 • Putnam • 2003 • 185 pp.

↪ *PRINTZ HONOR*

At six-foot-one and weighing almost 300 pounds, miserable and lonely, Troy Billings thinks of ways to end his life, but he's afraid people will laugh at his final moments. While contemplating jumping from a subway platform, he meets Curt MacCrae, a dirty, disheveled, self-destructive young man, who befriends him. When Curt isn't using drugs and searching for a place to sleep, he produces awesome guitar music. He decides that Troy, now T, will become the drummer for his punk-rock group, Rage/Tectonic. Although he's dabbled in drums, T doesn't really know how to play, but with some lessons from Curt, T starts to become a punk-rock legend. In the process, he not only saves himself but, with the help of his father, finds a way to save Curt as well.

In a character-driven novel — one of the funniest and most satisfying for teens in the last decade — two intriguing punk rockers take the stage and rule.

STEVE KLUGER

## Last Days of Summer

12–14 • Morrow • 1998 • 353 pp.

April 9, 1940. I have decided to turn to a life of crime. . . . Hitler is beginning to scare the holy heck out of me." In a novel told in letters, newspaper clippings, baseball scorecards, war dispatches, and telegrams, Joey Margolis, a twelve-year-old Jewish boy in Brooklyn, New York, worries about Hitler's rise to power, his parents' divorce, and his absent father. Since he craves a surrogate father, he decides to correspond with the New York Giants slugger Charlie Banks. Joey's smart-alecky, outrageous communications grab the reluctant attention of the superstar. Then Joey's best friend, Japanese-American Craig Nakamura, gets shipped off to an internment camp, and Joey's journey takes him to a meeting with President Roosevelt, whom he has written to frequently about national policy.

In a laugh-out-loud novel, with great one-liners on every page, the playwright Steve Kluger takes material that is serious at its core and keeps readers laughing and crying until the final page.

GORDON KORMAN

## *No More Dead Dogs*

12–14 • Hyperion • 2000 • 192 pp.

B ecause Wallace Wallace's father was continually exaggerating, Wallace tells the truth, nothing but the truth and always the truth. When he gives his honest opinion about a book assigned in English in which the dog dies — the teacher's favorite novel — it lands him in detention, off the football team, and into the drama club's production of that very same book.

Humor abounds as the story unfolds from several points of view: Wallace's, the drama teacher's, and that of two girls (one winds up being Wallace's love interest). A fresh approach to serious issues, the novel explores the role of authority and the meaning of friendship; it demonstrates that the truth can be very funny. This book also naturally appeals to those who find themselves weary of "dead dog" books.

Although a large number of writers for teens began their career as adolescents — S. E. Hinton, Maureen Daly, Christopher Paolini — Gordon Korman bloomed even earlier. He wrote his first draft of *This Can't Be Happening at Macdonald Hall!* when he was twelve. Because he collected the Scholastic Book Club money, he felt a loyalty to this publisher and submitted his novel to Scholastic in Canada. Although it was accepted, the book took a very long time to produce, which "didn't exactly mesh with a 7th grader's expectations." Korman went on to write dozens of novels — including *Son of the Mob* and *The 6th Grade Nickname Game* — the type of book he liked to read as a sixth- and seventh-grader. Thirty years later, he still has an incredible ability to find plots, characters, and subjects that keep his fans laughing.

CAROLYN MACKLER

## *The Earth, My Butt, and Other Big Round Things*

12–14 • Candlewick • 2003 • 246 pp.

↪ *PRINTZ HONOR*

Opening the story with the words "Froggy Welsh the Fourth is trying to get up my shirt," Carolyn Mackler keeps readers turning the pages to find out what will happen to her fifteen-year-old protagonist, Virginia. A fat girl in a family of skinny people, Virginia struggles with her self-image, her loneliness — her best friend has just moved away — and her relationship with Froggy Welsh the Fourth. In short, she faces every teen concern, but with great self-reflection and humor. She even has a set of rules for "The Fat Girl Code of Conduct."

In the end, Virginia learns that her parents and siblings may not be so perfect, and she discovers that she has real promise — with her sassy humor, honesty, and sensitivity. A likable protagonist, Virginia will be cheered on by readers as she moves toward the beginning of self-acceptance and self-love.

HILARY MCKAY

## *Indigo's Star*

12–14 • Simon & Schuster/McElderry • 2004 • 266 pp.

While Indigo is the focus of this second novel about the artistic, eccentric Casson family, which was introduced in *Saffy's Angel,* each character comes alive in this poignant, gently humorous novel. Indigo, peaceful and kind, is reluctant to return to school after a prolonged illness because he's the target of a red-haired boy and his gang. He befriends Tom, an American who has come to stay with his British grandmother to avoid his father's remarriage and the new family. Together, Tom and Indigo accept the inevitable changes in their lives and grow to appreciate their own unique families.

Although Hilary McKay tackles serious subjects — jealousy, realignment of families, bullying, and violence — she does so without solemnity. The interaction of the characters is often wildly funny. The hilarious Casson family saga continues in *Permanent Rose.*

JACLYN MORIARTY

## The Year of Secret Assignments

12–14 • Scholastic/Levine • 2004 • 344 pp.

The Australian high school students Lydia, Emily, and Cassie, as part of the Famous Ashbury-Brookfield Pen Pal Project, must write letters to three boys at Brookfield High. Even though they believe the project might be undermining their constitutional rights, making them associate with drug dealers and murderers, they quickly get swept up in a series of letters, e-mails, and diary entries as the three sets of pen pals get to know each other. But when Lydia and Emily discover that Cassie has been threatened by her correspondent, they declare an all-out war against the Brookfield boys.

With much humor and a bit of mystery and romance, the book has become a favorite of teens — often readers of Meg Cabot and Ann Brashares novels — who are attracted to both the fast-moving narrative and this modern comedy of manners.

GARY PAULSEN

## Harris and Me: A Summer Remembered

12–14 • Harcourt • 1993 • 157 pp.

An eleven-year-old city boy chronicles his summer with relatives on their hardscrabble farm. A description of his alcoholic parents begins this episodic, often rude, sometimes crude, but ultimately poignant saga. He and his cousin, Harris, become friends through their work and outrageous, bold, and totally impish antics. The boys explore the country, work on the farm, and torment the animals. In the most memorable scene, the narrator convinces his cousin to urinate on an electric fence.

Gary Paulsen has remained true to the characters, the place, and the setting. This fast-paced account provides a glimpse into a difficult life while exploring the meaning of home and family.

RICHARD PECK

## *The Teacher's Funeral: A Comedy in Three Parts*

12–14 • Dial • 2004 • 190 pp.

In a broadly humorous style, this book set in Indiana opens with a compelling first line: "If your teacher has to die, August isn't a bad time of year for it." And so Miss Myrt Arbuckle, the tyrant of Parke County's one-room schoolhouse, was laid to rest in 1904, her pointer in her hand and a grade book in her pocket. Within days, fifteen-year-old Russell Culver finds himself in a living nightmare when his older sister, Tansy, becomes the teacher of Russell himself and a ragtag group of students. Fire disrupts the first day of school, one set by Russell and his friend. During the next few months a lot happens, including two suitors for Tansy, but nothing heartrending occurs.

Inspired by Richard Peck's own Hoosier roots, the novel recreates the setting and spirit brilliantly. The text is spiced throughout with broad country humor — such as stories about the Hoosier who goes down to hell and has to come back for a blanket. With a last line that has a powerful kick, a very funny narrator, warmth, sweetness, lots of pranks and adventure, this book often gets returned with its young reader asking for "another one just like it." Because of its broad appeal, it reads aloud beautifully in a classroom or family setting.

DANIEL PINKWATER

## *5 Novels: Alan Mendelsohn, the Boy from Mars; Slaves of Spiegel; The Snarkout Boys and the Avocado of Death; The Last Guru; Young Adult Novel*

12–14 • Farrar, Straus • 1997 • 656 pp.

If readers are too old for Judy Blume and too young for Kafka, they might want to try these five novels written by someone with an outrageous sense of humor. Performing chickens, a New Jersey Martian, an orangutan orchestra — all these ridiculous ideas seem quite natural in this book. This volume of five of Pinkwater's funniest novels, perfect for a middle school reader, will keep readers laughing and arguing over which book they like the best. No one, absolutely no one, can be as funny in print as that comic genius Daniel Pinkwater.

JILL PINKWATER
## Buffalo Brenda
12–14 • Macmillan • 1989 • 203 pp.

India Ink Teidlebaum and Brenda Tuna, friends since seventh grade, want to be conspicuous as they begin their freshman year at Florence Senior High. Certainly their names make them different, but they want more than to be just a part of the crowd. Foisting themselves on the school newspaper staff, they publish attention-grabbing articles and reveal that the school cafeteria has been feeding the students horsemeat. After the principal shuts down the newspaper, they form the Florence High School Booster Club and raise enough money to adopt a bison as the school mascot.

Offbeat characters successfully bent on being different, lively dialogue, and a fast-paced plot distinguish this humorous examination of high school, authority, and the role of adults.

TERRY PRATCHETT
## The Wee Free Men
12–14 • HarperCollins • 2003 • 264 pp.

Nine-year-old Tiffany Aching, a dairy maid who also minds sheep, shows a great deal of common sense. When monsters from the fairy world begin arriving in her home on the Chalk, she sets out to stop them. Inheriting the Chalk and some powers of witchcraft from Granny Aching, Tiffany gets the support of the Wee Free Men; tiny, with red beards and blue tattoos, they excel in fighting, thieving, and drinking. When the Queen of the Elves kidnaps Tiffany's little brother, Wentworth, they set off to bring him back. The daftness of the little people makes a perfect foil for Tiffany's steady resolve.

Terry Pratchett began the book as a parody of 1980s fantasy, but he admits it took on its own form. Since he excels in humor, *The Wee Free Men* keeps readers laughing, along with offering bits of social commentary. Tiffany's adventures continue in *A Hat Full of Sky*.

LOUISE RENNISON

## *Angus, Thongs and Full-Frontal Snogging*

12–14 • HarperCollins • 2000 • 247 pp.

✧ *PRINTZ HONOR*

The reigning British queen of chick lit has captivated readers with a series of books that sound a good deal racier than they actually are. Her first one introduces Georgia Nicolson, a fourteen-year-old who exudes teenage angst. Georgia hates the way she looks, so she shaves off her eyebrows. She worries about her sexual identity — whether she will become a lesbian or develop breasts. Ultimately, she longs for full-frontal snogging — that is, kissing mouth to mouth, the real deal — so she practices with a kissing instructor. Told as a diary, the popular novel, peppered with teenage slang, requires a glossary to explain the British terms.

TOM ROBBINS

## *Skinny Legs and All*

14–18 • Bantam • 1990 • 432 pp.

In a richly complex and elegantly told tale, Ellen Cherry Charles, an aspiring artist, has moved to New York after marrying Boomer Petway, a redneck welder and the darling of the New York art scene. But when Boomer runs off to Jerusalem, Ellen takes up waitressing at Isaac and Ishmael's, a restaurant owned by an Arab and a Jew. The politically charged story brings an incredible number of colorful characters into its orbit: the nursing student Salome, who bumps and grinds in the Dance of the Seven Veils, and Can o' Beans, Dirty Sock, Spoon, Painted Stick, and Conch Shell, inanimate objects who travel to Jerusalem. Ellen's uncle Buddy, a radio evangelist, would like to get World War III started to hasten Armageddon. In this freewheeling exploration of Middle East politics, millennium frenzy, art, and religion, Tom Robbins keeps readers laughing because of his eclectic turn of phrase, the absurdity of the situations, and a wild mixture of tomfoolery and philosophy.

DYAN SHELDON

## *Confessions of a Teenage Drama Queen*

12–14 • Candlewick • 1999 • 272 pp.

Lola (a.k.a. Mary Elizabeth) Cep believes she is "a flamingo in a flock of pigeons." So when her mother moves to Dellwood, New Jersey, from New York City, Lola seizes the moment and reinvents herself for her new classmates. Everyone agrees she has a talent for acting, and she tap-dances her way through a lively, funny, and engaging story. As she takes on a rival, Carla Santini, Lola proves to be a worthy opponent to this mean girl who likes to run everything. Made into a movie in 2004, the book explores popularity, honesty, school cliques, and the ultimate triumph of a very engaging flamingo.

NEAL SHUSTERMAN

## *The Schwa Was Here*

12–14 • Dutton • 2004 • 228 pp.

Two individuals who feel invisible to or unnoticed by others become stars in this hilariously funny novel. Smart-mouthed Antsy Bonano of Brooklyn decides to become the agent for Calvin Schwa, an eighth-grader who seems almost invisible to those around him. Consequently, the "functionally invisible" Schwa can get away with things, such as entering the teachers' lounge, because he flies beneath everyone's radar. But one day the ingenious duo go too far. They accept a dare to enter the home of a legendary eccentric and his fourteen Afghan hounds; rather than a police record, they get a dog-walking sentence and companionship duties for the man's blind granddaughter, Lexie. Then the trouble really begins, for Lexie knows how to create some havoc of her own.

Because of Antsy's funny and street-smart voice, the reader keeps laughing until the story takes a more serious turn. The book explores why some people remain unnoticed and others get all the attention — a condition commonly experienced by teenagers. Great chapter titles, writing that pulls readers in immediately, and offbeat and marvelously quirky characters distinguish one of the best young adult titles of the past few years. An ideal book for the classroom or for adult-teen book discussion groups.

WILLIAM SLEATOR

## Oddballs: Stories

12–14 • Dutton • 1993 • 134 pp.

T en stories, based on William Sleator's own childhood, testify to his creativity and his family's insanity. In the course of the narrative, Sleator matures from nine to right out of high school. The stories are wacky and bizarre: his sister has a penchant for making dolls fight with each other; one brother hypnotizes another, who then drinks from the toilet; they play a game in the car, pretending to be "BMs" who tell their life stories as excrement. As a protagonist of his own story collection, Sleator emerges as inventive, curious, and thoughtful. He addresses many of the concerns of adolescents; talking about the popular clique, he writes: "Somehow they did not seem to understand that we, as oddballs and deliberate nonconformists, were far superior to them in every way."

Sleator dedicated the book "To my family: Please forgive me!" Selected for Jon Scieszka's "Guys Read" program, *Oddballs* keeps readers laughing about the Sleator family — and reminds them to do the same about their own idiosyncrasies.

STEPHANIE S. TOLAN

## Surviving the Applewhites

12–14 • HarperCollins • 2002 • 216 pp.

⬥ *NEWBERY HONOR*

T hirteen-year-old Jake Semple, an incipient hoodlum, thinks he can scare people. Then he gets placed in the unstructured Creative Academy home school of the Applewhite family, a chaotic group of artists, writers, poets, and furniture makers living in North Carolina. As Jake quickly learns, when you have no rules, you have no chance to rebel. And without rebellion, he has no idea who he is.

When the family takes over a production of *The Sound of Music* for the community theater, Jake becomes a convincing Nazi. Slowly, like the rest of the insane Applewhite family, he finds his passion — for acting.

With an enormous amount of humor and a cast of eccentric and lovable characters, including an Indian guru who delights in cooking, the book entertains readers while Jake gets transformed from a sociopath into a budding actor.

JOHN KENNEDY TOOLE

## *A Confederacy of Dunces*

14–18 • Louisiana State Press • 1980 • 338 pp.

↦ *PULITZER PRIZE*

One of the most off-putting and disgusting protagonists of modern literature, Ignatius Reilly lives on his mother's welfare checks in her home on a seedy back street of New Orleans. A deadbeat medievalist, he spends his time eating, going to movies, or sitting in his bedroom, talking and writing about his war against modernity. While waiting for his mother to return from the doctor, Ignatius gets hauled off by a cop who finds this huge, oddly dressed man suspicious. Then, because circumstances spin out of control, Ignatius must search for his first job, a journey that takes him into the seamy underbelly of New Orleans in the 1960s. After a series of hilarious episodes describing bad jobs gone wrong — at Levy Pants and as a hot dog vendor — Ignatius leads a workers' revolt and gets swept up in more insane events.

In the kind of ironic detail that the author himself might have written, John Kennedy Toole did not live to see his novel published or win the Pulitzer Prize. For two years, the legendary editor Robert Gottlieb worked with Toole on revising the book; ultimately, Gottlieb turned the manuscript down. Toole put the project away and, suffering from either paranoid schizophrenia or manic-depressive illness, committed suicide. In the late 1970s his mother pestered Walker Percy, then teaching at Loyola, to read the sprawling, messy manuscript. Impressed, Percy arranged for its publication and wrote a foreword relating its history.

However gross or ridiculous Ignatius may seem to some readers, many teens find themselves sympathizing with him, making the book a cult favorite. Adolescents particularly identify with the Jonathan Swift quotation that generated the title of the book: "When a true genius appears in the world, you may know him by this sign, that the dunces are all in confederacy against him."

SUE TOWNSEND

## *The Secret Diary of Adrian Mole, Aged 13¾*

14–18 • Grove/Atlantic • 1986 • 185 pp.

The bright but eccentric British teen Adrian Mole begins his first journal in January 1981 and continues it until April 1982, when Argentina invaded the Falklands and Britain became enmeshed in the conflict. Adrian's year is made remarkable by his erudition and his oblivion to what's going on around him. On May 12 he writes: "I am at the Crossroads of my life. The wrong decision now could result in a tragic loss to the veterinary world. I am hopeless at science. I asked Mr. Vann which O levels you need to write situation comedy for television. Mr. Vann said that you don't need qualifications at all, you just need to be a moron."

In this fast, funny, sophisticated, and totally irreverent novel, teenage angst has never been portrayed as so hilariously funny.

# Information

I HAVE OFTEN HEARD the following comment from parents or teachers about teens: "Oh, they don't read anything except information books." Such a remark indicates that the person making it believes that perusing information books, even complex works of prose nonfiction, does not count as reading. But many teens, who find life enough of a fantasy, often desire to read about real people and real events, and put their world in context. Fortunately for both adults and young adults, in the last decade scores of excellent nonfiction titles — written in prose rather than information nuggets — have been created for this audience.

By the time teenagers reach high school, most adult nonfiction falls within their grasp. The titles listed here and recommended in the booklist indicate the range of subjects and approaches available. Some of them focus on those fascinating, weird, bizarre, or gruesome topics always in fashion — gambling, cadavers, pirates, a serial killer, and a man with a hole in his head. But many deal with important lives and historical periods and contain some of the best literary writing available. Without question, anyone who picks them up and interacts with these titles is definitely reading.

STEPHEN E. AMBROSE

## Undaunted Courage: Meriwether Lewis, Thomas Jefferson, and the Opening of the American West

14–18 • Simon & Schuster • 1996 • 511 pp.

Having spent twenty summers with his family following in the footsteps of Lewis and Clark's 1803–1806 expedition, Stephen Ambrose chose to create a biography of Meriwether Lewis, Thomas Jefferson's secretary. Jefferson hand-picked Lewis for the journey; Lewis in turn asked William Clark to join him. On October 15, 1803, the two shook hands in Clarksville, Ohio, and headed west. Embarking on an incredible odyssey, they met all kinds of difficulties along the way; for instance, the boat builder, although always drunk, happened to be the only one available. In the narrative, Lewis, Jefferson, Clark, and Sacagawea, their Indian guide, emerge as individuals with strengths and weaknesses.

To write his detailed account, Ambrose incorporated much recent scholarship but made all of it accessible. The book abounds in facts about diplomacy, science, courage, and adventure; a fascinating picture of the American frontier in the nineteenth century emerges as Lewis and Clark move across the landscape. Although a work of history, *Undaunted Courage* reads like adventure fiction, engaging readers even though they already know the outcome.

MARC ARONSON

## Sir Walter Ralegh and the Quest for El Dorado

12–14 • Clarion • 2000 • 222 pp.

A courtier, a soldier, an explorer, a friend of playwrights, and a poet, Sir Walter Ralegh truly represented the Elizabethan Age. He helped crush the Irish resistance to English rule, led expeditions to South America, and raided Spanish merchant vessels. To accomplish all this, he moved from the lowly position of the younger son of a farmer into the center of Queen Elizabeth's court. But the arrogance and recklessness that helped him rise also caused his downfall. In a multilayered biography of this intriguing figure, Marc Aronson examines sixteenth-century England, with its religious friction, privateering disguised as colonization of the Americas, and the diplomatic maneuvers of the Elizabethan court.

Illustrations, portraits, and maps further enhance a biography that conveys a passion for the subject matter and contains a strong dramatic narrative. Aronson wrote two other equally intelligent volumes that, along with *Sir Walter Ralegh,* form a historical trilogy: *John Winthrop, Oliver Cromwell, and the Land of Promise* and *The Real Revolution: The Global Story of American Independence.*

## TRUMAN CAPOTE
### In Cold Blood

14–18 • Random House • 1965 • 368 pp.

On November 15, 1959, four members of the Clutter family were savagely murdered in the small town of Holcomb, Kansas. More than five years later, Richard Hickock and Perry Smith were hung in the Kansas State Penitentiary for this crime. A work of nonfiction — which often gets credited for inspiring a wave of New Journalism, nonfiction written with the language and structure of literature — explores these six deaths. *In Cold Blood* takes readers into the minds of the criminals, showing how random violence can and does happen.

Fascinated by a headline about the crime, Truman Capote explored the idea of a *New Yorker* piece with its editor, William Shawn. Encouraged, Capote headed to Kansas, taking along his childhood friend Harper Lee, the author of *To Kill a Mockingbird.* Lee helped with the interviews and with ingratiating Capote with the small community of Holcomb. After six years of research, Capote had gathered enough material for a two-thousand-page book. He focused it, gave it pace and drama, and wrote a true crime account.

A bestseller on its release, *In Cold Blood* inspired a motion picture and many authors to take nonfiction writing to new levels. Capote's literary style and his ability to make this crime real and vivid for the reader have helped keep the book popular and in print for forty years.

DAVID CORDINGLY

## Under the Black Flag: The Romance and the Reality of Life among the Pirates

14–18 • Random House • 1996 • 296 pp.

David Cordingly, a former curator at the National Maritime Museum in London, refutes the idea that pirates made their victims walk the plank. He then presents the real figures who inspired J. M. Barrie's *Peter Pan* and Robert Louis Stevenson's *Treasure Island*. This immensely readable book presents both the facts and folklore about pirates, what they wore, and how they were armed. Readers learn that most pirate ships worked as democracies, with elected captains, and that pirates did not devise cunning maps where *X* marked the spot. But they did engage in cutthroat raids and created terror on the high seas during the golden age of piracy (1650–1725). Distinctions get drawn between pirates, buccaneers, and privateers; Blackbeard, Captain Kidd, Calico Jack, Anne Bonny, and Mary Read all make appearances. The naturally dramatic subject matter and the thorough research have made this fascinating book a popular addition to summer reading lists.

CHRIS CROWE

## Getting Away with Murder: The True Story of the Emmett Till Case

12–14 • Penguin/Fogelman • 2003 • 128 pp.

In a chilling account of the 1955 murder of a fourteen-year-old black boy from Chicago by two white men in Mississippi, Chris Crowe presents a picture of a typical teenage boy — interested in the Chicago White Sox and girls. But on a summer visit to his great-uncle in Money, Mississippi, this northern boy failed to adhere to the southern way of life, which demanded that he treat whites in an appropriately submissive manner. Brutally murdered and then displayed by his bereaved mother in an open casket, Emmett Till and his plight became a rallying cry for the Civil Rights movement in the 1950s. The author believes that most African Americans remember the exact moment they learned of Till's death — in the same way that people would later recall the death of President John F. Kennedy.

With photographs of the murderers and the trial — which acquitted the men who later gave vivid accounts of the murder to *Life* — the book presents a piece of American history that, although not pleasant to read about, needs to be remembered. Because it provides excellent background, *Getting Away with Murder* works particularly well with Marilyn Nelson's stunning poetic rendering of the same events in *A Wreath for Emmett Till*.

JARED DIAMOND

## *Guns, Germs, and Steel:*
## *The Fates of Human Societies*

14–18 • Norton • 1997 • 480 pp.

↷ *PULITZER PRIZE*

Jared Diamond sought to answer a question posed by a New Guinea native: "Why is it that you white people developed so much cargo and brought it to New Guinea, but we black people had little cargo of our own?" Ultimately, Diamond identifies geographical placement and food production as the keys to the glaring inequalities of wealth and power in the modern world. He argues that dense, agriculture-based countries, unlike the hunter-gatherer communities, bred a hierarchy that transferred wealth. Farming societies could support craft specialists, who then developed weapons of steel. As a result, the European nations brought guns and diseases, overwhelming the native peoples on four continents — North and South America, Africa, and Australia. Refuting a racist explanation for European supremacy, Diamond argues that the differences in geography and environment basically shaped the disparate histories and populations in today's world.

Combining unconventional history, anthropology, archaeology, and technological development, this bold and ambitious work explores the rise of human civilization from 11,000 B.C. to the modern age. Widely adopted for high school reading, this impressive volume can be used to teach humanities, philosophy, biology, English, or history. Some schools have successfully chosen *Guns, Germs, and Steel* for every member of a class to read and discuss.

BARBARA EHRENREICH

## *Nickel and Dimed: On (Not) Getting By in America*

14–18 • Holt/Metropolitan • 2001 • 223 pp.

With millions of women being forced into the labor market because of welfare reform, the liberal cultural critic Barbara Ehrenreich joined them, trying to survive on a wage of $6 or $7 an hour. She traveled from an area close to her home in Florida through Maine to Minnesota, to see how the bottom third of wage earners live. At times funny and heartbreaking, her experiences as a waitress, cleaning woman, nursing home aide, and Wal-Mart employee parallel those encountered by most adolescents at their first jobs. Even with Ehrenreich's advantages of education, health, a car, and money saved for emergencies, she still had to work two jobs, seven days a week, to make ends meet.

Even more important, she saw how badly America treats its working poor, both personally and legally. A great discussion book for high school classes, *Nickel and Dimed* raises important issues about working when it serves solely as a means of survival.

JOSEPH J. ELLIS

## *Founding Brothers: The Revolutionary Generation*

14–18 • Knopf • 2000 • 290 pp.

↪ *PULITZER PRIZE*

Focusing on six political episodes during the 1790s, Joseph Ellis presents portraits of George Washington, Benjamin Franklin, Alexander Hamilton, Thomas Jefferson, Aaron Burr, James Madison, and John and Abigail Adams. All the essays underscore the fragility of the new nation; readers learn how vulnerable the founders felt their creation to be. Ellis even defines the 1790s as a long shouting match between Hamilton, who championed central government, and Jefferson, who defended states' rights. Although constantly bickering, they still felt they were part of a fraternity; Jefferson always called his peers "the band of brothers."

Believing that history and fiction have a great deal in common, Ellis creates well-rounded characters and a compelling, fascinating plot. Hence *Founding Brothers*, perfect for general readers, often finds its way onto summer reading lists and serves as an excellent introduction to the early history of the American nation.

TOM FEELINGS

## The Middle Passage: White Ships/Black Cargo

14–18 • Dial • 1995 • 80 pp.

This visual record of the Middle Passage shows the horrific transatlantic journey that brought enslaved Africans to the North American continent. In his introduction, John Henrik Clarke estimates that between thirty and sixty million Africans were captured and put on ships headed to the Americas; only about a third survived the journey. Wordless — illustrated with white tempera paint, black ink, and wet tissue paper art — the book shows the guns, yokes, chains, whips, and knives used on the slaves. The pain is so palpable that the reader can almost hear the slaves screaming. The white enslavers appear as mere wisps in the drawings, but the blacks have been rendered in sharp definition. From the forts on the West African coast to the markets, the perspective comes from the slaves themselves.

Often used in school units on slavery, *The Middle Passage* took Tom Feelings twenty years to create. Although the material was difficult to develop visually, in the end Feelings agreed with the writer James Baldwin when he said, "There's nothing that cannot be faced." The resulting book comes to terms with man's inhumanity to man and with a hideous chapter in American history.

DAVID HACKETT FISCHER

## Washington's Crossing

14–18 • Oxford • 2004 • 564 pp.

↪ NATIONAL BOOK AWARD FINALIST/PULITZER PRIZE

In a brilliantly researched and written account of George Washington's Delaware River crossing in 1776, David Hackett Fischer discusses the strategic, operational, and tactical factors involved. Until this point in the American Revolution, the patriots had been roundly defeated in New York, New Jersey, and Rhode Island. With many enlistments expiring and a lack of discipline in the troops, observers on both sides felt the rebellion had been broken. But in crossing the Delaware and at Trenton and Princeton, Washington and his generals, the men he himself had picked and relied on, showed the perseverance, inventiveness, and improvisation that would win the war. In *Washington's Crossing,* readers see the birth of the distinctively American form of war, in which civil and military leaders find themselves accountable to the people through their congressional representatives.

Fischer uses a form of writing he calls "braided narrative": statistical and factual reconstruction has been woven into the human side of the stories. Rarely has military history been presented with as much storytelling and psychological grasp of the combatants. Copious illustrations, maps, appendixes that discuss troops, weather, and battle order round out this superb study of military and American history.

JOHN FLEISCHMAN

## *Phineas Gage: A Gruesome but True Story About Brain Science*

12–14 • Houghton Mifflin • 2002 • 86 pp.

The foreman of a railroad blasting crew in Cavendish, Vermont, Phineas Gage had been tamping down black powder when an explosion occurred on September 13, 1848, and his thirteen-pound tamping iron shot through his head. Miraculously alive, he sat on a porch thirty minutes later, describing the event. To everyone's amazement, he recovered and lived for another eleven years. An ordinary man made extraordinary by an accident, Gage lived at a time when medical science was in its infancy.

John Fleischman reveals both his amazing story and information about the makeup and workings of the human brain. Historical photographs, a glossary, and clear diagrams complete this thorough exploration of the man with a hole in his head.

RUSSELL FREEDMAN

## *Eleanor Roosevelt: A Life of Discovery*

12–14 • Clarion • 1993 • 198 pp.

↦ *NEWBERY HONOR*

In this highly readable account of one of the country's most powerful first ladies, Russell Freedman shows how Eleanor Roosevelt transcended an unhappy childhood: an alcoholic father and parents who died while she was young. A timid and fearful child and an ugly duckling, Eleanor struggled to gain her own voice and become a champion for important social causes. After her husband contracted polio, she became his eyes and ears, touring the country and the world to win over his critics and promote new ideas about social policy and women's rights. Freedman discusses their marriage and FDR's infidelity, but he never sensationalizes, focusing mainly on Eleanor's public life, which is further highlighted in more than a hundred well-chosen photographs.

While Freedman was writing a biography of FDR, "a funny thing happened. . . . I fell in love with his wife." He wanted to capture the woman who "gave off light," portraying Eleanor as an honest, intelligent humanist, someone able to inspire loyalty and convey her passions. Her characteristic modesty comes through in her own statements: "'As for accomplishments, I just did what I had to do as things came along.'"

Ultimately, Freedman proves to be the consummate storyteller, sweeping readers up into Eleanor's life and taking them along. Although he himself has written a score of superb books for adolescents, nonfiction books for young adults simply don't get any better than *Eleanor Roosevelt*.

RUSSELL FREEDMAN

## The Voice That Challenged a Nation: Marian Anderson and the Struggle for Equal Rights

12–14 • Clarion • 2004 • 128 pp.

↪ *NEWBERY HONOR*

Beginning with Marian Anderson's concert at the Lincoln Memorial in 1939, Russell Freedman explores her childhood and teenage years as a music student. He covers her triumphs and setbacks and shows her love of classical music as well as spirituals. Someone who would have been noteworthy in any time — even Arturo Toscanini stated, "A voice like yours is heard once in a hundred years" — as an African American, Anderson also became an activist for equal rights. As she said, "I had become, whether I liked it or not, a symbol representing my people."

With exquisite photographs well placed throughout the text, the biography not only captures an extraordinary life but also describes the history and context of Anderson's era.

JAMES CROSS GIBLIN

## Good Brother, Bad Brother: The Story of Edwin Booth & John Wilkes Booth

12–14 • Clarion • 2005 • 220 pp.

James Giblin presents the story of two brothers — one, the greatest Shakespearean actor of his age; the other, the assassin of President Abraham Lincoln — in a highly readable photo essay. The saga begins and ends with Edwin, the good brother, who initially has problems with alcohol, then shifts back and forth between the two men. Throughout, the Civil War and its effect on Edwin and John Wilkes as well as the country serve as the backdrop, or stage setting. Both brothers follow in their father's footsteps and become actors; they are often compared to each other in press notices. After Lincoln's assassination, Edwin struggles with the devastating effect of living in the shadow of his bad brother. At one point Edwin, while was traveling in Germany, sent some articles to a friend to "show you how even here I am compelled to taste the bitter dregs of my past." However, he continues acting, sometimes receiving standing ovations and once being shot at on the stage. In his final days, Edwin established the Players Club in New York, which continues to this day on Gramercy Park.

Exquisite photographs, of the Booths and Lincoln conspirators, complement a text that works as a page-turner from beginning to end. The book not only reveals an incredible slice of history, it also leads to a discussion about how the choice of one member of a family can affect them all. As Giblin reminds us, in the end, the acts of the villain, the bad brother, live on, whereas the deeds of the good one have been long forgotten.

JAMES CROSS GIBLIN

## The Life and Death of Adolf Hitler

12–14 • Clarion • 2002 • 256 pp.

Because Adolf Hitler haunted James Giblin in his childhood, he decided to tackle the questions raised by this troubling political figure. Examining the rise and fall of the twentieth century's most dangerous and destructive dictator, Giblin initially focuses on Hitler's childhood and adolescent years, when he spent four years as a soldier in World War I. Increasingly able as a political speaker, Hitler began to accrue power; he wrote *Mein Kampf* while in jail and became committed to *Lebensraum,* the idea of additional living space for the Germans. The demonic qualities of this leader emerge: he loved dogs and opera but exterminated millions of innocent people. Beautifully written, well researched, illustrated with compelling photographs, *The Life and Death of Adolf Hitler* contains a final chilling chapter, "Hitler Lives," which explores neo-Nazism today in Europe and America.

JAN GREENBERG AND SANDRA JORDAN
## Andy Warhol: Prince of Pop
12–14 • Delacorte • 2004 • 208 pp.

Without making judgments or overdramatizing, Jan Greenberg and Sandra Jordan present the life of a highly original and controversial artist, following Andy Warhol from his youth in Pittsburgh to his decades in New York. Warhol predicted that everyone would be world-famous for fifteen minutes; he himself worked relentlessly for those few minutes of fame. The book presents all the facets of his life — his struggles with acne, his problems with self-image, and his infamous Factory studio, with its experimental sex and drugs culture. Readers learn of his gay lifestyle and his crush on Truman Capote, who believed Warhol to be a "born loser."

This highly readable, balanced, and fascinating study of an American icon will generate discussion and send those interested off to read more. Here and in their other books — such as *Runaway Girl,* about the sculptor Louise Bourgeois, or *Chuck Close, Up Close* — the authors present riveting biographies of nonconformists.

PHILLIP HOOSE
## The Race to Save the Lord God Bird
12–14 • Farrar, Straus/Kroupa • 2004 • 196 pp.

This photo essay, spanning two centuries, shows how science and society interact and how our approach to science evolves. At the heart of his narrative, with its heroes and villains, stands the elusive ivory-billed woodpecker, a creature scientists called "Lord God bird."

Much larger than the pileated woodpecker still sighted by bird enthusiasts, this huge creature lived in the southern states, and over time its
habitat shrunk to a small section of Louisiana, maintained by the
Singer Manufacturing Company.

In the beginning, the reader encounters Alexander Wilson, "the Father of Ornithology," on a mission to kill, capture, and catalogue birds.
But over time, a kinder, gentler approach to birds needed to be taken,
and the book walks us through those steps. We see how plumed hats
affected the bird population and how some Boston ladies of breeding
began the Audubon Society. Over time, museums of natural history
had to change the way they acquired specimens, and a new generation
of Junior Audubon members, including Roger Tory Peterson, headed
outdoors to catalogue what they saw.

In the end, the book — covering American history, social history,
biology, and ecology — will thrill conservationists, birders, budding
scientists, and those who want to study biodiversity. It has even convinced those who have never looked at birds to take up binoculars and
head into the field, as suggested by the conservationist James Tanner,
to "study nature, not books."

ERIK LARSON

## The Devil in the White City: Murder, Magic, and Madness at the Fair That Changed America

14–18 • Random House • 2003 • 447 pp.

↭ *NATIONAL BOOK AWARD FINALIST*

Shortly after Jack the Ripper haunted the streets of London, H. H.
Holmes murdered between 27 and 200 people, mostly single
women, in the growing metropolitan area of Chicago. Many of his victims had come to the city to visit its finest monument to date, the
World's Fair of 1893. Erik Larson shifts between the actions of this serial killer and Daniel H. Burnham, the architect responsible for the
fair. Managing thousands of workers and engineers and facing overwhelming obstacles from the weather, bureaucracy, illness, and death,
Burnham pulled this massive event together in two years, aided by
some of the most creative men of his day — Frederick Law Olmsted,
Louis Sullivan, and Richard M. Hunt.

This well-researched, fact-filled account reveals fascinating tidbits about Olmsted's landscapes, the antics of Buffalo Bill, the invention of Cracker Jack, and the creation of the first Ferris wheel. Larson also explores the rise in personal anonymity in this urban environment and how developing, sprawling cities caused a breakdown in community and created a new group of victims.

In a work of nonfiction that reads like a mystery novel, Larson keeps these two story lines running, building tension and pulling the reader along. Hence the book has made its way into high school history curriculums and has become a favorite of mystery readers — a testament to this multifaceted and intriguing book.

DAVID MACAULAY

## Mosque

12–14 • Houghton Mifflin • 2003 • 96 pp.

Over the years, David Macaulay has rendered the complex into simple terms, revealing the wonders of the architectural world in books such as *Cathedral, Castle,* and *Pyramid.* In *Mosque,* he focuses on the building of a fictional sixteenth-century mosque in Istanbul. With color and precision, he reveals how the mosque needs to be aligned with Mecca, examines its structural complexity, and shows its social functions. A college for religious education, a kitchen, a public bath, and a fountain nestle into a complex set of buildings. A master at explanation, Macaulay shows brick-making and stained-glass window construction; he also focuses on the people who make buildings and how these structures affect the community that grows up around them. All of Macaulay's books, ultimately, demonstrate awe and wonder about the design and engineering feats of societies.

When Macaulay worked on the PBS series *Building Big,* he began to appreciate the mosques of Istanbul. But after September 11, 2001, he felt an urgency to educate young adults about these incredible monuments. Never afraid of large subjects, always seeking those that stretch his own understanding, Macaulay struggled with cultural barriers and architectural questions before he could shape his project. But the resulting book, magnificent in its accomplishment, can be read to learn about another part of the world or can simply be appreciated for the breathtaking drawings. As one critic has written of Macaulay, "What he draws, he draws better than any other pen and ink illustrator in the world."

DAVID MCCULLOUGH

## *1776*

14–18 • Simon & Schuster • 2005 • 386 pp.

Covering basically one critical year of American history, *1776* focuses on the struggle between the world's greatest power, Great Britain, and one of its colonies. As the saga opens in October 1775, the House of Commons debates England's reaction to the American rebellion. Then the book explores how England found itself defeated by an undermanned, ill-trained, and badly equipped Continental Army. In the colonies, citizens had personal access to military leaders. So Henry Knox, a Boston bookseller, could meet with George Washington and propose bringing cannons from Fort Ticonderoga to Boston. Washington liked the ingeniousness of the plan; Knox — who possessed a particularly American blend of fortitude, perseverance, ability to suffer, and devotion to a cause — executed the amazing feat of transporting 120,000 pounds of artillery over 300 miles of inhospitable terrain, ultimately forcing the British to evacuate Boston.

Although untrained compared to British officers, the other American army leaders were certainly distinguished by their individuality — Charles Lee, called "Boiling Water" by the Native Americans; General Israel Putnam, "Old Put"; and Nathanael Greene, one of Washington's favorites, a Quaker who knew about fighting only through books. George III is treated more sympathetically than usual; Washington, still given a magnificent portrayal, voices some of his concerns, fears, and frustrations.

As we argue today about freedom, democracy, and security, the book reminds readers how and why America was born. Distinguished by its fascinating subject matter, expert research, and graceful and elegant prose, *1776* could easily become a classic on the American Revolution — the first volume any reader should pick up to understand America's fight for freedom.

BEN MEZRICH

## Bringing Down the House: The Inside Story of Six M.I.T. Students Who Took Vegas for Millions

14–18 • Free Press • 2002 • 257 pp.

In his exploration of the gambling industry and Las Vegas, Ben Mezrich focuses on Kevin Lewis, a shy, geeky M.I.T. student who gets caught up in a blackjack club that gambles in Vegas on weekends. As they train to be card counters and experts at blackjack, the group works together, with a battery of fake identifications, to amass a fortune of over $3 million. Some, like Kevin, try to use cards as a sideline; other brilliant students leave M.I.T. to make gambling their occupation. Much of the book focuses on their theory of card counting and the glitz and glory of winning massive sums. But then their fortunes turn. Not only do they see the seedier side of gambling, with lap dancers and ever-present security cameras, they find themselves thrown out of establishments, taken to backrooms, beaten up, and harassed by the IRS. In the process, a normal suburban boy with a priceless education gets diverted from what might have been his life.

An immensely popular book with older teens, *Bringing Down the House* sheds light — sometimes focused softly, sometimes neon and harsh — on one of America's most popular pastimes.

JIM MURPHY

## An American Plague: The True and Terrifying Story of the Yellow Fever Epidemic of 1793

12–14 • Clarion • 2003 • 166 pp.

↩ *NEWBERY HONOR/NATIONAL BOOK AWARD FINALIST*

In a terror-stricken city, a mysterious disease kills a hundred people every day. Unable to respond, government and medical workers have already fallen ill or died. Because no one else remains in the temporary capital, the secretary of war commands the country. This scenario may sound like a current medical thriller, but it actually took place in Philadelphia in 1793.

Beginning in the dock area, yellow fever stalked the citizens of the city, moving to its mansions. Once the epidemic struck, 20,000 people left for safer environs, including George Washington and his cabinet. While doctors, such as Benjamin Rush, argued about the best methods for treating the disease — ranging from severe blood-letting to herbal cures — over 5,000 people succumbed to it.

In a lavishly illustrated book with maps, newspaper columns, and period illustrations, Jim Murphy unflinchingly presents the horrors of the event as well as its heroes. He discusses the results of the plague — a traditional summer White House for the president — and the scientific research into this mosquito-born disease. But even today no cure exists; yellow fever remains "a modern-day time bomb."

Relying chiefly on his storytelling skills, Murphy recreates a time and place in a work of nonfiction that enthralls readers, young and old alike.

ELIZABETH PARTRIDGE

## *John Lennon: All I Want Is the Truth*

14–18 • Viking • 2005 • 232 pp.

After her fine biography of Woody Guthrie, *This Land Was Made for You and Me,* Elizabeth Partridge tackles another complex musical genius. Placing John Lennon's music in context, the book discusses Elvis, Chuck Berry, Little Richard, Bob Dylan, civil rights, Vietnam, and the peace movement. Although Lennon always takes center stage, the other Beatles get the spotlight from time to time — their boyhoods in Liverpool, their rise to the top-ten charts, and ultimately their divorce. Lennon emerges as brilliant, self-centered, and self-destructive. Yoko Ono, equally self-centered and disturbed, matched him in loneliness and rage. Chanting peace, John hit women and fought with men. Brashly independent, he needed someone strong, like Yoko Ono, to control him. Sex, drugs, and rock 'n' roll formed his life — and his era; all his habits get honest treatment in the book. In fact, the loss of so much of his life to heroin, alcohol, and a variety of drugs makes the account of his later years ultimately quite sad.

Illustrated with 150 photographs, some rarely seen before, the biography recreates time, place, and an incredibly talented and intriguing musician.

MARY ROACH

## *Stiff: The Curious Lives of Human Cadavers*

14–18 • Norton • 2003 • 304 pp.

T he way I see it, being dead is not terribly far off from being on a cruise ship. Most of your time is spent lying on your back . . . Nothing much new happens, and nothing is expected of you." With these opening lines, Mary Roach begins a witty and informative book on the subject of cadavers. She shows their productive use — medical research and organ transplants. Then she delves into more macabre subjects — cannibalism, or doctors practicing facelifts on decapitated heads. With entertaining bits of cadaver lore, the book thoroughly explores the history of this subject. Readers learn, for instance, that eighteenth-century students in a Scottish medical school could pay for their tuition in corpses.

A skilled journalist, the author exhibits a flair for the telling detail; in *Stiff* she has provided a fascinating account for anyone with even mild curiosity about the subject.

ERIC SCHLOSSER

## *Fast Food Nation:*
## *The Dark Side of the All-American Meal*

14–18 • Houghton Mifflin • 2001 • 356 pp.

A n award-winning journalist, Eric Schlosser spent three years studying the history of fast food. In this book, he makes a powerful case against an industry that exploits workers, destroys the environment, and creates an obese society. He takes readers on a tour of chemical factories and meatpacking plants; in the latter, one out of three migrant workers suffers a serious injury each year. He also explores many governmental issues, such as the influence of the meatpacking lobby in Congress. Much like Upton Sinclair's exposé *The Jungle*, Schlosser's book shows the shocking crimes against humanity committed by the fast food industry.

DAVA SOBEL

## Longitude: The True Story of a Lone Genius Who Solved the Greatest Scientific Problem of His Time

14–18 • Walker • 1995 • 192 pp.

Because the measurement of longitude eluded navigators for centuries, untold ships got lost at sea. Galileo, Newton, and Halley all attempted to solve this mathematical problem. But in 1714 England's Parliament offered a munificent prize for a solution. A self-educated clockmaker, John Harrison, invented a chronometer, a simple timepiece impervious to seas, temperature, and humidity. Although the Board of Longitude favored the astronomers over mechanics like Harrison, his approach ultimately triumphed.

This small volume — encompassing political intrigue, cultural history, scientific discovery, and the history of science — makes compelling reading even for those not usually attracted to these subjects. Experiencing great popularity and becoming a *New York Times* bestseller, the book has often been adopted for high school reading lists.

JANE RESH THOMAS

## Behind the Mask: The Life of Queen Elizabeth I

12–14 • Clarion • 1998 • 196 pp.

This life of England's legendary queen begins with Elizabeth's dramatic childhood as one of the children of Henry VIII and her younger years, some in prison, when her half-sister Mary sat on the throne. Learning from Mary's mistakes, Elizabeth took the throne at a time when women were considered unfit to rule. Nevertheless, she evaded pursuers, refusing to marry, and stood at the center of an empire and an age now considered synonymous with her name. By seeing the world through Elizabeth's eyes, readers can better understand her religious, political, and personal conflicts.

Thomas, who had been intrigued by her subject since she was a girl, tried to answer questions about how Elizabeth might have felt and how she became such a fierce and independent woman. This exciting biography, satisfying in its own right, will send readers to other sources.

## BARBARA W. TUCHMAN

## *A Distant Mirror: The Calamitous 14th Century*

14–18 · Knopf · 1978 · 677 pp.

In the fourteenth century, people experienced both natural and manmade disasters — the Hundred Years' War, the Crusades, massacres of Jewish people, and the Black Death, which killed thirty million Europeans. In this riveting account, Barbara Tuchman uses the relatively obscure French knight Enguerrand de Coucy as a focal point. The book not only serves as a recreation of a time but also explores the political and personal issues of the day. Because the ranks of the peasants were decimated, they became more assertive, which changed the relationship between laborer and landowner. Bankruptcies, crop failures, and plagues forced people apart; "emotional response, dulled by horrors, underwent a kind of atrophy."

This fascinating portrayal of a turbulent era has been enlivened by Tuchman's eye for the perfect quotation, arresting details, colorful scandals, lively events, and sensational acts. But Tuchman also finds in this era a message for our time — the possibilities for disaster and war in an age of collapsing assumptions.

## SIMON WINCHESTER

## *The Professor and the Madman: A Tale of Murder, Insanity, and the Making of the Oxford English Dictionary*

14–18 · HarperCollins · 1998 · 272 pp.

An erudite Civil War veteran, Dr. William C. Minor killed a man in England. Pronounced insane, the doctor was confined to a cell in Broadmoor Criminal Lunatic Asylum with his collection of rare books. Responding to a call for volunteers to create the *Oxford English Dictionary* in the early 1880s, Minor corresponded with its editor, Professor James Murray, a school dropout and self-educated man. As Minor provided Murray with the best definitions for 10,000 words, the two became friends as they pursued the dream of the *O.E.D.* together. Beginning each chapter with an entry from the original *O.E.D.*, the account also presents fascinating details about the dictionary, one of the greatest efforts since the invention of printing, and Victorian attitudes toward insanity.

This very readable chronicle of lexicography appeals to word lovers and history enthusiasts alike.

# Many Cultures, Many Realities

THE WORLD CONTAINS a rich tapestry of cultures: languages, races, and traditions. As a nation of immigrants, America comprises people from all different backgrounds. We have a rich legacy of what the African-American writer Virginia Hamilton once called parallel cultures, ones that exist side by side as equals.

The books recommended here represent writers from a variety of backgrounds. The stories excel in telling detail, presenting the struggles of a particular character or group of people. But the stories have many themes in common. Often they show teenagers caught between cultures when parents want to live in their old world and the adolescent wants to embrace a new one.

Since literature allows us to share others' experience vicariously, readers of multicultural books can grow to understand what it is like to live in another place, come from a different background, and be born in a different family. Ultimately, these books demonstrate the similarity of all human emotion. As the critic Rudine Sims Bishop has suggested, multicultural books provide both windows and mirrors: they allow adolescents to glimpse other cultures but also see themselves reflected in the experiences of those whose lives may seem completely different.

JULIA ALVAREZ

## *How the García Girls Lost Their Accents*

14–18 • Algonquin • 1991 • 290 pp.

This partly autobiographical tale about the adjustment to a strange new land is presented in fifteen stories that occur between 1956 and 1989, arranged in reverse chronological order. The daughters of Dr. García — Carla, Sandra, Yolanda, and Sofía — belong to the Dominican Republic's upper class. But as political exiles, these descendants of the Spanish conquistadors grow up in the Bronx and experience the clash between American and Hispanic cultures. In this new land they must figure out their own identity and "why the Irish kids whose grandparents had been micks were calling them spics."

With great humor and poignancy, Julia Alvarez shows how these four engaging young women rise to the challenges of their new country.

RUDOLFO ANAYA

## *Bless Me, Ultima*

14–18 • Quinto Sol • 1972 • 277 pp.

Antonio is almost seven when la Grande, Ultima, comes to live with his family in New Mexico. Ultima is a wise woman, a *curandera,* who knows the ways of herbs and healing; she holds the key to Antonio's future through her magic and wisdom. This classic coming-of-age story has been told from the Hispanic perspective as Antonio, searching for his own answers, finds himself torn between the different expectations of his mother and father. He struggles to come to terms with Spanish Catholic beliefs and Mexican Indian ones.

Rich storytelling combines with culture, history, belief systems, and language in this evocative story, as fresh today as when it was first written. The Spanish phrases have been integrated naturally, adding another dimension to the narrative. Although challenging for some readers, the book surprises others. As one high school student wrote: "I'm not sure I understand it, but I want to."

AN NA

## *A Step from Heaven*

14–18 • Front Street • 2001 • 160 pp.

↪ *PRINTZ AWARD/NATIONAL BOOK AWARD FINALIST*

In a much-praised first novel, An Na traces the life of a Korean immigrant, Young Ju Park, from the age of four through her teens. Told almost as a memoir, the book opens as Young's parents prepare to move to America. Flying on an airplane, the girl believes she is going to heaven. Eventually she learns that America, or California, although not actually heaven, may be "a step from heaven." But caught between two cultures, she must learn English at school and speak Korean at home. Her parents don't want her to become too American; she finds herself ashamed of them. Her disillusioned father becomes an alcoholic and increasingly abusive to his children and wife. But Young Ju grows into a strong, admirable young woman, full of hope and promise.

Often selected for English as a Second Language classes and an ideal book to read before Amy Tan's *The Joy Luck Club, A Step from Heaven* explores the classic immigrant story with great sensitivity and insight.

ANJALI BANERJEE

## *Maya Running*

12–14 • Random House/Lamb • 2005 • 224 pp.

In Manitoba, Canada, thirteen-year-old Maya experiences the dichotomy between her Indian and Canadian cultures. This fast-paced novel integrates fantasy and Hindu beliefs, particularly the elephant god Ganesh. Uncomfortable with her background, Maya becomes extremely jealous of her gorgeous cousin Pinky, who visits from India and steals the boy Maya fancies. But after she prays to a small statue of Ganesh, Maya learns to be more careful about her wishes.

Although set in the 1970s, this first novel seems contemporary; with humor, it demonstrates that all young people, no matter what their cultural background, deal with many of the same issues.

SANDRA CISNEROS

## *The House on Mango Street*

14–18 • Arte Público • 1984 • 128 pp.

In a series of spare, poignant, and powerful vignettes, this first-person narrative presents a year in the life of Esperanza, a Mexican-American girl about twelve years old. Esperanza moves to a house on Mango Street, in a Latino neighborhood of Chicago, the first home her parents actually own. In a novel that also presents a portrait of a neighborhood, Esperanza matures dramatically: she develops physically, experiences her first crush, and endures a sexual assault. Learning to write down her thoughts in order to escape her environment emotionally, she also resolves that someday she will leave Mango Street for a house of her own.

The forty-four vignettes, intertwined in the narrative, can be read in any order. Written as a story cycle while Sandra Cisneros was teaching English to high school dropouts, she included their stories, her mother's stories, and her own memory. But the emotions conveyed belong to her, and to communicate them she found "a poor girl's voice, a spoken voice, the voice of an American-Mexican."

JUDITH ORTIZ COFER

## *The Meaning of Consuelo*

14–18 • Farrar, Straus • 2003 • 187 pp.

A bookish child, Consuelo grows up in San Juan, Puerto Rico, during the 1950s. As she deals with the end of her parents' marriage, she cares for her younger sister, Mili, whose name comes from the word *milagros*, "miracle." Life grows steadily bleaker for Consuelo, for Mili starts speaking in tongues and descending into schizophrenia. With a father who loves all things American and a mother who adores the vanishing, tropical, and wild Puerto Rico, Consuelo experiences the political and social struggles besetting her native home. But after her best friend, a gay cousin, escapes from the confines of his family by going to New York, Consuelo decides to search for her own future in America, leaving the island and everything she has known.

In beautiful, poetic language, Consuelo moves through many transitions in her first-person narrative. In the end, rather than being a person who merely offers consolation to others, she becomes a young woman creating her own reality.

LINDA CREW

## *Children of the River*

12–14 • Delacorte • 1989 • 224 pp.

When the Khmer Rouge took power in Cambodia in 1975, Sundara, at thirteen, fled with her aunt and uncle and their newborn daughter to escape the horrors of the Communist regime. When their horrendous trip ends, Sundara moves in with her aunt's family in Oregon, where she must straddle the divide between being from Cambodia and being a typical seventeen-year-old American girl.

Told in a refreshing third-person narrative, the book presents both a broad overview and nonstop action at critical points, such as when Sundara and her family manage to escape from Cambodia. An unusual book about the refugee experience, *Children of the River* has been particularly effective in classrooms because of the issues it raises and its enthusiastic reception by young readers.

MICHAEL DORRIS

## *A Yellow Raft in Blue Water*

14–18 • Holt • 1987 • 384 pp.

This passionate and beautifully written novel explores three generations of Native American women. Rayona, fifteen, half-black and half-native, runs away from her home on a Montana reservation, where she lives with her grandmother, Aunt Ida. Supporting herself by working at Bear Paw Lake State Park and the rodeo, Rayona believes if she could stare long enough at a yellow wooden raft in the blue waters of the lake, her troubles would be resolved. But ultimately she returns to her mother, Christine, and the first-person narrative alternates between Christine and Ida, as they reveal some of their secrets.

Throughout his career, Michael Dorris sought to create Native American characters whom people could care about and love; *A Yellow Raft in Blue Water* succeeds brilliantly in this regard. Its multilayered family portrait draws readers into the lives of three very distinct characters as it reveals the rifts and the bonds between generations.

DEBORAH ELLIS

## The Breadwinner

12–14 • Groundwood • 2001 • 170 pp.

When her father is taken away by the Taliban, Parvana disguises herself as a boy so that she can become the family's breadwinner. This powerful portrayal of life under a repressive regime shows the impact of violence against dissenters and the continued subjugation of women, who cannot leave the house without a man. While providing a serious look at life in Afghanistan under the Taliban, the novel focuses on Parvana, an attractive and sympathetic heroine, and her daily struggles to survive and provide food for her family. Two other volumes, *Parvana's Journey* and *Mud City*, continue the saga of women in this war-torn country.

TANUJA DESAI HIDIER

## Born Confused

12–14 • Scholastic • 2002 • 512 pp.

The angst of growing up is exacerbated for Dimple Lala, who believes that she was born "backwards and clueless. In other words, born confused." A New Jersey teen born to Indian immigrant parents, Dimple struggles with her dual identity but also emerges as a normal teenager, struggling to understand friends and boyfriends. Tanuja Desai weaves discussions of Indian food, dress, and customs into the narrative and spices it with Dimple's commentary.

Reflecting the general concerns of all teenagers, the book especially appeals to readers from different backgrounds who find themselves confused by being part American and part something else.

KIMBERLY WILLIS HOLT

## Keeper of the Night

12–14 • Holt • 2003 • 309 pp.

At thirteen, Isabel Moreno finds her mother dead, praying on her knees with a bottle of sleeping pills beside her. Taking on more responsibilities at home in Malesso, Guam, Isabel struggles to have a normal life. But her father retreats into silence, her seven-year-old sister suffers from nightmares, and her brother becomes self-destructive. Told in very short chapters in Isabel's first-person voice, the story alternates between the here-and-now and haunting memories of Isabel's sad and beautiful mother, whose image begins to fade for her.

A master storyteller who writes lyrical and spare prose, Kimberly Willis Holt drew on childhood experience as well as extensive research to capture this Polynesian community and its cockfights and fiestas. Magnificent in its creation of the landscape and people, *Keeper of the Night* takes a tragic event in another culture and shows how individuals deal with it and ultimately heal.

ZORA NEALE HURSTON

## *Their Eyes Were Watching God*

14–18 • Lippincott • 1937 • 240 pp.

A proud, independent black woman, Janie Crawford, searches for her identity in a rural Florida community. Although her life contains terrors and difficulties, she always insists on her own terms, relying on her strength and passion. Raised by her grandmother, a former slave forced to marry an older farmer who runs away to marry again, Janie weds a much younger man, Tea Cake, a prelude to more tragedy.

An anthropologist and folklorist of the Harlem Renaissance, Zora Neale Hurston filled the novel with poetic language, full of rhythm, sound, and imagery. The first African-American feminist novel, *Their Eyes Were Watching God* relies not on philosophy but on character and language to beguile its readers. Ultimately, it speaks to all who want to define themselves on their own terms rather than society's. As Alice Walker, who revived an interest in Hurston's work, has written, "There is enough self-love in that one book — love of community, culture, traditions — to restore a world."

WITI IHIMAERA

## *The Whale Rider*

12–14 • Harcourt • 2003 • 152 pp.

E ight-year-old Kahu has always longed for her great-grandfather's approval. Koro Apirana, the chief of the Maori in Whangara, New Zealand, teaches the Maori ways to the boys and hunts for his successor. He cannot accept that his eldest and sole great-grandchild has turned out to be a girl. Kahu, who completely charms everyone else, forgives his dismissal of her time and time again, but she shows amazing abilities. When Koro leaves a stone deep in the ocean for a boy to discover, Kahu retrieves it instead. One day, when a group of whales beach themselves near the village, Kahu fulfills the ancient prophesies and becomes the whale rider who leads the whales to safety.

*The Whale Rider* alternates between the first-person narrative of Kahu's uncle and the mystical voices of the whales themselves. Tradition, sexism, faith, creation myths, and the Maori culture all combine in a simple, magical story that was quite effectively adapted for an independent film. The book will appeal to all those who believe they are destined for an important role in life.

JAMAICA KINCAID
## Annie John
14–18 • Farrar, Straus • 1985 • 148 pp.

Annie John describes her coming of age in her native Antigua and her growing awareness of those around her. She focuses obsessively on her love-hate relationship with her mother. In the course of the narrative, Annie changes from an obedient ten-year-old to a rebellious, hard-headed outcast.

Written in a style deceivingly simple for its complex material, the novel deals with the difference between public perception and private reality in a leisurely manner. Consequently, it provokes discussion among young readers — who often see their own lives reflected in Annie's experiences.

VICTOR MARTINEZ
## Parrot in the Oven: Mi Vida
14–18 • Harper • 1996 • 216 pp.
⮡ *NATIONAL BOOK AWARD*

A young Mexican-American teenager in the Central Valley of California, Manuel Hernandez, reveals the gritty details of his life in eleven chapters that also work as short stories. With an abusive alcoholic father who sometimes pulls out his gun, an older sister who gets pregnant, and the problems created by poverty, Manny still experiences typical teenage concerns — a crush on a white teacher and getting money to buy coveted items. But he also must decide whether to join the local gang; eventually he does, although basically he just wants to figure out how to make his own decisions. Marked by poetic language and metaphor, the book excels in its imagery and in its honest delineation of the problems faced by those standing outside the American dream.

KYOKO MORI

## Shizuko's Daughter

12–14 • Holt • 1993 • 238 pp.

After Shizuko commits suicide in her home in Kobe, Japan, twelve-year-old Yuki returns to find her mother's dead body on the kitchen floor. Shizuko's suicide note to Yuki reads: "People will tell you that I've done this because I did not love you. Don't listen to them. When you grow up to be a strong woman, you will know that this was for the best." Yuki must then face not only her mother's death but also her father's marriage to his mistress of many years. Deftly handling the tough issues raised, the novel follows Yuki for several years as she painfully grows and matures into a young woman. Kyoke Mori's poetic prose and beautiful imagery distinguish this autobiographical novel, making it both haunting and memorable.

NAOMI SHIHAB NYE

## Habibi

12–14 • Simon & Schuster • 1997 • 259 pp.

When Liyana Abboud turns fourteen, her father moves the family from St. Louis to his native Jerusalem. Liyana begins studying Arabic and learning the local customs from her Arab grandmother. In this story about Liyana's search for identity, Arab-Israeli tensions form a backdrop. Liyana falls in love with a boy who happens to be Jewish. Ultimately, she grows comfortable in her new community, surrounded with love from a large extended family.

Best known as a poet, Naomi Shihab Nye wrote *Habibi* as her first novel, basing it on some of her own experiences when, at fourteen, she moved to Jerusalem. In a slow, deliberate narrative, she explores political conflicts, a teenage romance, and a series of events in one person's life. The landscape comes alive in this novel — from Jerusalem itself to Bedouin camps. Often taught in multicultural units, *Habibi* explores the different cultures living side by side in Jerusalem, but it offers no simple solutions for their future.

CONNIE PORTER

## Imani All Mine

14–18 • Houghton Mifflin • 1999 • 212 pp.

At fifteen, Tasha has become a mother. She names her baby Imani, which means "faith" — something that is greatly needed in her tough, inner-city Buffalo, New York, neighborhood. Conceived when Tasha was raped, Imani is adored by her mother, who has little real meaning in her confused and confusing world as she struggles to provide for her baby while trying to continue at school.

Connie Porter herself grew up in poverty in a large family in Buffalo, and she wanted to write about some of the teenage girls she had known. Tasha's staccato narrative reveals a merciless place — as timely as today's newspaper headlines. The book explores the pain and violence of poverty while celebrating the unconquerable spirit of youth.

PAM MUÑOZ RYAN

## Esperanza Rising

12–14 • Scholastic • 2000 • 262 pp.

When Esperanza's grandmother teaches her how to crochet, she says, "Ten stitches up to the top of the mountain . . . Nine stitches down to the bottom of the valley." These might well have been the instructions for the girl's life. Born into privilege and wealth in Mexico, Esperanza watches her life disintegrate when bandits kill her father and greedy uncles take over the finances. With her mother, she sets out for the United States, where the two support themselves during the Depression in a company camp. Young readers grow to care for Esperanza and to feel her loneliness, sadness, pain, and wretched tiredness. An excellent teaching tool about the Depression, Mexican immigration, and forced repatriation, the book was inspired by the life of the author's grandmother.

BENJAMIN ALIRE SÁENZ

## Sammy and Juliana in Hollywood

14–18 • Cinco Puntos • 2004 • 240 pp.

During the 1960s Sammy Santos, a hard-working, bright, and responsible teenager, grows up in the Hollywood barrio of Las Cruces, New Mexico. Somehow he survives this period — although he faces the death of his first love, Juliana. Many of the issues and problems of the time are smoothly woven into the narrative — the role of the Church in barrio life, the loosening of school rules during the Vietnam era, the treatment of gay teens, and the effect of the draft on poor young men. But Sammy survives these turbulent times, maintaining a strong sense of self and the ability to hope for a better life.

Told in the first person, with Spanish woven into the text, the story presents a truly admirable protagonist. Benjamin Alire Sáenz has brought both the period of history and a compelling young man completely to life.

GARY SOTO

## Buried Onions

12–14 • Harcourt • 1997 • 149 pp.

Nineteen-year-old Eddie wants to break away from the poverty and gangs in his Fresno, California, neighborhood. When his cousin is killed, friends and family alike try to convince him to avenge the death with more violence. Ultimately, Eddie leaves his landscaping job to join the military in an attempt to get away — and, perhaps, start afresh.

This cheerless, almost hopeless novel captures the dark realities of growing up poor and Mexican American in the United States. Gary Soto's descriptions are staccato, gritty, and vivid — just like the smell of onions that pervades Eddie's very existence.

SUZANNE FISHER STAPLES

## *Shabanu: Daughter of the Wind*

12–14 • Knopf • 1989 • 288 pp.

↵ *NEWBERY HONOR*

Eleven-year-old Shabanu, part of a family of nomadic camel herd-
ers in the Cholistan Desert in Pakistan today, understands the
structure of her society. A daughter abides by her father's decisions,
and a wife obeys her husband. As wild as the wind, Shabanu considers
escaping from her own arranged marriage. But then disaster strikes,
and Shabanu and her sister are threatened with rape by a powerful
landowner. They escape and humiliate him, but they must face the
consequences.

In a first-person, present-tense narrative, *Shabanu* explores with
sensitivity and admiration the desert way of life and vividly captures
dust storms, camels mating and birthing, burials, wedding rituals, and
the rites of the Muslim faith. A newspaper correspondent who lived in
the area, Suzanne Fisher Staples based her characters on people she
met. Now with a half-million copies in print, the book has often been
a teenager's introduction to this part of the world and its culture.

ALLAN STRATTON

## *Chanda's Secrets*

12–14 • Annick Press • 2004 • 176 pp.

↵ *PRINTZ HONOR*

After her father dies in a diamond mind in sub-Saharan Africa, sixteen-year-old Chanda Kabelo finds that her life has changed forever. Her mother remarries several times; her best friend becomes a
prostitute. Although death from AIDS remains a constant threat, the
disease cannot be discussed. However, the girl begins to realize that
her mother has AIDS and that Chanda herself may be infected.

Although unrelenting, Chanda's story is not without hope; wise
and tenacious, Chanda manages to gain some control over her difficult life when she confronts the shame and its cause. The first-person, present-tense narrative in this raw and riveting novel brings daily
life in southern Africa into vivid detail.

AMY TAN

## *The Joy Luck Club*

14–18 • Putnam • 1989 • 288 pp.

In a novel filled with wisdom and compassion, four mothers and their Chinese-American daughters grapple with their cultural identity. Forming a mah-jong group in San Francisco, four Chinese immigrants provide a support group for themselves over the years. When one of them dies, her daughter joins the group and begins to understand her mother and herself. The chapters alternate between the eight voices of the mothers and daughters. The mothers attempt to fit into the American way of life; the daughters struggle with having immigrant parents. Intensely poetic and moving, the book reveals details of Chinese culture and heritage — vocabulary, festivals, food, and clothing — but because Amy Tan remains a storyteller, all these details simply enhance the narrative structure. Showing the tensions between mothers and daughters found in all ethnic groups, the book is ideal for classroom or mother-daughter book discussions.

ALICE WALKER

## *The Color Purple*

14–18 • Simon & Schuster • 1982 • 288 pp.

↪ *NATIONAL BOOK AWARD FINALIST/PULITZER PRIZE*

Celie, an indigent African-American woman who is fourteen when the novel begins, lives in rural Georgia during the early 1900s. She starts writing letters to God because Pa beats and rapes her. She even bears two of his children, whom he takes from her. Then she faces a horrible, turbulent marriage to a man she refers to as Mr. ____. Two independent women show Celie a different way to look at life, and she develops an intimate relationship with one of them. Although a pointed indictment of the men who abused and betrayed her, Celie's story also shows the strong bonds that exist between women and the resilience of the human spirit.

Certainly one of the most successful, if controversial, books written by a black woman, *The Color Purple* was an international bestseller and was made into a Steven Spielberg movie. Some found (and still find) Alice Walker's presentation of black men offensive. Walker herself believed that she simply broadened the trail blazed by her mentor, Zora Neale Hurston. Over the years, the novel has faced a multitude of censorship cases and made Walker — the second black woman to win a Pulitzer Prize — the mentor of many other writers.

GLORIA WHELAN

## Homeless Bird

12–14 • HarperCollins • 2000 • 192 pp.

↬ *NATIONAL BOOK AWARD*

Thirteen when her parents find her a husband, Koly leaves home to live in a distant Indian village. Having met neither the groom nor his in-laws, she finds the truth of her situation much worse than she could have feared. Her husband turns out to be sickly, and his parents wanted her dowry only so he could take a trip to bathe in the holy waters of the Ganges. Soon widowed and abandoned by her mother-in-law, this homeless bird exemplifies the plight of those Hindu women who have no status, family, or financial security. However, Gloria Whelan reverses the developing tragedy in the form of a young man, a benefactress, and an employer who appear just in time. Although the ending seems more American than Hindu, it helps make the book appealing to its young Western audience.

A strong heroine, fascinating cultural details, Hindu vocabulary, triumph over adversity, and romance all blend together in a deeply moving story.

RITA WILLIAMS-GARCIA

## Like Sisters on the Homefront

12–14 • Lodestar • 1995 • 166 pp.

When fourteen-year-old Gayle becomes pregnant the second time, her mother forces her to go to an abortion clinic and then to the family home in Georgia. So this young African American not only has to adapt to a new home but also face the disapproval of her relatives. Only Gayle's great-grandmother truly understands the girl: "When you lay down your deviling . . . you'll be stronger than those who lived by the rules all their lives." Gayle slowly gains that strength, moving beyond street smarts. Or, as Gayle writes about her future, "I'm gon to school. Beats being a house slave."

LAURENCE YEP

## Child of the Owl

12–14 • HarperCollins • 1977 • 288 pp.

In the 1960s, when her gambler father is hospitalized, likable and streetwise Casey temporarily moves to San Francisco's Chinatown to live with her grandmother. Casey comes to recognize her grandmother's strength and appreciate their shared culture. As Casey looks at Chinatown with native eyes, she brings the neighborhood alive.

In this book, one of the series about the Young family called the Golden Mountain Chronicles, Laurence Yep deftly blends Chinese traditions and lore into a contemporary coming-of-age novel. The struggle of Chinese Americans as outsiders is explored in many of Yep's fine novels, but he always presents it in ways that seem universal and understandable to all adolescents.

# Mystery and Thriller

EVER SINCE SIR ARTHUR Conan Doyle began spinning tales about a detective called Sherlock Holmes, teens have been reading mysteries and thrillers. As the Holmes mysteries suggest, this audience does not need an adolescent protagonist to attract them to a book.

Almost all of the adult bestsellers in this category have been written within the reading range of teens. Dan Brown, the author of *The Da Vinci Code,* has emerged in the last few years as one of teenagers' favorite writers. He is not only winning teen-voted awards but has found his way into high school curriculums as well. Another adult book, Mark Haddon's *The Curious Incident of the Dog in the Night-Time,* which features a fifteen-year-old protagonist, also quickly became a favorite book.

For a long time, mysteries and thrillers published specifically for their audience emerged as grade B fiction, attracting few creative writers. Fortunately, in the past few years that trend has been reversed, and many of the books listed — Kathleen Johnson's *A Fast and Brutal Wing,* Gail Giles's *Shattering Glass,* and Tim Wynne-Jones's *A Thief in the House of Memory* — feature not only interesting structures but superb literary writing as well.

In their honesty about contemporary issues, these books have moved a long way since Sherlock Holmes, but they all maintain that compelling, page-turning style that can make them enjoyable to read and hard to put down. I once heard a teenager say that a book was so boring it should be packaged with a fork so that readers could stick themselves from time to time to stay awake. In this group of books, forks are rarely if ever necessary.

---

PETER ABRAHAMS

## Down the Rabbit Hole: An Echo Falls Mystery

12–14 • HarperCollins/Geringer • 2005 • 375 pp.

In a mystery that develops in a leisurely manner, thirteen-year-old Ingrid visits with Cracked-up Katie right before Katie gets murdered. In fact, Ingrid leaves her beloved red soccer shoes at the scene of the crime. When she returns to get them, she discovers another intruder at the crime scene — who may very well be the murderer. Even though the police chief in her small town of Echo Falls talks to Ingrid frequently, she decides to pursue the murderer privately, drawing on her reading of Sherlock Holmes. At the same time, Ingrid plays her favorite sport, gets the main role in *Alice in Wonderland*, begins a romance with the son of the police chief, and helps her grandfather save land from development.

A modern Nancy Drew, Ingrid is an attractive heroine with great reader appeal; she solves her crime and narrowly escapes becoming the next murder victim in this light but entertaining mystery, the first of a series.

KEVIN BROOKS

## Lucas

14–18 • Scholastic/Chicken House • 2003 • 423 pp.

Fifteen-year-old Cait lives on a small island off the coast of England. Suspicious of everyone, the islanders outdo themselves in their insularity when a sixteen-year-old drifter, Lucas, comes to the island. A beautiful, mysterious boy who seems oddly clairvoyant, Lucas understands what being an outsider means. Cait befriends him, falls in love with him — and watches in horror as members of the hidebound community start to pin crimes on Lucas that he has not committed. When another islander tries to rape Cait, Lucas comes to her defense; although he can save her, he cannot save himself.

Fast-paced and absorbing, the novel moves inevitably toward its tragic end. The dreamlike quality of island life has been juxtaposed with very believable violence and fear as Kevin Brooks explores the hideous consequences of prejudice and hatred.

### DAN BROWN

## *The Da Vinci Code*

14–18 • Doubleday • 2003 • 454 pp.

The plot of Dan Brown's bestseller rests on the premise that Jesus Christ had an affair with Mary Magdalene and that their child became the first of a royal bloodline. When the Louvre's chief curator is murdered, Sophie Neveu, a French police cryptologist, and Harvard's symbol expert, Robert Langdon, try to solve the case. As the search moves to England, they find themselves caught between two powerful groups: the Priory of Sion, an ancient secret society whose members included Sir Isaac Newton, Da Vinci, and Botticelli, and the conservative Catholic organization Opus Dei.

Including an enormous amount of art history, *The Da Vinci Code* blends fact and fiction in a breathtaking manner. The book often sends readers to do further research — on the Knights Templar, the Holy Grail, the early history of the Christian Church — to determine what the author invented; it has been taught in high schools for exactly that reason. Because of the controversy surrounding it, other volumes, including a special illustrated edition, have been published to support or refute the claims in the book.

With a fascinating, page-turning plot, the book intrigues many readers who do not normally pick up thrillers. Heading the bestseller list for two years, *The Da Vinci Code* has sold over 20 million copies. An enormous number of those readers are teenagers; consequently, many of them — who also enjoy *Angels & Demons* and *Deception Point* — now list Dan Brown as one of their favorite authors.

### ROBERT CORMIER

## *The Rag and Bone Shop*

12–14 • Delacorte • 2001 • 176 pp.

In his last novel, Robert Cormier gave his fans the kind of taut, powerful, and compelling story that had been his trademark since *The*

*Chocolate War*. A seven-year-old girl has been brutally murdered, and a shy and sweet twelve-year-old boy, Jason, was the last person to see her alive. Since the case has attracted so much local attention, a man named Trent, a special kind of police officer, has been brought to town, for he always gets a confession. His prey, this time, happens to be an innocent boy.

Most of the novel focuses on Trent's interrogation and his pursuit of a confession. The reader feels Jason's confusion, discomfort, and finally defeat as he admits to what he has not done. Then Cormier, the master of the unexpected ending, pulls a few more punches.

This brief page-turner explores guilt, redemption, and all of the evil that lurks, as described by the poet William Butler Yeats, in "the foul rag-and-bone shop of the heart."

SIR ARTHUR CONAN DOYLE

## The Hound of the Baskervilles

12–18 • McClure's • 1902 • 256 pp.

Critics of young adult literature often proclaim the irrefutable truth that these books must feature a young adult protagonist. However, they forget one of the most popular books for young adults over the last century. In one of the classic mysteries of all time, Sherlock Holmes sends Dr. Watson to Baskerville Hall, in Dartmoor, Devonshire, England, in 1889. Sir Charles Baskerville has just died, seemingly killed by the legendary and mysterious black hound that has plagued the Baskerville line. Holmes, in the meantime, disguises himself so that he can roam the moors at night. The estate borders a moor that includes the Grimpen Mire, a deadly quicksand bog; a mysterious butler, an escaped killer, and the spectral hounds complete the gothic atmosphere.

A brilliant book, deftly constructed with no wasted words, *The Hound of the Baskervilles* displays the talents of Sherlock Holmes, Sir Arthur Conan Doyle's great creation. A century's time has not dulled the thrill of this tale, which gets assigned to students summer after summer. Once engaged in the book, no one seems to miss a young adult protagonist; almost all who encounter the story happily move on to Conan Doyle's many brilliant stories about the great detective.

LOIS DUNCAN

## Killing Mr. Griffin

12–14 • Little, Brown • 1978 • 223 pp.

A former college teacher, now a high school English instructor, Brian Griffin tortures his students with his high standards and unbending principles. One day Mark Kinney, a persuasive teenager with a personality that resembles a psychopath's, convinces four others to help him in a "prank" — to kidnap Mr. Griffin and make him miserable for a few hours. But after leaving Mr. Griffin tied up in the dark, the pranksters return to find him dead. They all begin to deal with their actions then, ultimately turning on one another.

Made into a movie, *Killing Mr. Griffin* is a perennial crowd-pleaser, although it may seem a bit ludicrous in places, such as the kidnapping scene. But the book builds tension and fear and keeps readers engrossed until the final, surprising ending. As more than one person has learned, the lesson of the book is: "Never, I repeat NEVER! kidnap your teacher."

In this novel and many of her other popular mysteries, such as *I Know What You Did Last Summer,* Lois Duncan knows how to build suspense and keep young teens reading breathlessly until the final page.

GAIL GILES

## Shattering Glass

12–14 • Roaring Brook • 2002 • 215 pp.

In the opening paragraph, readers learn that Simon Glass has been killed; on the last page, they learn how. But the rest of the book builds suspense, with twists and turns, as Gail Giles shows a high school clique gone amuck. When Rob Haynes transfers to a new high school, he quickly becomes the leader of the pack. Handsome, removed, manipulative, and angry, he sets out to turn the school on its ear. His main project becomes Simon Glass, the school nerd, or goat, whom Rob decides to transform into the "class favorite." But Glass, wealthy and brilliant, has some plans of his own, which ultimately cause his murder. Told by Young Steward, who goes to jail for the crime, the novel builds tension page by page, leading the reader to the horrifying if inevitable conclusion.

Darker than Lois Duncan's *Killing Mr. Griffin* but covering some of the same territory, *Shattering Glass* examines a sinister high school environment and the ultimate danger of going along with the crowd.

JOHN GRISHAM
## The Last Juror
14–18 • Doubleday • 2004 • 485 pp.

John Grisham remains perennially popular with adolescents; often their lists of favorite books include one if not two Grisham titles. Because he creates exciting, fast-paced plots filled with colorful characters, he has fashioned thriller after thriller that has been adapted well for the movies and attracted teens.

*The Last Juror* takes place in the small town of Clanton, Mississippi, in the 1970s. A long-haired Yankee and college dropout, Willie Traynor takes control of the only newspaper in Ford County. With the brutal murder of a young mother, he brings the paper into the maelstrom that the crime creates. The town of Clayton, those who live outside the law, and the events of history that slowly change the South all become a focus for the narrative. But ultimately the story returns to what happens when the convicted murderer is released and the jurors start to die.

In a funny, suspenseful, and heartfelt novel, Grisham presents the tensions between the old and new South and a young man's transformation when he chose to live in small-town Mississippi.

LEV GROSSMAN
## Codex
14–18 • Harcourt • 2004 • 348 pp.

Edward Wozny, an investment banker on a two-week vacation between jobs, becomes drawn into the murky world of medieval literature. Cataloguing a rare book collection, he is solicited by the Duke and Duchess of Bowmry to find a codex by Gervase of Langford — which may not even exist. Edward pulls a passionate young scholar, Margaret Napier, into the quest, and the two are quickly drawn into events that spin out of control as the duke and duchess vie against each other. When not searching for the mysterious document, Edward plays MOMUS, an intricate, addictive computer game that starts to mirror his real adventures as he looks for the codex.

This literary historical thriller offers an exciting plot, an attractive young scholar, and an intriguing subplot for technophiles.

### DAVID GUTERSON

## *Snow Falling on Cedars*

14–18 · Harcourt · 1994 · 480 pp.

In 1954 a small island community off the coast of Washington State tries a Japanese-American man for the murder of Carl Heine, another fisherman on the island. The entire community had been severely affected during World War II when its Japanese citizens had been forced into internment camps. The accused murderer, Kabuo Miyamoto, and the newspaperman, Ishmael Chambers, resume seemingly normal lives after the war. But Chambers's childhood sweetheart was now married to Miyamoto. So when Chambers finds information that could alter the verdict of the trial, he must face a private battle as powerful as the public one.

An English teacher who adored *To Kill a Mockingbird*, David Guterson took its structure — two separate stories that become one — and kept many of the same elements: a murder trial, a courtroom drama, a racial conflict, an identifiable regional setting, and a particular time in American history. Guterson felt so indebted to Harper Lee that when he won the prestigious PEN/Faulkner Award, he offered to fly the aging author to Washington, D.C., for the ceremonies.

With over three million copies in print and now translated into twenty-five languages, *Snow Falling on Cedars* works particularly well in high school literature classes or social studies units on the Japanese-American internment. A leisurely novel, it opens like a tight rosebud and blooms in full by the end.

### MARK HADDON

## *The Curious Incident of the Dog in the Night-Time*

14–18 · Doubleday · 2003 · 226 pp.

*The Curious Incident of the Dog in the Night-Time*, Yann Martel's *Life of Pi*, and Philip Pullman's *The Golden Compass* serve as the current standard-bearers for "crossover books." Publishers generally use that term to mean those books that feature a young adult protagonist — or sometimes even a child protagonist — and can be read with equal enthusiasm by adults and young adults. In England, *Curious Incident* was released simultaneously as both a young adult and an adult title, but it won the prestigious Whitbread Book of the Year Award as an adult novel. In the United States, it appeared only on an adult list and became a *New York Times* bestseller. But the book has gained a wide and enthusiastic audience of all ages on both sides of the Atlantic.

Fifteen-year-old Christopher John Francis Boone, of Swindon, Wiltshire, England, knows "all the countries of the world and their capital cities and every prime number up to 7,057." Out walking at midnight, Christopher discovers a dead poodle with a pitchfork sticking through it. As a devotee of Sherlock Holmes, Christopher sets out to solve this mystery as if he himself were the great detective. Very smart when it comes to logic, Christopher suffers from Asperger's syndrome, a form of autism marked by emotional detachment, which makes him unable to understand human beings or typical emotions. He therefore does not see where his investigation is taking him and cannot see his effect on others — including his increasingly frustrated parents, who can barely handle him. But he's a whiz at other things: he spends whole chapters discussing mathematical problems, deep space, and the nature of perception.

Amazing in his portrayal of an emotionally dissociated, or autistic, mind, Mark Haddon shows a rare gift of empathy; like his character, he can be wise, funny, and thought-provoking. As he has written, the book "has a very simple surface, but there are layers of irony and paradox all the way through it. Here is a fiction about a character who says he can only tell the truth, he can't tell lies — but he gets everything wrong."

Some find this novel hilarious, some weep, but most find themselves intrigued by Christopher, one of the freshest, most lovable adolescents ever to appear in fiction. Although a recent title, this young adult pleaser will be adopted for high school English classes well into the future.

VIRGINIA HAMILTON

## The House of Dies Drear

12–14 • Macmillan • 1968 • 256 pp.

Thirteen-year-old Thomas Small arrives in an Ohio town because his father has been hired to teach history at the college. They move into a long-empty house; with secret tunnels, it once served as an important station on the Underground Railroad run by the abolitionist Dies Drear. But after they move in, ghosts walk, walls slide back to reveal secret passages, and Thomas and his father find hidden treasure.

Since Virginia Hamilton's grandfather traveled to Ohio as a fugitive slave on the Underground Railroad, she had always been fascinated by his story. Although she wrote many critically acclaimed books, she continued to love this title because it was full of "excitement, mystery, black history, the strong, black family." With a compelling plot, a gothic setting, and an attractive protagonist, *The House of Dies Drear* makes history tangible, so it is often included in American history units on slavery.

TONY HILLERMAN

## The Wailing Wind

14–18 • HarperCollins • 2002 • 334 pp.

Over the years, Tony Hillerman has garnered a large adolescent following; his delightful books always combine a Native American cultural journey, police methods, and a mystery. For a reader new to Hillerman, *The Wailing Wind* is an excellent place to start. The Navajo Tribal Police lieutenant Joe Leaphorn has retired, leaving his companion, Sergeant Jim Chee, in command. Chee's assistant, Officer Bernadette Manuelito, bungles her first appearance at a homicide crime scene, and Leaphorn comes into the case to help them cover her mishap. All three start hunting for an alleged gold deposit on Native land — trying to find it and stay alive before the killer strikes again. During the investigation, a romance develops between Chee and Manuelito, who are both devoted to their people and way of life.

But relating the plot of a Hillerman novel never captures its texture. In this New Mexico landscape, a different sense of time, a connection to the natural world, and a unique way of looking at reality emerge as well. Readers learn about the history of the West and the indigenous ways of its people in books that keep them coming back. Many Hillerman novels appear on summer reading lists; however, they also work well for independent reading or for parent-teen book discussions.

### KATHLEEN JEFFRIE JOHNSON

## *A Fast and Brutal Wing*

12–14 • Roaring Brook • 2004 • 191 pp.

In a mystery that remains ambiguous from beginning to end, a series of memos, newspaper articles, and a journal unfold a disturbing set of events. On a Halloween night, three teenagers awake to find themselves naked and bloody in the deserted woods near the house of a now-vanished writer. In the process of unraveling this potential crime without a body, Kathleen Jeffrie Johnson reveals information about the family of one of the teens and about a father who also vanished. The girl believes that she can transform herself into a cat and that her brother becomes a hawk. In the end, the line between psychosis and reality remains blurry — only the vanished writer is perfectly fine, having merely taken a trip.

Certainly the book expands the possibilities of mysteries written with adolescent characters; readers focus not on who committed a crime but whether anything actually happened — except in the mind of a disturbed teenage protagonist. Some love this powerful blend of fantasy and mystery, and some hate it—but few forget it.

### LAURIE R. KING

## *The Beekeeper's Apprentice*

14–18 • St. Martin's • 1994 • 405 pp.

Sir Arthur Conan Doyle's Sherlock Holmes has inspired a legion of writers to further develop his character. But none has crafted as beguiling and exciting mysteries about him as Laurie R. King.

During World War I, Holmes has retired to a Sussex farm to raise bees, occasionally investigating cases for the government. Fifteen-year-old Mary Russell, whose wit, ego, and sleuthing gifts match those of Holmes, stumbles into him on Sussex Downs one day. Since Watson has been relegated to a role as a butler, Holmes and Mary make a detective team, working on some cases together until Mary leaves to study theology at Oxford. Ultimately, the two must solve the case of the kidnapping of Jessica Simpson, the daughter of an American senator, and Holmes and Mary find themselves pitted against the daughter of the diabolical Professor Moriarty.

A book for Holmes fans and those who love history, humor, adventure, and mystery, *The Beekeeper's Apprentice* and its sequels keep readers craving more about Mary Russell. Although the book can simply be read for enjoyment or in adult-teen discussion groups, it has even been used in high schools to teach math.

### E. L. KONIGSBURG

## Silent to the Bone

12–14 · Atheneum/Karl · 2000 · 261 pp.

A frantic call to the police opens this novel: a woman says that her baby won't wake up. Since the baby's accident, thirteen-year-old Branwell remains silent, refusing or unable to speak about what happened to his half-sister. Confined to the Clarion County Juvenile Behavioral Center, Branwell often sees his best friend, Connor, who narrates the novel and tries to help him. Connor uses a set of written flashcards to cut through the silence; eventually, Bran starts spelling out words in his desire to communicate his thoughts. Although everyone holds Bran responsible for the baby's coma, he had simply covered up for the irresponsible actions of the seductive British au pair.

Just as in *From the Mixed-Up Files of Mrs. Basil E. Frankweiler*, E. L. Konigsburg develops two smart, savvy protagonists. With an incisive understanding of psychology and the human heart, she keeps the narrative tense and taut until the final upbeat ending.

### SHARYN MCCRUMB

## Ghost Riders

14–18 · Dutton · 2003 · 401 pp.

E arly in the Civil War, the mountain dwellers of western North Carolina and eastern Tennessee worked to stay neutral, believing the war a rich man's argument. But once the Union sympathizer Keith

Blalock gets drafted into the Confederacy, Malinda Blalock decides not to wait out the war. She cuts off her hair and enlists as Sam, Keith's younger brother. Getting themselves discharged, the two then join the Union ranks, avenging Confederate raids on their friends and relatives. Sam's Confederate colonel, Zebulon Baird Vance, goes on to serve as the governor of North Carolina during the war — events also covered in the narrative.

In a parallel story line, modern Civil War reenactment troops camp in this area of the Appalachians. But as they recreate Southern history, the ghosts of fallen soldiers begin appearing at their campsites and to residents. Two area locals, who possess the gift of "sight," must quell these ghosts.

One of the best novelists exploring Appalachian history today, Sharon McCrumb also brings to life another, little-known aspect of the Civil War — the hundreds of women disguised as men who participated in the war. For *Ghost Riders*, McCrumb used the true stories of the Blalocks and Zebulon Baird Vance, mixed it with local history, and added a fictitious current community.

McCrumb's ballad novels, based on lore passed through the generations — *The Ballad of Frankie Silver, She Walks These Hills,* and *The Rosewood Casket* — are often included in high school curriculums. With compelling plots, eccentric characters, and a great deal of history, the books resemble Appalachian quilts; her scraps of legends, ballads, rural life, and local tragedy present deeper truths about the culture of the South's mountain region.

JOYCE MCDONALD

## Shades of Simon Gray

12–14 • Delacorte • 2001 • 248 pp.

In 1798, the citizens of Bellehaven hung Jessup Wildemere from the Liberty Tree without benefit of a trial. On a strange night two hundred years later, Simon Gray, a seemingly model student, drives his car at high speed into that tree and arrives in the hospital in a coma. Is it an accident or intentional? What is Simon hiding? Three seniors panic about Simon's crash; Simon had been illegally entering the computer system at school, gaining valuable tests for them. They had therefore been accepted by their chosen colleges without doing the necessary work. As Simon remains suspended in a coma, he travels back in time, meets Jessup Wildemere, and gains the necessary evidence to learn the truth about this centuries-old crime. Using elements of a ghost story, a thriller, and a romance, Joyce McDonald excels in pacing and drama, keeping readers riveted as all the details come together.

JOYCE MCDONALD

## Swallowing Stones

12–14 • Delacorte • 1997 • 245 pp.

At a Fourth of July party, teenage Michael MacKenzie tests a Winchester rifle he was given. The bullet kills Charlie Ward, who is working on his roof four blocks away. For most of the narrative Michael, basically a likable and decent young man, attempts to hide his crime. But slowly his guilt isolates him from those around him. In alternating sections, fifteen-year-old Jenna faces the tremendous loss caused by her father's horrifying death. In an ending not as explicit as some teens have wanted, readers see Michael ready to confess to Jenna.

Exploring guilt and the repercussions of an accidental crime, this highly emotional book keeps readers riveted as they wait for Michael to make the right choice.

GRAHAM MCNAMEE

## Acceleration

12–14 • Random House/Lamb • 2003 • 213 pp.

While working in the lost-and-found department of the Toronto Transit Commission, seventeen-year-old Duncan finds an unclaimed journal that appears to have been written by a serial killer. At first he tries to ignore it, then he tries to get the attention of the police; finally he and one of his best friends work through the journal to locate this madman. Duncan has been haunted by an incident in which he could not save the life of a drowning swimmer near him in the pool. He decides that this time he won't fail the women stalked by this killer, even though his friend, Vinny, feels that hunting for this man is a bit like the Hardy boys going after Hannibal Lecter.

This fast-paced, thrilling exploration of the mind of a cold-blooded killer has been leavened by humor and the sarcasm and bantering of teenage boys. But it is taut, compelling, totally believable, and almost impossible to put down.

CAROL PLUM-UCCI

## The Body of Christopher Creed

12–14 • Harcourt • 2000 • 331 pp.

↩ *PRINTZ HONOR*

Christopher Creed has been considered a freak all his life, an outsider, the target of all the bullies in his small town in South New Jersey. But when he disappears without a trace, the town wonders if he has been murdered or if his last e-mail indicates a suicide. In this final communication, Chris reveals his envy of others, like golden boy sixteen-year-old Torey Adams. Torey finds himself haunted by Creed's disappearance and tries to figure out what happened with Chris's neighbor Ali and her boyfriend, Bo, a guy from the wrong side of the tracks who has a criminal record. Their search takes Torey into a Native American burial grounds and old secrets in his town.

The author of other fine mysteries for young adults, including *What Happened to Lani Garver*, Carol Plum-Ucci has crafted a suspenseful and compelling novel that explores the effects of intolerance in a community.

PHILIP PULLMAN

## The Ruby in the Smoke

12–14 • Knopf • 1987 • 230 pp.

Featuring sixteen-year-old Sally Lockhart, *The Ruby in the Smoke* takes place in the back alleys, wharves, sewers, and opium dens of Victorian London. A pistol-packing, adventurous heroine, Sally has been raised unconventionally by her father. When he dies in a shipwreck, she fends for herself and even discovers how he was murdered. The book includes an evil villainess, a maharajah's ruby, Chinese pirates, a secret society, and many unsavory denizens of the London underworld.

The page-turning story sends readers quickly to the next two installments, *The Shadow in the North* and *The Tiger in the Well*.

ELLEN RASKIN

## *The Westing Game*

12–14 • Dutton • 1978 • 216 pp.

⊖ *NEWBERY MEDAL*

In the bicentennial year of 1976, Ellen Raskin began drafting a novel that took almost two years to write and had a few distinct components: a historical background, a puzzle mystery, the forging of wills, the death of a millionaire, and imperfect heirs. With a working title of "Eight Imperfect Pairs of Heirs," the book that evolved surprised her. This apparently simple story chronicles how the will of Samuel W. Westing, an eccentric millionaire, sends his heirs searching for his murderer. Before the end of the book, the simple plot grows amazingly complex with aliases, disguises, word games, and trickery.

Raskin came to writing through her work as an artist. After designing about a thousand book jackets, she began to illustrate children's books. She moved on to writing and illustrating books with word drawings; then she shifted to prose. She had always hoped to win the Caldecott Medal for illustration. Instead, she won a Newbery Medal for *The Westing Game,* a book that many people thought was simply too much fun to win the highest literary award.

Because young readers enjoy the twists and turns of her plots, this book has become a staple for middle schools and independent reading.

ALICE SEBOLD

## *The Lovely Bones*

14–18 • Little, Brown • 2002 • 330 pp.

On December 6, 1973, fourteen-year-old Susie Salmon was brutally raped and murdered. Placed in an interim heaven until she can let go of earthly concerns, Susie narrates her own story as she watches her grief-stricken family and friends come to terms with this crime in a suburban community. Her mother escapes her pain through adultery; her sister constantly thinks about Susie; her shattered father seeks the murderer with vengeance, even when the police have given up.

As family and friends start to create "the lovely bones" knitted around the empty space left by Susie's death, she stays fourteen in heaven, savoring her life on Earth and viewing those she loves. A modern version of Thornton Wilder's *Our Town,* the novel remains uplifting, funny, and sweet, despite the murder at its core. In this *New York Times* bestseller, Alice Sebold has taken a neighborhood tragedy and turned it into compelling and satisfying literature that works well in high school English classes and adult-teen book discussion groups.

ALEXANDER MCCALL SMITH
## The No. 1 Ladies' Detective Agency
14–18 • Anchor • 2002 • 235 pp.

Not a conventional mystery, Alexander McCall Smith's novel tells the story of a female private detective. Whatever the category, readers have become enchanted with his creation, Precious Ramotswe, of Botswana, who optimistically sets up the first detection agency in her country. At first her cases come slowly — women who believe they have cheating husbands, a missing child who might have been murdered by witch doctors. Without training but with great intuition, sometimes working from a detective manual, Mma Ramotswe develops her conclusions in a desultory way and focuses on several investigations at once, weaving them in and out of the narrative. Her love of Africa, particularly Botswana, her humanity, her goodness, and her humor enliven every page.

Mma Ramotswe's saga appeared in the United States several years after its publication in England, where two sequels, *Tears of the Giraffe* and *Morality for Beautiful Girls,* had already been published. The author, who taught law at the University of Botswana, had written more than fifty books when he started to develop his story about a cheerful woman with "a traditional build." Like his readers, he became so enthralled with his detective that he continued writing. He believes that his books, whose popularity spread by word of mouth, provide an antidote to the terrible times after September 11, 2001. Mma Ramotswe truly lives a kinder, gentler life as she enjoys bush tea with her friends and clients.

A unique setting, a totally engaging heroine, and a gentle, lyrical style, *The No. 1 Ladies' Detective Agency* and its sequels have quickly become bestsellers in the United States. Because older teens also enjoy them, the books have started to appear on high school reading lists and make excellent choices for teen-adult discussions.

DONNA TARTT

## *The Secret History*

14–18 • Knopf • 1992 • 559 pp.

From the Prologue of the book, in which five of his college friends recount the murder of Bunny Corcoran, to the final pages, where the fate of these five is revealed, *The Secret History* moves with a slow, enthralling, but impeccably controlled pace. When Richard Papen arrives at Hamden College in Vermont, he is quickly seduced and taken into an elite group of Greek scholars, who get private tutoring from the world-famous Julian Morrow. With trust funds, lots of time, and lots of pretensions, the group enjoys long weekends in New England manors and engages in a sybaritic life. But slowly Richard realizes that they are not what they seem on the surface. In a move to cover up an inadvertent murder, four of them plot Bunny's demise because he has discovered their deed and has been blackmailing them. Although devoid of conscience, whether engaging in incest or group sex, the young murderers find themselves haunted by their undetected crime. In fact, it shapes what remains of their lives.

On reading some of Donna Tartt's stories, published when she was a freshman in college, one faculty member introduced himself, saying, "My name is Willie Morris and I think you're a genius." Twenty-eight when the book was published, Tartt had worked for ten years on a thousand-page manuscript, begun when she was a student at Bennington College, the model for Hamden. Her admiration for Greek literature influenced the work, but she also admitted her indebtedness to certain children's novels, such as *Mary Poppins,* in which the young live in a world of their own, largely unsupervised. This first novel became an immediate success and headed up the *New York Times* bestseller list; over a million copies have been printed in the United States alone, and it has been translated into twenty-three languages.

With its mesmerizing college-age protagonists and its elements of Greek tragedy — beauty, unrequited love, betrayal, mystery, and murder — *The Secret History* has developed a cult following among adolescents, much like *The Catcher in the Rye* and *Catch-22.*

ELEANOR UPDALE

## Montmorency: Thief, Liar, Gentleman?

12–14 • Orchard • 2004 • 233 pp.

Readers first meet the adult narrator, Montmorency, in 1875 as a convict, badly bruised and scarred from his life of crime. Because a kind doctor decides to repair him, give him new life, and put him on display at the Scientific Society, the criminal hears a lecture on the new underground systems in Victorian London. Hence, when released from prison, he begins a whole new wave of crime. Establishing two personalities, he lives as both Scarper, an assistant, and Scarper's master, Montmorency, who dresses in expensive clothes and gradually insinuates himself into the best circles of society. But in the very process of acting like a gentleman, Montmorency changes his character. The reader watches a satisfying progress from a liar and thief to a man who uses his espionage skills in the service of his country — although in the end, Montmorency keeps Scarper's boots under his bed — just in case.

In the same way that the viewer starts to side with the criminals in *Bonnie and Clyde,* the reader begins to identify with Montmorency and hope for his escape. Consequently, at the end, when he returns stolen objects and makes restitution, they can celebrate. This delightful and unusual novel of unpunished crime also reveals a great deal about Victorian England, its dark back streets and alleys, and its class system; it has been successfully continued in sequels.

NANCY WERLIN

## The Killer's Cousin

12–14 • Delacorte • 1998 • 231 pp.

Seventeen-year-old David Yaffe, recently acquitted of his girlfriend's murder, moves in with his aunt, uncle, and cousin so he can complete his senior year of high school in a new location. Uncle Vic has some sympathy for David's plight, for his own daughter, Kathy, had died four years earlier. But his eleven-year-old cousin, Lily, exhibits extremely malicious behavior and starts entering David's apartment to destroy computer files and his possessions. Although neither of her parents understand that she may be a bad seed, David begins to realize that her behavior has something to do with Kathy's death. In a riveting climax, the expertly paced thriller brings David and Lily together; as two people who have killed the things they love, they must ultimately help each other move toward healing.

TIM WYNNE-JONES

## A Thief in the House of Memory

12–14 • Farrar, Straus/Kroupa • 2005 • 210 pp.

When Dec Steeple was ten, his beautiful mother, Lindy, disappeared. After he turned sixteen, a mysterious intruder — who entered the family mansion of Steeple Hall — was crushed under a bookcase. Although the case has been dismissed by the town court, Dec finds himself obsessing about this man and his missing mother. As other objects — a long-lost watch, a yearbook — appear and disappear, Dec experiences vivid dreams, memories, and visions of his mother. He even starts believing that his boring and mild-mannered father may actually be a killer.

With subtlety and ambiguity, Tim Wynne-Jones has woven a spellbinding tale of old wealth, old memories, and old pain. In this exploration of the shifting reality of memory, the enticing story and the sympathetic protagonist keep readers engaged until the emotional and believable resolution.

# *Plays*

PLAYS OFTEN STAY longer in memory than many other forms of literature. Who can forget *Our Town* and its characters George and Emily?

Some of the plays in this section feature teenage characters or those in their early twenties; some get read in high school or have been staged for years by drama clubs — *A Raisin in the Sun, Inherit the Wind,* and *You Can't Take It with You.* An occasional play like *Rent* has become so immensely popular with adolescents that its fans call themselves "Rent-heads."

Nearly all of the plays concern young people finding their identity, whether in their family, such as *Brighton Beach Memoirs,* or in their culture, such as *Golden Child.* Sometimes adolescents turn against their own family, to become true to themselves, as they do in *The Effect of Gamma Rays on Man-in-the-Moon Marigolds;* on occasion, the realization of who they are may not always be pleasant, as seen in *"Master Harold" . . . and the boys.*

Whether to read or perform, these plays, from classics to contemporary, contain a great deal to intrigue and excite teenagers.

-------------------------

DAVID AUBURN

## Proof

14–18 • Faber • 2001 • 96 pp.

✧ *PULITZER PRIZE*

Twenty-five-year-old Catherine sacrificed college to care for her father, a mathematician, during his final illness. Now that he's dead, her isolation is interrupted by the arrival of two visitors: her concerned older sister, who would like to take Catherine back to New York, and a former student of their father's, who wants to study his mentor's notebooks. The discovery of an amazing mathematical proof among the father's papers and the burgeoning relationship between Catherine and the researcher propel the plot of this play. Reviewers of the original production noted that the story's twists would often elicit audible gasps from the audience; readers will be equally engaged by this intelligent, exceptionally well crafted, and always surprising drama about love, loss, family ties, and the nature of genius.

ATHOL FUGARD

## "Master Harold" . . . and the boys

14–18 • Knopf • 1982 • 60 pp.

Athol Fugard has chronicled the horrors of South Africa's past in more than two dozen well-regarded plays, but none is as personal as this emotionally wrenching drama set in 1950. Hally, a white seventeen-year-old, makes his regular afterschool visit to the St. George's Park Tea Room, which is owned by his family and staffed by two black employees, Sam and Willie. Sam has always been a substitute parent for Hally, who has a love-hate relationship with his own disabled, alcoholic father. What begins as a jovial rainy afternoon filled with homework, ballroom dance practice, and ice cream sodas changes when news about Hally's father causes the boy to explode with anger. Hally casts racial aspersions on his two friends; in a devastating climax, he spits in Sam's face and demands to be called "Master Harold." Fugard, whose actual first name is Harold, based this unforgettable play on events from his own youth. Though the setting is specific and Hally, Sam, and Willie are wonderfully individualized, this tearoom and its three inhabitants serve as a microcosm of apartheid society.

## WILLIAM GIBSON
### *The Miracle Worker*
14–18 • Knopf • 1957 • 128 pp.

Originally presented as a television drama, *The Miracle Worker* later enjoyed tremendous success as a Broadway play and motion picture; it continues to be performed and read today. Gibson has taken the intrinsically fascinating story of Helen Keller — the blind, deaf, and mute girl freed from her physical prison by her teacher, Annie Sullivan — and crafted a rousing play. The fight scenes between Helen and Annie are described in action-packed detail; the story reaches a devastating climax when young Helen grasps the concept of language. *The Miracle Worker* celebrates the tenacity of the human spirit, the powerful bonds between teacher and student, and the gift of human communication.

## LORRAINE HANSBERRY
### *A Raisin in the Sun*
14–18 • Random House • 1959 • 154 pp.

The first play by an African-American woman to appear on Broadway, *A Raisin in the Sun* explores the hopes and dreams of a family living in an apartment on Chicago's Southside. Anticipating an insurance payment after his father's death, Walter Lee Younger, married with a small child, would like to invest the money in a liquor store. His sister hopes it will pay her medical school tuition; their mother dreams of buying a home for the family. The Youngers lose part of the money to theft, encounter prejudice from their future neighbors, and deal with an unexpected pregnancy, yet are sustained by their pride and love for one another in this powerful domestic drama. Though the amazingly gifted Lorraine Hansberry died young, her best-known work continues to speak to modern audiences. *A Raisin in the Sun* is frequently staged by schools, community groups, and on the professional stage. Students also read the printed text in high schools across the country.

MOSS HART AND GEORGE S. KAUFMAN

## *You Can't Take It with You*

14–18 • Farrar, Straus • 1937 • 96 pp.

⤖ *PULITZER PRIZE*

A perennial favorite of high school drama departments, this comedy features a memorable cast of eccentrics: Grandpa Vanderhof, who doesn't believe in paying taxes; his daughter Penny, an aspiring playwright; her husband, Paul, who makes fireworks in the basement; granddaughters Essie, a klutzy ballerina, and Alice, the most conventional member of this madcap family. When Alice invites her boyfriend and his staid parents home to dinner, the evening is filled with ribald party games, unexpected guests, and all manner of fireworks. Despite its age, *You Can't Take It with You* remains fresh and lively, thanks to its character-driven humor and still timely celebration of nonconformity, love, and laughter.

BETH HENLEY

## *Crimes of the Heart*

14–18 • Viking • 1982 • 106 pp.

⤖ *PULITZER PRIZE*

On Lenny McGrath's thirtieth birthday, there isn't much to celebrate. Her pet horse was just hit by lightning; her younger sister Babe is in jail for shooting her husband; their wild middle sister, Meg, didn't make it big in Hollywood; and Old Granddaddy has been hospitalized with yet another stroke. The plot may sound depressing, yet the reunion of these three sisters in Hazelhurst, Mississippi, is a laugh-a-minute comedy about the importance of family ties and trying to make the best of every situation. The play tackles some weighty subjects — including suicide, infidelity, and attempted murder — with off-the-wall southern-fried humor, reminding us that sometimes the only thing separating comedy and tragedy is perspective. Nearly every aspect of this play — the plot, the characters, the dialogue — is perfectly poised between laughter and tears.

DAVID HENRY HWANG

## Golden Child

14–18 • Theatre Communications • 1998 • 62 pp.

Long before it was popular to record the oral histories of older family members, ten-year-old David Henry Hwang realized the importance of preserving the memories of his grandmother, who was born in China and immigrated to the United States as a young woman. Asked to spend his summer vacation with her, Hwang taped her memories and later compiled a ninety-page family history. Nearly thirty years passed before he returned to that document and began writing *Golden Child*. In his play, a middle-aged Chinese-American man, married and expecting his first child, is visited by the ghost of his mother, Eng Ahn, who recounts events from her childhood. Most of the story is set in Southeast China in 1918–1919; at that time, the family converted from Confucianism to Christianity — an event that had tragic consequences. But that change also made possible the unbinding of Ahn's feet and the possibility of her attending school, choosing her own spouse, and immigrating to America. This deeply moving play paints an insightful picture of how shared traditions and cultural changes affect several generations of one family.

JONATHAN LARSON

## Rent

14–18 • Morrow • 1997 • 160 pp.

↭ PULITZER PRIZE

A musical that has inspired devotion from many young adults, *Rent* is an updating of the opera *La Bohème*, moved to New York's East Village in the 1980s. The heroes of the opera, a poet and a painter, are now a rocker and a filmmaker. The heroine, previously a ballet dancer with tuberculosis, is a club dancer with AIDS. Larson's contemporary version is gritty and hard-hitting, yet it features an element of hope not found in the original work. *Rent* contains very little dialogue, and one of the pleasures of seeing it onstage or listening to the recording is hearing its diverse musical styles, which include rock, country, pop anthems, and even a tango. However, reading the complete libretto is equally rewarding — an experience similar to reading a novel-in-poems. The book also includes photographs from the stage production and an oral history of the show's evolution. Tragically, thirty-five-year-old Jonathan Larson died of an undiagnosed heart ailment hours after the final dress rehearsal; this groundbreaking play went on to run for years on Broadway, become a major motion picture, and attract a generation of young fans.

JEROME LAWRENCE AND ROBERT E. LEE

## Inherit the Wind

14–18 • Random House • 1955 • 144 pp.

Jerome Lawrence and Robert E. Lee dramatize the 1925 "Scopes Monkey Trial," in which a Tennessee science teacher was tried for teaching evolution in a public school. Though the play changed the names of the real people — in the actual court case, Clarence Darrow served as defense attorney and William Jennings Bryan as the prosecutor — it remains a fairly accurate summation of the trial. Highlighted by engaging characterizations and literate dialogue, this bracing courtroom drama presents both sides of the creationism versus evolutionism debate still being waged today.

ARTHUR MILLER

## The Crucible

14–18 • Viking • 1953 • 176 pp.

Though far from an accurate account of the 1692 Salem witch trials, Arthur Miller's historical drama works brilliantly as theater. The play offers convincing characterizations, forbidden love, unsettling scenes of teenage hysteria, courtroom battles, a tragic hero, and a plot that moves, with mounting suspense, toward its gripping and inevitable conclusion. That Miller's story of community hysteria and rumormongering was also a pointed allegory of McCarthyism — the anti-Communist "witch-hunting" crusades of the early 1950s — adds another layer of history and significance to this towering drama.

EUGENE O'NEILL

## Ah, Wilderness!

14–18 • Random House • 1933 • 141 pp.

E ugene O'Neill's autobiographical masterpiece, *Long Day's Journey into Night*, may depict the most tormented family in theater history, yet his earlier *Ah, Wilderness!* contains one of the warmest family portraits that has ever graced the stage or page. Set in 1906 small-town Connecticut, O'Neill's only comedy concerns sixteen-year-old Richard Miller, a lovestruck kid with outsized emotions. Living with his wise parents, numerous siblings, a charmingly alcoholic uncle, and a sad but understanding spinster aunt, Richard — given to quoting poetry and making grandiloquent statements about life — becomes distraught when a misunderstanding ends his first romance. He responds to his heartbreak by going on a date with a wild older woman and returning home drunk, but it's just a small misstep on the road to maturity. Richard soon patches up things with his girl and regains the respect of his parents. This gentle family comedy, which takes place over the Fourth of July holiday, represents old-fashioned Americana at its best.

WILLIAM SHAKESPEARE, ARTHUR LAURENTS (LIBRETTO), AND STEPHEN SONDHEIM (LYRICS)

## Romeo and Juliet and West Side Story

14–18 • Laurel Leaf • 1965 • 256 pp.

I n print for over forty years, this paperback volume pairs two plays with a particular appeal for young adults: Shakespeare's sixteenth-century tragedy of star-crossed young lovers from rival families in Verona and the twentieth-century musical that borrowed the same plot to tell the tale of a doomed teenage romance played out against a background of gang warfare in New York City. Introduced by Norris Houghton and often used in classrooms, the book gives readers the opportunity to compare two theatrical works written nearly four hundred years apart; both still have the power to grab emotions, and their texts sing with poetry and song.

NEIL SIMON

## *Brighton Beach Memoirs*

14–18 • Random House • 1984 • 130 pp.

Fifteen-year-old Eugene Morris Jerome, a baseball fanatic and aspiring writer, serves as the wisecracking narrator of this heartwarming yet wickedly funny autobiographical play. In the fall of 1937, his Brooklyn home is crowded with an overworked father, a harried mother, an irresponsible older brother, and a widowed aunt with two daughters. Eugene, enduring the physical and psychological trials of adolescence, wryly observes his relatives' often-serious ordeals. Dad has a heart attack, and his brother Stanley gambles away his paycheck. But Eugene quietly recognizes the underlying love and support that keep the family united despite their occasional quarrels and teasing. Neil Simon continues this story in two more highly regarded plays: *Biloxi Blues,* which describes Eugene's boot camp experiences in World War II, and *Broadway Bound,* in which Eugene and his older brother begin writing comedy.

NEIL SIMON

## *Lost in Yonkers*

14–18 • Random House • 1991 • 128 pp.

⮞ *PULITZER PRIZE*

After writing a score of hit Broadway comedies, Neil Simon won the Pulitzer Prize for this more serious effort, a touching family drama that still features his usual humorous dialogue. After their mother's death, a pair of teenage brothers are sent to spend several months with their stern, German-immigrant grandmother and her mentally disturbed daughter, Bella. Arty and Jay slowly come to understand how Grandma Kurnitz's cold, domineering personality has emotionally stunted each of her children, particularly childlike Aunt Bella, who longs for love despite her disability. Set during World War II, this sensitive play will provoke both laughter and tears as it looks deep into the heart of this damaged family.

ALFRED UHRY

## The Last Night of Ballyhoo

14–18 • Theatre Communications • 1997 • 99 pp.

For the Freitag family of Atlanta, Georgia, December 1939 means trimming the Christmas tree, attending the premiere of *Gone With the Wind,* and planning for Ballyhoo, an annual series of parties, dinners, and dances that draw Jewish young people from all over the South. Twenty-year-old Sunny Freitag, home from Wellesley College for the winter break, is unexpectedly asked to Ballyhoo by a brash, charismatic New Yorker, while her cousin Lala, a college dropout, is invited by a knavish family acquaintance. Alfred Uhry writes about a delicate subject — the assimilation of a southern Jewish family that embraces Christian traditions and expresses disdain for Eastern European Jews — with honesty and humor. The play's setting on the eve of World War II adds a poignant element; the concluding scene of a family Sabbath dinner — which may be viewed realistically or as Sunny's dream for the future — caps the drama with a perfect note of grace.

THORNTON WILDER

## Our Town: A Play in Three Acts

14–18 • Coward-McCann • 1938 • 128 pp.

Though specifically set in Grover's Corners, New Hampshire, in the early twentieth century, *Our Town* maintains a timeless, otherworldly quality. This unconventional play, narrated by a character known as "the Stage Manager" and traditionally performed without props, explores such monumental subjects as life, love, and death. The central characters — George Gibbs and Emily Webb — grow up, fall in love, and marry. Then Emily dies in childbirth, joining the other dead souls who calmly chat and reminisce in the windy, hilltop cemetery outside the town. Given the opportunity to revisit her past, Emily returns to observe her twelfth birthday, but she is so overwhelmed by the fleeting, everyday beauty of life that she gratefully returns to the cemetery. A work of amazing depth and resonance, *Our Town* is among the greatest and most enduring of all American plays.

TENNESSEE WILLIAMS

## *The Glass Menagerie*

14–18 • Random House • 1945 • 105 pp.

The first major success of Tennessee Williams's illustrious theater career, *The Glass Menagerie* remains one of his most poetic and heartfelt works. This autobiographical "memory play" concerns a discontented young man, his handicapped sister, and a mother who revels in the past yet is anxious to find a "gentleman caller" for her painfully shy daughter. Lyrically written, this delicate domestic drama is nearly impossible to forget.

PAUL ZINDEL

## *The Effect of Gamma Rays on Man-in-the-Moon Marigolds*

14–18 • HarperCollins • 1971 • 128 pp.

↬ *PULITZER PRIZE*

When the editor Charlotte Zolotow saw an early production of this drama on public television, she immediately recognized Paul Zindel's keen understanding of adolescent psychology and invited him to try writing books for young adults. His success as a novelist (*The Pigman; My Darling, My Hamburger*) eventually eclipsed his career as a playwright, though this drama remains one of his finest works in any medium. In it, an embittered, self-pitying divorcée rages at the universe and her two teenage daughters, one of whom seeks refuge in the world of science. Simple and heartbreaking, Zindel's drama is a testament to the human spirit, which — like the marigolds exposed to radiation in Tillie's school science project — struggles to grow and thrive under the bleakest conditions.

# Poetry and Poetic Novels

MOST OF US first encounter poetry while still in the crib in the form of classic nursery rhymes; our childhood years are filled with jump rope ditties, schoolyard chants, and silly limericks. Unfortunately, this innate love of verse is often lost by the time we become teenagers. Many young adults regard poetry as something only to be studied and analyzed for English class.

These selections highlight poetry that will especially appeal to teenagers — both in and out of the classroom. They include standard works by writers such as Robert Frost and Langston Hughes, as well as unusual recent books that document the life of George Washington Carver and the streets of Harlem. These books pair poems on similar topics by male and female authors, provide multicultural perspectives, and present poems in graphic formats. They use diverse poetic forms — rhyming, free verse, blank verse, concrete poetry — and cover an amazing range of subjects. Because the novel in free verse has become a favorite of young adult writers over the last decade, several fine examples — such as Virginia Euwer Wolff's *Make Lemonade* and Karen Hesse's *Out of the Dust* — have been included.

Young adults who think of poetry as something relegated to dusty textbooks may be surprised by the fresh insights, emotional impact, and pure entertainment found in many of these titles.

LORI CARLSON, EDITOR

## Cool Salsa: Bilingual Poems on Growing Up Latino in the United States

12–14 • Holt • 1994 • 160 pp.

Some of the poets represented in this volume were born in Argentina, Guatemala, and Venezuela but now live in the United States. Others are second- and third-generation Americans of Cuban, Mexican, and Bolivian descent. All celebrate their heritage in this collection of poems about the Latino experience in the United States. Pablo Medina describes the life of a young immigrant in New York City. Abelardo B. Delgado contrasts Mexican and American perspectives on the Day of the Dead. Sandra Cisneros extols the joy of pig roasts and hot dogs. Each poem is presented in both English and Spanish except for a handful that blend the two. Frequently studied in multicultural poetry units and in English as a Second Language classes, this book was followed in 2005 by *Red Hot Salsa: Poems on Being Young and Latino in the United States*.

CATHERINE CLINTON, EDITOR
STEPHEN ALCORN, ILLUSTRATOR

## I, Too, Sing America: Three Centuries of African American Poetry

12–14 • Houghton Mifflin • 1998 • 112 pp.

Lucy Terry was the first known African-American poet. Her 1746 verse, "Bars Fight," was passed down orally for generations before being published in 1855; now it forms the cornerstone of this historical survey. Presented chronologically, each entry contains a brief biography, a few words about the author's skills, goals, and influence, and an example of his or her work. The volume includes, among others, Phillis Wheatley's last poem, "Liberty and Peace"; selections by Paul Laurence Dunbar, Langston Hughes, and Countee Cullen; Gwendolyn Brooks's tributes to Martin Luther King, Jr., and Malcolm X; and entries by the contemporary poets Maya Angelou, Alice Walker, and Rita Dove. Most, though not all, explore racial identity and experience in a volume that serves as a solid introduction to African-American poetry.

SHARON CREECH

## *Love That Dog*

12–14 • Harper • 2001 • 105 pp.

People often argue about which book written by the highly versatile author Sharon Creech they like the most — her Newbery Medal–winning *Walk Two Moons*, *The Wanderer*, *Absolutely Normal Chaos*, or *Heartbeat*. But her slim love letter to teachers, poetry, and poets — *Love That Dog* — may well prove her most enduring title. In a free verse journal chronicling a school year, Jack at first insists that poetry belongs to girls. But his teacher, Miss Stretchberry, gradually engages his interest and gets him to develop his own poem. As his journal entries get longer and longer, Jack tackles complex works. William Carlos Williams, William Blake, Robert Frost, and particularly Walter Dean Myers convince Jack that poetry can be appreciated by boys as well as girls. When Myers himself visits the class, Jack develops a severe case of hero worship.

With a title inspired by the Walter Dean Myers poem "Love That Boy" and its obvious appeal for a classroom unit, *Love That Dog* has made its way into the hearts of its readers and has convinced many a young person to give poetry a chance.

HELEN FROST

## *Keesha's House*

12–14 • Farrar, Straus • 2003 • 128 pp.

✒ *PRINTZ HONOR*

Seven troubled adolescents end up at Keesha's house, which offers shelter, safety, and comfort. Stephie and Jason are about to become parents; Carmen's drinking problem has taken her to juvenile detention; Harris has been thrown out of his house because he is gay; Katie has been abused by her stepfather; Dortay is negotiating the foster care system. Keesha, determined to support herself and go to school, has brought them all together. Some teens simply pass through the house; others form a family. Although all of these themes have been explored many times in fiction for the young, Helen Frost makes her characters and their lives vibrant by her use of sestinas and sonnets to convey their thoughts: "All my questions are like wind-tossed / papers in the street."

Touching on the issues of race and class, this spare and eloquent novel has been performed onstage. Most frequently, it appears on poetry reading lists; taking poetic forms most often associated with romantic writings, Frost has given them new life and vitality in this original, thought-provoking novel.

ROBERT FROST, AUTHOR
THOMAS W. NASON, ILLUSTRATOR

## You Come Too: Favorite Poems for Readers of All Ages

14–18 · Holt · 1959 · 112 pp.

One of the twentieth century's most beloved and respected poets, Robert Frost won the Pulitzer Prize four times for his verse. This sampling includes some of his greatest triumphs, including "Stopping by Woods on a Snowy Evening," "The Death of the Hired Man," and "The Road Not Taken." Because his poems frequently focus on birch trees, fireflies, and farm life, many view Frost as a folksy nature poet — and his work can certainly be enjoyed on that level. But repeated readings reveal layers of meaning just below each homespun surface, as Frost explores such weighty themes as mortality, alienation, and heartbreak. He is also a stylist of the highest order, using not just standard rhyme patterns but frequently blank verse (unrhymed iambic pentameter) in poems such as "Mending Wall." This volume provides a brief, accessible introduction to Frost's work.

JAN GREENBERG, EDITOR

## Heart to Heart: New Poems Inspired by Twentieth-Century American Art

12–14 · Abrams · 2001 · 80 pp.
⊰ PRINTZ HONOR

Jan Greenberg — a novelist who, with Sandra Jordan, has also written excellent biographies of the artists Jackson Pollock, Andy Warhol, and Vincent Van Gogh — combines her love of art and literature in a volume that pairs works of modern American art with new poems by over forty contemporary writers. The poets themselves selected the works they wanted to write about, resulting in a dazzling array of artistic formats (including paintings, photographs, and sculpture) and poetic styles (from sonnets to free verse.) Nancy Willard writes about a pair of carousel horses captured in a photograph by Eric Lindbloom. David Harrison's "It's Me!" assumes the voice of Marilyn Monroe, represented multiple times in Andy Warhol's famous silkscreen. Jane Yolen tackles Grant Wood's "American Gothic." The artwork is well reproduced and the poems are fresh and engaging in a book that inspires readers to put words to their own favorite art.

KAREN HESSE

## *Out of the Dust*

12–14 • Scholastic • 1997 • 227 pp.

✎ *NEWBERY MEDAL*

Set in the Dust Bowl of Oklahoma in the 1930s, *Out of the Dust* concentrates on fourteen-year-old Billie Jo. When her mother dies in a tragic accident, Billie Jo's and her father's lives are changed forever. In a text marked by rhythm, even music, every word and every line break have been selected with care — from the opening sentence to the final lines: "And I stretch my fingers over the keys, / and I play."

For this book, Karen Hesse conducted extensive research in newspapers of the period, careful observing the daily weather reports. As she wrote, her narrative evolved. In the original manuscript, Billie Jo wrote poetry and played the piano, but those talents seemed inconsistent with her training and life. Because Hesse wanted to show a child who experienced a simple life, she decided that free verse would be the ideal form to convey the sparseness.

Many authors have the ability to create books quite popular with young people; some can write complex books not always accessible to the young. A few, like Hesse, combine exceptional quality with great appeal. She tackles subjects of significance in her books and does not hesitate to examine them honestly. In *Out of the Dust*, the heat, the dust, the longing, the anguish, the pain of living, and the healing from tragedy have all been presented in spare, haunting verse.

LANGSTON HUGHES

## Selected Poems of Langston Hughes

14–18 • Knopf • 1959 • 320 pp.

An iconic figure of the Harlem Renaissance — the cultural explosion of African-American art, literature, and music in 1920s New York — Langston Hughes continues to be read and enjoyed in the twenty-first century. This compilation of his work, selected by Hughes himself, draws verse from seven volumes as well as several that never appeared in book form. Some, such as "The Weary Blues," are "jazz poems" — originally written to be accompanied by music at Harlem nightclubs. There are religious poems, spiritual meditations, and gospel shouts. A group of seriocomic, first-person poems explains how feisty Madam Alberta K. Johnson survives the Depression. Many of the entries, including the much-anthologized "I, Too" and "The Negro Speaks of Rivers," celebrate the poet's heritage. This stylistically diverse and emotionally powerful collection demonstrates why Hughes is considered one of America's great poets.

PAUL B. JANECZKO, SELECTOR

## The Place My Words Are Looking For: What Poets Say About and Through Their Work

12–14 • Bradbury • 1990 • 133 pp.

This volume contains poems by some major names in children's and young adult books, including Eve Merriam, Jack Prelutsky, Nancy Willard, Karla Kuskin, and X. J. Kennedy. Written in both rhymed and free verse, the poems — some whimsical, some serious, some laugh-out-loud funny — concern kid-friendly topics such as skate-boarding, soda pop, and surviving sixth grade. What makes the collection especially appealing is that most of the entries are followed by author's notes; they explain why the creators write poetry, reveal what inspired a particular piece, or offer advice to readers and aspiring young poets.

PAUL B. JANECZKO, SELECTOR
CHRIS RASCHKA, ILLUSTRATOR

## A Poke in the I: A Collection of Concrete Poems

12–14 • Candlewick • 2001 • 48 pp.

A treat for both the ear and the eye, this unusual, highly browsable volume contains thirty concrete poems — verses whose typography, spacing, and graphic arrangement add an extra layer of meaning and enjoyment to the words on the page. The lines in Roger McGough's "A Weak Poem" trail feebly toward the bottom of the book. Sylvia Cassedy visibly demonstrates the importance of not stepping out of line in "Queue." Words shuttle across a double-page spread in Monica Kulling's "Tennis Anyone?" Other poems follow the trajectory of a pigeon's flight and a sled's downhill slide, while others mimic the shapes of Popsicles, dandelions, and giraffes. Chris Raschka's splashy color illustrations add to the appeal of this volume; it may even inspire readers to create their own concrete poems.

GARRISON KEILLOR, EDITOR

## Good Poems

14–18 • Viking • 2002 • 504 pp.

This aptly titled volume gathers nearly three hundred poems under such far-flung categories as "Day's Work," "Sons and Daughters," "Failure," and "Snow." The breadth of material is amazing, ranging from Shakespearean sonnets to classics from Emily Dickinson and Robert Frost to new poems by contemporary, still largely unknown writers. The subject matter, themes, and poetic styles are diverse, but these accessible poems all share compelling language and a narrative line or emotional impact that lingers in the memory. Readers of every age and sophistication will discover literary gold here, but *Good Poems* may be especially prized by young adult readers as a favorite volume of verse to be studied and underlined, memorized, quoted aloud, and shared with friends as it gets carried from high school classroom to college dorm to a permanent place on the family bookshelf.

WALTER DEAN MYERS

## *Here in Harlem: Poems in Many Voices*

12–14 • Holiday House • 2004 • 88 pp.

Walter Dean Myers, who grew up in Harlem, reaches back to his youth with a collection of first-person poems that represent various citizens from that vibrant New York neighborhood in the late 1940s. Each of the poems — untitled, but identified by the name of the speaker, along with his or her age and occupation — is based on someone the author personally knew, or knew about, as he was growing up. Framed by the memories of an eighty-seven-year-old retired singer, the book also introduces the local undertaker, several veterans, a newsstand dealer, a numbers runner, a party girl, and a handful of high school and college students. The mostly free verse poems reveal the dreams, disappointments, and daily experiences of these well-defined yet prototypal characters in a collection that brings an entire community to life in verse.

MARILYN NELSON

## *Carver: A Life in Poems*

12–14 • Front Street • 2001 • 103 pp.

↜ *NEWBERY HONOR/NATIONAL BOOK AWARD FINALIST*

In a collage of fifty-nine free verse poems, George Washington Carver emerges as a private, scholarly man of great personal faith and social purpose. A child of enslaved parents who was raised by a white couple, Carver became a chemist and devoted his life to the betterment of black Americans. That journey has been told in poems from the various points of view of those he encountered along the way. But the emotion, the heart and soul of Carver and those around him, distinguish these verses:

> It was 1915, the year
> of trenches and poison gas
> when Booker T. Washington
> rushed home from New Haven
> to die in his own bed.
> For the first days after the funeral
> Carver sat and rocked, sat

and rocked. For months
he could not teach,
would not go into the lab.
. . . . He had seen Washington and Carver together
winning back the birthright of the disinherited.
This is how a dream dies.

Someone who had always written poetry for adults, Marilyn Nelson believed she was creating another volume for them. But Stephen Roxburgh, her editor, thought this collection would work well with an adolescent audience and designed the book accordingly, adding photographs to enhance the poetry. The resulting slim volume, winner of numerous awards, combines free verse and biography in a totally satisfying and unprecedented manner, ideal for reading aloud and discussing.

NAOMI SHIHAB NYE AND PAUL B. JANECZKO, EDITORS

## *I Feel a Little Jumpy Around You: Her Poems and His Poems Collected in Pairs*

12–14 • Simon & Schuster • 1996 • 261 pp.

In an intriguing format, Naomi Nye and Paul Janeczko pair similarly themed poems by male and female writers. These dual entries explore topics ranging from first kisses and marriage to apples and tomatoes, reflecting the similarities and differences between the way each sex perceives and experiences the subject. Sophisticated and occasionally enigmatic, the poems are written in a variety of styles — with nearly two hundred entries, there is sure to be something for every taste. Refreshingly, a number of unknown and undiscovered poets are represented, and the contributors' notes, in which the poets describe how gender has influenced their work, will fuel classroom discussion and debate.

NAOMI SHIHAB NYE

## *19 Varieties of Gazelle: Poems of the Middle East*

12–14 • Greenwillow • 2002 • 142 pp.

↝ *NATIONAL BOOK AWARD FINALIST*

The daughter of an American mother and a Palestinian father, Naomi Shihab Nye was born and raised in the United States, but she has celebrated her Middle Eastern heritage in fiction, autobiographical essays, and poetry. These sixty poems, collected here for the first time, help fill a void in young adult literature as they describe the warm details of Middle Eastern family life, which endure despite the region's political divisions, and recount the conflicted experiences of Arab Americans growing up in the United States. Published within a year of the September 11 terrorist attacks — an event acknowledged in the author's introduction and the volume's first poem — the book makes a poignant plea for peace and healing.

MARY OLIVER

## *New and Selected Poems: Volume One*

14–18 • Beacon • 1992 • 272 pp.

◁○ *NATIONAL BOOK AWARD FINALIST*

## *New and Selected Poems: Volume Two*

14–18 • Beacon • 2005 • 178 pp.

The titles of the individual poems evoke pastoral images: "Lonely, White Fields," "Hummingbird Pauses at the Trumpet Vine," "The Lilies Break Open Over the Dark Water," "Skunk Cabbage." America's preeminent nature poet presents dozens of minutely observed free and blank verse poems that offer fresh, often startling images of crows and kookaburras, poppies and peonies, spring azures, late summer roses, and the first snows of winter while asking the reader to consider life, mortality, and the human experience in the natural world. Mary Oliver has won the Pulitzer Prize and National Book Award for her poetry, and these volumes — which also include a few entries about her youth ("Spring in the Classroom") and the lives of assorted grandparents, aunts, and uncles — demonstrate her mastery of the form. After reading these thoughtful and penetrating poems, readers may find themselves looking at the natural world with a newfound sense of wonder.

LIZ ROSENBERG

## The Invisible Ladder: An Anthology of Contemporary American Poems for Young Readers

12–14 • Holt • 1996 • 144 pp.

Despite being Pulitzer Prize winners, poets such as Rita Dove, Galway Kinnell, Carolyn Kizer, and Maxine Kumin are generally unknown to teenagers. This volume helps rectify the situation by introducing forty modern American poets to young adults. Arranged alphabetically, each entry is accompanied by two photographs — one showing the poet as a child, the other as an adult — and includes a first-person statement about how the writer came to discover poetry as a young person. Each poet is represented by one to five selections of sophisticated yet generally accessible free verse poems on subjects ranging from eating blackberries to loneliness and death. A final "Ways to Use This Book" suggests how young people can better appreciate poetry through memorization and recitation, by writing "answering poems" to published verses, and finding inspiration in the specific subjects, themes, and formats used by the poems in this volume.

CYNTHIA RYLANT, AUTHOR
WALKER EVANS, PHOTOGRAPHER

## Something Permanent

12–14 • Harcourt • 1994 • 64 pp.

Walker Evans's stunning black-and-white photographs inspire over two dozen poems that poignantly capture moments of both despair and hopefulness during the Depression. Cynthia Rylant's stark free verse uses a minimum of words to explore entire life stories: a rural boy acquires a sense of self-esteem when he is asked to pose for a photographer; a pair of empty shoes helps a grieving family through their sadness; a young man's job at a filling station first inspires jealousy, then compassion, among his rivals. Though the book concerns a long-gone era, the mesmerizing quality of the stark photographs and plainspoken poems will strike a visceral chord with today's young adults.

ALLAN WOLF

## *New Found Land*

12–14 • Candlewick • 2004 • 501 pp.

In a blank verse epic, Allan Wolf presents the Lewis and Clark expedition through fourteen alternating narrators. Although the expected participants have been given their due — the two men and Sacagawea — Lewis's dog, a Newfoundland named Seaman (who says his true name is Oolum), serves as the narrator and sets the stage for some of the key events on the journey.

Successfully combining historic research with a compelling narrative form, the author has written a challenging and unique book. It expands the possibilities of the free verse novel, demonstrating how history and poetry can be successfully intertwined.

VIRGINIA EUWER WOLFF

## *Make Lemonade*

12–14 • Holt • 1993 • 200 pp.

## *True Believer*

12–14 • Atheneum • 2001 • 264 pp.

⟿ *PRINTZ HONOR/NATIONAL BOOK AWARD*

In *Make Lemonade,* an inner-city fourteen-year-old girl, LaVaughn, desperately wants a ticket out of her housing project, so she agrees to baby-sit for the two children of a seventeen-year-old unwed mother, Jolly. Ultimately Jolly loses her factory job. But LaVaughn prods Jolly to return to school, where she can save herself and her children — make lemonade from the lemons of her life. In *True Believer,* LaVaughn, now fifteen, once again narrates a story in blank verse, but this time it is her own. "Me and Myrtle & Annie, / we all want to save our bodies for our right husband / when he comes along." Annie and Myrtle join "Cross Your Legs for Jesus," but LaVaughn begins her own solo journey toward faith. Along the way, this attractive protagonist falls in love, finds a vocation, and continues to work toward college.

Because of Virginia Euwer Wolff's brilliant use of blank verse, readers move along, totally in sync with LaVaughn; they laugh, cry, celebrate, and worry with her. Because the author, deliberately, never identifies the ethnicity of the characters, some have assumed LaVaughn to be white; others, black; still others, Asian. Consequently these two volumes have as many different interpretations as they have readers, again a testament to their subtlety and craft.

# Politics and Social Conscience

OFTEN THE CRITICAL QUESTIONS of the adolescent years revolve around three areas — sex, religion, and politics. Sexual questions have been addressed in books for teens since the 1970s, and religious and spiritual issues have become a current favorite topic in books for adolescents. But if a Martian read the body of books for adolescents, he would be convinced that they hung out in shopping malls, with no political or social connection to their society. Rarely do books for teenagers show them engaged in larger issues or focused outside themselves.

There are some exceptions to this trend, and all the books cited here give an idea of what authors might choose to write about. It can only be hoped that they address this last taboo in young adult literature. At a time when teens have been observed in increasing numbers to volunteer, work for a politician, or argue about issues such as the environment, their literature needs to reflect their increased participation in the community and society.

......................

JULIA ALVAREZ

### *In the Time of the Butterflies*

14–18 • Algonquin • 1994 • 325 pp.

In the Dominican Republic during the Trujillo dictatorship, the Mirabal sisters became heroines in the cause of freedom; in 1960 three of the sisters were murdered for their part in an underground plot to overthrow the government. Julia Alvarez breathes life into the stories of Patria, Minerva, and Maria Terese, who were known as "las mariposas" (butterflies) in the underground. Beginning with the recollections of the surviving sister, the novel develops each of the sisters in her own distinct voice. Alvarez builds the narrative gradually, allowing readers to empathize with the characters. These ordinary children consciously take action and become heroic because of their choices.

Alvarez brilliantly captures the terror-filled atmosphere of a police state. But this rich story, filled with a strong sense of place, has been steeped in actual events and filled with hope and love.

AVI

## *Nothing but the Truth*

12–14 • Orchard • 1991 • 179 pp.

⟡ *NEWBERY HONOR*

Freshman Philip Malloy wants to be on the track team, but his failing grade in English makes him ineligible. In a class with the teacher he wishes to escape, Miss Narwin, Philip begins each morning humming "The Star-Spangled Banner" when the students have been asked to remain silent. Suspended from school, Philip finds that things quickly go out of control when his minor infraction becomes a national scandal.

Taking place over a few weeks and structured as a series of diary entries, memos, letters, radio transcripts, and dialogues, the novel shows the events from different points of view. Hence the reader serves as the detective, trying to discover where the truth really lies.

Widely read in schools, *Nothing but the Truth* naturally encourages class discussions about freedom of speech, the Bill of Rights, censorship, and piecing together the truth from media coverage. But it also works for independent reading — a powerful, entertaining novel from beginning to end.

CAROLYN COMAN

## *Many Stones*

12–14 • Front Street • 2000 • 158 pp.

⟡ *PRINTZ HONOR/NATIONAL BOOK AWARD FINALIST*

Berry Morgan's older sister, Laura, has been murdered in South Africa; she went there to teach to try to help Nelson Mandela's new government. Obliged to travel with her divorced father for the memorial service, Berry does not look forward to their trip. But after she and her father encounter South Africans who search for ways to forgive apartheid, Berry realizes she must begin her own reconciliation. Her problems, in fact, begin to decrease in size the more she realizes what has happened to those in South Africa: "Nothing I know comes close to being a matter of life and death."

In a quiet ode to the grieving process that connects the personal and political, *Many Stones* focuses on the inner landscape of a confused and unhappy teenager, grappling with the issues of a foreign country in transition.

ROBERT CORMIER

## *I Am the Cheese*

12–14 • Pantheon • 1977 • 234 pp.

I am riding the bicycle and I am on Route 31 in Monument, Massachusetts, on my way to Rutterburg, Vermont, and I'm pedaling furiously." With these innocent words, Robert Cormier begins a story of deception and lies. Next an official transcript appears, an interview between fourteen-year-old Adam Farmer, the protagonist, and Brint, an interrogator. The narrative shifts again, to a third-person omniscient voice. Skillfully weaving these three points of view, Cormier builds a story full of tension, mystery, and secrets. Living in a small New England city, Adam begins to realize that something seems odd about his family. He then discovers two birth certificates in his name and begins to wonder about his family. His father reveals that they have lived under an alias because of his testimony at a special Senate committee. On a trip to Vermont to avoid their enemies, a deliberate car accident kills Adam's mother. Adam is transported to a "confinement facility," where he is constantly drugged and brutally interviewed about details his father may have revealed. Only in his own mind does he ride the bike, in freedom, to Vermont; in the end, the reader understands that Adam's first-person narration has been completely unreliable.

Disillusioned by Nixon and the Watergate era, Cormier chose to write about a corrupt government agency. He actually published his own telephone number in the book and got thousands of calls from his fans over his lifetime. Often they just wanted to speak to a real writer, but sometimes they needed to discuss serious problems; Cormier loved having a personal connection with his readers.

Brilliantly executed, *I Am the Cheese* explores how evil often is inflicted on the young and the innocent. A sophisticated, cunningly developed psychological thriller, it raises important questions about the misuse and corruption of government.

CHRIS CRUTCHER

## The Sledding Hill

12–14 • Greenwillow • 2005 • 230 pp.

Eddie Proffit loses both his father and his best friend, Billy, in freak accidents within weeks of each other. He's also about to lose his favorite class, *Really* Modern Literature, taught by an almost-militant but likable librarian. To make things even worse, his mother has been spending time with the nefarious Sanford Tarter. A repressive, bordering-on-sadistic English teacher at Eddie's school, Tarter is also the manipulative minister at the fundamentalist church that Eddie's mother has embraced. When a Chris Crutcher novel taught in *Really* Modern Literature is challenged by one of Tarter's minions, a campaign begins to rid the library of all of Crutcher's books.

The novel is narrated by the dead Billy — in a manner reminiscent of Alice Sebold's *Lovely Bones*. A lot of issues are covered: one Youth for Christ member comes out of the closet, and Crutcher presents his view of censorship and reading in general: "Stories aren't good or evil . . . just reflections of one person's perception of the world. One kid might read that story and feel recognized, might find a connection. Another kid might read the same story and be offended or angered or bored. If those two students got together and talked about their reactions to the story, they'd know each other a little better."

Ultimately, a group of determined young people speak about this particular book and censorship. Their impassioned speeches give another dimension to the novel, presenting adolescents who take action that has political consequences.

KHALED HOSSEINI

## *The Kite Runner*

14–18 • Riverhead • 2003 • 372 pp.

A deeply flawed protagonist, Amir — a writer raised in Kabul, Afghanistan, in the 1960s and 1970s — moves to California and becomes a successful novelist. He remains haunted by a childhood incident in which he betrayed the trust of his best friend, Hassan, the son of the family servant; consequently Hassan was brutally beaten and raped by a neighborhood gang. In 2001 Amir learns that Hassan and his wife have been murdered by the Taliban and their son, Sohrab, needs to be rescued. As it turns out, the boy has been enslaved by the head of the gang, now a prominent Taliban official.

Although the book chiefly delineates the culture and politics of Afghanistan, it also serves as a deeply personal story about how choices made in childhood affect adult lives. It is rare that a book can be so brilliant from a literary point of view yet so timely. Often disturbing, *The Kite Runner* begs to be discussed with other readers. For that reason, it often gets chosen for parent-teen discussion groups or for an entire school or town to read.

NORMA HOWE

## *The Adventures of Blue Avenger*

12–14 • Holt • 1999 • 230 pp.

On the morning of his sixteenth birthday, David Bruce Schumacher, a modest and ordinary boy, legally changes his name to Blue Avenger. Blue, the secret champion of the underdog who even looks taller, can easily tell Omaha Nebraska Brown that he loves her. He then in quick order saves his principal from killer bees and helps his best friend, suffering from terrible skin problems, get free treatment. He even manages to get bullets outlawed in Oakland, California. Wonder of all wonders, Blue creates a lemon meringue pie that doesn't "weep." Throughout these adventures, Blue and Omaha, now a duo, discuss free will versus fate, a topic dear to both of them.

Funny, fast-paced, with two delightful protagonists, *The Adventures of Blue Avenger* takes comic book sensibility into the novel format. Because Blue fancies himself a hero, he willingly disturbs the universe

and rights personal and social wrongs. His wild story, with many ex-
traneous details, is wrapped up beautifully at the end; the tale continues in *Blue Avenger Cracks the Code* and *Blue Avenger and the Theory of
Everything.*

KEN KESEY

## One Flew Over the Cuckoo's Nest

14–18 • Viking • 1962 • 272 pp.

Narrated by the paranoid Chief Bromden — a huge man of mixed
Native American and European blood who fakes being deaf and
mute — the story takes place in an Oregon psychiatric hospital where
the Chief has lived for ten years. A swaggering former Marine, Randle
Patrick McMurphy, arrives; a prison farm inmate, he has had himself
committed to a mental institution to avoid work. Soon McMurphy
engages in a power struggle with "Big Nurse" Ratched, a twisted ad-
ministrator who gets patients to attack one another so that she can
stay in control. Although McMurphy wins some of the battles, ultimately, the nurse has him lobotomized. At the end of the book, Chief
Bromden, now a sane individual, escapes from the hospital and makes
his way to Canada.

Although the title comes from a nursery rhyme ("One flew east,
one flew west, and one flew over the cuckoo's nest"), the book works
best with sophisticated teens or adults. Based on Ken Kesey's experiences as an attendant in a psychiatric hospital just after graduating
from Stanford's creative writing program, the novel inspired an Os-
car-winning movie, starring Jack Nicholson. Through the years,
*One Flew Over the Cuckoo's Nest* has been read by adolescents as an
allegory about repressive institutions in America that pretend to be
benevolent.

BARBARA KINGSOLVER

## The Poisonwood Bible

14–18 • Harper • 1998 • 653 pp.

In 1959, an evangelical Baptist minister's family moves from Georgia
to the Belgian Congo (now Zaire) for three turbulent decades. Na-
than Price's determination to convert the natives to Christianity turns

out to be both foolhardy and even dangerous. A church angel and house devil, Price abuses his wife and daughters both physically and emotionally, and he refuses to understand why river baptism offends the natives in the village of Kalinga.

The story evolves through the points of view of Orelanna Price and her four daughters, each of them beautifully delineated. Fifteen-year-old Rachel resents her separation from normal teen life. Adah, who does not speak because of a birth injury, shrewdly observes the world around her. Leah, Adah's passionate and idealistic twin, throws herself into their new life, but the realities of the Congo erode her religious faith. Five-year-old Ruth May, excited and frightened, ultimately pays for this excursion with her life. Through the eyes of the women, we observe how the American and African cultures collide. The family saga takes place against the world backdrop of the election of Patrice Lumumba, the involvement of the Eisenhower administration in his assassination, and the dictatorship of Joseph Mobutu.

Barbara Kingsolver, who spent part of her own childhood in the Congo, took almost a year to hone five distinct narrative voices to represent different philosophical positions. Basically, she wanted to write a book that addressed the question: "What did we do to Africa, and how do we feel about it?" The women's responses represent extreme guilt, denial, social activism, empirical analysis, and spirituality. Even the title of the book contains a compelling metaphor. A poisonwood tree grows near the Prices' African home; although beautiful, it causes rashes and boils on the skin.

In Kingsolver's novel, the characters emerge as quirky, fallible human beings. Readers become swept up in their experiences, their observations, and their tragedies. Few modern novels have ever blended the political and the personal so brilliantly. Older readers often lament that they did not read *The Poisonwood Bible* in their high school English class; now many of this generation do.

GABRIEL GARCÍA MÁRQUEZ

## *One Hundred Years of Solitude*

14–18 • Harper • 1970 • 383 pp.

With no single plot or timeline, *One Hundred Years of Solitude* moves in circles. Both the history of Macondo, a small town in South America, and the founders of that town, the Buendía family, serve as protagonists; the story follows seven generations of Buendías and the rise and fall of the town. The patriarch, José Arcadio Buendía, marries his cousin Úrsula Iguarán; their fear of bearing deformed children lingers throughout the story.

Their children become both land usurpers and rebels during a period of civil war. Although Úrsula lives so long she cannot remember her age, none of the female Buendías matches her fortitude. Later generations combat foreign imperialism and set up banana plantations. In the end, the older generations are lost in nostalgia; the young people, in debauchery and isolation. The novel reflects the political, social, and economic ills of South America but contains fantastic events as well.

Having had a vision while driving one day, Gabriel García Márquez wrote the book barricaded in his study in Mexico. He imagined the entire story that had been plaguing him since 1942 and knew that he had to tell it the way his grandmother used to tell tales: she had an uncanny talent for relating the fantastic with deadpan seriousness. Fifteen months later, García Márquez emerged with a manuscript — and his wife presented him with a stack of bills. To write his masterpiece, García Márquez drew on memories of his grandparents, who married despite being cousins, and their household. But he mixed his personal experience with his political beliefs and concerns, and the economic history of Latin America became part of the novel.

An immediate commercial and critical success when it appeared in 1967, *Cien Años de Soledad* sold 50,000 copies in its first two weeks. Since then, the book has been translated into thirty languages, has sold over 30 million copies, and led to the Nobel Prize for literature for García Márquez.

With a labyrinthine structure and epic scope, the book has made its way onto summer reading lists across the nation; for most students, it provides a door to the incredible world of Latin American magical realism. According to one reviewer, it "is the first piece of literature since the Book of Genesis that should be required reading for the entire human race."

PHILIP ROTH

## The Plot Against America

14–18 • Houghton Mifflin • 2004 • 392 pp.

In his first foray into alternate history — or *uchronie,* time that doesn't exist — Philip Roth envisions a mesmerizing alternate world. In 1940 Charles Lindbergh defeats FDR in the presidential election, and young Philip, age seven, and his family face the consequences in their Weequahic neighborhood of Newark, New Jersey. Lindbergh's blatant anti-Semitism leads him to sign a nonaggression pact with Hitler; he holds a dinner party for von Ribbentrop, Hitler's foreign minister. Enacting new laws, the isolationists create an atmosphere of religious hatred, which ultimately leads to pogroms in America.

But the eerily logical narrative also provides a family portrait as the Roths respond to events that divide them personally and politically. The stable Jewish neighborhood descends into a nightmare of confusion, fear, and unpredictability. Written in the first person, with the adult Roth looking back on his childhood, the narrative alternates between his intensely personal world and these horrific national events.

Although Roth altered the presidential election, he tried to keep "everything else as close to factual truth" as he could in the years 1940–1942, the framework of the book. Historical figures such as Henry Ford and Walter Winchell inhabit this world. Roth uses, verbatim, Lindbergh's 1941 America First speech in Des Moines, Iowa. The end of the book contains pages of historical and biographical information, the true chronology of those years. In the book, however, Roth challenges how we look at history: "Turned wrong way round, the relentless unforeseen was what we school children studied as 'History,' harmless history, where everything unexpected in its own time is chronicled on the page as inevitable. The terror of the unforeseen is what the science of history hides."

In this novel Roth forces readers to assess aspects of the American culture — its worship of celebrities like Lindbergh, its support of government policy, no matter how wrong, and its willingness to descend into prejudice and hatred of various groups. Suspenseful as a thriller and one of the most accessible of Roth's recent books, *The Plot Against America* provides a wealth of material for classroom discussion.

JANET TASHJIAN

## The Gospel According to Larry

12–14 • Holt • 2001 • 227 pp.

Claiming that a manuscript was handed to her by a young man, Janet Tashjian presents his story to the reader. Seventeen-year-old Josh Swensen sees his mission quite clearly: "I've only wanted one thing my whole life — to contribute, to help make the world a better place." Josh sets up a Web site (www.thegospelaccordingtolarry.com) that delivers sermons against consumerism and about returning to nature. Although he's the son of an advertising executive, Josh owns only seventy-five possessions, so his sermons reflect how he actually lives. His best friend, Beth, whom he loves secretly, becomes an early advocate of the Web site; fan clubs are set up, the rock band U2 endorses Larry, and a huge Larryfest occurs. Suddenly, through Larry, Josh has become a celebrity. Although he tries to hide his identity, his nemesis lands on his doorstep with cameras, and Josh is hounded by the press day and night. In the end, Josh goes so far as to fake his own suicide, to give himself some space in his life. Fortunately, this utterly engaging protagonist returns in *Vote for Larry*.

Geekish, independent, longing for his mother (who has died), Josh wins over his readers quickly, and Beth proves an equally dynamic and believable supporting character. Josh's desire to make a difference, his inventiveness, and his passion make him a unique protagonist in the young adult canon. The book is ideal for adult-teen book groups and classroom discussion.

MARKUS ZUSAK

## I Am the Messenger

14–18 • Knopf • 2005 • 359 pp.

↬ *PRINTZ HONOR*

Nineteen-year-old Ed Kennedy, a cab driver, drifts aimlessly through life. His father has died of alcoholism; his mother verbally abuses him whenever she gets a chance. Only an attachment to an aging, odiferous dog and three friends with whom he plays cards connect him to the human race. But one day Ed inadvertently stops a bank robbery, after which strange messages are delivered to him in the form of playing cards. As he follows the instructions from his mysterious correspondent, he ends up helping people, entering the lonely or broken spaces of their lives. He rescues a woman who gets raped nightly by her drunken husband, reads to a widow who believes him her long-dead husband, and helps a priest gain Sunday attendance by throwing a huge party with free beer. As Ed completes his assignments, he grows in wisdom and humanity, and in the end, he starts to be a positive force in the lives of those closest to him.

Brilliantly structured, with four sections organized as a deck of cards, the story tracks the change of a very likable protagonist from a loser to someone readers would like as a friend. Ed has learned to take action in his own community and now understands that social conscience begins with those around him.

# Realistic Fiction

WHEN S. E. HINTON talked about teenagers in the 1960s and 1970s, she firmly believed that they wanted to read books about people exactly like them, living as they lived. In fact, since *The Catcher in the Rye* and *The Outsiders* appeared, realism has been the preferred form of writing for teens.

But over the next three decades, realistic novels became all too formulaic. Particularly during the 1990s they degenerated into an endless discussion of various teen dilemmas. All suffered from "problem novelitis" — where the problems overwhelmed the story and were the only reason for the fiction. Overly dramatic, emotional, pumped up on steroids, they served basically a therapeutic rather than a literary mission.

Although not completely absent in the twenty-first century, such books have definitely been on the wane. We see fewer first-person, angst-ridden novels, fewer descendants of Salinger's protagonist, Holden Caulfield, and more emphasis on plot, character, and storytelling. Since Harry Potter brought fresh air into books for adolescents, today's teens often seek to pick up humor, fantasy, science fiction, mystery, and romance a bit more frequently than they do books about teenagers just like themselves.

Whether the pendulum of publishing is swinging toward or away from this group of books, the following titles still work with the audience and function as fiction rather than therapy. Sometimes touched by magical realism — as in *Kit's Wilderness* or *Freak the Mighty* — they all possess a truth of emotion that characterizes the best of this genre.

··········—————————··········

DAVID ALMOND

## Kit's Wilderness

12–14 • Delacorte • 2000 • 240 pp.

⊸ *PRINTZ AWARD*

K it Watson, the thirteen-year-old narrator, and his two classmates, John Askew and Allie Keenan, live in a rural coal mining town in England. Kit and John come from a long line of miners, and Kit has recently come to the area to help care for his widowed grandfather. John pressures Kit to take part in a game called Death. When a spinning knife points to someone, they "die" — live alone in the dark and go to join the ghosts of boys killed in the coal mining accident in 1821. Although many of the participants consider this exercise a fantasy, Kit senses something more dangerous and makes a profound connection to these boys and the past.

Although written about David Almond's own town, three hundred miles north of London, the setting has appealed to many American readers because of its similarities to West Virginia and Pennsylvania coal towns. With haunting, lyrical prose and appealing supernatural elements, the book combines a realistic portrayal of the town with magical realism. A challenging book, *Kit's Wilderness* holds many surprises and rewards for those who come under its spell.

RUSSELL BANKS

## Rule of the Bone

14–18 • Harper • 1995 • 400 pp.

Y ou'll probably think I'm making a lot of this up just to make me sound better than I really am or smarter or even luckier but I'm not." In this totally authentic voice, fourteen-year-old Chappie Dorset relates the story of his life. He has a litany of miseries — divorced parents, an abusive stepfather, and an indifferent mother. Since he relieves the torpor of his existence with alcohol and marijuana, he steals money from his mother. As a result, he gets kicked out of his home in upstate New York, changes his name to Bone, and begins to hang around with people even more disreputable than he is. In time Bone heads down to Jamaica with a Rastafarian called I-Man in search of his real father.

Structured much like a modern *Adventures of Huckleberry Finn,* the novel takes place in the shopping mall culture of the late twentieth century and touches on issues of class and race. This poignant and riveting book succeeds because its readers empathize with Bone, a believable and insightful young man, and get swept up in his spiritual quest.

MARTHA BROOKS

## *True Confessions of a Heartless Girl*

14–18 • Farrar, Straus/Kroupa • 2003 • 181 pp.

Seventeen-year-old Noreen, a heartless girl, pregnant, untrusting and untrustworthy, has such low self-esteem that she has walked from one disaster to another. One stormy night, she leaves her most recent boyfriend and finds her way to a rundown café in a small town in Manitoba, Canada. There Lynda, a single mother, offers her lodging, because Lynda, once in trouble herself, had been befriended by Dolores, a seventy-six-year-old Native American. But continuing to cause problems for those she meets, Noreen starts a fire in the cabin she's given and loses her baby. Told from the viewpoints of all three women, the story looks at the power of community and how troubled teens can cope with their lives.

PAT CONROY

## *The Great Santini*

14–18 • Houghton Mifflin • 1976 • 448 pp.

A first novel replete with autobiography, *The Great Santini* features two amazing protagonists — or antagonists: Ben Meecham, seventeen at the beginning of the novel, and his fighter pilot father, Bull, a colonel in the U.S. Marine Corps. Bull calls himself "the Great Santini," a man who loves his flying and drinking buddies and his Catholic religion. But he abuses his wife and children, and Ben, the oldest son, suffers the most. Basically a nice kid, he struggles with his father's domineering and difficult ways. In one unforgettable scene, they battle on the basketball court; Ben says, "Do you know, Dad, that not one of us here has ever beaten you in a single game? Not checkers, not dominoes, not softball, nothing." When Colonel Meecham is killed in a plane crash, Ben must come to terms with his father in a completely different way.

Motivated by Pat Conroy's own adolescence and his relationship with his father, who "would make John Wayne look like a pansy," *The Great Santini* inspired the 1979 movie of the same name starring Robert Duvall. When Conroy's mother sued for divorce, she used the novel as evidence. But Conroy has also stated that he was raised by a man "who made all the United States of America the safest country on earth in the bloodiest century in all recorded history." This conflict of vision and emotion sits at the heart of this unforgettable novel.

## JULIE REECE DEAVER

### Say Goodnight, Gracie

12–14 • Harper/Zolotow • 1988 • 214 pp.

Morgan and her best friend, Jimmy, have been together since infancy; now seventeen-year-olds in high school, they share the same interests. Morgan takes acting workshops at Second City in Chicago; Jimmy dances in musicals, a modern Fred Astaire. When Jimmy tries out for a new play, Morgan cuts class to go with him; inseparable, they understand each other completely. Then the unthinkable happens: Jimmy is killed by a drunken driver, and Morgan has to piece together a life without him.

Julie Reece Deaver spends half the book developing Jimmy and Morgan and in the second part shows how everyone involved chooses a different manner in which to deal with their grief. Although Morgan does not choose a particularly healthy path of coping from a psychological point of view, her actions seems consistent with her character; she refuses to talk to anyone, experiences panic attacks and depression, and sleeps with Jimmy's jacket wrapped around her. Unique for its honest portrayal of the grieving process, this touching and highly emotional book helps readers understand what it means to suffer and survive a deep loss.

SHARON M. DRAPER

## Tears of a Tiger

12–14 • Atheneum • 1994 • 180 pp.

The author pulls no punches in this starkly realistic novel, which begins with the death of a teen in a car accident and ends with a suicide. Although a fine high school basketball player, Andy Jackson already suffers from low self-esteem before his best friend, Robert, is killed in the car Andy has been driving while drunk. The two other black teenagers in the accident manage to deal with their guilt — one finds God, the other a supportive girlfriend. But although Andy sees a therapist and explores his guilt — and the impact of the white society on him — he ultimately goes under and chooses suicide.

The book alternates between news clippings, student writings, Andy's first-person narrative, and school announcements in a mélange of voices. A schoolteacher for most of her career, Sharon Draper truly captures what can go wrong in school as well as the tensions that can exist between black and white students in any school. This short yet very sad novel, often a favorite in middle schools, was followed by two books about the same characters, *Forged by Fire* and *Darkness Before Dawn*.

JANET FITCH

## White Oleander

14–18 • Little, Brown • 1999 • 464 pp.

Astrid Magnussen, who ages from twelve to eighteen in the course of the novel, loses her mother, Ingrid, a feminist poet who is thrown into prison for murdering her ex-lover. Through years of foster care in Los Angeles, Astrid experiences unspeakable horrors — being shot at and mauled by dogs, searching for food in garbage cans, and many varieties of neglect. Yet she views her life with gratitude: as she has been sent from one foster mother to another, Astrid has learned about many women and how they suffer. Through all her struggles, she remains in touch with her mother. Over time Ingrid, as deadly as the white oleander plant of the title, has become a feminist icon and earns her freedom. Astrid then must face her greatest struggle — breaking free from her mother.

This story of a fierce power struggle between mother and daughter is often passed from one adolescent to another; despite its disturbing content, readers find this book powerful and mesmerizing, like a fevered dream.

JOHN GREEN

## Looking for Alaska

14–18 • Dutton • 2005 • 237 pp.

∽ *PRINTZ AWARD*

M iles Halter collects famous last words. He loves to discover and use these ending phrases as a possible road map for life. Hence he uses Rabelais's final phrase, "I go to seek a Great Perhaps," to explain why he left a public high school to attend a private prep school in rural Alabama. Like all prep school novels, *Looking for Alaska* presents the school environment, with tough classes, pranks, and hard drinking. Here Miles becomes infatuated with Alaska Young — mean, moody, and sexy — who leads him on, always promising more. But when Alaska is killed in a car accident, Miles and his friends must deal with her possible suicide and their own guilt.

With an engaging, unreliable narrator, the natural attraction of prep school life, and a cast of smart-talking intelligent teens, *Looking for Alaska* combines a protagonist who might have hung out with Holden Caulfield with the kind of moral questions that characterize *A Separate Peace*.

KENT HARUF

## Plainsong

14–18 • Knopf • 1999 • 301 pp.

∽ *NATIONAL BOOK AWARD FINALIST*

T he title of the book refers to the simple vocal melodies, sometimes sung by alternating voices, that have been used by Christian churches for centuries. In the novel, six compassionately rendered major characters from Holt, Colorado, and several minor ones present their own songs, which blend together to create a picture of a single year in this prairie town. The depressed wife of high school teacher Tom Guthrie moves out of their home, leaving him to care for their young sons, Ike and Bobby. A pregnant teenager, Victoria, thrown out into the street by her mother, takes refuge with another teacher until she goes to live with some elderly bachelor brothers. Gruff and socially awkward, they still try to make Victoria feel at home; ultimately they form a nontraditional family, caring for one another.

The simple and understated narrative beautifully describes the landscape, sunsets, birdsongs, and natural world of the prairie. Ranchers check cows for babies and conduct an autopsy on a horse. In this portrait of small-town life, everyone knows everyone else's business. Like the plains, the story has been stripped down to essentials; it brilliantly conveys all the human emotions — grief, bereavement, loneliness, anger, kindness, benevolence, and love.

KAREN HESSE

## The Music of Dolphins

12–14 • Scholastic • 1996 • 183 pp.

The narrator of this eloquent, poetic novel, Mila, has been living as a feral child with dolphins for eleven years. At fifteen, she is rescued by humans and becomes part of a government study — examined and taught language, music, and computer skills. However, although Mila bonds with the humans and thinks of them as family, she continues to long for the ocean. Like many feral children, she fails to thrive completely in her new environment, and in a very powerful dénouement, the research team returns her to her dolphin group.

The book begins with her rudimentary sentences and progresses in complexity as Mila's language skills develop — an extraordinarily difficult task that the writer accomplishes seamlessly. Although the book maintains a deceptively simple format, it explores complex and demanding issues. Hence it has been a favorite for classroom discussion and independent reading for a decade.

KIMBERLY WILLIS HOLT

## When Zachary Beaver Came to Town

12–14 • Holt • 1999 • 231 pp.

↭ *NATIONAL BOOK AWARD*

In 1971, a quirky group of individuals inhabit the town of Antler, Texas. Since nothing ever happens in Antler, the townspeople pay two dollars and line up to examine a recently arrived trailer decked out with Christmas lights. In the trailer resides Zachary Beaver, who proclaims himself, at 643 pounds, to be the world's fattest boy. Thirteen-year-old Toby Wilson narrates the events of that summer; Toby and his best friend, Cal, help Zachary step outside his trailer and realize one of his dreams — getting baptized. In a character-driven novel, the author brilliantly captures small-town Texas life, its idiosyncratic characters, and the gifts such towns provide for their citizens.

### A. M. HOMES

## *Jack*

12–14 • Macmillan • 1989 • 221 pp.

In a story written with humor and panache, the protagonist, fifteen-year-old Jack, struggles with the realities presented by his parents' divorce. On a weekly outing with his father, Jack discovers that his father is gay. At first Jack responds with hostility — he adopts a macho façade but worries about his own sexual identity. His peers react to the news brutally, calling him "fag baby." Gradually, however, as he matures, Jack gains insight into his family and himself and realizes that all families face different problems.

A book that captures the feelings, actions, and speech patterns of adolescent boys, it was written when the author was nineteen. This basically sweet and gentle story, with a nice young man at its center, has gained a wide audience because it deals with questions about identity — issues close to the heart of every adolescent.

### NICK HORNBY

## *A Long Way Down*

14–18 • Riverhead • 2005 • 335 pp.

At the beginning the author quotes Elizabeth McCracken: "The cure for unhappiness is happiness." In a wry novel, Nick Hornby brings four protagonists together on New Year's Eve at Toppers' House, where people in London go to jump to their death. They are definitely individuals who would not ordinarily meet: a television personality, a single mother of a disabled son, a distraught teenage girl, and an American rock musician. All four come down from the roof alive; making a pact to reassess their options, they start meeting regularly, since they now have the others to talk to. Rather than a book on suicide, the novel really deals with what happens when you decide not to kill yourself.

This well-executed and thoughtful tale — narrated in turn by each of the four individuals — never denigrates the seriousness of the protagonists' troubles. But with his characteristic humor and lively storytelling, Hornby takes on the grimmest of subjects, making it funny and surprising as well. Consequently, he has written a book now being passed from one teen to another. As one young reader admitted, all teens have thoughts of suicide from time to time; this book allows them to explore the topic — and enjoy an optimistic and happy ending.

DAVIDA WILLS HURWIN
## *A Time for Dancing*
12–14 • Little, Brown • 1995 • 272 pp.

A narrative that alternates between a sixteen-year-old dancer, Juliana, and her best friend, Samantha, grapples with the reality of an adolescent struggling with death and dying. When Jules is diagnosed with histiocytic lymphoma, she must deal with endless sessions of chemotherapy and emergency runs to the hospital; occasionally she escapes into a dream state. Samantha watches as her friend embarks on a solo journey toward death.

In this hauntingly real book, the subject matter may be too intense for some; others appreciate the book's honesty, as it presents the feelings and emotions of a very believable young woman and her best friend. Definitely a "three-handkerchief" book, the novel will satisfy anyone hunting for a sad story. Some teens admit that *A Time for Dancing* was the only book that ever really made them cry.

A. M. JENKINS
## *Damage*
12–14 • Harper • 2001 • 186 pp.

In a believable and powerful story a seventeen-year-old boy, called on the football field "the Pride of the Panthers," struggles with clinical depression. In a second-person voice, Austin Reid brings readers into his life, which on the outside seems ideal. The most beautiful girl in the school pursues him; eventually they become involved sexually. But even with Heather in his life, Austin continues to spiral downward — pulling away from friends, missing key plays on the football field, contemplating suicide with a razor. Although the author never explores what recovery from depression might mean, the novel ends hopefully, with Austin reaching for help by getting honest with his best friend.

Few novels for adolescents have presented the feelings and thoughts of a depressed individual so accurately and believably. Because Austin happens to be such a nice individual and an attractive protagonist, his worsening condition seems all the more horrible. Dedicated to "those who are struggling; . . . those who have made it through; . . . those who have been left behind," this riveting novel has actually saved lives.

ANGELA JOHNSON

## *The First Part Last*

12–14 • Simon & Schuster • 2003 • 132 pp.

⟜ *PRINTZ AWARD*

Sixteen-year-old Bobby and his girlfriend, Nia, intend to put their baby, Feather, up for adoption. But Bobby ends up caring for the child, after Nia goes into a coma. With a narrative alternating between short chapters entitled "then" and "now," readers follow Bobby's absorption with Feather, the sacrifices he makes to give her constant care, his loss of sleep, and his mental anguish. Only in the end does the narrative reveal why he has decided to keep Feather. In poetic, lyrical prose, Angela Johnson, one of only a handful of children's book creators to become a MacArthur Fellow, has created an amazingly sensitive and caring African-American boy, who tries, desperately, to do the right thing.

RON KOERTGE

## *Arizona Kid*

12–14 • Little, Brown/Joy Street • 1988 • 304 pp.

Sixteen-year-old Billy believes that he is too short, too pale, and much too wimpy. Then he spends a summer with his gay uncle in Tucson, Arizona, working with racehorses. Billy finds romance with a girl who adores him and work that he absolutely loves. His uncle, who has struggled to find his own path in life, becomes a positive influence, helping Billy find his own solutions. When Billy returns home, he has developed a new self-confidence and sense of direction.

Often called on to defend his books in censorship cases, Ron Koertge always insists in his usual modest but firm style, "I write what I write and take the heat." Young readers have appreciated him for his candor. Funny, emotionally satisfying, *Arizona Kid* — now available in an attractive edition from Candlewick Press — remains one of the best-loved books by this popular author, who understands adolescents as few writers do. Once these readers find him, they can continue with his many fine novels — including *The Brimstone Journals*, *Stoner & Spaz*, and *Margaux with an X*.

WALLY LAMB

## *I Know This Much Is True*

14–18 • Harper/Regan • 1998 • 912 pp.

A forty-year-old house painter in Three Rivers, Connecticut, Dominick Birdsey has spent his entire life dealing with his twin brother, Thomas, a paranoid schizophrenic. From childhood on, Dominick fights for his own space in a house dominated by his abusive stepfather, Ray, who bullies both boys. When Thomas chops off his own hand, Dominick turns to the pages of his grandfather's handwritten memoir to try to make sense out of his life and his brother's.

Reminiscent of the work of Pat Conroy, the novel contains strong character studies and alternates between the recent present and flashbacks to Dominick's tortured childhood and adolescence. Excerpts from the grandfather's memoir are interpolated throughout the main text. Many teenagers have found this literary tour de force particularly compelling, one of their favorites of all time.

IAIN LAWRENCE

## *The Lightkeeper's Daughter*

12–14 • Delacorte • 2002 • 249 pp.

Seventeen-year-old Elizabeth (Squid) McCrae returns to her childhood home on Lizzie Island, a remote location off the coast of British Columbia, in Canada. After fleeing from the island as a pregnant teenager, Squid brings her three-year-old daughter with her as well. While visiting her family, Squid pieces together the events surrounding the death of her brother, Alistair, who drowned when his kayak overturned. Obsessed with whales, Alistair believed that he could understand their language. By reading his journal and calling forth memories, Squid recounts the family history as the reader moves from contemporary events to flashbacks. Although her father wanted only to live out his life as the lightkeeper on the island, her mother worried about the consequences of their children being raised in its narrow confines. This emotionally charged story of blame, guilt, and recrimination has been set against a magnificently beautiful and imagined landscape.

With its detailed look at the childhood and adolescence of Squid and her brother, *The Lightkeeper's Daughter* allows young readers to imagine a life utterly different from their own. In this ideal book for teen-adult book groups, both the adolescent and adult characters have been well rendered.

ANN M. MARTIN

## *A Corner of the Universe*

12–14 • Scholastic • 2002 • 181 pp.

✏ *NEWBERY HONOR*

Although Hattie does not exactly have a normal life — she lives with her father, an artist, her mother, and a group of eccentric boarders — Hattie enjoys her interaction with everyone in her home. In 1960 when summer comes, right before she turns twelve, Hattie looks forward to long lazy days, trips to the library, and the pleasures of a carnival visiting her small town.

But that summer she discovers a family secret: she has an uncle no one has mentioned. Because the institution where he lives is closing, Adam comes back to live with her grandparents. Although everyone else considers him a freak, Hattie enjoys his company, his strange way of talking — filled with references to television programs — and believes that she understands her mentally deficient uncle when no one else does. But when she treats him as just another child, encouraging him to sneak out of his house and go with her to the carnival, Hattie finds that her actions lead to terrible consequences.

Both Hattie and Uncle Adam emerge as truly likable and compelling characters. A book about friendship and being an outsider, *A Corner of the Universe* has quickly become one of those books teens embrace, cherish, and remember.

NORMA FOX MAZER
## After the Rain
12–14 • Morrow • 1987 • 290 pp.
⭯ *NEWBERY HONOR*

Fifteen-year-old Rachel does not happen to be fond of her grandfather — critical, unaffectionate, and ornery. Although her parents try to care for him by shopping for groceries and cooking meals, he does not accept help gracefully. One day, doctors tell the family that he has only a few months to live — and Rachel finds herself spending every afternoon with him. She even begins to sacrifice time with her friends and boyfriend to prepare meals for him and be with him at the hospital when he dies.

A powerful book about death and dying and the strength of family ties, *After the Rain* often is recommended to adolescents who are struggling with the loss of a family member and the grief that follows.

PHYLLIS REYNOLDS NAYLOR
## The Agony of Alice
12–14 • Atheneum • 1985 • 144 pp.

When Alice McKinley was four, her mother died, and in sixth grade she finds little understanding in her all-male household for the problems of growing up female. Searching for a mentor, she discovers that a physically unattractive teacher, Mrs. Plotkin, actually has the qualities that Alice would like to emulate. Filled with humor, narrated in the first person by Alice, the novel presents an honest, enthusiastic, and vital heroine. Alice asks questions — about sex, for example — that young readers themselves would like to ask. Phyllis Naylor's frankness attracts her audience but has dismayed some adults. In 2002, the Alice books followed Harry Potter as the second most challenged series in America.

Thanks to modern technology, the author has used the letters and responses posted on her Web site to help her write subsequent books. Although she doesn't have a real daughter, she considers the novels a way to raise her fictional daughter, Alice McKinley. Readers who first meet Alice as a sixth-grader can watch her mature gradually. She becomes a freshman in *Alice Alone* and writes for the high school paper in *Simply Alice*. *Including Alice* takes her into her sophomore year, when she deals with the romantic entanglements of her family and peers — including a lesbian relationship between two of her friends. In *Alice on Her Way,* Alice learns how to drive and celebrates her sixteenth birthday. Several more planned books will take the heroine through high school. Because Naylor doesn't want to disappoint her fans, she has actually written the final volume, in which Alice ages from eighteen to sixty, and it resides in a fireproof box in the author's office. Certainly to date, Naylor hasn't let her readers down; they all remain eager to find out what happens to Alice.

KATHERINE PATERSON

## *Jacob Have I Loved*

12–14 • Crowell • 1980 • 228 pp.

↪ *NEWBERY MEDAL*

Katherine Paterson's most complex book, *Jacob Have I Loved,* takes place on the imaginary island of Rass in the Chesapeake Bay during World War II. At thirteen, Sara Louise Bradshaw has been blessed with health and strength, but her twin sister, Caroline, a frail human being, happens to be both beautiful and musically talented. Like Esau in the Bible, Sara Louise feels she has been deprived of her birthright as the elder by a few minutes. Blaming God, she stops going to church, and she discovers she is in love with Captain Wallace, an older man who has returned to the island. As the war progresses, Sara Louise takes on more work, gathering oysters and crabs. But only after she leaves the island does she really face her sibling rivalry and come to terms with it in a completely different way.

Often used with a wide range of students, the book required three years of struggle for Paterson to achieve a final manuscript that she herself could admire. Beautiful in its prose, a story of quiet but dramatic power, *Jacob Have I Loved* not only recreates a time and place, but it also captures the universal tension between siblings.

RODMAN PHILBRICK

## *Freak the Mighty*

12–14 • Blue Sky • 1993 • 169 pp.

Maxwell Kane has several strikes against him: he is learning disabled, unusually large for his age, and the son of Killer Kane, who murdered his wife. So Max often prefers the solitude of his basement room in his grandparents' house. But when a boy moves in next door who is even more disabled than Max because he cannot grow, the two become inseparable. In fact, Max often puts the brilliant Kevin, or Freak, on his shoulders, and as "Freak the Mighty" the two share celebrations, exchange stories, and attend class together, where Max steadily improves. When Max's father returns and kidnaps his son, it takes all of the Freak's genius to save his friend from a nightmare.

Touching in its portrayal of an unusual friendship, fast-paced, and funny — until its tragic dénouement — *Freak the Mighty* has become a staple of middle school curriculums.

ANITA SHREVE

## *Light on Snow*

14–18 • Little, Brown • 2004 • 307 pp.

In a small, idyllic New Hampshire town, a father and his twelve-year-old daughter, Nicky, set out one late afternoon on snowshoes. Soon, hearing cries, they find an abandoned infant, whom they rush to the hospital. The father has lived as a recluse since he left his architectural career in New York and took up furniture-making in the country. Consequently, he attracts the suspicion of the local crime investigator. When the mother of the child shows up on their doorstep during a blizzard and they harbor her, they become accomplices to the crime. As Nicky and her father come to terms with this teenage mother's life, they must also face their own decisions and memories about another baby. Nicky's infant sister, Clara, and her mother had been killed two years earlier in an automobile accident — an event that neither Nicky nor her father has completely faced.

Nicky emerges as an engaging heroine. She can identify with the baby, with the mother, and even accept the struggles her father has gone through. As she matures, she also learns to speak her heart and her mind. In the end, although one child has lost her life, Nicky and her father have saved another one — and possibly even their own.

Powerful, beautiful in its spare but exact telling, a tour de force by one of our finest contemporary writers, *Light on Snow* explores coming of age in a unique and totally mesmerizing way.

TERRY TRUEMAN

## Stuck in Neutral

12–14 • Harper • 2000 • 116 pp.

↬ *PRINTZ HONOR*

In a first-person present tense, Shawn McDaniel, age fourteen, explains that when he was born, a tiny blood vessel burst in his brain; suffering from cerebral palsy, he cannot control a single muscle in his body. But he has a secret, an exciting inner life that no one could imagine, and he remembers everything he has ever heard. Shawn's father, who has written a Pulitzer Prize–winning poem about his experience as a parent, becomes increasingly fascinated with euthanasia as a way to end Shawn's pain. Unable to communicate any of his thoughts, Shawn wonders if his father intends to kill him. While raising the ethical and emotional issues surrounding such an event, the story leaves the outcome unclear.

The father of a profoundly disabled son, like the character of Shawn, the author wrote the novel from his emotions and feelings, trying to come to terms with his son and himself. The resulting book engenders a lot of discussion and hence has been included on many middle school reading lists.

CYNTHIA VOIGT

## Izzy, Willy-Nilly

12–14 • Atheneum • 1986 • 274 pp.

A kind, generous, popular, and pretty cheerleader, Izzy loses most of her right leg in a car crash caused by a drunken date. Now, at fifteen, she must learn to live in a way that she never thought possible.

Although she cries only at night, she faces abandonment by her friends, then grief, denial, depression, and anger. But ultimately a former acquaintance becomes the friend who allows Izzy to come to terms with her circumstances; Izzy faces school again, dealing with the now-challenging relationships with her peers.

Readers see the mental anguish through Izzy's eyes; the slow pace of the narrative mirrors the actual time needed for the healing process. A compelling and likable heroine and the book's many insights into the life of an amputee have made *Izzy, Willy-Nilly* popular with younger teens for two decades.

# Religion and Spirituality

IN THE TWENTY-FIRST CENTURY, teens have been turning increasingly to books that explore large philosophical or spiritual questions. Who am I? What is the right way to live? What should I do with my life? Is there a God, and if so, what does that mean in terms of my life?

For about three decades, although sex was completely acceptable in books for teens, these books rarely presented young people who thought about religion or spirituality. Certainly some fantasies — by J.R.R. Tolkien, C. S. Lewis, Marion Zimmer Bradley, and Phillip Pullman — explored religious questions and the classic themes of good and evil. However, realistic stories in which teens attended church or thought about their relationship to God were difficult to find except in books produced by religious publishers. Today, however, young adult literature has taken on a quest for spiritual or religious answers.

Obviously, teens following a particular religious or spiritual path will have been recommended volumes by their church or religious group. The books that follow explore the issues of religion and spirituality in general and will be appreciated best by those who still have a lot of questions rather than those who believe that for now they have found their own answers.

DAVID ALMOND

## *Skellig*

12–14 • Delacorte • 1998 • 182 pp.

↪ *PRINTZ HONOR*

The British author David Almond has written many compelling and memorable novels for teens, including *The Fire-Eaters*. But his debut as a young adult novelist, for which he won both the Carnegie Medal and Whitbread Award, remains one of his most popular books.

After his parents move to a new but rundown house, ten-year-old Michael struggles with a different neighborhood and the deteriorating health of his baby sister. One day, in their ramshackle garage, Michael discovers an extraordinary creature covered in dust and spider webs, his face thin and pale, his food consisting of bugs and mice.

With the help of his neighbor Mina, Michael tries to rescue Skellig, finds food and medicine for him, and transports him to a safer place to live. In one brilliant scene, as they remove his decrepit black clothing, they discover that he has wings where his shoulder blades should be. And they begin to wonder who he might be — a human being, an angel, a bird, or a creature never before seen.

The book alternates between dreamlike scenes with Skellig to completely realistic ones in which Michael goes to school in this small English town, plays soccer, and learns about Darwinian evolution. As Mina and Michael care for the desiccated stranger, Michael himself gains some power and mastery in his own life. Then one incredible night the three dance together in a circle, and both Michael and Mina seem to grow their own wings. Finally, before Skellig leaves on the next part of his journey, he visits the hospital and helps save Michael's sister.

Lyrical, magical, and highly emotional, with a very real boy as the protagonist, the story makes frequent references to William Blake. In fact, Skellig can be characterized as a Blake drawing brought to life in prose. Although Michael is ten years old, the book works better with a slightly older reader because of the complexity of the issues involved. Both a mystery and an adventure story, it poses questions about faith, angels, life, spirituality, and creativity that linger with the reader. A great book for classroom discussion, book groups, or independent reading.

MARION ZIMMER BRADLEY

## The Mists of Avalon

14–18 • Knopf • 1982 • 876 pp.

No saga has captured the imagination of English-speaking countries as powerfully as the romance of King Arthur and the Round Table; Mary Stewart's and T. H. White's versions have been included in the Fantasy section of *500 Great Books for Teens*. But King Arthur's story most frequently has been told from a male perspective; Marion Zimmer Bradley imagines it from the point of view of the women in Arthur's life. Hence the landscape seems familiar to readers, but the perspective is unique and breathtaking.

Viviane, the Lady of the Lake, High Priestess of Avalon, has foreseen a united Britain under a high king who will remain true to Avalon and the old religion of Druid Goddess worship. However, across this land a new religion, worshipping a male Christ, has begun to take hold. Viviane chooses and trains Morgaine (Morgan Le Fay), Arthur's half-sister, to succeed her as priestess. Then, in sacred rites, Viviane brings the two together for mating; although Arthur's son Mordred comes from this union, Morgaine leaves Avalon, horrified by the incest she has unwittingly committed.

Arthur's queen Gwenhwyfar, frustrated over her barrenness, searches for solace in piety and the Christian religion. Ultimately she demands that Arthur fly the banner of Christ rather than that of the pagan Dragon. But when the Christians take the sacred cup of the Druids to use in their mass, the Goddess herself appears, inspiring the Knights of the Round Table to take up the quest of the Holy Grail. Basically, the author sides with the pagans in the struggle between the two religions, although she does present the first Christians in a positive light, for they engaged in a theology far different from that of their descendants.

Add to all these details the traditional jousts, love permutations, sexual liaisons, and battles, and the large, sprawling work often seems far too short for readers. Bradley continued the saga in *The Forest House, Lady of Avalon*, and *Priestess of Avalon*, which was completed after her death by her writing partner, Diana L. Paxson. The book weaves feminism with religious discussion and speculation — never forgetting, however, to tell an exciting and spellbinding tale.

PAULO COELHO

## *The Alchemist*

14–18 • Harper • 1993 • 174 pp.

Written by a Brazilian novelist, the story of Santiago, a Spanish shepherd boy, reads like an exotic fable. Driven by a need to travel, Santiago wants to pursue a recurring dream in which he goes to Egypt and finds hidden treasure. An old man advises him to pursue his own Personal Legend, claiming that "when you want something, all the universe conspires in helping you to achieve it." So with courage Santiago sells his flock and goes to Tangier, where a thief steals his money. There he works in a crystal shop, prospers, and then travels with an Englishman to find a famous alchemist. Finally, Santiago makes the last leg of his journey to the pyramids and learns that the treasure he sought is waiting in the place he least expects it.

Having studied alchemy for eleven years, Paulo Coelho wrote *The Alchemist* in two weeks. First published in Portuguese in 1988, the book sold a mere 900 copies, and the Brazilian publishing house decided not to reprint it. But Coelho's next novel received a great deal of attention, bringing *The Alchemist* to the top of the bestseller list. Over time this small book, translated into almost sixty languages, sold over 20 million copies — more than any other book from Brazil and any book written in Portuguese.

In a narrative that speaks to following one's own heart and dreams, Coelho teaches his lessons with originality and restraint. He explores spirituality and faith, how everything has a soul, how God resides in a grain of sand or a flower. The book has proven so popular with young readers that textbook editions have been created, with a guidebook for teachers, in countries all over the world.

ANITA DIAMANT

## *The Red Tent*

14–18 • St. Martin's • 1997 • 321 pp.

The only daughter of the biblical Jacob, Dinah finds herself cherished by Jacob's four wives. In her first-person account of her life, readers are immersed in the biblical world of Israel and Egypt around 1500 B.C., and they watch how Jacob's marriages to Rachel, Leah,

Zilpah, and Bilhah affect the community of women. Through songs and stories, the mothers and grandmothers pass their wisdom on to the next generation. They exchange these stories in the red tent, where women sequester themselves at times of monthly cycles, birthing, and illness. There they enjoy one another's companionship, trade secrets like bracelets, and worship household gods. Eventually, Dinah goes to Canaan, witnesses the reunion of Jacob and Esau, becomes a midwife, and flees to Egypt.

Taking liberties with the strict biblical account, Anita Diamant weaves a fascinating tale, filled with flawed and very human and sensuous people. Dinah, who does not have a voice in the Bible, has been given a powerful one here, providing texture and content to the sketchy biblical stories. Published quietly and with little fanfare, *The Red Tent* became a word-of-mouth bestseller, supported by the clergy of various denominations. Those who prefer biblical history unadulterated tend not to embrace this work, but for those teens struggling to understand religion and their relationship to God, it can be highly effective and memorable.

LEIF ENGER

## *Peace Like a River*

14–18 • Atlantic • 2001 • 312 pp.

Asthmatic Reuben Land has been dead for twelve minutes when his father, Jeremiah, orders him to breathe "in the name of the living God." Hence Reuben believes in miracles and has no problem talking about them. But after he turns eleven, he needs this faith more than ever. For after his brother, Davy, is jailed for the murder of two intruders into the family home, Davy escapes to the Badlands of North Dakota. Reuben, his younger sister Swede, and his father head out to find him; so does the FBI. But it appears that the family has support from a higher power. Narrated by Reuben, but including a heroic story of the cowboy Sunny Sundown written by Swede, the book sweeps readers along in a story where biblical allusions abound.

The author wrote *Peace Like a River* for his entire family and created a story that can be enjoyed by a wide readership. Often chosen for an entire community or area to read, the book also works extremely well in teen-adult discussion groups. This beautiful and evocative novel, with a title from a traditional American hymn, celebrates family, faith, and miracles.

ANNE FADIMAN

## The Spirit Catches You and You Fall Down: A Hmong Child, Her American Doctors, and the Collision of Two Cultures

14–18 • Farrar, Straus • 1997 • 339 pp.

This compelling nonfiction study chronicles the clash between a Hmong family and the American medical community, a conflict between Western medicine and Eastern spirituality. Lia Lee's family immigrated to California from Laos in 1980. Born in 1982, Lia was diagnosed as epileptic by American doctors at three months, but her family called her disease "the spirit catches you and you fall down." Western doctors prescribed twenty-three different types of medicine over four years; her family wanted to practice holistic healing and hire shamans. Because the two cultures did not come together, Lia became brain dead after a massive seizure, although her parents continued to care for her. The book serves as a cautionary tale about the importance of "cross-cultural medicine."

Vivid, deeply felt, and well researched, the story shows the encounter of two disparate cultures as the author sympathizes with each point of view. *The Spirit Catches You and You Fall Down* works well for an entire school to read, because it raises important issues about different approaches to medicine, healing, spirituality, community, and culture.

PAUL FLEISCHMAN

## Whirligig

12–14 • Holt • 1998 • 133 pp.

Right before his seventeenth birthday, Brent Bishop attempts suicide driving his car while drunk. Although he lives, he kills another teenager, Lea Zamora. As restitution, Lea's mother asks that Brent honor her daughter by placing four whirligigs, built by him and featuring Lea, in the four corners of the country. Seeing a chance for atonement, Brent sets out by bus on this strange mission that not only transforms his life but that starts to affect, positively, the lives of others. As he travels to Washington, California, Florida, and Maine, he takes an inward journey and begins to reflect about how both good and bad actions can have a ripple effect. As he builds his whirligigs, they become more complex, more beautiful, more a true homage to Lea's life and spirit.

Paul Fleischman weaves Brent's first-person narrative with the stories of four individuals, dramatically different in background (a young violinist, an immigrant from Puerto Rico, a survivor of Auschwitz, a Maine teenager), who come upon the whirligigs and find the answers they have been seeking. In other hands, this mélange of viewpoints and five protagonists would prove confusing, but Fleischman — as he did in *Seek* and *Breakout* — once again proves his mastery of using multiple voices to create a narrative.

In the end, Brent confesses his thoughts and feelings to a painter in Maine, and she provides the perspective and the forgiveness that he has been desperately seeking on his journey. In a unique story, Brent and young readers learn how small, positive deeds can have powerful consequences and how a single action can reverberate — just like a whirligig, turning in the wind.

MARGARET GEORGE

## *Mary, Called Magdalene*

14–18 • Viking • 2002 • 630 pp.

As someone who had written many sprawling historical and biographical novels, Margaret George turned her hand to a fictional account of the life of Mary Magdalene, since scant historical material exists about her. Possessed by demons as a young girl, Mary desperately sought a cure; then a prophet named Jesus cast out these devils. Mary finally chose to leave her family and children to become a disciple of Jesus. Basing some of the novel on the Gnostic accounts, such as the Gospel of Mary, George brings Mary to the center of Christ's work, showing sixteen disciples, four of them women, as the closest followers. Mary remains at the center of the early Christian church in this novel, and George has done enough research to make her version credible. Certainly *Mary, Called Magdalene* opens up discussion —

and often sends young readers in search of other material about the early Christian church.

## MYLA GOLDBERG

### *Bee Season*

14–18 • Doubleday • 2000 • 275 pp.

Eliza Naumann, at nine, believes herself to be the dullest member of her intellectual Jewish family. With a lawyer mother, brilliant older brother, and her father, a cantor at the synagogue, Elly seems only to have a rare aptitude for spelling. When she competes at local contests, the letters take on a life of their own and she experiences mystical insight into words. Consequently her father shifts all his attention to her because of this rare gift, believing that she can fulfill the teachings of the Kabbalah scholar Abulafia, a Jewish mystic who taught enlightenment through the alignment of letters and words. As they pursue these studies and the spelling bee circuit, Elly's brother joins the Hare Krishnas, and her mother descends into madness.

The novel, which explores religious devotion, love, and family dynamics, captures as well as any work of fiction the obsessive personality and its consequences. In the end, Elly must declare her own independence from her father and her family, which she does during the national spelling bee. In *Bee Season*, the spelling bee becomes a metaphor for childhood; desperately trying to please her parents, Elly realizes, ultimately, that she never can.

## MAREK HALTER

### *Sarah*

14–18 • Crown • 2004 • 295 pp.

In the tradition of Diamant's *The Red Tent*, the French author Marek Halter weaves a tale of the wife of Abraham, Sarah, who remained barren until she was an old woman. Born to one of the lords of Ur, Sarah flees her wedding in distress. She becomes a priestess of Ishtar and leaves the city with Abraham, who has been called by his God to find a new land for his people. Abraham, acting only on faith, sets off with Sarah, who leaves the comforts of civilization to wander through the wilderness.

In this theological fantasy or fictional portrait of a biblical figure, Sarah and her sexuality, feelings, and emotions are explored; she emerges as a complex and extremely sympathetic heroine. The striking jacket image draws readers into this feminist saga; the story then keeps them engrossed in Sarah and her journey.

PETE HAMILL

## Snow in August

14–18 • Little, Brown • 1997 • 384 pp.

In 1947, during a raging snowstorm, an eleven-year-old Catholic altar boy, Michael Devlin, ends up assisting the aging rabbi Judah Hirsch with the Sabbath duties at his synagogue. Michael thereby becomes the *Shabbos goy* for the temple, lighting fires and doing other work forbidden to Orthodox Jews on the Sabbath. Fatherless because of World War II but with a wonderful relationship with his mother, Michael clearly needs the conversation, wisdom, and attention of the rabbi. Michael learns Yiddish; the rabbi, a refugee from Prague, learns English. In their anti-Semitic, gang-ridden Brooklyn neighborhood, Michael has to hide his motives for spending so much time with his friend. Witnessing the brutal beating of a Jewish shopkeeper, Michael must also decide whether to remain silent or come forward, knowing that he and his mother will face recrimination if he does the honorable thing.

But this harsh landscape has been lit with miracles. At the rabbi's first baseball game, he and Michael see Jackie Robinson play for the Dodgers. Michael discovers the Kabbalah; he builds a rare and beautiful friendship with the old man. In an ending shaped by magical realism, Michael summons forth the ancient Golem from Prague, who helps solve the neighborhood's problems during a snowstorm in August. Although some have difficulty with the ending, *Snow in August* — a book about faith, belief, and magic — is often chosen as a multigenerational Community Reads title.

PETE HAUTMAN

## *Godless*

12–14 • Simon & Schuster • 2004 • 198 pp.

↬ *NATIONAL BOOK AWARD*

Contemporary literature for adolescents too rarely presents a young person struggling with God and spirituality. But that is the primary concern of the protagonist of *Godless,* sixteen-year-old Jason Bock. Raised in a Roman Catholic family and in absolute rebellion against the Church, Jason decides to invent a religion of his own. He worships the town's water tower and invents a cult: "Chutengodianism — a religion with no church, no money, and only one member. I have a religion, but I have no faith. Maybe one day I'll find a deity I can believe in. Until then, my god is made of steel and rust."

However, Jason finds others willing to follow him, and one night they ascend the sides of the "Ten-legged God" to celebrate midnight mass and swim in the dark, vast water reserve. These antics send one member to the hospital, one to a psychiatric ward, and Jason to prison and 210 hours of community service. Bloodied but unbowed, Jason holds fast to his rebellion until the end of the book, continuing to walk what his father calls "a long, lonely road."

With a lot of smart, snappy dialogue and an intriguing central figure, *Godless* may not solve any of the questions raised by Jason's spiritual journey, but at least this thought-provoking novel opens those issues up for discussion.

JOHN IRVING

## *A Prayer for Owen Meany*

14–18 • Morrow • 1989 • 543 pp.

While playing a Little League game in a small New Hampshire town, Owen Meany, a social outcast with a high-pitched voice, hits a foul ball that strikes Johnny Wheelwright's mother on the head and instantly kills her. Narrating the story, Johnny shows how the boys still cling to their friendship. Owen even cuts off his friend's fingers to keep Johnny from having to serve in Vietnam. In time Owen, a latter-day prophet and Christ figure, inspires true Christian belief in Johnny.

Written with political anger about American society at the end of the 1980s, the novel has survived because of its portrait of a friendship and its central question — why does Johnny become a Christian because of Owen Meany? The novel also contains John Irving's trademark characters — oddballs, freaks, and true originals — which have earned this book, as well as *The Cider House Rules* and *The World According to Garp,* many devoted readers.

BEN MIKAELSEN

## Touching Spirit Bear

12–14 • Harper • 2001 • 241 pp.

At fifteen, Cole Matthews seethes with anger. He hates his abusive alcoholic father and his distant mother. One day, when his rage goes out of control, he attacks a classmate and severely damages him. Instead of a jail sentence, Cole is sent to live by himself on an island off the coast of Alaska. Mauled by a huge white bear, he almost loses his life. But when he returns from the hospital, a Tlingit elder shows him how to use meditation, dancing, wood carving, and action to heal from anger and hatred. As Cole struggles to live in isolation, he undergoes a spiritual transformation that changes his vision of himself and those around him.

Unusual in its plot, *Touching Spirit Bear* combines the elements of a survival novel with those of an intriguing spiritual journey.

CHAIM POTOK

## The Chosen

14–18 • Simon & Schuster • 1967 • 304 pp.

Set in the Williamsburg section of Brooklyn, New York, from the end of World War II until about 1950, *The Chosen* begins on a baseball field with a group of boys around fifteen years old. One team, from the school of Hasidic Jews, regards the other, composed of Orthodox Jews, with scorn; they compete with the ferocity of a holy war. Danny Saunders, the son of the rabbi of the Hasids, hits a ball so hard that it strikes the eye of the narrator, Reuven Malter, the son of an Orthodox Jew and teacher of the Talmud. After this hostile first encounter, a friendship develops between the two boys. The novel explores the growth of these extraordinary young men, their relationships with their fathers, the closed community in which they live, and their struggle to sustain their religious life and tradition in a secular age.

Chaim Potok's first novel, published for adults, deals with reverence, responsibility, holiness, learning, tradition, and the pain of defending these ideals against the world. Ultimately, the characters struggle with universal issues: "A man must fill his life with meaning, meaning is not automatically given to life. It is hard work to fill one's life with meaning." Because of its subject matter and its brilliant execution, the novel has become a staple of high school reading lists over the last four decades.

SHARON SHINN

## *Archangel*

14–18 • Ace • 1996 • 390 pp.

In the land of Samaria, the angel Gabriel stands next in line to become Archangel. But before he does, he needs to find his wife, marry her, and sing with her in the annual Gloria, the festival of song to praise Jovah. A homing device on his wrist, called the Kiss of the God, brings him together with his wife, a common slave girl named Rachel. But Rachel quickly becomes a thorn in his side; with a lot of bickering, the two disaffected but predestined lovers at last bring about the removal of the evil Archangel Raphael and start to put the kingdom in order.

With many names that sound like those of ancient Israel and with a cast of angels and archangels, this book and the other volumes of the Samaria series — *Jovah's Angel, The Alleluia Files, Angelica,* and *Angel-Seeker* — have become favorites in the religious community because they present characters with strong faith and discuss the nature of God. However, in these books Jovah happens to be a spaceship controlling the actions of a colony. Still, this combined romance, science fiction, and religious novel sweeps readers up in a highly inventive fantasy world and in some beautifully described angel wings.

ELIZABETH GEORGE SPEARE

## *The Bronze Bow*

12–14 • Houghton Mifflin • 1961 • 256 pp.

✧ *NEWBERY MEDAL*

For ten years, since the death of his father at the hands of the Romans, eighteen-year-old Daniel bar Jamin of Galilee has lived on hatred, wanting only to avenge his loss. While apprenticed to the village blacksmith, Daniel is treated so badly that he runs away to the mountains. There, he lives with a band of refugees directed by Rosh. Some consider Rosh a savior, others, a bandit. After the blacksmith dies, Daniel goes back to his village to care for his sister, Leah. There he and his friend Joel recruit young men who will become part of a liberating army. But in this war-torn land, another messiah has been preaching, a man named Jesus, who encourages love rather than vengeance. In the final chapter, Jesus heals Leah, and Daniel sets out on a path quite different from the one he had previously embraced.

Elizabeth George Speare wrote *The Bronze Bow* as a Sunday school supplement; she disliked the portrayals of Jesus in the media at the time and wanted to make Christ a real human being. Although a superb historical novel — which vividly recreates the time period and won for Speare a second Newbery Medal — the book fell into disfavor for many years because of the appearance of Jesus Christ as a character. However, recently it has been appearing on middle school reading lists — for many of the same reasons that books such as Anita Diamant's *The Red Tent* have made their way onto high school reading lists. A brilliant historian, Speare generally wrote from her head; the most emotionally satisfying of all of her work, *The Bronze Bow* definitely came from her heart.

# Romance

A S SIGMUND FREUD reminded us, all we have is love and work. Without question, teenagers would much rather focus on the former than the latter; however, teenage romance in literature, just as in real life, may not have a happy ending. Ever since Shakespeare introduced us to those star-crossed lovers Romeo and Juliet, teenage romance has often taken a turn for the worse.

Before *The Catcher in the Rye* and *The Outsiders* introduced a new realism and focus into young adult novels, romance novels ruled the day. Two of the gems of the 1940s, Maureen Daly's *Seventeenth Summer* and Benedict and Nancy Freedman's *Mrs. Mike,* have actually stood the test of time and are still picked up today. However, most of the romances of this era by writers such as Phyllis Whitney and Betty Cavanna have long been out of print because teenage manners and fashion change so quickly.

Because stark and harsh realism became the acceptable coinage in young adult fiction, romance novels even seemed a form of the past. But recently those working with adolescents have noticed an increase in the demand for gentle romances. In the twenty-first century, all kinds of love are explored — boys and girls, girls and girls, and boys and boys — but the basic constructs have not changed: love requited, love unrequited, infatuation, people meant for each other, those kept apart by families.

Love may be all we need, but even teenagers know it is not necessarily easy to find the right person to love.

------------

LIZ BERRY

## *The China Garden*

14–18 • Farrar, Straus • 1996 • 285 pp.

Against her will, seventeen-year-old Clare Meredith goes with her mother from London to Ravensmere, a historic English estate, to relax before Clare enters university. She finds the place mysterious: everyone seems to have expectations of her, and her mother appears to withhold information. Then a tall, dark, and handsome biker, Mark, enters the equation. For unknown reasons, Clare takes midnight walks in the abandoned China Garden — framed by the magnificent Moon Gates.

Magic, mystery, suspense, an ecological message, and romance combine to make a book that teenagers find hard to put down.

OLIVE ANN BURNS

## *Cold Sassy Tree*

14–18 • Ticknor & Fields • 1984 • 400 pp.

Fourteen-year-old Will Tweedy narrates this contemporary classic set in Cold Sassy, Georgia, in 1906–1907. His grandfather Rucker has decided to get married, because he needs a housekeeper, to a woman much younger than he. Since his wife has been dead for only three weeks, Rucker's daughters worry about what the people of this small southern community will think and say. Although the intended bride comes from Baltimore and is hence practically a Yankee, Will likes her and supports his grandfather's desire to marry. Surviving a near-death experience involving a train, Will becomes a sensation in the town, but when everyone comes to ask him about the incident, Rucker arrives with his new bride. Although originally agreeing to a marriage of convenience, the two actually fall in love; shortly before Rucker dies, they produce a child who will continue to live in Cold Sassy, no matter what the gossips say.

This story of an unorthodox marriage, as seen through the eyes of a fourteen-year-old, took the author over eight years to complete while she battled the side effects of chemotherapy. Basing the story on her father's life in Commerce, Georgia, and grounding it in family history, Olive Ann Burns was at work on another novel about the characters,

*Leaving Cold Sassy,* which her editor had to pull together after her death. Burns's colorful characters, her detailed setting, and her humor have endeared *Cold Sassy Tree* to adolescents for over two decades.

## ANDREW CLEMENTS
### *Things Not Seen*
12–14 • Philomel • 2002 • 251 pp.

In a very innocent and modern rendition of H. G. Wells's *The Invisible Man,* fifteen-year-old Bobby wakes up one morning in Chicago's Hyde Park to discover that he has become totally invisible. At first his parents refuse to cope with the situation, going off to work and leaving him at home. But he finally convinces them of the seriousness of his plight just before they get into an automobile accident and are seriously injured. Bobby then copes alone with being an invisible teenager and in the process develops a friendship with a beautiful blind girl, Alicia, whom he meets at the library. With their mutual disabilities, they start to help each other; in the process, Alicia provides Bobby with the information he needs to reverse his invisibility. Although they don't quite kiss at the end, they set the stage for the relationship to develop now that Bobby has become visible again.

Andrew Clements works out the details of invisibility quite thoroughly, hence the fantasy and the realism blend together smoothly. Fresh, engaging, written with a likable protagonist with a very real problem, *Things Not Seen* has become a staple of middle school reading lists because of its universal appeal.

## MAUREEN DALY
### *Seventeenth Summer*
12–14 • Dodd, Mead • 1942 • 291 pp.

In a first-person voice, Angie Morrow, one of four daughters, tells about three iridescent summer months in Fond du Lac, Wisconsin, when she goes on her first date and experiences her first kiss. Both love and heartache surround her relationship with handsome Jack Duluth, the son of a baker. Quite innocent, Angie has a couple of beers, gets "tight," and never drinks again; she worries about people being fast and the man dating her sister Lorraine. But during this pivotal summer, Angie basically goes to parties, dances, and Fourth of July parades, watches fireworks, sails on Jack's boat, and enjoys the experience of a young man's falling in love with her. The book captures the awkward feelings and missteps of a developing relationship — the wonder and uncertainty, the concern about exposing a boyfriend to family. Angie constantly tells us that we'd like someone or something, and by the end of the book readers find they like Angie, a decent, lovely girl with ambition, who heads off to college.

Maureen Daly captures both the social structure of small-town America before World War II and the innocence of a young girl who matures. As Angie says in the last line, "Never again would there ever be anything quite as wonderful as that seventeenth summer!"

Having won a short story contest in high school, Daly began to write this autobiographical novel while in college. She submitted the manuscript to Dodd, Mead for its college literary fellowship, and the book, published when Daly herself was only twenty-one, was quickly adopted by teenagers even though it had been published for adults. In a detail that she might have written, Daly herself found romance when she met her husband at a book autographing party.

Real romance, a lot of ambience, and a good deal of genuine emotion have kept this book in print all these years, with several million copies sold. One of the few young adult novels that can truly be called a classic, *Seventeenth Summer* has been, and continues to be, shared by grandmothers and granddaughters.

LOUIS DE BERNIÈRES

## *Corelli's Mandolin*

14–18 • Pantheon • 1994 • 448 pp.

During World War II, the Greek island of Cephallonia was occupied by Italian troops who ultimately turned against fascism and joined the native Greeks. The unconsummated love affair between young Pelagia, the daughter of the patriotic doctor on the island, and the amiable Italian captain, Antonio Corelli, a mandolin player, seems difficult enough, given the shifting allegiances of those on the island. But it is shattered when the Germans invade. Although Corelli escapes from the island to fight the Germans on the mainland, the Nazi troops slaughter thousands of the resident Italian soldiers.

With elements of magical realism and black comedy, the book contains multiple viewpoints and includes chapters of letters, speeches, and political pamphlets. Based on a true episode during the Nazis' occupation of Cephalonia, *Corelli's Mandolin* is an enchanting literary tour de force and an epic wartime love story. Although published for adults, the love story, history, and magnificent setting have endeared it to teenage readers, who frequently pick it up for independent reading.

SARAH DESSEN

## Dreamland

14–18 • Viking • 2000 • 250 pp.

As a younger sister, Caitlin always thought she never measured up to her perfect sibling, Cass. Then Cass abruptly runs off with a boy, and sixteen-year-old Caitlin struggles to fill the void left in the family. One day at a party she meets Rogerson Biscoe, a wild-haired, BMW-driving, drug-dealing bad boy, and she sees in him a chance to reinvent herself. As Caitlin struggles with this developing relationship, she doesn't know how to set boundaries. Then Rogerson begins hitting her, slapping her, abusing her, and she cannot pull away.

Deft at creating character and building events, Sarah Dessen explores teenage romance gone awry — when a relationship really becomes harmful. The reader feels Caitlin's pain and watches, horrified, as the adults ignore the signs of her abuse. Although it deals with an important issue, this powerful, provocative story never seems clinical; it often appeals, however, to girls who have stayed in emotionally or physically abusive relationships. Ultimately positive, *Dreamland* presents Caitlin's recovery in an institution and her survival and triumph as a human being.

BENEDICT AND NANCY FREEDMAN

## Mrs. Mike

12–14 • Coward-McCann • 1947 • 284 pp.

Even teens who admit to being devotees of the horror writer R. L. Stine find themselves swept away by this lush romance. In 1907, Katherine Mary O'Fallon of Boston goes to visit her uncle in Canada. There she meets and quickly falls in love with Sgt. Mike Flannigan of the Royal Canadian Mounted Police. Married to him at sixteen,

Kathy dogsleds with Mike several hundred miles north, to an isolated, dangerous, and brutal land where Mike serves as magistrate, doctor, priest, and counselor to all in the area. Traumatized by some of the horrible events that occur, including the death of their children, Kathy goes back to Boston, not knowing if she will return. But she longs for Mike, goes back to him, and starts another family in the wilderness.

Believing that her life should be recorded for posterity, Katherine Mary Flannigan pulled together a five-page outline, which, through an agent, was given to Benedict and Nancy Freedman, two writers in their midtwenties. They interviewed Mrs. Flannigan for three months and undertook massive newspaper research. Each wrote different scenes but went over the other's work sentence by sentence. Receiving enthusiastic reviews, the novel often appeared on both the fiction and nonfiction bestseller lists at the same time.

With sweeping romance yet tremendous honesty about the fragility of love, *Mrs. Mike* has enchanted teens for many years. An excellent choice for mother-daughter reading groups, it contains an immensely attractive heroine — not to mention a handsome, sensitive, strong, and chivalrous hero.

GARRET FREYMANN-WEYR

## *My Heartbeat*

12–14 • Houghton Mifflin • 2002 • 160 pp.

⤏ *PRINTZ HONOR*

Love triangles have always dominated romance literature, but *My Heartbeat* presents an unusual twist on this theme. Fourteen-year-old Ellen idolizes her brother, Link, and loves his best friend, James. For years these two wealthy New York private school chums have watched foreign films together, read complex novels, and attended concerts. But in high school, as the boys struggle with the exact nature of their relationship, Link decides to break it off. Ellen takes up with James, who is bisexual, and moves toward a sexual relationship with him. But as she does, Link starts falling apart mentally.

Exploring issues of self-discovery and the ambiguity of sexual relationships, the novel excels in presenting the emotional life of these three young lovers in a totally believable, compelling fashion.

NANCY GARDEN

## Annie on My Mind

14–18 • Farrar, Straus • 1982 • 234 pp.

Two seventeen-year-old New Yorkers, Liza and Annie, meet at the Metropolitan Museum of Art. Devoted museum-goers, both love medieval history, and they find themselves instantly drawn to each other. But they have different backgrounds: Liza attends a privileged prep school; Annie lives in an Italian working-class neighborhood. As their friendship deepens, they slowly realize their sexual attraction to each other, but after their relationship becomes public, they each have to handle the emotional stress with their peers and family. In the end, Liza and Annie resume contact, hoping to revive a relationship that means a great deal to each of them.

Absolutely groundbreaking when it was published, because of Nancy Garden's acceptance of lesbian love, *Annie on My Mind* got removed from libraries and was even burned in some communities. Garden's *The Year They Burned the Books* was inspired by her experiences fighting censorship cases. Although clearly written over two decades ago, the book still works with readers as a gentle romance, showing the healing powers of love.

PATRICE KINDL

## Owl in Love

12–14 • Houghton Mifflin • 1993 • 214 pp.

A wereowl, a girl by day and owl by night, fourteen-year-old Owl Tycho loves her science teacher; at night she perches on a tree outside his house, pining away for him. Since Owl isn't doing enough hunting, her parents worry about her health. At school, Owl is tormented because she never eats in front of her classmates, but she knows that her normal rodent fare wouldn't impress the cafeteria crowd. In a lovely ending, Owl survives her crush, actually helps a pale and starving young man, and makes a true friend, one she can trust. In the course of the narrative, she moves from being an outsider to someone who interacts with her community.

This delightful fantasy shows the problems of being a misfit in an original and totally delightful way. Patrice Kindl also explores the ability of adolescents to shift from one personality to another, trying to find one that fits them. Consequently, Owl emerges as a character that alienated or confused teenagers can take to heart and appreciate.

GAIL CARSON LEVINE

## *Ella Enchanted*

12–14 • Harper • 1997 • 233 pp.

⌁ *NEWBERY HONOR*

In a modern Cinderella story, Ella, at birth, receives a terrible gift from an addled fairy: henceforth, she cannot disobey a command. Her mother protects Ella, but when her mother dies, the teenage Ella must contend with her father's new fiancé. She is sent to a finishing school, where one of her despicable stepsisters discovers her secret and uses it against her. Determined to reverse the spell, Ella runs away and encounters ogres, giants, and a company of knights, led by Prince Charmont, or Char. After she is placed with her new stepmother, Ella must serve in the kitchen as a scullery maid. But in a happy ending, which requires her to face her greatest weakness, Ella attends three royal balls and ends up with her prince, just as we knew she would.

With a quite avaricious, mean-spirited, and selfish stepmother and stepsisters, and with a spunky, intelligent heroine and a prince to die for, *Ella Enchanted* appeals to readers who love retold fairy tales, such as Robin McKinley's *Beauty* and Donna Jo Napoli's *Zel*.

DAVID LEVITHAN

## *Boy Meets Boy*

12–14 • Knopf • 2003 • 186 pp.

A romance story as sweet as they come, showing only the exchange of kisses, conjures up the innocence of Maureen Daly's *Seventeenth Summer*. But this love story focuses on two high school boys. Paul, aware since kindergarten that he is gay, possesses self-confidence in abundance and lives in a family, community, and school that have completely accepted him. With a strong gay-straight alliance that boasts more members than the football team, the school elects a homecoming queen who also happens to be the star quarterback, an intriguing character called Infinite Darlene, and the cheerleaders ride

Harleys. In this amazing world, Paul's attraction to the artistic new boy in town, Noah, follows the natural progression — falling in love, losing the romance, then reuniting. Paul shows universal feelings and fears as his romance deepens with Noah.

In a novel that seems part fantasy and part reality, David Levithan claims he wrote a book "about where we're going, and where we should be," a world where sexual preferences carry as much stigma as the color of someone's eyes or hair. A funny and insightful book, *Boy Meets Boy* presents a cast of original and highly entertaining characters. Even taught in college gender studies classes, it can be read by anyone seeking a very happy and tender love story.

MARGARET MAHY

## The Catalogue of the Universe

12–14 • Atheneum • 1986 • 185 pp.

Beautiful Angela May lives alone with her mother and has heard stories all her life about the man who fathered her. A high school senior, she becomes determined to meet him, although her best friend, Tycho, tries to dissuade her. Although things don't work out when Angela faces her father, she and Tycho, a New Zealand version of the frog prince, develop a romance; they share a love of ideas and speak of books, astronomy, the Ionians, and math in a very sexy way.

With a distinct New Zealand setting and two unusual protagonists, *The Catalogue of the Universe* explores the age-old topic of teenage love and romance, treating adolescents with an inherent respect for their intelligence.

MARGARET MAHY

## The Changeover: A Supernatural Romance

12–14 • Atheneum • 1984 • 214 pp.

Fourteen-year-old Laura Chant resents her divorced mother's new love interest, Chris Holly. While taking care of her three-year-old brother, Laura takes him to a strange store, and the villainous owner imprints Jacko's hand with a stamp. Since Jacko becomes ill immediately afterward and needs to go to the hospital, Laura believes that he has had a supernatural encounter. She seeks out the advice of Sonny

Carlisle, a classmate who dabbles in the occult. Not only does one of his white witchcraft rituals seem to help Jacko improve, but Laura and Sonny develop a love relationship of their own.

Margaret Mahy has an uncanny ability to mix the ordinary with the mysterious, challenging ideas of time, space, and identity. In a part-horror, part-fantasy, and part-romance story, Laura battles to save her brother and in the process transforms herself.

IAN MCEWAN

## *Atonement*

14–18 • Doubleday • 2002 • 353 pp.

On a hot summer's day in 1935, thirteen-year-old Briony Tallis stands by her window on an English country estate and observes her sister, Cecilia, and the cleaning woman's son, Robbie. Arguing by an ancient fountain, the two break a valuable porcelain vase. In a fury, Cecilia strips her clothes off, leaps into the fountain, and retrieves the fragment. But in Briony's innocent and muddled mind, she believes that Robbie, a brilliant scholar whose education at Cambridge has been financed by the family, has done something shameful. Telling a blatant lie, she accuses Robbie of rape, gets him jailed, and brings disaster to her sister as well, for Cecilia loves the young man.

In the second part of the novel, Robbie, now a private in the British Army in World War II, witnesses all the atrocities of the campaign at Dunkirk. Abandoning her family, Cecilia has become a nursing sister in a veterans' hospital in London and struggles with the brutality and horror of war. Later Briony herself becomes a nursing student, comes to terms with what she did as a youth, and tries to make amends to Robbie and Cecilia, now living together as lovers. But no apology seems good enough. With an epilogue written in the first person by Briony in 1999, the outcome of the story remains in doubt.

*Atonement* explores in detail how an adolescent's moral sense and judgment can be so vastly different from an adult's. Ian McEwan had always been drawn to Jane Austen's *Northanger Abbey*, in which a young woman's reading of gothic novels causes her to misunderstand the events around her. He wanted to explore the idea of a young girl with imagination causing havoc, to see if he could develop her fully as the central character in his novel, and to write a simple love story in the twenty-first century.

Although by no means simple, *Atonement* captivates readers, as they hope the lovers will reunite and be whole again. A master of the language, McEwan always finds the unexpected word or adjective: a litigious couple defend "their good names with a most expensive ferocity." As well as any work of fiction, this luminous novel explores guilt, remorse, misunderstanding, and forgiveness — for ourselves and for others.

ROBIN MCKINLEY

## *Beauty: A Retelling of the Story of Beauty and the Beast*

12–14 • Harper • 1978 • 247 pp.

Written in the first person with frankness and humor, this retelling of the French story recasts the three daughters as Grace, Hope, and Honour. But the youngest is always called Beauty, even when she becomes a mousy, thin teenager who loves books and hopes to become a scholar. With her family in financial decline, Beauty moves with her horse, Greatheart, to a new home on the edge of a mysterious forest. In the center of the forest lives a monster, who gives rose seeds to Beauty's father — and in return demands a daughter. So Beauty goes to meet her Beast in a castle that conjures up whatever she needs and a library that yields books not yet written. Full of lush detail, magic, invention, and romance, *Beauty* makes the family members real and human and serves as a fine antidote to the Disney version of this fairy tale. Many fans read this well-written and well-conceived book many times, savoring it again and again.

DONNA JO NAPOLI

## *Zel*

12–14 • Dutton • 1996 • 228 pp.

In a sixteenth-century Swiss village, Zel goes to the market with her mother anticipating only her usual pleasures, of talking to vendors and special treats. But after she helps a nobleman, Konrad, with his horse, he asks what gift she would like in return. She requests a goose egg, to comfort a frustrated goose who has been building a nest with stones. That goose egg changes his and her life forever. Zel turns out to be no ordinary child. She lives alone with her mother, who believes that they have everything they need since they have each other. Actually a witch, however, she acquired Zel by making a pact with the devil and will do anything necessary to keep the girl all to herself. In one horrific scene, Mother convinces the thirteen-year-old to climb a walnut tree into a tower and abandons her there. For the next two years, Zel spends endless time in captivity, descending into madness. Having searched all that time, Konrad finds her, enters the tower on her long hair, makes love to her, and plans for her escape so that they can wed.

The narrative deftly alternates between Mother's first-person voice and the third-person present-tense voices of Zel and Konrad. Donna Jo Napoli has adapted "Rapunzel" and given it new psychological meaning for young readers. In a text that makes the witch of the story quite human, she explores the issues of dysfunctional mother-daughter relationships and the healing power of love and family. For in the end Zel "believes in life, in all its beauty and fragility. She has her daughters. She has her art. She feels rich. Her soul mends." A haunting story with romantic and lyrical prose, *Zel* stands as an excellent introduction to Napoli's many fine novels, which adapt fairy tales but add history and richness all her own — such as *The Magic Circle* ("Hansel and Gretel"), *Crazy Jack* ("Jack and the Beanstalk"), *Beast* ("Beauty and the Beast"), and *Bound* ("Cinderella").

ANN PACKER

## The Dive from Clausen's Pier

14–18 • Knopf • 2002 • 413 pp.

Twenty-three-year-old Carrie Bell finds her reality completely altered when her fiancée, and boyfriend from age fourteen, Mike Mayer, dives into Clausen's Reservoir and becomes a quadriplegic. Carrie at first tries to escape into sewing, something she loves. But, having lived in Madison, Wisconsin, all her life, she runs away precipitously, to New York City, where she takes fashion courses at Parsons and meets an older Holden Caulfield type, unable to come to terms with his own past. Eventually, Carrie returns to Mike and Madison.

By the end of the book, Carrie remains somewhat confused about her own path as she struggles to gain the confidence of her friends and family. But she serves as an acute observer of others, and hence a wide

variety of characters come vividly to life, as does the difference between small-town and big-city mores. With a sure sense of pace, the
book explores two young lovers faced with real tragedy as it raises the
moral issue of what one person owes another human being.

## EDITH PATTOU

### *East*

12–14 • Harcourt • 2003 • 508 pp.

In a beautifully told story, Edith Pattou adapts the Norwegian fairy
tale "East of the Sun, West of the Moon" into a lush, romantic story.
Set in Norway in the 1500s, *East* alternates among several voices as it
builds tension and plot. Born to a very superstitious mother, Rose frequently sees a white bear as she plays and has had one as an imaginary
friend since she was small. One night a white bear appears, promising
to give the family prosperity and cure a sick child if he can take Rose.
When he returns, Rose chooses to go with him — a journey that takes
her over land and sea into a mysterious castle. There her every need
gets attended to; in this magical setting lamps light, succulent food appears, and a magnificent loom has been set up for her weaving, for
Rose loves the craft. Slowly she and the bear become comfortable with
each other. However, one night she sneaks a look at the bear — really a
handsome man under a spell — spills candle wax on him, and seals his
fate; he now belongs to the beautiful troll queen. Horrified by what
she has done, Rose sets out on a long journey, over the ocean and
through the icebound land, to be reunited with her bearman.

With magnificent descriptions of the icy and northern terrain, an
examination of love, loss, and betrayal, and the universal language of
fairy tales, *East* has already proved popular with both adults and
young readers and has been adopted for summer reading lists. An excellent choice for mother-daughter reading groups.

## LOUISE PLUMMER

### *The Unlikely Romance of Kate Bjorkman*

12–14 • Delacorte • 1995 • 184 pp.

In a modern romance just as innocent as *Seventeenth Summer*, Kate
Bjorkman writes about her perfect Christmas, when she and her

brother's best friend fall in love. The setting, St. Paul, Minnesota, conjures up scenes from *It's a Wonderful Life*. With two parents devoted to each other and a creative and supportive family, Kate has a normal life that could be considered ideal. An unlikely romance heroine, she considers herself an Amazon at six feet in height; she wears thick glasses and shares her father's passion for linguistics. But when her brother, his new wife, and his best friend, Richard, visit from California at Christmas, Kate begins a romance with Richard that looks like it could last — or at least has lasted for all of six weeks.

Kate fills her saga, written as a romance novel, with tension and a betrayal by her own friend; with humor, she also provides notes for revising her story that add depth to the characters. But in the end, this sensible young woman, who plans to go to Columbia University after high school, writes long and delicious passages about kissing.

This old-fashioned, charming romance contains appealing characters, a very happy ending, and much holiday cheer.

ELIZABETH MARIE POPE

## The Sherwood Ring

12–14 • Houghton Mifflin • 1958 • 266 pp.

The guerrilla fighting in upper New York State during the Revolutionary War has seldom been explored in fiction; Elizabeth Marie Pope uses that background for a superb romance and ghost story set in Orange County, New York, where the author lived. Orphaned Peggy Grahame goes to live with her uncle at the old family farm, but soon she makes friends with the ghosts who linger at her ancestral home. They tell fabulous stories about the Revolution, when bands of American Patriots and British Loyalists roamed the countryside. Peggy watches her ancestor Barbara fall in love with a clever British officer — even his name, Peaceable Drummond Sherwood, could cause hearts to flutter.

Pope wrote books "connected in some way with history, magic, love, and intelligence." She created only one other novel, *The Perilous Gard*; both books are gems; both make readers long for other books by Pope.

Although Peggy pales a bit as a protagonist, her ancestors shine. Lush and rich, a well-paced story with a lot of history, *The Sherwood Ring* will answer any request for a gentle romance.

RANDY POWELL

## Is Kissing a Girl Who Smokes Like Licking an Ashtray?

12–14 • Farrar, Straus • 1992 • 208 pp.

A shy, geeky high school senior, Biff fantasizes about a romantic involvement with the girl of his dreams, Tommie Isaac. But a fifteen-year-old wisecracking and cigarette-smoking rebel, Heidi, enters his life, and the two develop a platonic relationship. Most of the action takes place over one weekend; at the end of this romantic comedy, it remains unclear if Biff will abandon his fantasy girl for the reality of Heidi.

Superb descriptions of the Seattle area and realistic dialogue round out this rare examination of a male adolescent in the throes of a crush.

DODIE SMITH

## I Capture the Castle

14–18 • Atlantic • 1948 • 352 pp.

In a dilapidated, rural English castle, seventeen-year-old Cassandra Mortmain, an aspiring writer, begins a journal, describing her unusual family and her feelings about them. Although the Mortmains purchased the castle when they were rich, they have watched their resources dwindle and now lack food and other necessities. At the beginning of the narrative, Cassandra's sister Rose jokingly invokes a spell to change their fortunes; then the wealthy American Cotton family takes over the nearby estate. With romance, disappointments, and a happy ending, the old-fashioned story easily captures readers' hearts and often is compared to the works of Jane Austen.

Written when the British author Dodie Smith was living in Pennsylvania, homesick for England, the book was out of print in America for many years. But in the 1990s J. K. Rowling called attention to the novel, one of her favorites; reissued, it also served as the basis for a 2003 film. Now it appears on many high school reading lists and has been embraced by a modern audience, enchanted by the protagonist, the genteel poverty, and life in a castle.

JERRY SPINELLI

## Stargirl

12–14 • Knopf • 2000 • 186 pp.

Although Jerry Spinelli once got a letter saying, "So you wrote a book. Big deal," *Stargirl* has been voted the favorite book of young readers in several states. The book contains two of Spinelli's most memorable characters, Leo and Stargirl, a free spirit. Homeschooled, with a purpose all her own, Stargirl completely alters an Arizona high school where "all wore the same clothes, talked the same way, ate the same food." Wearing long pioneer skirts and carrying a pet rat, Stargirl truly seems to comes from another planet — but "She is who we really are. Or were." This innocent love story explores teenage culture and nonconformity, and with a character inspired by Spinelli's wife, Eileen, it shows the heart and wit of one of our most gifted writers for young readers.

WENDELIN VAN DRAANEN

## Flipped

12–14 • Knopf • 2001 • 212 pp.

Ever since Juli looked into Bryce's dreamy blue eyes in second grade, she has been smitten. Finding Juli and her family a bit freakish, Bryce immediately begins to avoid her. Juli is definitely unique. She sits in the ancient sycamore tree on the block; she raises chickens in her backyard and delivers eggs. But by eighth grade, everything changes. Bryce starts thinking about Juli all the time, and she begins to wonder if he isn't handsome but shallow; he starts pursuing her, and she starts running away.

Told in chapters by Juli's and Bryce's alternating first-person voices, the contrasting points of view — he-said, she-said — round out two intriguing and very believable characters. Breezy, funny, yet true to eighth-grade life, *Flipped* captures young lovers, their insecurities, their emotional roller-coaster rides, and their insanity.

LAURA WHITCOMB

## *A Certain Slant of Light*

14–18 • Houghton Mifflin • 2005 • 282 pp.

Like any other star-crossed teenage lovers, Billy and Jennifer come from families that oppose their developing relationship. With his father in the penitentiary and his mother in the hospital, Billy is ordered around by his older brother, who forbids him to bring Jennifer to the house. Jennifer comes from a devout but completely controlling Christian family, and her parents believe that she should date only people from the church. So the teens grab spare moments, find secret places in the theater to make love, and skip classes to have a chance to be together, for they know they are the only beings on earth who can truly understand and appreciate each other.

Such has been the standard plot of teenage romance since *Romeo and Juliet,* but Laura Whitcomb adds a peculiar twist. For these two teenagers happen to be old spirits, or Lights, who have yet to find their way to God and heaven. Jennifer's body is appropriated by Helen, who has been around for 130 years; Billy has been taken over by a younger spirit, James. At first, they exchange what they know and have learned about roaming the earth since their deaths. In time they have to find ways to leave their human bodies and be reunited in the spirit. In fact, the book's ending — "We touched now soul to soul, both of us Light. And when we kissed, the garden rocked, floating upstream" — contains a kiss that sends them both literally into heaven.

Raising many questions, the book explores controversial territory: Jennifer is accused of having an affair with a teacher, and the lovers have unbridled and totally fulfilling sex. But because of the fantasy in the book, these details seem less stark than they would in a totally realistic story.

This stunning debut novel keeps readers turning the pages to find out what happens.

CONNIE WILLIS

## *To Say Nothing of the Dog*

14–18 • Bantam • 1998 • 424 pp.

In this sequel to *The Doomsday Book,* Connie Willis delivers an incredibly funny screwball romance. By 2057, Oxford University has made great advancements in time travel but lacks funding. Hence it takes on the project of Lady Schrapnell, a wealthy American who wants to rebuild Coventry Cathedral — destroyed in 1940 in the Blitz. The historian Ned Henry has been through so many drops, hunting for a hideous item called "the bishop's bird stump," that he finds himself badly time-lagged and senseless. Since a young student, Verity Kindle, miraculously transported a cat into the present, something no one thought possible, Ned is sent back to 1888 to repair the space-time continuum. But because of his mental condition, he fails to understand any of his instructions. As he basks in the Victorian world, meeting an amazing number of eccentric characters (including Charles Darwin, who keeps jumping out of trees), Ned falls in love with Verity. With chaos and confusion, they attempt to put the right couples together, because one produces an RAF grandson who engaged in critical bombings against the Germans. But the time-travel system seems to be breaking down, and at points they are not sure they will ever get back to their own Oxford.

In this fast-moving winner of the Hugo Award, filled with information about chaos theory, the Victorian age, World War II, Dorothy Sayers, and séances, the author provides a lot of excitement and humor and unites three pairs of lovers. In the final pages, Ned and Verity experience their first kiss, which lasts for 169 years. This book is a good choice for those who love tales of time travel, historical fiction, mysteries, or complex but totally rewarding romances.

ELLEN WITTLINGER

## Hard Love

14–18 • Simon & Schuster • 1999 • 227 pp.

↪ PRINTZ HONOR

Sixteen-year-old John shuffles between his depressed mother, who won't even touch him, and absent, playboy father, with whom John spends weekends. Because of his interest in zine writing and publishing, he meets Marisol, who writes *Escape Velocity,* a zine he admires. Although John struggles with his own identity and has always stayed away from the opposite sex, Marisol has always had a strong grasp on her own lesbianism. In this modern saga of unrequited love, John knows from the beginning that the girl he grows to love and care for cannot, and does not, return his feelings. At the end another girl emerges, and readers believe that John will finally heal, recovering from "hard love."

With pages that look like authentic zines, handwritten poems, and letters, the narrative moves at a snappy pace as it provides a compelling portrait of an adolescent writer experiencing a quixotic first love. The format works particularly well for reluctant readers. As one teen has written, "I HATED reading . . . But this book has changed that forever."

JACQUELINE WOODSON
## If You Come Softly
12–14 • Putnam • 1998 • 181 pp.

In a contemporary interracial romance, two fifteen-year-olds at an elite New York City prep school fall in love at first sight. Ellie, an upper-middle-class Jewish girl, tells the story in the first person, and the experiences of Jeremiah, the African-American son of a movie producer and famous writer, have been related in the third person. The author has rendered their situation with delicacy and subtlety: the intensity of their emotions, their developing trust in each other, and the problems that come from a perfect love in a deeply flawed society. Even though tragedy has been forecast, it still doesn't soften the impact of the heart-wrenching ending when Jeremiah is killed as he runs in a white neighborhood.

Jacqueline Woodson wanted to create a modern Romeo and Juliet, but in her book the enemies of the young lovers are racism and police brutality. She crafted a book that haunts readers, who find themselves turning the events of the novel over and over again in their minds.

CARLOS RUIZ ZAFÓN
## The Shadow of the Wind
14–18 • Penguin • 2004 • 487 pp.

This blend of thriller, historical fiction, mystery, and love story has been set in Barcelona, Spain, in the 1940s and 1950s. In 1945 ten-year-old Daniel Sempere, the son of a rare book dealer, is taken to the Cemetery of Forgotten Books, a secret vault containing a labyrinth of passageways and crammed bookshelves. There he adopts one volume, *The Shadow of the Wind* by Julián Carax, making sure it will stay alive. Even though another bookseller immediately offers to buy it from him at great cost, he holds on to it and cherishes it. But he does so at great risk because a malignant figure, Laín Coubert, has bought up or stolen every available copy and burned them.

In a book where the subplots have subplots, Daniel comes to spend time with the bookseller and falls in love with his blind niece, Clara. He reads to her and worships her from afar. Ultimately he goes on a quest to find Carax; in that process he discovers unpleasant details about Spain during the Civil War and World War II. As Daniel delves into Carax's past, his own story, as he becomes involved with his best friend's sister, starts to strangely mirror the life of Carax himself.

On the bestseller list in Spain, *The Shadow of the Wind* has been given a masterful translation, full of wit and wisdom: "Destiny is usually around the corner. . . . But what destiny does not do is home visits. You have to go for it."

The novel, like Cornelia Funke's *Inkheart,* appeals particularly to those who love books just as much as those who enjoy a complex and magnificent love story. This multifaceted novel — scary, erotic, tragic, thrilling, and emotionally satisfying — shows Daniel's coming of age, his first sexual experience, and his growth into a compassionate and believable young man.

# Science Fiction

A CHANCE TO LIVE in a completely different world has always appealed to teenagers; hence they have been one of the most enthusiastic audiences for science fiction. The genre began with the dystopian novels of Aldous Huxley and George Orwell; in their imaginary states the condition of life was extremely bad, the opposite of a utopia. *Brave New World* and *1984* predict a future, based on tendencies in the present, that a reader would not want to embrace.

But science fiction evolved to include a variety of intriguing forms: novels with fully created alternate worlds, such as Frank Herbert's *Dune;* complex time travel, as explored by Octavia Butler and Connie Willis; and alternate history. In the last category, called *uchronia,* the novelist asks the question: "If some pivotal event in history had taken a slightly different turn, how would it have affected later events?" Jasper Fforde in *The Eyre Affair* and Harry Turtledove in *The Guns of the South* seek to answer that question. The best examples of the genre have indeed aged very well; many of them are still teen favorites.

Although certainly grounded in this rich tradition, most of the science fiction novels published directly for teens have been dystopian. However, these works, including M. T. Anderson's *Feed* and Lois Lowry's *The Giver,* happen to be among the best works of fiction crafted for this audience in the last dozen years.

We live in an era with a spectrum of problems that can easily be explored in futuristic novels or alternate histories. What kind of world will we have in the future? Will our ecological destruction of the planet bring about its ultimate demise? What tendencies in our society will cause its destruction? Although books for teenagers rarely deal with political questions, the science fiction novels cited here not only explore serious issues but also keep teens excitedly turning the pages as well.

············——————··········

DOUGLAS ADAMS

## *The Hitchhiker's Guide to the Galaxy*

14–18 • Harmony • 1982 • 216 pp.

One of the most hapless heroes in the canon of literature, Arthur Dent gets plucked off the earth, seconds before it is pulverized, by his friend Ford Prefect, who for fifteen years has been posing as an out-of-work actor. In reality Ford conducts research for a new edition of *The Hitchhiker's Guide to the Galaxy*. The two begin their trek among the stars, meeting a variety of characters: Zaphod Beeblebrox, the president of the galaxy, with two heads and three arms; Trillian, his girlfriend, the former Tricia McMillan of Earth; Marvin, the depressed robot; and a few laboratory mice. The story moves with the speed of light from one punch line to the next. The most devoted fans of the book believe that it changes the way readers look at their own lives; others simply enjoy the adroit turns of phrase and idiosyncratic characters. Broadly humorous, much like Monty Python and British sitcoms, the adventures of Arthur and Ford have kept teens and adults laughing for a couple of decades and have spawned multiple sequels and a movie.

M. T. ANDERSON

## *Feed*

14–18 • Candlewick • 2002 • 234 pp.

✧ *NATIONAL BOOK AWARD FINALIST*

In a futuristic society, a communication "feed" provides a constant stream of media content hardwired directly into the brain. The teen narrator, Titus, accepts this world, where parents select their children's attributes and corporations control the stream of information and advertising. But during a spring break on the moon, Titus meets a homeschooled teenager, Violet, who rejects the idea of the feed and does her own thinking and research. In time, Violet's feed malfunctions, and because she is too perceptive and rebellious, no one will repair it.

Inspired by the black humor of Evelyn Waugh's early novels, such as *Decline and Fall*, M. T. Anderson naturally drew on the tradition of dystopian fiction, including *Gulliver's Travels, 1984,* and one of his childhood favorites, H. G. Wells's *The Time Machine.* Anderson's intense dislike of mass market culture provided the emotional center for the novel; his incredible ear for teenage slang — "Dude, the truffle is totally undervalued!" — creates much of the humor.

In this deft combination of contemporary teen life — their slang, profanity, and shopping mall subculture — and fantasy, the book explores the problems of our conspicuous consumer age taken to a new and frightening level. A severely flawed protagonist, Titus at first denies the truth, then finally awakens to it. Yet the book causes readers to question what might happen, and is now occurring, in a media-dominated culture. Like the best of speculative fiction, *Feed* leaves its readers uncomfortable and disturbed long after they have finished the last page.

MARGARET ATWOOD

## The Handmaid's Tale

14–18 • Houghton Mifflin • 1986 • 312 pp.

Offred, the protagonist of the story, serves as a handmaid, a woman who will produce children in the Republic of Gilead, an American community set sometime in the future. Because of exposure to pesticides, nuclear waste, or leakage from chemical weapons, many women have become infertile. Hence, the few fertile women get trained as birth mothers for the upper class. Lower-class women either clean up the toxic waste or become "Marthas," house servants. In the new Republic, a feminist's nightmare, women are strictly controlled, unable to have jobs or possessions, and are assigned to various classes. Sex is allowed only for reproduction; handmaids turn the children they bear over to morally fit wives, who raise them.

After trying to escape from Gilead, Offred gets placed in the service of the Commander and his wife, Serena Joy. Serena finds herself jealous and would happily send Offred away if she does not become pregnant. Offred develops an unexpected relationship with the Commander, who is also lonely and isolated. Told by Offred, a somewhat unreliable narrator, the story reveals her eventual escape from this horrendous regime.

Margaret Atwood, a Canadian, set the novel in the United States because she believed her story more in keeping with the American political landscape than with what could happen in Canada. Writing in 1984, the year of Orwell's brilliant speculative fiction, she studied various utopian and dystopian novels and imagined what would occur if conservative Christians took control of the American government and established a dictatorship. She believed the book looked only at what has already happened in the United States and gave it a slight, futuristic twist.

Certainly controversial, *The Handmaid's Tale* has also become one of the books that adolescents remember with passion from their high school reading. It particularly affects young women who are trying to understand their society and their role in it.

GARY BLACKWOOD

## Second Sight

12–14 • Dutton • 2005 • 279 pp.

In a rare alternate history actually written for adolescents, Gary Blackwood chooses Washington, D.C., in 1864 as his setting. There Nicholas and Joseph Ehrlich perfect a father-and-son mind-reading act that they use to entrance theatergoers. Joseph meets many of the performers of the day, including John Wilkes Booth, and becomes acquainted with Cassandra Quinn, a girl with clairvoyant powers. She senses various plots against President Lincoln, and Joseph becomes her go-between to the president's office. Ultimately Cassandra and Joseph need to intervene to keep Lincoln alive.

With a witty omniscient narrator, a fine twist on history, and fascinating, behind-the-scenes information about the theater and performers, *Second Sight* provides a page-turning plot, a lesson in history, and a great deal to discuss — in book groups or in classes. Enthusiastic readers will also want to pick up Blackwood's *The Year of the Hang-*

*man;* set in 1777, this alternate history is based on the concept that the British captured George Washington and the Americans lost the Revolutionary War.

RAY BRADBURY
## *Fahrenheit 451*
14–18 • Ballantine • 1953 • 173 pp.

A lthough some science fiction ages badly — because the future arrives and looks nothing like the author's predictions — Ray Bradbury's *Fahrenheit 451* seems amazingly contemporary. In this novel the United States has been involved in an ongoing, free-floating war. Day and night, combat jets streak overhead. The rest of the world hates us, and Americans don't understand why. They don't understand much of anything, really; they stay surrounded all day long by electronic stimuli that talk back to them and serve as their family.

At the center of this novel set in the twenty-fourth century stands Montag, a fireman. But in this society firemen don't protect homes from fires, they start them. "It was a pleasure to burn," Montag believes, and like his fellow firemen, he sets out to destroy homes that contain dangerous objects — books. He devotes his days and nights to removing all of the printed material in society. A powerful, provocative book, *Fahrenheit 451* presents a world where books have to be hidden or no longer exist, where enemies of the state get hunted down by a Mechanical Hound, and where those who love literature have fled to the countryside and commit their lives to reciting great literature from memory.

Over the years, editors inappropriately removed material in seventy-five different sections of the novel; in 1982 all the "damns" and "hells" were reinstated. Some fifty years after publication, the book about the dangers of censorship still has the power to make both young readers and adults think and respond. Ray Bradbury once said, when asked what adults could do to encourage teenage reading, "Hand them a book. . . . Give one of my books to a twelve-year-old boy who doesn't like to read, and that boy will fall in love and start to read." And for over fifty years *Fahrenheit 451* has done just that — helped young and old alike fall in love with reading and books all over again.

ANTHONY BURGESS

## *A Clockwork Orange*

14–18 • Norton • 1962 • 192 pp.

Written in the vernacular of street gangs, *A Clockwork Orange* begins: "'What's it going to be then, eh?' There was me, that is Alex, and my three droogs, that is Pete, Georgie, and Dim, Dim being really dim, and we sat in the Korova Milkbar." In this future world these teenagers speak a special language (Nadsat) and spend their time robbing and terrorizing London's citizens. At a cottage called HOME, they beat up the author of "A Clockwork Orange," a manuscript celebrating human free will, and rape his wife. After murdering a woman, Alex spends two years in a state jail; the government uses him as a guinea pig in a new treatment, Ludovico's Technique, which eliminates a person's power to choose. Released from jail, Alex simply wants to get away from the violence of his youth, settle down, marry, and have a son.

When *A Clockwork Orange* was published in the United States, the twenty-first chapter, showing Alex's move to nonviolence, was dropped. Finally, in 1986, the original book appeared in America. Anthony Burgess always claimed that his publisher insisted on the altered version. The editor maintained that he merely made a suggestion to improve the book: he did not believe that Alex — with a lifetime of alienation, rape, torture, random brutality, and rebellion — could get so quickly brainwashed into morality and a sense of social order.

Made popular by a Stanley Kubrick film, the book appeals to those who enjoy black humor, original language, and details of the grotesque. Burgess's underlying questions about government, free will, choice, and humanity continue to make the novel an intriguing one to discuss in adult-teen groups or in classes.

OCTAVIA E. BUTLER

## *Kindred*

14–18 • Doubleday • 1979 • 264 pp.

The second half of the twentieth century saw the publication of several neo-slave narratives, including such works as Margaret

Walker's *Jubilee* and Toni Morrison's *Beloved*. One of the most impressive remains Octavia Butler's *Kindred*, in which Dana, a black woman, gets transported from Los Angeles in 1976 onto a slave plantation in Maryland in the early 1800s. Whenever Dana's ancestor Rufus finds himself in harm's way or almost dead, she suddenly appears, after getting dizzy and woozy in the "real" world. At first Dana stays only to help Rufus, who becomes a white slaveowner in the immediate situation. But she starts spending longer and longer time periods on the plantation, and at one point her white husband, Kevin, comes with her.

Because of Dana's modern sensibilities, she experiences the reality of slavery even more brutally than those of the period might have — the savage beatings, people becoming chattel or property, and families being torn asunder. Dana finally returns to the modern world — physically damaged, missing part of an arm — and psychologically changed. But the reader has also been altered in the course of this narrative: slavery becomes more than an institution; readers have grown to identify with real people and real pain.

When Butler wrote the book at the beginning of her career, few black protagonists existed in science fiction or time travel fantasy, and blacks did not write books in the genre. Butler's passion for her subject matter, her characters, and her compelling, page-turning story have gained a growing audience for *Kindred*, which has been most recently reissued as part of Beacon Press's Bluestreak series.

ORSON SCOTT CARD

## *Ender's Game*

12–14 • Tom Doherty • 1985 • 324 pp.

As Earth prepares for the coming war with an alien insectoid race, six-year-old Ender Wiggin trains feverishly for military command. The third child in a family — with a sister, Valentine, who loves him and a brother, Peter, who doesn't — Ender gets taken one day to the International Fleet battle school. Using games and simulators in the Battle Room, Ender succeeds at various scenarios thrown his way where other children have failed. Learning to balance a need for winning and aggression against intelligence and compassion, he becomes the last, best hope for saving Earth. Can he be trained in time? Will he master the command or will the Buggers decimate the human race? Are these only games — or more real than they seem? These tensions form one of the most popular science fiction novels ever published for young readers.

Orson Scott Card wrote the short story "Ender's Game," which first appeared in 1977 in the science fiction magazine *Analog*. He had been thinking about how military training might change in the future and imagined a battle room where soldiers could use 3-D simulators. Choosing a child as a protagonist, Card transformed his story into a book for adults in about four weeks, and *Ender's Game* won both the Hugo and Nebula awards when it appeared. Its sequel, *Speaker for the Dead*, again won both awards the following year.

Quickly, the book became a staple for teenagers; it beguiles even those who don't usually enjoy science fiction. Many admit to multiple readings, and the book has even been used in military schools to train new cadets in military thinking and in college leadership classes. With several popular sequels, the book combines game play, an intriguing character, and fascinating philosophical concepts in a fast-paced thriller, full of surprises to the very end.

JOHN CHRISTOPHER

## The White Mountains

12–14 • Macmillan • 1967 • 214 pp.

In a future world, Tripods control the earth. Some say these machines, invented by men, revolted against the human race and enslaved them. Some believe that the Tripods came from another planet. But all know that when boys reach fourteen, they experience a "capping" ceremony, when a metal plate gets inserted into their head. After that, they become the servants of the Tripods. In order to avoid capping, two boys, Will, who narrates the story, and his cousin Henry in England join up with Beanpole (Jean Paul) in France. Hiking through Switzerland, they follow a map to join the mountain men, free men who are preparing to destroy the Tripods.

Including two sequels, *The City of Gold and Lead* and *The Pool of Fire*, and a prequel, *When the Tripods Came*, John Christopher's Tripods Trilogy presents a basic boys' adventure tale with a light touch of science fiction. The swift-moving narrative, told with originality and grace, has remained popular with young readers for some forty years.

ROBERT CORMIER

## Fade

14–18 • Delacorte • 1988 • 310 pp.

As Stephen King wrote before *Fade* was published: "Imagine what might happen if Holden Caulfield stepped into H. G. Wells's *The Invisible Man*." In the summer of 1938 Paul Moreaux, a French-Canadian teenager, lives in a Massachusetts mill town. At first he seems like an ordinary thirteen-year-old, attending parochial school and fitting into the town's structure. But in time he discovers that, like his uncle Adelard, he has inherited the family trait of "fading" — he can become invisible at will. Although this gift might seem exciting, it proves a heavy burden for Paul, as it had for other members of his family, bringing much disappointment and heartache.

In a complex novel, multiple narrative voices piece together the story: Paul, his nephew Ozzie, who also inherited the trait, and his cousin Susan, who finds Paul's manuscript about the events. But the book includes thirty-three developed characters, and fifty-five more get mentioned by name. Details of the landscape and life in this factory town, gritty and gray, emerge with great clarity. Because the setting seems so completely drawn, these descriptions add to the borderless and disturbing interweaving of reality and fiction.

By the time he started writing the book, Robert Cormier had built a firm reputation as a realist. He then began to explore an autobiographic novel with an added element — what would happen if he and his main character could become invisible? The resulting science fiction novel rests firmly in reality. In fact, on the surface it appears to be so truthful that friends would often pull Cormier aside and say, "Bob, *can* you fade?"

Like so many of Cormier's novels, *Fade* provokes endless discussion because of its ambiguity and intrigue. In this book Cormier proved once again that he could write like an angel — even when he explored the devil's own world.

MICHAEL CRICHTON

## Jurassic Park

12–14 • Knopf • 1990 • 400 pp.

On an isolated island off the coast of Costa Rica, a group of businessmen and scientists have been scheming to build the world's most incredible and ambitious theme park. Using the cutting edge of DNA research, they recreate a variety of dinosaurs — some peaceful, some vicious — and cage them in the spectacular Jurassic Park. However, a series of mishaps causes the inventors to call in a team from the outside to validate their work; it includes a paleontologist, his research partner, and a mathematician. John Hammond, the mastermind behind the group, also spontaneously decides to include his grandchildren in the weekend expedition. But in this modern rendition of the Frankenstein story, the almost three hundred dinosaurs quickly start to act as they naturally would, not as their creators envisioned.

Taking readers on a roller-coaster ride, page after page, Michael Crichton not only provides an original and exciting plot but also includes a great deal of scientific information: Chaos Theory, DNA, a host of magnificent creatures — their attributes and social instincts — as well as the moral and philosophical issues surrounding scientific research. Infinitely more intriguing than the films it has inspired, *Jurassic Park* can be enjoyed by readers of all ages; even after they stop hunting for dinosaurs under the bed, they will never think about them in quite the same way again.

PETER DICKINSON

## Eva

12–14 • Delacorte • 1989 • 220 pp.

With a vastly overpopulated planet on which the wilderness has disappeared, people spend most of their time indoors, watching the huge "shaper." Thirteen-year-old Eva Adamson, the daughter of a zoologist, lies in an irreversible coma resulting from a terrible car accident. One of her father's colleagues performs a successful experiment and implants Eva's own neuron memory into the brain and able body of a female chimpanzee. When she finally leaves the hospital, Eva finds herself besieged by the media. She also begins to adjust to her half chimp–half human existence. In time, she decides to lead the chimps away from their captors to a remote island. There she teaches them the rudiments of survival; she becomes a new Eve, son of Adam, for chimpanzees.

This novel, which covers nearly a quarter of a century, deals with many of the issues common to young adults — the replacement of a small, smooth body with a large, unrecognizable one, the discovery that parents can be weak, the loss of parental affection, and leaving the known to strike out on one's own.

Peter Dickinson found in writing the novel that it took unexpected twists and turns. He began by exploring the person scientists refer to as "African Eve," the ancestress of humankind suggested by mitochondrial research. Dedicating the book to Jane Goodall, the chimpanzee expert, Dickinson brought in the issues of animal rights, although that had never been his intention. All of these random elements finally come together in the cauldron of story, creating a book memorable, eerie, and haunting.

JEANNE DUPRAU

## *The City of Ember*

12–14 • Random House • 2003 • 274 pp.

Set in a post-apocalyptic underground world, the city of Ember exists without natural light and with diminishing resources. "Running out of light bulbs, running out of power, running out of time — disaster was right around the corner." As twelve-year-old Doon repairs leaks in the Pipeworks, he learns about the city's malfunctioning generator. So, with his schoolmate Lina, he sets out to save the city. Readers are kept on the edge of their seats by the spare and suspenseful storytelling, with a lot of cliffhangers, as he and Lina find their way outside Ember to a world that had been left behind.

Both Doon and Lina make attractive characters, for they care about each other and remain persistent in the face of difficulties. The futuristic landscape — inspired by the author's childhood, when people built backyard bomb shelters — can easily be imagined as well as the underlying problem: how people react to a scarcity of resources. Followed by *The People of Sparks* and with more room for sequels, the book has quickly established itself as a favorite of young readers and works extremely well with reluctant readers.

SYLVIA LOUISE ENGDAHL

## *Enchantress from the Stars*

12–14 • Atheneum • 1970 • 288 pp.

✎ *NEWBERY HONOR*

In a science fiction novel more concerned with philosophy than technology, Elana comes from an advanced civilization where they can communicate by extrasensory perception and move objects by psychokinesis. A Student of the Federation Anthropological Service, Elana and other members of the service help protect Younglings — those societies that might be wiped out by others in the cosmos. Hence she gets sent to Andrecia, where people still believe in magic and feel that a dragon has been ravaging the land. In fact, the dragon happens to be the Imperial Exploration Corps from another planet. Elana must work with Georyn, a woodsman on the planet, to frighten off the invaders. Ultimately he saves Andrecia with the aid of the woman he sees as an Enchantress from the Stars.

The complex narrative offers three points of view: Elana's first-person account; the omniscient prose of Jarel, a member of the Imperial Exploration Corps; and the impressions of Georyn, which read like a fairy tale.

In 2001, when the book had been out of print for many years, Walker reissued it with an attractive cover by Leo and Diane Dillon and an essay by Lois Lowry. This well-designed volume has introduced a new generation to a thought-provoking and imaginative journey into the future, where the fate of planets rests on the shoulders of teenagers.

NANCY FARMER

## *The Ear, the Eye and the Arm*

12–14 • Orchard • 1994 • 312 pp.

✎ *NEWBERY HONOR*

Working for a publishing company in Zimbabwe, Nancy Farmer had been creating stories for African schoolchildren. Then, with her son, Daniel, as the model for a four-year-old character, she wrote a story combining a lot of disparate elements, including Shona mythology and folklore. In *The Ear, the Eye and the Arm,* thirteen-year-old Tendai, his sister, and his brother, Kuda, have been sheltered all their lives because their father, chief of security for Zimbabwe in 2194, has always been a constant target for criminals. However, they are captured by an enormous woman named She Elephant and forced to work in a toxic waste dump. Although they manage to escape, they keep getting trapped. Eventually, the family enlists the aid of some detectives with paranormal powers — the Ear, the Eye, and the Arm — who provide some comic relief in the story.

A glossary aids with both traditional African and futuristic terms. Bringing all the fantasy and futuristic strands together seamlessly, this novel, with an unusual mélange of elements, cannot be mistaken for any other book.

NANCY FARMER

## *The House of the Scorpion*

12–14 • Atheneum • 2002 • 382 pp.

↦ *NEWBERY HONOR/PRINTZ HONOR/NATIONAL BOOK AWARD*

In the near future, in the evil country of Opium, young Matteo Alácran experiences a privileged life as the clone of the drug lord El Patrón, now 142 years old. Generally clones are despised, used only for medical purposes and for tending the poppy fields. As he grows older, Matt tries to reconcile his love for the drug lord with the evil the substances have produced — humans and animals who become zombies, clones slaughtered for their organs. Matt must flee after El Patròn dies, but ultimately he chooses to come back in an attempt to alter the drug kingdom.

In this futuristic story that evokes the landscape of the Mexican border, Nancy Farmer raises questions about the nature of our responsibility to others and the meaning of life and death. A combination of adventure, survival lore, and science fiction, *The House of the Scorpion* moves into the territory of Huxley's *Brave New World* to present a chilling modern dystopia.

JASPER FFORDE

## The Eyre Affair

14–18 • Viking • 2002 • 374 pp.

In a hilarious alternate history that contains some of the madcap humor of Douglas Adams novels, Special Operative Thursday Next, a literary detective, takes on a case involving a stolen Dickens manuscript. In England circa 1985, the Crimean War has been dragging on for about 130 years; literature, however, holds a prominent place in everyday lives — hence the stealing of a manuscript takes on extreme importance. The evil Acheron Hades intends not only to steal original manuscripts but plans to alter them forever, since he has discovered a portal that takes people in and out of books. At first a minor Dickens character gets murdered, but then this mastermind sets out to kidnap Jane Eyre and change the plot of one of England's most beloved books forever.

Much as characters wander in and out of books in Cornelia Funke's *Inkheart*, the line between reality and fiction has been blurred in *The Eyre Affair*. Romance, adventure, mystery, and literary allusions play out over the course of the narrative as the author provides a totally happy and satisfying ending to this clever work of fiction.

MARGARET PETERSON HADDIX

## Running Out of Time

12–14 • Simon & Schuster • 1995 • 184 pp.

Thirteen-year-old Jessie believes that she lives in Clifton, Indiana, in 1840. When her mother asks her to leave the village to get help for a diphtheria epidemic, Jessie discovers a horrible fact: she really lives in Clifton, Indiana, in a reconstructed village in 1996. The site has been used by unethical scientists and gets viewed daily by tourists. As Jessie tries to help the inhabitants of the village, she must struggle with phenomena she has never encountered — cars, telephones, and television.

Not only has Margaret Peterson Haddix invented a fascinating premise, she keeps the action moving swiftly as Jessie manages to escape from the village and the evil men who have incarcerated all of them. Because the book explores authentic Midwestern life in 1840, it can be used for classroom discussions. Combining time travel, histori-cal fiction, and a contemporary setting, it appeals to a wide range of readers. Those who enjoy it will definitely want to read Haddix's im-mensely popular Shadow Children series.

FRANK HERBERT

## Dune

14–18 • Chilton • 1965 • 537 pp.

In a complex society 8,000 years in the future, human beings have colonized planets throughout the universe. From his own planet, Duke Leto prepares to leave for his new position as governor of a desert planet, Arrakis (Dune), in order to harvest a valuable spice drug found only in this environment. Although he takes his concubine, Jessica, and his fifteen-year-old son, Paul, Leto has been warned by his men that his rivals, the Harkonnens, led by Baron Harkonnen, may be setting a trap for him.

Although Leto gets killed, Jessica and Paul escape. The natives of the desert, the Fremen, believe that these two are their saviors and have come to create a lush paradise on the planet. Jessica becomes their reverend mother. Paul discovers that, by eating the spice drug, he can see into the future and the past, and he teaches the Fremen to fight in a special style, "the weirding." When Paul and the Fremen prevail over massive odds, Paul becomes the new emperor.

Frank Herbert began his research on sand dunes in Oregon in 1957, and by 1963 had sent his agent an outline for a book entitled *Dune World.* John W. Campbell, Jr., of *Analog* magazine, bought the manuscript in days. But the serialization would be the easiest part of the publishing process for Herbert. Twenty-three publishers turned down this massive volume, complaining about everything from the unfamiliar technology in the first ten pages to the length of the text. Consequently Chilton, best known for its auto repair manuals, had the honor of putting this classic into print. After winning both the Nebula and Hugo awards, *Dune* began to reach its audience; today, over 20 million copies have been sold.

Taking real elements from history, casting them in a new light, and incorporating an ecological message, Herbert created a richly tex-tured, fascinating, and exotic world in *Dune;* because of the complexity of its universe, the book, which contains several appendixes, including an extensive glossary, often gets compared to Tolkien's Lord of the Rings trilogy. This superb blend of adventure, invention, mysticism, environmentalism, and politics was followed by five sequels. Brian Herbert, with the help of his father's notes, has added several prequels. The books have inspired a movie, a television series, classroom units for teaching, an encyclopedia, music — and legions of fans for the past forty years.

ALDOUS HUXLEY

## Brave New World

14–18 • Doubleday • 1932 • 259 pp.

In the year 2540, 632 years after the invention of the Model T Ford, children get produced in the Central London Hatching and Conditioning Centre as part of various castes — Alphas, Betas, Gammas, Deltas, and Epsilons. They also get thoroughly conditioned by injection and socialization. Although everything in the population has been controlled, even happiness, Bernard finds himself dissatisfied. On vacation on a New Mexico savage reservation, he encounters John, the Savage, born viviparously. When Bernard transports John and his mother back to England, the novel focuses on the contrast between the old ways and the new civilization. In this mechanized world, sex is rampant but emotion disdained.

Inspired by the Russian novel *We*, by Yevgeny Zamyatin, *Brave New World* ushered in a century of dystopian fiction. Novels of the future, such as Edward Bellamy's *Looking Backward*, tended to paint the coming world in rosy hues. Obviously affected by the rise of Marxism and Communism in Europe and the stock market crash, Aldous Huxley, although he came from a family that had championed Darwin, saw the new state order as something quite horrific. When the book appeared, it received negative, even vituperative, reviews ("a lugubrious and heavy-handed piece of propaganda"); the novelist E. M. Forster once called Huxley "a humanist who disliked humanity." But if Huxley's harsh vision was a bit ahead of its time, readers found themselves intrigued by his landscape, an eerie combination of totalitarian and omnipresent feel-good drugs and sex. In *Brave New World*, Huxley gives readers a disturbing vision of a scientifically engineered dystopia — one that proved prescient in many ways and that still engenders heated discussion when read in high school or college.

## DANIEL KEYES
### *Flowers for Algernon*
14–18 • Harcourt • 1966 • 311 pp.

In a touching, suspenseful, and convincing story, Charlie Gordon, a janitor–delivery boy in his thirties, possesses an I.Q. of 68. But through neurosurgery he is transformed into a genius. As he moves from barely literate to eloquent, he records this journey in his journal. Because he has been used as a guinea pig, the doctors simply don't know what such a leap in intellect will mean for a person formerly functioning as a six-year-old. The only subject so far has been the white mouse Algernon, who can at first execute mazes with ease. As Charlie progresses intellectually, he begins to remember his former self and the happiness that now eludes him. Then Algernon suddenly deteriorates, and Charlie discovers a terrible flaw in the scientist's calculations.

Winner of the Nebula and Hugo awards and the basis of the movie *Charly*, the book has been widely adopted for classroom use for four decades. Some students even run mazes to get inside Charlie's head. Ultimately, *Flowers for Algernon* encourages discussion of the idea that led Daniel Keyes to write it: "What would happen if it were possible to increase human intelligence artificially?"

## LOIS LOWRY
### *The Giver*
12–14 • Houghton Mifflin • 1993 • 208 pp.
↪ *NEWBERY MEDAL*

In 1993 Lois Lowry found herself frequently visiting a nursing home, with her mother and father each in a separate section. Going blind, her mother would relate tales of childhood. Although in better physical condition, her father slowly lost his memory. As a result, Lowry started to think about the importance of memory.

At the same time, she took her nine-year-old grandson to ride the Swan Boats in Boston's Public Garden. He asked her, "Have you ever noticed that when people think they are manipulating ducks, actually ducks are manipulating people?" This comment haunted Lowry, and she began wondering what kind of world her grandchildren would inherit.

With these images in mind, Lowry began writing a novel about a future utopia. But after a while she saw the dark side of the world she had been creating. Eventually, she realized — as readers of *The Giver* grow to understand — that she had created a dystopian novel.

From the opening sentence, "It was almost December, and Jonas was beginning to be frightened," readers get pulled along by the sweep of the narrative. Set in a futuristic world that appears to have solved all the world's problems — poverty, inequality, loneliness, and old age — *The Giver* chronicles the coming-of-age of twelve-year-old Jonas. Jonas gets assigned as an apprentice to The Giver, the keeper of all the memories that the community has abandoned to achieve its current stability. In the process, he begins to question the choices made by his community and what it means for his own future. One of literature's most impassioned young protagonists, Jonas must finally face the inadequacies and hypocrisies of his parents' generation.

Some reviewers expressed concern about the ambiguous ending of the book. However, the ending allows each reader to determine the fate of Jonas: "For the first time, he heard something that he knew to be music. He heard people singing . . . But perhaps it was only an echo." Lowry always intended the ending to be optimistic. In the sequels, *Gathering Blue* and *The Messenger,* readers learn what actually happens to Jonas.

Provocative, moving, and haunting, from the moment of its publication *The Giver* emerged as an ideal book to read and share, whether in parent-teen book groups or in the classroom. Now, with millions of copies in print, it has taken its place as one of the greatest speculative novels of the twentieth century.

JOHN MARSDEN

## Tomorrow, When the War Began

12–14 • Houghton Mifflin • 1995 • 286 pp.

In one of Australia's best-selling titles for teenagers, Ellie and six of her friends go off camping in a wilderness area. Returning a week later, they find their houses empty, their pets dead, and the country invaded by an unnamed enemy. Slowly they deduce that their town has been captured, and they go into hiding, amass provisions, and harass the invaders in guerrilla warfare. In these adventures, Ellie kills two men and finds she no longer can be called a polite, obedient kid but has changed into a complex and stronger person. In this strange new land, the teenagers pair up and fall in love, but they also find new meaning and purpose in their lives. At the end of the book they blow up a strategic bridge, and their harrowing escapades continue for seven more volumes in this popular series.

*Tomorrow, When the War Began* allows young readers to ponder what they might be called on to do if their country were ever invaded. It's superb for parent-teen or teenage book discussion groups.

ROBERT C. O'BRIEN

## *Z for Zachariah*

12–14 • Atheneum • 1975 • 249 pp.

Ann Burden, sixteen, tells in a diary how she has survived an atomic war by living in her family home in Pennsylvania farm country. Ann emerges as a sensitive yet resourceful young woman, in love with nature, close to the earth, with strong religious feelings. While she cares for her cows and chickens and tends the vegetable garden, John Loomis, a chemist from Cornell, arrives in a plastic "safe suit." Although suspicious of him, Ann also longs for companionship. She takes care of him during a long illness, but he later attempts to rape her. Showing great courage, Ann steals the safe suit and sets out to find another place to live.

Because the author worked at the *National Geographic*, which frowned on outside writing by staff members, Robert Leslie Conly adopted a pseudonym, his mother's name, and published his novels covertly. Without book tours, media interviews, meeting and greeting people, talking to readers, or any other kind of public appearance, Robert C. O'Brien gained his devoted following solely by his writing. Although he died shortly before finishing this novel, his daughter Jane finished it and prepared it for publication. Hence both a male and female writer shaped one of science fiction's most attractive female protagonists.

Although published more than thirty years ago, this combination of survival story and science fiction frequently shows up on lists of teenagers' favorite books. Certainly, it is one of the greatest father-daughter collaborations of all time.

GEORGE ORWELL

## *1984*

14–18 • Harcourt • 1949 • 279 pp.

Winston Smith works for the Ministry of Truth in London. His totalitarian society controls people's lives completely; privacy does not exist in any form; everyone is watched from telescreens. Rewriting history for the benefit of the government, Winston alters newspapers and all records, including books. A low-ranking member of The Party, he tries to break away. First he writes in a diary, a forbidden activity, and then has an affair with another party member. But Big Brother always watches: Winston gets caught, imprisoned, and reprogrammed. No one can escape from the system.

Written after the death of his wife and when he himself suffered from tuberculosis, George Orwell found himself in a bleak frame of mind and created a book that maintains a mood of hopelessness about the future of mankind. The first readers of *1984* applied the novel to events in the Soviet Union; but Orwell insisted that any society, including England and America, could easily develop a totalitarian, all-controlling government.

Although the actual year of the title occurred more than two decades ago, George Orwell's speculative novel continues in the twenty-first century to captivate young readers, make headlines, and even be part of the political election process. For over fifty years, it has warned against all-invasive government, "Big Brother," and the "Thought Police" and what they mean for individual freedom.

RODMAN PHILBRICK

## *The Last Book in the Universe*

12–14 • Scholastic/Blue Sky • 2000 • 223 pp.

Taking place after the Big Shake destroys the world, the story focuses on a young epileptic hoodlum, Spaz, who sets out to rob an old man, Ryter. Much of the planet has been taken over by rival gangs and ganglords; however, a select few — the proovs, or genetically improved — live in the idyllic Eden. Stealing merely happens to be Spaz's job, but Ryter begins to have a profound influence on this troubled young man. When they go on a long journey to see Spaz's dying "sister," they get the help of a gorgeous proov, Lanaya, in the process. She takes them to Eden, something forbidden, and it looks remarkably like the earth today. Spaz ultimately becomes "the last book in the universe," and he sets out, like Ryter, to record a story on paper.

Clearly influenced by Anthony Burgess's *A Clockwork Orange* in both its language and world of gang warfare, *The Last Book in the Universe* raises many issues about life on earth by positing a rather grim future. A classroom and summer reading favorite, this novel causes adolescents to think and turn the pages excitedly at the same time.

PHILIP REEVE

## Mortal Engines

12–14 • Harper/Eos • 2003 • 311 pp.

Long after the Sixty Minute War that destroyed civilization and its technology, London has become a "Traction City," one capable of moving all over the landscape and seizing other municipalities. After one successful capture, the city historian, Thaddeus Valentine, gets attacked by a girl with a horribly disfigured face. When Tom Natsworthy saves Valentine, however, much to Tom's surprise, Valentine shoves him down a waste chute into the wilderness. Teaming up with the girl, Hester Shaw, Tom traverses the sky and land, learning about life before the war, the true nature of Valentine and his enemy, the Anti-Traction advocates, and the limitations of "municipal Darwinism." Along the way, he encounters a group of pirates who have taken over Turnbridge Wheels, a dashing aviatrix, and the reconstructed robot-man Grike, who stalks Hester and Tom.

Filled with lots of action, hairbreadth escapes, tension, battles, and deaths, the book occupies a gritty post-apocalyptic world but still contains dollops of humor. One of the pirates, Mr. Ames, had once been a teacher but thought being a pirate "was a lot more fun, and the hours were better, and Peavey's ruffians were better behaved than most of his old pupils." Reminiscent of Philip Pullman's Dark Materials trilogy and Stroud's Amulet of Samarkand titles, the book ends with room for sequels, the first being *Predator's Gold.*

MEG ROSOFF

## *How I Live Now*

12–14 • Random House/Lamb • 2004 • 208 pp.

↪ *PRINTZ AWARD*

Sent by her incompetent father, fifteen-year-old Daisy goes to live with her cousins on a remote English farm. Soon after Daisy arrives, her aunt gets stranded in Oslo, and hostile forces invade England. With no adult supervision, the teenagers at first enjoy their freedom; in this environment, Daisy falls in love and has a sexual relationship with her cousin Edmond. In the course of a few months, after the enemy takes over the farm, Daisy moves slowly from a self-centered, whiny teenager to a survivor of a terrible war.

In *How I Live Now,* the reader learns few details of the actual warfare or how the country gets captured. Rather, the narrative focuses on personal matters, such as Daisy's eating disorder. However, like John Marsden's Tomorrow series, *How I Live Now* can be used to encourage teenagers to think about how they might behave at the outbreak of another major war.

NEAL SHUSTERMAN

## *The Dark Side of Nowhere*

12–14 • Little, Brown • 1997 • 185 pp.

In an eerie science fiction thriller, Jason at first believes he lives in one of the most boring towns and belongs to one of the most boring families ever found. But then the death of a classmate starts him on a quest; with Paula, a new girl in town from New Jersey, Jason researches what happened in the town a few years earlier. Suddenly, his life moves from boring to thrilling; it turns out he and his dull parents come from another planet, the first of a convoy sent to take over Earth. Because more aliens will soon arrive, Jason and others train with advanced weaponry; they get shots to turn them back into aliens. But as they prepare for the glorious day when Earth will be ruled by others, Jason begins to ponder what it means to be human.

Fast-paced and funny, the book keeps building tension. In the end, it might even convince a teen or two that boring isn't so bad after all.

WILLIAM SLEATOR
## House of Stairs
12–14 • Dutton • 1974 • 169 pp.

In a haunting novel, five sixteen-year-old orphans have been confined in the creepy house of stairs and are being subjected to Pavlovian conditioning exercises, based on blinking red and green lights. At first all five learn to dance for their meals; then a new phase of the experiment calls for them to be cruel to one another. Two of the teens, Peter and Lola, resist the attempts to modify their personalities. They pull themselves away from the group and care for each other as they slowly starve. Ultimately, all five get transported to a hospital for care. However, the full impact of what has happened becomes evident in the last scene, when three of the teens begin to dance at the sight of a blinking green traffic light.

The idea for the book's setting and title came from an M. C. Escher print that shows endless stairways with wormlike creatures crawling around them. But William Sleator's mother actually came up with the reason for the novel's experiment: it has been sanctioned by a warlike society to train people to be without human feelings so that they can direct concentration camps and serve as secret agents and interrogators.

Because of the book's vague futuristic setting and the issues it explores, *House of Stairs* has remained a powerful reading experience for teens, a cult book often remembered well into adulthood.

WILLIAM SLEATOR
## Interstellar Pig
12–14 • Dutton • 1984 • 197 pp.

While vacationing on Cape Cod with two friends, Joan and Frank, William Sleator decided to use their home as a setting for a book he was writing. He then transformed the three vacationers into the alien characters of *Interstellar Pig*. While working on the book, he would read snatches of what he was writing and placate his friend

Joan with a description of her character as "Woman so beautiful." But in the end Joan became an evil spider woman, Zena, and Frank served as the model for Manny, an alien. Slater finished the book by the time of their wedding and presented them with a bound copy. Since they all remained friends, one can only assume that the couple had a sense of humor — or at least understood the creative process.

For two decades, this book has captivated young teens. Sixteen-year-old Barney finds himself attracted to three neighbors, Zena, Manny, and Joe, who are totally absorbed in a board game, Interstellar Pig. In this game, players assume the identities of aliens and try to obtain a playing card that features a pig. When the game ends, all the players who have failed to capture "Piggy" are destroyed, and so are their home planets. Barney slowly comprehends that his three neighbors are extraterrestrial creatures. With an intelligence level well below those of his adversaries, he represents human beings. And he also begins to sense that this game may be more real than he ever imagined.

A master storyteller, Sleator draws readers into Barney's first-person account, and they feel his fear and inadequacy during the intense competition. With numerous twists and turns, the game and the book keep readers enthralled.

HARRY TURTLEDOVE

## The Guns of the South

14–18 • Del Rey • 1992 • 519 pp.

From its initial premise, *The Guns of the South* naturally intrigues readers. In 1864, with the Confederacy's resources at a low ebb, Robert E. Lee meets Andries Rhoodie, who demonstrates an amazing new weapon, the AK-47. Rhoodie and his colleagues agree to supply these guns and their ammunition to the South at a minimal cost. As Lee learns, they represent a white, racist, supremacist organization from the twenty-first century; they therefore want Lee to win the war and change the course of racial and political history.

Completely grounded in the actual history, the story begins with the fighting of the 47th North Carolina regiment as it and other groups receive these miracle weapons and march on Washington; the second half takes place after the war. With an unflinching portrayal of prejudice and racial hatred, the narrative shows how the supremacists underestimate Lee, just as the Union generals always did. But it also provides a framework in which to discuss military tactics, politics, war, racial attitudes, and history.

Considered one of the best alternate or counterfactual histories, *The Guns of the South* proves to be the ideal volume for anyone wanting to explore the age-old question "What would have happened if the South had won the Civil War?" Many agree with the Civil War expert James McPherson, who believed this book to be one of the most fascinating Civil War novels ever written.

## SCOTT WESTERFELD
### Uglies
12–14 • Simon & Schuster • 2005 • 425 pp.

In a dystopian trilogy — including *Pretties* and *Specials* — Scott Westerfeld imagines a fantasy world ideal for teenagers. At the age of sixteen, everyone gets an operation; with a new skin and new bones, they become supermodel gorgeous. Then they go to live and party in a high-tech town, New Pretty Town. A few months before her sixteenth birthday, Tally can't wait for this transformation. While trying to sneak around New Pretty Town, she discovers another prowler, Shay. Shay shows her how to hoverboard — skateboard in the air — and they go to the remains of an older civilization, which has been ruined by war and other forms of destruction. A rebel, Shay does not want to get the operation, and she vanishes before Tally does. Tally agrees to find Shay and betray her because otherwise the community won't allow Tally to become pretty. In her quest, she finds out that what she has been taught in school may not be the truth — the operation not only changes the way people look, it also changes how they think.

Soundly based on the fantasy life of teenagers, *Uglies* creates a future world inhabited by Paris Hilton and her friends — and a band of outlaws trying to save them from themselves.

## CONNIE WILLIS
### Doomsday Book
14–18 • Bantam • 1992 • 578 pp.

In 2054 Oxford University takes students, via time travel, to different locations to perform research. Hence a young historian, Kivrin, prepares for a trip to the Middle Ages with amazing thoroughness. She studies Middle English and a variety of other languages, learns all kinds of skills, and helps on an archaeological dig of a place she hopes to find by traveling to the 1300s. During the Christmas holiday, Kivrin sets out to spend two weeks in a small village near Oxford in 1320.

But things begin to go wrong when Badri, the technician on the project, comes down with serious influenza and infects the others. Kivrin herself arrives incoherent, feverish, and unable to function. The chapters switch back and forth between twenty-first-century Oxford and a village near fourteenth-century Oxford. Only slowly does Kivrin understand that a catastrophic error has been made; she has been sent to 1348, the year the Black Death struck this part of the world. A doctor in Oxford searches around the clock for the source of the influenza — which will kill almost 20 percent of those quarantined in the city — and finally realizes that the archaeological dig has brought a strain of virus from the 1300s into the future.

The book combines the best of a medical thriller with well-researched, well-grounded historical fiction. The small village of forty people — with its priest, noble family, and servants — all die; in the process of the narrative, readers and Kivrin have grown to know and care for them. Kivrin herself, an adolescent with a great head and heart, shows amazing resilience and fortitude. When, in the end, her mentor comes into the 1300s to save her, the entire saga gets rounded out in a believable and satisfying manner.

This science fiction tour de force, winner of both the Hugo and Nebula awards, easily convinces those who believe they do not like the genre to pay more attention to it. With its focus on pandemics and the inadequacies of the medical community, the book provokes discussion about one of our most important current issues.

# Short Stories

ARBARA KINGSOLVER CALLS short stories "Large truths in tight spaces," and those who love the form agree. In a fast-paced world, the short story can be read in one sitting, providing complete satisfaction for the reader; it doesn't give readers the whole enchilada, just the hot sauce.

The popularity of the short story has undergone peaks and valleys throughout its history; certainly most adults remember classics from their adolescent years — Sherwood Anderson's *Winesburg, Ohio,* O. Henry's "The Gift of the Magi," the tales of Edgar Allan Poe, and Shirley Jackson's "The Lottery." For a period of time the publication of original short stories fell on hard times, but Jhumpa Lahiri's *Interpreter of Maladies,* which won the Pulitzer Prize in 2000, inspired both writers and publishers to work in this format. The result has been an avalanche of short story collections in the twenty-first century aimed at adolescent readers. In the world of teens, constantly bombarded by electronic media, the short story works with a short attention span, and is ideal, as the critic Michael Cart has written, for those who might be best described as "hummingbirds on twelve cups of coffee."

Many short story collections — like Hazel Rochman's *Somehow Tenderness Survives* — bring together the work of various authors on different topics. I've included many of these volumes in the booklist. Most of my selections focus on short story collections by individual authors, those who have shown a particular mastery of this genre.

SHERWOOD ANDERSON

## *Winesburg, Ohio*

14–18 • Huebsch • 1919 • 256 pp.

In a series of unflinching and unsentimental character studies, Sherwood Anderson explores the hopes and heartbreaks of the citizens of a northern Ohio village at the turn of the twentieth century. The two dozen interlinked stories introduce a disgraced schoolteacher, a religious zealot, alcoholics, unhappy families, doomed lovers, and the young cub reporter George Willard, who has observed the sad lives of his neighbors and will someday, we suspect, commit their stories to paper. *Winesburg, Ohio* helped usher in a new era of naturalistic writing and influenced authors such as Hemingway, but it is still read today for its uncanny observations of human behavior and timeless themes. Once considered somewhat scandalous for its frank treatment of sexuality, within a generation or two the book was studied in high schools. Today's students have the option of reading Anderson's stories from either a bound volume or off the computer screen; Project Gutenberg has provided free public access to the entire text on the Internet, giving the lazy midwestern town of Winesburg, Ohio, a new home in cyberspace.

MARION DANE BAUER, EDITOR

## *Am I Blue?: Coming Out from the Silence*

14–18 • Harper • 1994 • 273 pp.

A groundbreaking anthology, *Am I Blue?* deals frankly and honestly with gay issues from a young adult perspective. Many of the sixteen stories concern teenagers coming to terms with their own sexuality; others focus on the acceptance of gay friends and relatives. Some of the finest writers for young adults have contributed selections, including M. E. Kerr, Francesca Lia Block, Jacqueline Woodson, Gregory Maguire, and Lois Lowry. These well-written stories encompass a wide range of styles and genres, from the title story, Bruce Coville's comic fantasy, to tales set in other times and places. In her introduction, Bauer states, "It is my dream that ten years from now such an anthology will not be needed, that gay and lesbian characters will be as integrated into juvenile literature as they are in life." These stories provide a powerful commentary about societal and emotional responses to homosexuality.

RAY BRADBURY

## Dandelion Wine: A Novel

12–14 • Knopf • 1957 • 267 pp.

Though *Dandelion Wine* is subtitled "a novel," many readers consider it a collection of short fiction connected by place (Green Town, Illinois), time (the summer of 1928), and a central character (twelve-year-old Douglas Spaulding — though he does not appear in all of the stories). Ray Bradbury wrote the book over the course of twelve years, beginning each morning by jotting down random words, then using free association to recall images and scenes from his own childhood in Waukegan, Illinois. The resulting stories — many originally published in magazines before being collected here — recall the everyday wonders of getting a new pair of tennis shoes, making wine in the cellar, and playing kick-the-can after supper. They also recount the bittersweet times of losing friends and loved ones, taking the last ride on the town trolley, and fearing "The Lonely One," a menacing figure who terrorizes the town. Bradbury is best known for his science fiction and fantasy, and while this book has a realistic setting, the imagery-laden prose is so evocative and pleasurable that readers may feel they've been transported to a bygone era, suffused with the magic of summertime.

TRUMAN CAPOTE

## Breakfast at Tiffany's

14–18 • Random House • 1958 • 178 pp.

The four stories in Truman Capote's *Breakfast at Tiffany's* represent the wide range of this author's craft. The novella-length title piece tells the story of the appealingly enigmatic Holly Golightly, formerly of Tulip, Texas, and now living the madcap life of a New York sophisticate. Readers familiar with her only from the 1961 Audrey Hepburn film may be surprised at how much more powerful — and emotionally haunting — her story seems in its original incarnation. Two brief narratives (an offbeat romance set in Haiti and the tale of friendship between two inmates in a rural prison farm) are followed by "A Christmas Memory," an autobiographical story so perfectly written that it has achieved classic status. Individually, each story is a unique and memorable reading experience; collectively, they demonstrate Capote's stylistic diversity and keen insight into a broad gamut of human nature.

MICHAEL CART, EDITOR
## Rush Hour: A Journal of Contemporary Voices
12–16 • Delacorte • 2004–2006 • 144–240 pp.

In the four volumes of *Rush Hour,* Michael Cart set out to publish offbeat, unprecedented fiction, written with authenticity for young adults. Each volume combines seasoned veterans with those unknown to the audience and brings together graphic novels, short stories, poetry, excerpts from novels, flash fiction, and art around a theme. Eclectic and bold in its concept, *Rush Hour* provides compelling short material guaranteed to capture the interest of teens.

JUDITH ORTIZ COFER
## An Island Like You: Stories of the Barrio
12–14 • Orchard • 1995 • 165 pp.

In the first story in this collection, an American teenager spends the summer with her mother's relatives in Puerto Rico; the rest of the dozen tales take place in her New Jersey barrio where Spanish is spoken among neighbors, music and dancing fill the sometimes-dangerous streets, and American-raised teenagers butt heads with their more traditional parents. Against this colorful backdrop, overwhelmed Arturo seeks refuge in a local church, Luis offers a gift to a beautiful girl who lives in a funeral home, and Teresa and Anita find summer jobs. Each polished story stands alone, but one of the pleasures of this collection comes from seeing the characters reappear throughout, often demonstrating their continuing growth and change. Doris — introduced as a shy and self-described invisible girl — later emerges as a leader, creating a teen theater program and arranging a party to honor a neighborhood outcast. This vibrant and engaging volume helps fill a gap in young adult fiction, presenting an all-too-rare look at Hispanic themes and characters.

CHRIS CRUTCHER

## Athletic Shorts: Six Short Stories

14–18 • Greenwillow • 1991 • 154 pp.

Best known for his hard-hitting young adult novels that use sports as a metaphor for life and growing up, Chris Crutcher tackles the short story in this collection of involving tales. The best known, "A Brief Moment in the Life of Angus Bethune," was also the first story Crutcher ever tried writing. In it, an overweight high school student with two pairs of gay parents gets elected Winter Ball King as a class joke. This story, which has an unexpectedly touching conclusion, was made into the 1995 film *Angus.* The other entries all concern characters introduced in Crutcher's novels — *Running Loose, Stotan!,* and *The Crazy Horse Electric Game* — as they face athletic challenges (wrestling Dad or a female opponent) and confront their own fears and prejudices. In one story, for instance, teenage Louie Banks befriends a young man with AIDS. Fans of Crutcher's novels will enjoy checking in on these familiar characters; those who simply enjoy short stories will find this volume an excellent introduction to the author's work.

DAVE EGGERS, EDITOR

## The Best American Nonrequired Reading

14–18 • Houghton Mifflin • annual series • around 400 pp.

For students bogged down with school assignments, the concept of "pleasure reading" may seem unlikely. Yet young adults can read this annual series without fear of due dates or exam questions — a collection of short fiction and essays that celebrate the sheer enjoyment and entertainment of good writing. Begun in 2002 and edited by Dave Eggers, *The Best American Nonrequired Reading* gathers material from mainstream magazines such as *The New Yorker* and *Esquire,* as well as alternative literary journals and an occasional online publication. The result is an annual filled with edgy short stories by new writers; hip essays — both comic and serious — by authors such as David Sedaris and David Mamet; Lynda Barry comic strips; and thought-provoking investigative journalism that delves into fast-food cravings and traces the journey of a T-shirt from its original owner in New York City to an impoverished man in rural Uganda. With approximately two dozen selections in each volume, these eminently browsable books are sure to offer something for every taste.

ALICE HOFFMAN

## Blackbird House

14–18 • Doubleday • 2004 • 225 pp.

When the *Boston Globe* asked Alice Hoffman to write a short story about summer on Cape Cod, she submitted "The Summer Kitchen," a tale of a family moving into a new vacation home as their young daughter recovers from cancer. Hoffman set the story in her own summer house on Cape Cod and began to wonder about the experiences of other families who had lived there in past generations. *Blackbird House* is a collection of twelve interlinked stories set in the same New England farmhouse at different points in history. During the British occupation, a boy and his father go off to sea. In a story with a twist at the end, a young man buys a farm with money he was paid for taking another man's place in the Civil War. During a blizzard, a twentieth-century teenager stumbles on the murder of an abusive neighbor. Hoffman's rich, dreamy prose begs to be read aloud and savored in stories that often have the raw, simple power of folklore and fairy tales.

SHIRLEY JACKSON

## The Lottery and Other Stories

14–18 • Farrar, Straus • 1949 • 302 pp.

Many teens know the much-anthologized title story, but this volume provides a broader look at Shirley Jackson. Although not always as shocking as "The Lottery," which speaks to anyone who has ever felt like an outcast, the more than twenty stories in this collection almost always introduce an element of horror or madness into ordinary domestic situations. They include Jackson's classic tale of her son's first days of kindergarten (the darkly comic "Charles") as well as several entries that expose the racial and religious prejudices of seemingly well-bred middle-class characters. Though written in the 1940s, these often subtle studies of intolerance still retain power for modern readers. Threaded throughout the volume are a number of stories about the enigmatic James Harris, who appears in various guises, including an absent bridegroom and a four-year-old boy playing in a sandbox, and who disrupts and destroys the lives of nearly everyone he encounters. At their best, Jackson's disquieting tales of everyday horror linger in the imagination like impossible-to-forget bad dreams.

JHUMPA LAHIRI

## Interpreter of Maladies

14–18 • Houghton Mifflin • 1999 • 198 pp.

⇔ *PULITZER PRIZE*

When the Pulitzers were announced in the spring of 2000, many were surprised when the fiction award went to a paperback book written by a young, first-time author of East Indian descent. The award brought immediate attention — and bestseller status — to Jhumpa Lahiri's collection of nine stories that highlight the Indian experience both at home and abroad. With a handful set on the Indian subcontinent, the best entries concern first- and second-generation Indians living in the United States. Several poignantly describe defining moments that either strengthen or destroy a beginning marriage. Some are written from the perspective of children: a ten-year-old girl sees the impact of Pakistan's civil war on a family friend; young Eliot observes the loneliness and homesickness of his babysitter, an immigrant faculty wife from India. Lahiri's themes of identity, displacement, and love are a natural fit for young adult readers, as is her accessible, well-crafted prose.

NORMAN MACLEAN

## A River Runs Through It and Other Stories

14–18 • University of Chicago • 1976 • 239 pp.

Norman Maclean's book contains only three stories. Two concern his youthful experiences at a logging camp working for the U.S. Forest Service. The title piece is a novella-length account of fly-fishing with his father and younger brother. Maclean describes how his minister father taught his sons to fish at an early age, and he recalls the summer, years later, when the two brothers made a series of fly-fishing trips accompanied by a troublesome in-law and, on one occasion, by their now-elderly father. The Montana setting is brilliantly evoked, and fly-fishing serves as an excellent metaphor for life, family, and the relationship between Maclean and his tragic, hard-drinking brother in this wise and unforgettable story. A former university professor, Maclean recorded these stories at the urging of his children. No mainstream publisher was interested, but the University of Chicago Press issued the book as its first work of fiction. The book enjoyed great success and was a frontrunner for the Pulitzer Prize in letters, although, according to reports, the Pulitzer board rejected it because they felt it was a memoir, not fiction. A movie directed by Robert Redford, starring Brad Pitt, also helped attract readers to this title, much beloved by both adolescents and adults.

NORMA FOX MAZER

## Dear Bill, Remember Me? and Other Stories

12–14 • Delacorte • 1976 • 195 pp.

Romance, family relationships, and the quest for independence and identity are the themes of these eight stories about teenage girls. Norma Fox Mazer's collection is written in a variety of narrative styles, with some tales related in the first person, others from an omniscient perspective, one written in the form of journal entries, and another as a series of unsent letters. The plots and characterizations are equally wide-ranging, though Mazer especially excels at exploring the lives of working-class characters: sheltered Zoe makes a new friend during secret visits to a neighborhood park; Chrissy shares a trailer home with her father and uncle. Readers will identify with Mazer's protagonists as they experience change and personal growth.

WALTER DEAN MYERS

## 145th Street: Short Stories

12–14 • Delacorte • 2000 • 151 pp.

Walter Dean Myers, who grew up in Harlem, returns to his roots in this collection of ten stories set in the neighborhood surrounding 145th Street. Each of the lean, engaging tales introduces intriguing characters: an old man who plans and attends his own funeral; a Hispanic girl who may be experiencing a series of prophetic dreams; an elderly African-American woman who shares her Christmas with a Caucasian policeman and his family; and a studious girl and a jock who fall in love and stay in love against all odds. Vibrant characterizations, an authentic setting, and a strong sense of community distinguish this collection. Though several of the stories realistically — and sometimes grimly — concern crime and gang violence, the general tone is optimistic and spirited. Harlem and 145th Street have been depicted without adulation but with great affection.

## JOYCE CAROL OATES
### Small Avalanches and Other Stories
14–18 • Harper • 2003 • 400 pp.

Besides being one of today's most honored novelists, Joyce Carol Oates is considered a master of the short story form. This volume collects twelve tales that have a special resonance for young adults. Two of the entries, "Where Are You Going, Where Have You Been?" (the basis of the Laura Dern and Treat Williams film, *Smooth Talk*) and "How I Contemplated the World from the Detroit House of Corrections and Began My Life Over Again," are among the author's best-known and critically acclaimed short stories. The others, psychologically harrowing, often violent, and unrelievedly grim, are vintage Oates. Though not for every reader, this mature and thought-provoking collection serves as a solid introduction to this major American author and can lead young readers to seek out some of her adult novels that have particular teen appeal — *Foxfire: Confessions of a Girl Gang, Them,* and *We Were the Mulvaneys.*

## TIM O'BRIEN
### The Things They Carried
14–18 • Houghton Mifflin • 1990 • 272 pp.

Tim O'Brien, who was drafted into the military after graduating from college in 1968, has crafted a harrowing, highly personal collection of short fiction based on his own experiences in Vietnam. Gripping vignettes recall the fears, casual cruelty, and madness of young men during wartime. O'Brien graphically describes the deaths of several members of his platoon, repeats a stunning story of a medic's girlfriend who reportedly joined him in country, and tells the haunting tale of the man he killed. These narratives are occasionally interrupted by sections in which O'Brien looks back at the war from a distance of twenty years, providing additional background information on his experiences, updating the lives of the servicemen introduced in the stories, and sometimes even refuting the events that he has just presented in fictional form. This gripping, multilayered volume can be read on many different levels. While young readers may not quite comprehend the implications of the forty-three-year-old author's recalling and rewriting scenes from his past, they will surely relate to the honestly portrayed emotions and actions of O'Brien's fellow soldiers, many of whom were still in their own late teens while serving in Vietnam.

RICHARD PECK

## Past Perfect, Present Tense: New and Collected Stories

12–14 • Dial • 2004 • 177 pp.

Throughout his career as an award-winning novelist, Richard Peck has demonstrated a knack for creating pithy short stories for anthologies. In this book he collects a baker's dozen, categorizing them into sections labeled *The First, The Past, Supernatural,* and *The Present.* What makes this collection notable, besides the general high quality of the prose, is that Peck provides an author's perspective on how each of the stories came to be written. His best-known story came into existence mainly because an editor promised him $300; others are based on places the author has visited or events he has experienced; still others introduce characters that later found their way into his novels. Peck's dry commentary — which includes a brief afterword, "How to Write a Short Story," followed by a few helpful hints — gives this collection a personal touch and may inspire fledgling authors.

HAZEL ROCHMAN, EDITOR

## Somehow Tenderness Survives: Stories of Southern Africa

12–14 • Harper • 1988 • 147 pp.

Hazel Rochman, who was born and raised in Johannesburg, South Africa, introduces this collection with an incisive portrait of life under apartheid, followed by ten stories — five by black authors and five by white — that illustrate the grim, soul-crushing impact of institutionalized racism. Doris Lessing describes a white girl's encounters with an African chief. Nadine Gordimer tells of an ill-fated interracial romance. Peter Abrahams and Mark Mathabane contribute autobiographical accounts of police brutality. Though sometimes graphically violent, the stories demonstrate that, even under the worst regimes, somehow tenderness, human dignity, and even hope can survive. This volume was originally published when apartheid was the law in South Africa. Though times have changed, it still deserves attention — much like Holocaust literature — to remind readers of the political horrors that existed in the not-too-distant past and that still cast their shadow on twenty-first-century Africa.

J. D. SALINGER

## Nine Stories

14–18 • Little, Brown • 1953 • 208 pp.

Fans of *The Catcher in the Rye*, drawn to this book by J. D. Salinger's name, will discover a volume substantially different from that landmark young adult novel. Most of these subtle tales were originally published in *The New Yorker* and reflect the postwar malaise of the late 1940s and early 1950s. Readers lulled by the stories' everyday events and innocuous conversations will be startled by the emotional landmines just below each placid surface, such as when the fancifully titled "A Perfect Day for Bananafish" and "Uncle Wiggily in Connecticut" unravel into dark tales of suicide and alcoholism. A number of stories speak directly to the young adult experience: a private school student has an unsettling encounter with her classmate's brother in "Just Before the War with the Eskimos"; a young soldier meets an odd British girl in "For Esmé — with Love and Squalor"; a nineteen-year-old lies his way into a job as an art teacher in "De Daumier-Smith's Blue Period." Though not as accessible to young readers as *The Catcher in the Rye*, these urbane, edgy stories will intrigue and disturb sophisticated teenagers.

TIM WYNNE-JONES

## *Lord of the Fries and Other Stories*

12–14 • DK/Kroupa • 1999 • 214 pp.

Called the "master of the glimpse," Tim Wynne-Jones in his third collection of stories presents seven tales of striking originality. With his corkscrew logic and sublime turns of phrases, each story immediately grabs the reader's attention from the first sentence. In "The Fallen Angel," the mysterious Luc, with a voice like an angel, turns satanic. And in one of the finest stories, "The Bermuda Triangle," a young boy, Jim, who turned mute when his father disappeared, finds his own voice.

*Lord of the Fries and Other Stories* quickly reveals why this Canadian author is considered one of the contemporary masters of the short story — someone who writes original, fresh, and vibrant tales, with an emotional twist at the end.

# Sports

THE NATURAL CONFLICT of sports, man against man or woman against woman, appeals not only to young adults in reality, it has tremendous vitality in fiction. But the literary sports novel, where sports are used to present greater issues, has gone in and out of fashion. One of the groundbreaking young adult novels in the 1960s, Robert Lipsyte's *The Contender,* set the bar for excellence of craft and writing. In the 1980s, writers such as Bruce Brooks and Chris Crutcher combined their passion for sports and fiction to provide some brilliant examples of the literary sports novel.

But in the last few years good sports fiction — which depends on the writer's getting the details of the game accurate but also telling another story — has waned. Some critics saw hope for this genre in 2005, when a few fine books, such as Matt de la Peña's *Ball Don't Lie,* appeared.

Always popular with readers, great sports literature, as these writers have demonstrated, can explore the central adolescent issues of coming of age and growing up in the context of a basketball court, swimming pool, or baseball field.

EDWARD BLOOR

## *Tangerine*

12–14 • Harcourt • 1997 • 294 pp.

Although legally blind, Paul Fisher still observes things that others don't. He understands how evil his older brother, Erik, can be, even though their parents believe only in the "Erik Fisher Football Dream." In diary entries, Paul tells about their new home in the strange Florida town of Tangerine, with muck fires, deadly lightning, killer mosquitoes, and huge sinkholes that swallow up half the school. Even though Paul might be described as a geeky freak in prescription goggles, he still wants to play soccer. So when his school won't let him on the team because of his legal blindness, he transfers to Tangerine Middle School, a rougher environment with some tough Latino characters. But Paul's decency, humor, sports ability, and true love for the smells and beauty of the citrus fields gain him gradual acceptance. In this new setting, against great odds, Paul becomes a true hero and starts to piece together the chilling history of his family.

Adolescent readers can easily identify with Paul's problems — how parents don't see the strengths and weaknesses of their own children and the plight of being a younger brother of a star who is also a bully. They enjoy the action and suspense as well as the details of the soccer games.

As a novelist, Edward Bloor does everything extraordinarily well. He writes with wit and heart and provides a fast-paced plot, intriguing characters, and a fascinating setting that some think resembles a science fiction backdrop but Bloor claims is the Florida he observes on the nightly news. In *Tangerine* he has created a coming-of-age story, suspense thriller, mystery, and one of the best young adult novels of the 1990s.

BRUCE BROOKS

## *The Moves Make the Man*

12–14 • Harper • 1984 • 280 pp.

↬ *NEWBERY HONOR*

Thirteen-year-old Jerome Foxworthy, a gifted black athlete, exults in basketball and the fakes and moves of the game. Segregation has made "the Jayfox" the token black in an otherwise white junior high school in North Carolina. Jerome teaches basketball to one of his classmates, Bix Rivers, who excels in baseball but makes a pact with his stepfather to take up a man's sport. Bix balks at the dishonesty, even deceit, of basketball fakes; he has an obsession with truth. In the end, both boys need to come to terms with truth and fakery, both on the basketball court and off. As Jerome says, "The fact is — if you are faking, somebody is taking . . . there are no moves you truly make alone."

In a feisty, first-person narrative, Jerome brings basketball to life, with the "bammata bammata bammata bam" resounding through the bottom of the players' feet. Some of the adult characters display racist behavior that reflects the time, but the book belongs to the two boys, both compelling and likable characters, and the friendship they develop. In fact, Jerome so enters the imagination of readers that sometimes young fans of the book, attending signings by the author, have been disappointed to learn that Bruce Brooks is not a black basketball dude. Brooks has excelled, however, as a thoughtful, literary writer for adolescents. *The Moves Make the Man*, his debut novel, won the Boston Globe–Horn Book Award for fiction and has attracted legions of fans over the years.

CHRIS CRUTCHER

## *Ironman*

12–14 • Greenwillow • 1995 • 181 pp.

When Bo Brewster was nine, his father banished him from the family and confined him in his room after school. Now a high school senior, Bo questions all authority, constantly battles with his father, and thrives on isolation. Finally, an outburst at school lands him in an Anger Management class, and he must spend two mornings a week discussing emotional issues with the group — which he initially believes to be populated with future serial killers. Here Bo meets and falls in love with Shelly, someone whose passion for physical challenge matches his own. The rest of the time he trains to become the best triathlete in the state of Washington. Eventually he takes part in the triathlon — with support from his Anger Management group.

The story has been told from Bo's hyperbolic letters alternately to the broadcaster Larry King and an omniscient, third-person narrator. A therapist who has worked with young people, Chris Crutcher always catches the nuances of teen language and behavior brilliantly in his crisp, funny, and fast-moving prose. In this book, as in many of his others, he uses the natural excitement of sports to present larger, philosophical issues — divorce, child abuse, anger, and homosexuality.

CHRIS CRUTCHER

## *Running Loose*

12–14 • Greenwillow • 1983 • 224 pp.

Seventeen-year-old Louie Banks appears to have everything a teen could want — a promising academic career, athletic ability, friends, part-time work, great parents, and a pretty and smart girlfriend. But when his football coach decides to take out the opposing team's star player, Louie considers the action immoral, and he will not play for the coach. So in his high school he moves from hero to goat. Then his girlfriend dies in a car accident.

Crutcher's first novel contains many autobiographical elements. The parents in *Running Loose* are based on his own, and Crutcher developed Louie from his memories of himself as a teen. The resulting honest portrayal of teenage life and struggles has been popular for over two decades.

CHRIS CRUTCHER

## *Stotan!*

12–14 • Greenwillow • 1986 • 183 pp.

Told in a diary format, this account of several months in a senior year has been narrated by Walker Dupree, captain of the swim team. Before that year, he and three of his teammates experience a week-long endurance training, called Stotan. During this week they pull together, share details of their sometimes brutalized lives, and learn to trust their own abilities. "'When it's time to meet the Dragon . . . you can't fight him head on. . . . But you can go *with* him and beat him.'"

In a novel with tough language and a tough situation, the sickness and death of one of the team members, the story has been sprinkled with humor and contains memorable and fully formed characters.

CHRIS CRUTCHER

## *Whale Talk*

14–18 • Greenwillow • 2001 • 220 pp.

In a story about small-town prejudice, seventeen-year-old The Tao Jones (T.J.) represents various minority populations: he's black, white, and Japanese. Despite his athletic ability, T.J. has stayed away from organized sports, but in his senior year, to help his favorite teacher, he joins the swim team and gets other outcasts to participate — "a muscle man, a giant, a chameleon, and a one-legged psychopath." Although this motley crew meets the derision of the other swimmers, their dedication to one another and the sport strengthens at each meet.

Although the plot seems a bit messy — with a multitude of problems and issues — Chris Crutcher has always proven himself a genius in capturing the emotions and feelings of teenagers. Hence *Whale Talk* — as well as Crutcher's other sports novels — has become extremely popular with readers.

MATT DE LA PEÑA

## *Ball Don't Lie*

12–14 • Delacorte • 2005 • 282 pp.

Written by a former college basketball player, *Ball Don't Lie* takes place, in part, on the basketball court. In a dark gym in Los Angeles, Lincoln Rec, seasoned and would-be players compete. In this arena Sticky, a seventeen-year-old white boy, plays with obsession and passion. Rejected from several foster homes, he has lived without advantages or possibilities all of his life. But on the ball court he has a genius, a talent, and it may just be his ticket to someplace great, like the NBA.

The author alternates compelling, believable sports scenes with details from Sticky's life: his mother's suicide, his abuse by others, the people who bring him into their homes and then return him. But this bleakness has been leavened by the possibilities now developing for this hero who suffers from obsessive-compulsive disorder — a beautiful girlfriend who loves him, a chance for an elite basketball camp, and college scouts who have been paying attention.

In his debut novel, Matt de la Peña gives readers everything they could want in a sports thriller — an unusual but vibrant character whom they grow to care for, lots of sports action and lingo, and a hopeful ending for a teenager whose life has been filled with pain. This gritty urban story will appeal to everyone who loves sports — and to everyone who gets swept up in poetic writing and brilliant characterization.

## CARL DEUKER

### On the Devil's Court

12–14 • Little, Brown • 1988 • 252 pp.

The son of someone famous, seventeen-year-old Joe Faust dreams of playing basketball at a public school with a great team. But his life of privilege condemns him to private schools and their lackluster sports. When the family moves to Seattle in his senior year, however, Joe doesn't even make the school's basketball team. One day, practicing on an abandoned court, he decides he'd sell his soul to the devil for twenty-four great games on that team. Although the devil has nothing to do with it, Joe secures a berth on the team, which is headed for the state championship. But he keeps worrying that his success might be the result of a pact with the devil.

A basketball lover's book, *On the Devil's Court* also explores the relationship of fathers and sons and the sacrifices people make for their obsessions. In the end, Joe learns a great deal about teamwork, being a member of a family and a community, and charting his own course.

## W. P. KINSELLA

### Shoeless Joe

14–18 • Houghton Mifflin • 1982 • 265 pp.

If you build it, he will come." When the former insurance salesman turned Iowa farmer Ray Kinsella hears these words, as if spoken by a baseball announcer, he decides to turn part of his cornfield into a baseball diamond. And one day, just as he had hoped, Shoeless Joe Jackson, one of the greatest hitters of the game but banned because of the Chicago Black Sox scandal, appears in the baseball park being created. Later Joe's fellow White Sox players join him, and Ray goes on a cross-country trip to round up his idol, J. D. Salinger, who's living in seclusion in New Hampshire, and bring him back to the game that's developing in the Iowa cornfield.

Magical realism and baseball, the heritage passed from fathers to sons and daughters, and the history of the sport that ties America together all come together in an extraordinarily beautiful book, which was made into the movie *Field of Dreams*. Kinsella spins an incredible story — part dream and part vision — and keeps readers enthralled as he displays his magic.

ROBERT LIPSYTE

## *The Contender*

12–14 • Harper • 1967 • 227 pp.

Seventeen-year-old Alfred Brooks, a high school dropout, works at a dead-end job in a grocery store. Gangs roam the streets of his Harlem neighborhood, and one night Alfred gets beaten senseless. Now, motivated, he acts to change the pattern of his life and starts to train as a boxer in a local club. He wants to know if he can become a contender, someone who might be a champion. In the process of learning this brutal and difficult sport, Alfred gains self-respect and competence. After three fights, Alfred retires from the ring. Having discovered that he can, indeed, be a contender, he sets out to help a friend get off drugs.

While covering the 1965 fight in Las Vegas between Muhammad Ali and Lloyd Patterson for the *New York Times*, Robert Lipsyte talked to a boxing manager who ran a gym in a Manhattan slum. The manager would sit at the top of the stairs at night, waiting for a motivated and desperate kid to come up those stairs. Using this idea as the premise for a book, Lipsyte drew on his understanding of the sports world for a powerful narrative with some gut-wrenching scenes of boxers in the ring. Three more volumes continue the story, *The Brave, The Chief,* and *Warrior Angel.* For several decades, young readers have found *The Contender* honest, real, and true to teenage emotions, and they have also appreciated the positive and upbeat ending.

WALTER DEAN MYERS

## Hoops

12–14 • Delacorte • 1981 • 183 pp.

A black teenager from Harlem, Lonnie Jackson loves the feeling he gets playing street basketball. Working at a dead-end job with no prospects before him, he agrees to sign on with a team that will play in the citywide Tournament of Champions, rumored to be attractive to NBA scouts. At first he doesn't always like his sometimes sober, sometimes drunken coach, Cal, but Lonnie grows to admire him, learning of Cal's own pro basketball past. Then the shadow of Cal's past starts to come into the present, for Cal lost his game, basketball, because he trafficked with gamblers. Now it appears that they want to get involved in the Tournament of Champions as well.

In *Hoops,* Walter Dean Myers portrays the street life, the slang, and the crime of Harlem, as well as a boy's dream to escape it. This sad and poignant book contains a great deal of exciting basketball play as well as an emphasis on connecting with other human beings, love, and relationships.

GARY PAULSEN

## Winterdance: The Fine Madness of Running the Iditarod

12–18 • Harcourt • 1994 • 272 pp.

In the tradition of Jack London and Farley Mowat, Gary Paulsen spins a tale of himself and his dog team, surviving in the Arctic wilderness. Paulsen ran his first Iditarod, an approximately 1,200-mile dogsled race from Anchorage to Nome, Alaska, in 1983. *Winterdance* not only focuses on the life-threatening disasters of the race — strong winds, blinding snow, subzero temperatures — but also explores the attraction of the race and its meaning to those who attempt it. Ultimately, Paulsen highlights the dogs that made it possible for him to finish.

With simple prose reminiscent of Hemingway and with action and terror, this nonfiction account may not encourage readers to become participants, but it will definitely satisfy the needs of any armchair adventurers.

CYNTHIA VOIGT

## *The Runner*

12–14 • Atheneum • 1985 • 281 pp.

Set on the Maryland shore in 1967, *The Runner* stands as a prequel to Cynthia Voigt's Tillerman saga, portrayed in *Homecoming* and *Dicey's Song*. Although he was the state cross-country champion for the past two years, Samuel "Bullet" Tillerman, seventeen, runs for the joy of it, not to win. A loner, Bullet rages against his father's inflexibleness, his mother's submission, and his absent siblings. Stubbornly defiant, Bullet lives by his own rules and his own unrelenting discipline. While he waits for his eighteenth birthday, Bullet keeps busy — farmwork, running, and hauling crabs and oysters. During this time, he overcomes his racial prejudice and becomes friends with Tamer Shipp, a promising black runner whom Bullet's coach wants him to train. In the end, Bullet moves from being an antisocial misfit to being someone who prizes personal connections; then he heads to Vietnam, becoming a casualty of the war.

Although told through Bullet's eyes, the narrative has been crafted in the third person. Ultimately, *The Runner* talks as much about connections — denied, sustained, or treasured — as it does about the sport of running. It also addresses many serious subjects: racism, war, growing up and becoming the person someone wants to be, friendship, values, and parental conflicts.

RICH WALLACE

## *Wrestling Sturbridge*

12–14 • Knopf • 1996 • 136 pp.

Ben and his three friends have been wrestling together since sixth grade. Although Ben has strengths as a contender, he does not excel like his friend Al. Now they have to vie for a position on the team, and Al has always beaten him. Consequently, Ben finds himself in his last year of high school without a spot on the team. He has always viewed wrestling as a way to escape from Sturbridge, Pennsylvania, a smothering small town built around the concrete plant and high school sports. He begins dating Kim, a girl from outside the town who believes in him and believes that young people can change their lives.

In an exciting, energetic, and suspenseful book — as much about direction and choices as it is about wrestling — Rich Wallace puts a spin on the usual sports story: his hero doesn't win the final match.

As one young reader summed up the book: "An excellent book that makes you think about your own life . . . Read it instead of watching *The X-Files, Homicide,* or old tapes of *Twin Peaks.*"

VIRGINIA EUWER WOLFF

## Bat 6

12–14 • Scholastic • 1998 • 230 pp.

The sixth-grade girls from two small schools in Oregon spend their year practicing for the fiftieth annual softball game between the two rivals. In 1949 the effects of World War II still linger in these small communities — with war injuries and hatred of the Japanese. Because the book has been told by twenty-one team members in their own voices, the reader gets to know details about each of these players as they train for the big game: Shazam, a troubled girl who lost her father in the attack on Pearl Harbor; Aki, a Japanese American recently returned from an internment camp; and Manzanita, who has a conversion experience and has found God. During the game, the town watches in horror as Shazam attacks and severely injures Aki; then all of them — adults, coaches, and players — wonder about their share of guilt in this event.

Simply because of the twenty-one voices that must be followed, *Bat 6* proves more challenging to read than most sports stories. But for those willing to take the time, it has tremendous power as it presents a historical period and game (ladies' softball) not often encountered in books. Even more important, *Bat 6,* ideal for discussion in parent-child book groups or in a classroom, explores honestly what hatred of a wartime enemy can mean in a time of peace.

# War and Conflict

W AR. IT CAN HAPPEN on a school bus full of kids. On a city street. In Europe or the Pacific. When wars begin, they conjure up images of heroism, easy victory, and a way to distinguish oneself. But as a war plays out, it brings with it destruction, death, pain. It changes, forever, those who become involved with it.

In our books about war, social class often plays a significant role. Those with status become commissioned officers and lead others into battle. Those with fewer resources see opportunities to gain skills or become someone. On the battlefield, bullets are the great equalizer. Everyone — rich and poor, educated and ignorant, large and small, young and old — can die.

Most of our war literature for teenagers, although sometimes cynical, is reflective and honest. Many of the characters in these books note what Jack Raab said in Harry Mazer's *The Last Mission:* "War is not like the movies. It's not fun and songs. It's not about heroes. It's about awful, sad things . . . I hope war never happens again."

But in a world where it does happen again, the vast majority of those who fight happen to be the young. Hence, books about war and conflict remain an essential part of reading for young adults.

MARK BOWDEN

## *Black Hawk Down: A Story of Modern War*

14–18 • Atlantic • 1999 • 486 pp.

With the skill and alacrity of a seasoned journalist, Mark Bowden provides a powerful account of the Americans' failure on a U.N. peacekeeping operation in 1993. Attempting to capture key warlords in Mogadishu, Somalia, the elite troops met with huge and unexpected resistance. By the end of the fight, eighteen American soldiers and five hundred Somali civilians had died; countless more had been wounded. Relying on hundreds of interviews with young soldiers and Delta Force veterans, official reports, and radio transcripts, Bowden turns this nonfiction account into a piece of writing that reads like a novel. Readers can smell, taste, hear, and almost touch this grueling battle.

Revealing the details of modern warfare, the book also raises important ethical, political, and military questions.

JAMES BRADLEY WITH RON POWERS

## *Flags of Our Fathers: Heroes of Iwo Jima*

12–14 • Delacorte • 2001 • 211 pp.

In the fierce World War II battle for the island of Iwo Jima in the Pacific — which took place over thirty-six days, beginning on February 19, 1945 — nearly 7,000 Americans died and over 18,000 fell wounded. In fact, two of every three Americans who set foot on the island became casualties. Of strategic importance — Iwo Jima gave the United States access to airfields close to the Japanese shore — the battle produced one striking and enduring photographic image: six Marines raising the American flag on this volcanic island.

James Bradley, the son of one of those men, looks at each man individually, from his childhood on, but he also explores the battle itself, the high cost to the soldiers, and the lingering effects. This version, adapted with adolescents in mind by Michael French, captures the essence of what Bradley accomplished in his longer, adult nonfiction book but has pared the material down to its essential story. Ultimately, both books show how all of the troops on Iwo Jima, many of them teenagers or men in their early twenties, exhibited heroism and courage under the most trying circumstances. For many — certainly any-one whose father or grandfather fought on Iwo Jima — the book will literally leave them sobbing because of the amazing sacrifices of these heroic young men.

## ROBERT CORMIER
### *After the First Death*
14–18 • Pantheon • 1979 • 233 pp.

A bus carrying sixteen children gets hijacked by terrorists. As the narrative probes the events and individuals involved in the "Bus and the Bridge" incident, the terrorists and their secret agency pursue their objectives ruthlessly, with no regard for lives. Faced with a living nightmare, the teenage bus driver, Kate Forrester, emerges as a truly believable and admirable heroine. A superb craftsman who shifts points of view and interior dialogue with great skill, Robert Cormier narrates the story from many perspectives, including that of one of the terrorists, Miro, who must prove his manhood by killing for the cause.

In a riveting, shocking, and totally plausible book, Cormier puts a face on terrorists, terrorism, and death by terrorism. Although written in the 1970s, the book remains as chilling and timely today.

## L. M. ELLIOTT
### *Under a War-Torn Sky*
12–14 • Hyperion • 2001 • 284 pp.

On his fifteenth World War II bombing mission, nineteen-year-old Henry "Hank" Forester gets shot down over Alsace, France, near the Swiss border. As he parachutes, he encounters machine gun fire, which injures his left leg. Lost, hungry, and in enemy territory, Hank travels toward the Allied troops; he survives in the countryside with the help of those brave enough to be part of the French Resistance. Speaking in dialogue that contains many French words, these individuals emerge as the true heroes and heroines of the novel.

Based on the experiences of L. M. Elliott's father during the war, this tense story combines adventure, action, intrigue, and suspense. Paired with Don Wulffson's *Soldier X*, the two novels show both sides of World War II from the point of view of a soldier traveling behind enemy lines.

## ADÈLE GERAS
### *Troy*
14–18 • Harcourt • 2001 • 341 pp.

Narrating the events of the Trojan War from a fresh point of view, Adèle Geras presents the conflict as seen by the women of Troy. Most of the story focuses on two sisters: Xanthe, who serves Hector's wife, Andromache, and Marpessa, a maid to Helen of Troy, the most beautiful woman in the world. The sisters watch closely how these two women handle the ten years of conflict. The Greek gods and goddesses drift in and out of the story, interfering with the people in the city and on the battlefield. Just to keep things interesting, Eros and Aphrodite cause both sisters to fall in love with Alastor, a wounded warrior.

By the end, the women experience war as grief, destruction, sacrifice, and horror. In this sensual, atmospheric, and violent retelling, the Homeric stories take on new life and meaning.

## JOSEPH HELLER
### *Catch-22*
14–18 • Simon & Schuster • 1961 • 453 pp.

In a hilarious satire about the insanity of war and modern bureaucracy, the hero, or antihero, John Yossarian becomes an everyman fighting the system. Yossarian serves in the Air Force's 256th squadron during World War II, stationed on an island off the coast of Italy. Basically afraid of death, he wants to stop flying to avoid being killed and uses extreme means to get excused — poisoning his squadron with soap, altering a combat map, even sabotaging his own plane. He asks the squadron's doctor to declare him unfit because of insanity, but the doctor cites "Catch-22" — if Yossarian asks to be let out of his duties, he must be sane. John's nemesis, Colonel Cathcart, keeps increasing the number of missions that he must accomplish before he can be rotated out.

Like his protagonist, Joseph Heller served in a B-25 bomber group in Europe during World War II. After completing sixty missions, he received an honorable discharge and several accolades. Disillusioned by America's role in Korea and the Cold War, around 1953 he began to structure a novel that would explore duty, personal responsibility, and the legitimacy of war itself. But the novel emerged slowly; Heller wrote only an hour or two at a time. Finally, working with a young editor, Robert Gottlieb, he spent several years revising the book. (Gottlieb always believed that "22" happened to be a funnier number than "14" or "18," as originally intended.)

At first met with savage reviews, the book gained its widest audience in paperback in the 1960s. *Catch-22* became the antiwar novel of its generation and the inspiration for a popular movie; it has sold over 10 million copies to date. Set in the forties, written in the fifties, published in the sixties, the novel defined American frustration with the Vietnam War in the sixties and seventies. With its broad scope, its brutal truths, and its dazzling wit, it has remained popular with adolescents and one of the premier antiwar novels of all time.

JOSEF HOLUB

## *An Innocent Soldier*

12–14 • Scholastic/Levine • 2005 • 232 pp.

In a novel featuring Napoleon's Grande Armée, a young farmhand, just sixteen, gets substituted as a conscript for the farmer's son. Young Adam may not be a totally reliable narrator, and he certainly is not the brightest bulb around, as his commander observes. But as someone loyal, determined, and courageous, Adam ultimately becomes the servant of a well-born lieutenant, himself just a boy.

The heart of the novel focuses not so much on the fighting — the duo miss the major battles of the Russian campaign — as it does on the friendship that develops between these two young men thrown together in the worst of times. Again and again Adam saves the life of his master; eventually they consider themselves brothers, and their partnership makes it possible for them both to return from the campaign alive.

The horrors of the war, the hideous cold, the chronic sickness, and the misuse of military power are explored in the novel. But the book shows how comradeship and companionship become possible, even necessary, in the worst conditions.

PNINA MOED KASS

## Real Time

14–18 • Clarion • 2004 • 192 pp.

A sixteen-year-old German boy tries to exorcise his past as the grandson of a World War II soldier; a young Russian girl reclaims her Jewish heritage on an Israeli kibbutz; a teenage Palestinian seeks stability for his family. These perspectives and others converge when a suicide bomb explodes on a crowded Israeli bus. Pnina Moed Kass deftly explores contemporary events in Israel and Palestine while providing a multiple set of viewpoints on that war.

Sophisticated in its construction, *Real Time* contains a fast-paced, stunning, and insightful exploration of terrorism — with an unusual setting and range of perspectives.

IAIN LAWRENCE

## B for Buster

12–14 • Delacorte • 2004 • 336 pp.

In order to escape an abusive father, Kak, a sixteen-year-old from Kakabeka, Canada, lies about his age and joins the Canadian Air Force during World War II. Stationed in Yorkshire, England, Kak befriends Bert, the man who cares for homing pigeons. Bert sends the birds on each mission so that the RAF can track when the planes have been shot down.

Using a little-known piece of history — the inclusion of homing pigeons in World War II bombers — Lawrence tells a taut coming-of-age story that shows the evolution of an idealistic and naïve young man into a war-scarred veteran.

HARRY MAZER

## The Last Mission

12–14 • Delacorte • 1979 • 188 pp.

A fifteen-year-old Jewish boy from the Bronx, Jack Raab decides to use his older brother's birth certificate to enlist in the army because he wants to fight Hitler. Becoming a member of the B-17 bombing squad for the 8th Air Force, Jack completes twenty-four successful missions over Germany. When his plane goes down over Czechoslovakia, however, he alone survives. Taken prisoner, Jack returns to the United States with a revulsion against war, and he remains unable to forget the death of his best friend in battle.

As a seventeen-year-old in the Army Air Force, Harry Mazer flew twenty-six missions on a B-17 bomber in World War II. When his plane went down over Czechoslovakia, he and the only other survivor were captured by Germans and taken as prisoners of war. When Mazer returned to the United States, at times he felt ashamed to still be living when so many others had died, and he told his story compulsively to anyone who would listen. Finally, he transformed his memories and experiences into *The Last Mission* and later wrote a trilogy about World War II in the Pacific — *A Boy at War, A Boy No More,* and *Heroes Don't Run.*

*The Last Mission* shows both the heroism of a teenager and the terrible price of war. Young readers often embrace the line toward the end of the story: "War is one stupid thing after another."

## MICHAEL MORPURGO
### *Private Peaceful*
12–14 • Scholastic • 2004 • 202 pp.

Since Thomas Peaceful, called Tommo, is too young to fight in World War I, he lies about his age and joins his brother on the front. Tommo and Charlie have done everything together. But the narrative moves over a night when Tommo holds a vigil alone, recounting the events of his and Charlie's lives as they grew up in rural England. For at dawn, his beloved brother will be executed by a British firing squad for desertion.

Hearing about World War I from veterans, Michael Morpurgo traveled to the front and found a tombstone, providing the ironic name of his protagonist. Shocked by the killing of around three hundred British soldiers by British firing squads, men probably suffering from shell shock, Morpurgo wrote this impassioned novel for teens.

Stylistically sophisticated and powerful, it explores the physical and psychological horrors of war.

WALTER DEAN MYERS

## *Fallen Angels*

14–18 • Scholastic • 1988 • 309 pp.

Richie Perry, a seventeen-year-old African American from Harlem, joins the army during the Vietnam War. Although he was supposed to be spared combat, Perry gets sent into action in 1967; quickly he learns that he must kill the Vietcong before they kill him. He experiences hours of boredom marked by seconds of terror. Ultimately, "the real question was what I was doing, what any of us were doing, in Nam." As Perry begins to comprehend that survival depends on more than just staying alive, he watches how each person in his platoon deals with the stress of warfare. But he also learns that they share many things in common, in life and in death. After being wounded and hospitalized, surviving the Tet offensive, Perry returns home, psychologically shattered.

Inspired by Walter Dean Myers's own experience and that of his brother, who was killed on his first day of combat in Vietnam, the author worked to make sure the narrative reflected the combat experience of young soldiers, including their frequent cursing. Because of the first-person perspective and realistic detail, readers get drawn into the battles and bunkrooms as if they themselves were in Vietnam. Vividly showing a young soldier amid the carnage and chaos of war, Myers has crafted a modern classic, reminiscent of Stephen Crane's *The Red Badge of Courage*.

WALTER DEAN MYERS

## *Shooter*

14–18 • Harper/Amistad • 2004 • 223 pp.

Madison High School in Harrison County has become the setting for a high school shooting. Through interviews, conversations, newspaper articles, police reports, and the journal of the gunman himself, readers learn what led up to this terrible event. Two of the shooter's closest friends, Carla and Cameron, are interviewed at length. Are they co-conspirators, also guilty of this crime?

Trying to understand the events at Columbine and schools in a dozen other places, Walter Dean Myers attempted to get inside the minds of those who might become involved in a shooting. How would they and their friends think? What would bring someone to pull the trigger?

The resulting book has been met with great enthusiasm by teenagers, who find themselves, as they usually do in the Myers canon, reflected in this novel.

PATRICK O'BRIAN

## *Master and Commander*

14–18 • Lippincott • 1969 • 411 pp.

Never out of favor but certainly made more popular by a recent movie, the first of the series about Captain Jack Aubrey focuses on his friendship with Stephen Maturin, the ship's surgeon and intelligence agent. On the foundation of this friendship, Patrick O'Brian creates an entire civilization. At the beginning of the nineteenth century, Britain is at war with Napoleonic France. A young lieutenant in Nelson's navy, Jack gets promoted to captain and inherits command of HMS *Sophie*, engaging in one thrilling battle after another. But the reader also learns intimate details about life on the ship, the conversation of officers, the food, the rigging, and the sounds as great ships draw in close for battle.

While it vividly recreates the time and period, the book also explores the political, philosophical, and social temper of the era. Followed by twenty other titles absolutely adored by readers, the books have been called "the best historical novels ever written." Certainly, reading *Master and Commander* and the other volumes allows readers to believe that they have actually served on a man-of-war under Lord Nelson.

MICHAEL SHAARA

## *The Killer Angels*

14–18 • McKay • 1974 • 376 pp.
⇨ *PULITZER PRIZE*

In one of the best novels ever written about the Civil War, Michael Shaara initially presents his cast of characters, those who actually participated in the battle. In the afterword, he tells what happened to these men. In between, he so vividly fashions historical figures that the reader grows to know and understand them. To see the battle of Gettysburg, the reader follows a group of men, hears their interior monologues, and views the battlefield from their eyes. For the South, Lee, Longstreet, Armistead, Pickett, and Stuart all emerge with their concerns, their common beliefs, and their differences. Shaara highlights the disagreement between Lee and Longstreet over strategy at the battle of Gettysburg. On the Union side Buford (whose hunt for the high ground may have saved the Union) and Hancock (Lew Armistead's best friend, a brave and skillful general) get their day in the sun. But certainly the starring Union role falls to Col. Joshua Lawrence Chamberlain, commander of the 20th Maine, who held the Union's left flank on the second day at Little Round Top.

*The Killer Angels* can be appreciated by any reader, even those who do not think themselves Civil War devotees. Some have admitted that it has changed their lives; certainly, it changes the way anyone looks at the battle of Gettysburg and the Civil War. So brilliantly does Shaara create character and context that the reader grows to see these men as real human beings. A decade after reading the book, I found myself weeping at Gettysburg as I stood on the spot where Lewis Armistead fell.

Carefully rendered by Civil War reenactors in the epic film *Gettysburg*, the book also was continued by Shaara's son Jeffrey in two very popular Civil War novels, *Gods and Generals* and *The Last Full Measure*. But nothing, absolutely nothing, holds a candle to this brilliant, passionate, intelligent novel about real men who emerge as true heroes — on both sides of the war.

HAMPTON SIDES

## Ghost Soldiers: The Epic Account of World War II's Greatest Rescue Mission

14–18 • Doubleday • 2001 • 345 pp.

World War II's famous Bataan Death March was only the beginning of the trauma faced by the American soldiers who had been captured by the Japanese in the Philippines. Because the Japanese believed that anyone who surrendered was less than honorable, they tortured and treated these prisoners brutally. For three years, these ghost soldiers suffered at the hands of their captors and experienced a host of illnesses from malaria to dysentery. When the Army Rangers arrived in the Philippines under Gen. Douglas MacArthur, they executed a daring mission to liberate the 513 captives still alive. Penetrating thirty miles behind enemy lines, these special forces brought hundreds of prisoners to safety, with the angry Japanese in pursuit.

After extensively interviewing survivors, Hampton Sides in a thrilling nonfiction narrative explains and celebrates this famous rescue. As he acknowledges, Bataan veterans, to this day, feel a sense of bitterness and still cling to their company slogan: "No mama, no papa, no Uncle Sam . . . and nobody gives a damn." However, this book has certainly raised the American consciousness about how this company suffered during and after World War II and pays tribute to the men who fought, struggled, and often died in the Pacific.

GEERT SPILLEBEEN
## Kipling's Choice
14–18 • Houghton Mifflin • 2005 • 160 pp.

It is Monday, September 27, 1915. John Kipling turned eighteen just six weeks ago. He is screaming from terror and pain." A lieutenant in the Irish Guard in World War I, Kipling goes into his first battle in France, and it turns out to be his last. A powerful chronicle, in which John dies slowly from his wounds, has been expertly intertwined with the story of how he came to be a soldier. Gaining a commission as an officer, John sought to please his famous father, Rudyard, who wrote *The Jungle Book* and *Kim*. In the end, John's life is cut short; his father dies, a broken man.

One of the most compelling examinations of why men choose to go to war, *Kipling's Choice* also looks at the hopes and heartaches of families as they send their sons off to the battlefield.

ROSEMARY SUTCLIFF
## The Shining Company
12–14 • Farrar, Straus • 1990 • 296 pp.

Drawing on the earliest surviving North British poem, *The Go-doddin*, Rosemary Sutcliff presents seventh-century Britain from the point of view of a teenager, Prosper, the second son of a feudal chieftain. Fulfilling a dream, Prosper joins three hundred warriors and their shield-bearers in an expedition against the Saxons. Even as a shield-bearer, he undergoes a year's preparation for combat. Despite their training, this band of warriors, the Shining Company, gets destroyed in a bloody battle.

Although these British weapons and customs differ from our own, the fighting, fears, and loyalties of company members parallel those of modern soldiers. Beautifully crafted, the book delineates a piece of history with a character whom any contemporary teenager can understand.

KURT VONNEGUT

## *Slaughterhouse-Five or The Children's Crusade*

14–18 • Delacorte/Lawrence • 1969 • 205 pp.

The protagonist of the novel, Billy Pilgrim, becomes unstuck in time, so in random order he travels between periods of his life. Hence the narrative jumps back and forth in time and place but does have a basic linear sequence. Born in 1922, Billy gets drafted into the army, thrown into the Battle of the Bulge in Belgium, and immediately becomes a prisoner of war. Just before being captured, he experiences his first time shift and sees his entire life in one sweep. Sent to work in a former slaughterhouse in Dresden, Billy and his fellow POWs survive but must excavate corpses from the rubble when Dresden is bombed. Back in the United States, Billy experiences a nervous breakdown, staying in a mental hospital. Then in 1967 he gets abducted by two-foot-high aliens, Tralfamadorians, who look like upside-down toilet plungers. Traveling to New York, Billy tells his story on radio to let the world know what he has learned from their intriguing society. They believe that although a person may be dead in one moment of their life, they are alive in all others.

For his sixth novel, Kurt Vonnegut drew on his own experience as a young soldier in Europe during World War II. In 1945 he witnessed the bombing of Dresden and the thousands who died there; he "dug corpses from cellars and carried them, unidentified, their names recorded nowhere, to monumental funeral pyres." Because of the emotional difficulty of working with the material, it took Vonnegut over twenty years to sift through his memory and transform it into fiction. Although in 1969 his other books had sold fewer than 6,000 copies,

*Slaughterhouse-Five,* along with Philip Roth's *Portnoy's Complaint* and Mario Puzo's *The Godfather,* vied for positions on the bestseller list.

Like many of Vonnegut's dark, sardonic books, *Slaughterhouse-Five* — part science fiction, part autobiography, and part history — records man's inhumanity to man. Although published for adults, the book got adopted by young readers, many of whom were involved in the anti-Vietnam movement. His absurd humor, his cynicism, and his irony appeal to adolescents who challenge the actions of those who came before them.

DON WULFFSON

## Soldier X

12–14 • Viking • 2001 • 227 pp.

In an unusual perspective on World War II, *Soldier X* shows the war through the eyes of Erik Brandt, a sixteen-year-old German boy drafted into the army. Not committed to the Nazi cause, Erik, who has a Russian mother and grandparents and speaks the language, immediately gets sent to the Russian front. When the Russians overrun the Germans, he dons a Russian uniform, feigns amnesia, and is taken to a hospital. There he "recovers," becomes an orderly, and falls in love with a young nurse, Tamara. When the hospital comes under attack by the Germans, Erik and Tamara escape and set off through the countryside. Both manage to survive, changing alliances more frequently than they change their clothes as they move over the landscape.

*Soldier X* clearly presents the horrors of war, the brutality of the conflict, and the price to those who fought it. Like Harry Mazer's *The Last Mission,* this book brings readers close to the thoughts and feelings of a teenage combatant, this time on the other side of the conflict.

Beyond the 500:
Additional Titles of Interest

•

Books by
Geographic Location

•

Books by
Historical Time Line

•

Recommended Audio Books

•

Index

# Beyond the 500:
## Additional Titles of Interest

## Adventure/Survival

*Shipwreck at the Bottom of the World* by Jennifer Armstrong
*The True Confessions of Charlotte Doyle* by Avi
*Two Years Before the Mast* by Richard Henry Dana
*Incident at Hawk's Hill* by Allan W. Eckert
*Julie of the Wolves* by Jean Craighead George
*Far North* by Will Hobbs
*Island of the Blue Dolphins* by Scott O'Dell
*The Long Walk: The True Story of a Trek to Freedom* by Slavomir Rawicz
*Alive: The Story of the Andes Survivors* by Piers Paul Read
*Pirates!* by Celia Rees
*Call It Courage* by Armstrong Sperry
*Treasure Island* by Robert Louis Stevenson

## Autobiography/Memoir

*Growing Up* by Russell Baker
*The Basketball Diaries* by Jim Carroll
*Stop-Time* by Frank Conroy
*King of the Mild Frontier* by Chris Crutcher
*Funny in Farsi* by FirooZeh DuMas

*Sickened: The Memoir of a Munchausen by Proxy Childhood*
  by Julie Gregory
*Woman Warrior* by Maxine Hong Kingston
*No Pretty Pictures* by Anita Lobel
*Coming of Age in Mississippi* by Anne Moody
*Lost in Place: Growing Up Absurd in Suburbia* by Mark Salzman
*Lucky* by Alice Sebold
*Old School* by Tobias Wolff

## Classic Titles

*Pride and Prejudice* by Jane Austen
*Little Women* by Louisa May Alcott
*Jane Eyre* by Charlotte Brontë
*Wuthering Heights* by Emily Brontë
*The Good Earth* by Pearl Buck
*Alice in Wonderland* by Lewis Carroll
*My Antonia* by Willa Cather
*O Pioneers!* by Willa Cather
*The Awakening* by Kate Chopin
*David Copperfield* by Charles Dickens
*Oliver Twist* by Charles Dickens
*A Tale of Two Cities* by Charles Dickens
*Crime and Punishment* by Fyodor Dostoyevsky
*The Three Musketeers* by Alexander Dumas
*The Great Gatsby* by F. Scott Fitzgerald
*Mythology* by Edith Hamilton
*A Farewell to Arms* by Ernest Hemingway
*The Old Man and the Sea* by Ernest Hemingway
*The Sun Also Rises* by Ernest Hemingway
*A Bell for Adano* by John Hersey
*Andersonville* by MacKinley Kantor
*On the Road* by Jack Kerouac
*Kim* by Rudyard Kipling
*The Jungle Book* by Rudyard Kipling
*The Call of the Wild* by Jack London
*White Fang* by Jack London
*A Night to Remember* by Walker Lord
*Moby Dick* by Herman Melville
*Gone With the Wind* by Margaret Mitchell
*Never Cry Wolf* by Farley Mowat

*My Friend Flicka* by John O'Hara
*Cry, the Beloved Country* by Alan Paton
*Atlas Shrugged* by Ayn Rand
*The Fountainhead* by Ayn Rand
*East of Eden* by John Steinbeck
*The Grapes of Wrath* by John Steinbeck
*Of Mice and Men* by John Steinbeck
*Uncle Tom's Cabin* by Harriet Beecher Stowe
*The Adventures of Huckleberry Finn* by Mark Twain
*The Adventures of Tom Sawyer* by Mark Twain
*A Connecticut Yankee in King Arthur's Court* by Mark Twain
*Miss Lonelyhearts/Day of the Locust* by Nathanael West
*The House of Mirth* by Edith Wharton
*Black Boy* by Richard Wright
*Native Son* by Richard Wright

## Edgy, Trendsetting Novels

*3 NBs of Julian Drew* by James Deem
*Middlesex* by Jeffrey Eugenides
*Seek* by Paul Fleischman
*Extremely Loud and Incredibly Close* by Jonathan Safran Foer
*Inexcusable* by Chris Lynch
*Autobiography of My Dead Brother* by Walter Dean Myers
*Fight Club* by Chuck Palahniuk
*33 Snowfish* by Adam Rapp

## Fantasy

*Time Cat* by Lloyd Alexander
*Tuck Everlasting* by Natalie Babbitt
*Flame* by Hilari Bell
*The Folk Keeper* by Franny Billingsley
*Firegold* by Dia Calhoun
*Gregor the Overlander* by Suzanne Collins
*Into the Land of the Unicorn* by Bruce Coville
*The Cup of the World* by John Dickinson
*The Conch Bearer* by Chitra Banerjee Divakaruni
*The Neverending Story* by Michael Ende
*The Oracle Betrayed* by Catherine Fisher
*Red Shift* by Alan Garner

*The Weirdstones of Brisingamen* by Alan Garner
*Across the Nightingale Floor* by Lian Hearn
*Secret Sacrament* by Sheryl Jordan
*Children of the Lamp* by P. B. Kerr
*Arrows of the Queen* by Mercedes Lackey
*The Arm of the Starfish* by Madeleine L'Engle
*Wicked: The Life and Times of the Wicked Witch of the West*
    by Gregory Maguire
*The Squire's Tale* by Gerald Morris
*Magic Circle* by Donna Jo Napoli
*The Wind Singer* by William Nicholson
*Wolf Brother* by Michelle Paver
*Trickster's Choice* by Tamora Pierce
*The Perilous Gard* by Elizabeth Marie Pope
*Haroun and the Sea of Stories* by Salman Rushdie
*Wringer* by Jerry Spinelli
*The Wishing Moon* by Michael O. Tunnell
*The Winter Prince* by Elizabeth Wein
*Borderland* and its sequels, edited by Terri Windling and
    Mark Alan Arnold
*Dealing with Dragons* by Patricia C. Wrede
*The Grand Tour* by Patricia C. Wrede and Caroline Stevermer

## Graphic Novels

*One! Hundred! Demons!* by Lynda Barry
*Electric Girl* by Michael Brennan
*Concrete* by Paul Chadwick
*Clan Apis* by Jay Hosler
*Zero Girl* by Sam Kieth
*Finder* by Carla Speed MacNeil
*The Complete DR and Quinch* by Alan Moore and Alan Davis
*The League of Extraordinary Gentlemen* by Alan Moore
*Palestine and Safe Area Gorazde* by Joe Sacco
*Usagi Yojimbo* by Stan Sakai
*Pedro and Me* by Jude Winick

## Historical Fiction

*Year of Wonders* by Geraldine Brooks
*My Brother Sam Is Dead* by James Lincoln and Christopher Collier

*Johnny Tremain* by Esther Forbes
*Black Jack* by Leon Garfield
*Smith* by Leon Garfield
*Samurai's Tale* by Erik Christian Haugaard
*The Minister's Daughter* by Julie Hearn
*Across Five Aprils* by Irene Hunt
*Rifles by Watie* by Harold Keith
*Goodnight, Mr. Tom* by Michelle Magorian
*Kit's Law* by Donna Morrissey
*The Abduction* by Mette Newthe
*Year Down Yonder* by Richard Peck
*A Day No Pigs Would Die* by Robert Newton Peck
*Breath* by Donna Jo Napoli
*The Yearling* by Marjorie Kinnan Rawlings
*Where the Red Fern Grows* by Wilson Rawls
*The Light in the Forest* by Conrad Richter
*Girl in Blue* by Ann Rinaldi
*Taking Liberty: The Story of Oney Judge, George Washington's Runaway Slave* by Ann Rinaldi
*The Witch of Blackbird Pond* by Elizabeth George Speare
*No Shame, No Fear* by Ann Turnbull
*The Devil's Arithmetic* by Jane Yolen
*Girl in a Cage* by Jane Yolen and Robert J. Harris

## Horror, Ghosts, Gothic

*Jaws* by Peter Benchley
*Tithe* by Holly Black
*The Exorcist* by William Peter Blatty
*Something Wicked This Way Comes* by Ray Bradbury
*Down a Dark Hall* by Lois Duncan
*Locked in Time* by Lois Duncan
*Coraline* by Neil Gaiman
*A Stir of Bones* by Nina Kiriki Hoffman
*The Turn of the Screw* by Henry James
*The Silver Kiss* by Annette Curtis Klause
*Gothic!* by Deborah Noyes
*Witch Child* by Celia Rees
*Vampire High* by Douglas Rees
*Interview with the Vampire* by Anne Rice
*Queen of the Damned* by Anne Rice

*A Density of Souls* by Christopher Rice
*All That Lives* by Melissa Sanderson-Self
*Frankenstein* by Mary Shelley
*The Strange Case of Dr. Jeckyll and Mr. Hyde* by Robert Louis Stevenson
*Dracula* by Bram Stoker
*Blue Is for Nightmares* by Laurie Faria Stolarz
*The Haunting of Alaizabel Cray* by Chris Wooding
*Poison* by Chris Wooding

## Humor

*Prom* by Laurie Halse Anderson
*The Fall of Fergal* by Philip Ardaugh
*Hope Was Here* by Joan Bauer
*Worst Enemies/Best Friends* by Annie Bryant
*The BFG* by Roald Dahl
*The World According to Garp* by John Irving
*Son of the Mob* by Gordon Korman
*Saffy's Angel* by Hilary McKay
*The Education of Robert Nifkin* by Daniel Pinkwater
*Freaky Friday* by Mary Rodgers
*Breakfast of Champions* by Kurt Vonnegut
*Cat's Cradle* by Kurt Vonnegut
*Welcome to the Monkey House* by Kurt Vonnegut
*Girls for Breakfast* by David Yoo

## Information

*The Real Revolution* by Marc Aronson
*Hitler Youth* by Susan Campbell Bartoletti
*Beyond the Myth* by Polly S. Brooks
*Bury My Heart at Wounded Knee* by Dee Brown
*Shadow Life* by Barry Denenberg
*Blink* by Malcolm Gladwell
*Seabiscuit* by Laura Hillenbrand
*Profiles in Courage* by John F. Kennedy
*A Sand County Almanac* by Aldo Leopold
*Darkness over Denmark* by Ellen Levine
*Never to Forget* by Milton Meltzer

*Left for Dead: A Young Man's Search for Justice for the USS Indianapolis*
   by Pete Nelson
*The Orchid Thief: A True Story of Beauty and Obsession* by Susan Orlean
*This Land Was Made for You and Me* by Elizabeth Partridge
*Standing Like a Stone Wall* by James I. Robertson Jr.
*The Planets* by Dava Sobel
*Fear and Loathing on the Campaign Trail* by Hunter Thompson

## Many Cultures/Many Realities

*Go and Come Back* by Joan Abelove
*Things Fall Apart* by Chinua Achebe
*The Fire Next Time* by James Baldwin
*A Hero Ain't Nothing But a Sandwich* by Alice Childress
*The Birchbark House* by Louise Erdrich
*Invisible Man* by Ralph Ellison
*Like Water for Chocolate* by Laura Esquivel
*Seedfolk* by Paul Fleischman
*The Friends* by Rosa Guy
*Roots* by Alex Haley
*Jazz Country* by Nat Hentoff
*Memories of Sun* by Jane Kurtz
*El Bronx Remembered* by Nicholasa Mohr
*House Made of Dawn* by M. Scott Momaday
*The Other Side of Truth* by Beverly Naidoo
*Cuba 15* by Nancy Osa
*When I Was Puerto Rican* by Esmeralda Santiago
*Under the Persimmon Tree* by Suzanne Fisher Staples
*Flyy Girl* by Omar Tyree
*The Star Fisher* by Laurence Yep

## Mystery/Thriller

*Wolf Rider* by Avi
*Angels and Demons* by Dan Brown
*Calling Home* by Michael Cadnum
*The Big Sleep* by Raymond Chandler
*And Then There Were None* by Agatha Christie
*Death on the Nile* by Agatha Christie
*Murder on the Orient Express* by Agatha Christie

*The Face on the Milk Carton* by Caroline B. Cooney
*The Terrorist* by Caroline B. Cooney
*The Great Train Robbery* by Michael Crichton
*I Know What You Did Last Summer* by Lois Duncan
*Playing in Traffic* by Gail Giles
*The Chamber* by John Grisham
*Runaway Jury* by John Grisham
*Deep Waters* by John Herman
*Listening Woman* by Tony Hillerman
*In Darkness, Death* by Dorothy and Thomas Hoobler
*Fell* by M. E. Kerr
*A Deadly Game of Magic* by Joan Lowry Nixon
*The Kidnapping of Christina Lattimore* by Joan Lowry Nixon
*The Boy in the Burning House* by Tim Wynne-Jones

## Plays

*A Taste of Honey* by Shelagh Delaney
*The Diary of Anne Frank* by Frances Goodrich and Albert Hackett
*The Diviners* by Jim Leonard
*The Member of the Wedding* by Carson McCullers
*Awake and Sing!* by Clifford Odets
*The Elephant Man* by Bernard Pomerance
*The Book of Liz* by Amy Sedaris and David Sedaris
*The Foreigner* by Larry Shue
*The Nerd* by Larry Shue
*1776* by Peter Stone and Sherman Edwards
*The Exact Center of the Universe* by Joan Vail Thorne
*The Skin of Our Teeth* by Thornton Wilder
*Fences* by August Wilson

## Poetry and Poetic Novels

*Life Doesn't Frighten Me at All* by John Agard
*My Father's Summers* by Kathi Appelt
*Annie Allen* by Gwendolyn Brooks
*North of Everything* by Craig Crist-Evans
*Witness* by Karen Hesse
*Worlds Afire* by Paul Janeczko
*Shakespeare Bats Cleanup* by Ron Koertge

*The Realm of Possibility* by David Levithan
*A Wreath for Emmett Till* by Marilyn Nelson
*Ariel* by Sylvia Plath
*God Went to Beauty School* by Cynthia Rylant
*The Spoken Revolution: Slam Hip Hop and the Poetry of a New Generation*
   by Marc Smith, editor
*Stop Pretending* by Sonya Sones
*What My Mother Doesn't Know* by Sonya Sones
*Learning to Swim* by Ann Warner Turner
*The Child's Calendar* by John Updike

## Politics and Social Conscience

*The Fire Next Time* by James Baldwin
*Hoot* by Carl Hiassen
*St. Ursula's Girls Against the Atomic Bomb* by Valerie Hurley
*Middle Passage* by Charles Johnson
*The Prince* by Niccolo Machiavelli

## Realistic Fiction

*Durable Goods* by Elizabeth Berg
*Home Before Dark* by Sue Ellen Bridgers
*Gingerbread* by Rachel Cohn
*Celine* by Brock Cole
*Sex Education* by Jenny Davis
*The Skin I'm In* by Sharon G. Flake
*Breakout* by Paul Fleischman
*Breathing Underwater* by Alex Flinn
*The Moonlight Man* by Paula Fox
*One-Eyed Cat* by Paula Fox
*America* by E. R. Frank
*Ellen Foster* by Kaye Gibbons
*I Never Promised You a Rose Garden* by Joanne Greenberg
*Takeoffs and Landings* by Margaret Peterson Haddix
*Geography Club* by Brent Hartinger
*Invisible* by Pete Hautman
*Mr. and Mrs. Bo Jo Jones* by Ann Head
*Looking for Alibrandi* by Melina Marchetta
*When She Was Good* by Norma Fox Mazer

*All the Pretty Horses* by Cormac McCarthy
*Feeling Sorry for Celia* by Jaclyn Moriarty
*Way Past Cool* by Jess Mowry
*Scorpions* by Walter Dean Myers
*Dancing on the Edge* by Han Nolan
*The Language of Goldfish* by Zibby O'Neal
*Bridge to Terabithia* by Katherine Paterson
*A Room on Lorelei Street* by Mary E. Pearson
*Criss Cross* by Lynne Rae Perkins
*My Sister's Keeper* by Jody Picoult
*Bel Canto* by Ann Patchett
*Prep* by Curtis Sittenfeld
*When She Hollers* by Cynthia Voigt
*From the Notebooks of Melanin Sun* by Jacqueline Woodson
*The Dear One* by Jacqueline Woodson

## Religion and Spirituality

*When We Were Saints* by Han Nolan
*Not the End of the World* by Geraldine McCaughrean
*In the Shadow of the Ark* by Anne Provoost
*I Believe in Water: Twelve Brushes with Religion* by Marilyn Singer
*Shadowmancer* by G. P. Taylor

## Romance

*This Lullaby* by Sarah Dessen
*The Grand Sophy* by Georgette Heyer
*These Old Shades* by Georgette Heyer
*Kissing Kate* by Lauren Myracle
*Beast* by Donna Jo Napoli
*The Notebook* by Nicholas Sparks

## Science Fiction

*The Diary of Pelly D.* by L. J. Adlington
*The Foundation* series by Isaac Asimov
*I, Robot* by Isaac Asimov
*The Year of the Hangman* by Gary Blackwood

*The Martian Chronicles* by Ray Bradbury
*2001: A Space Odyssey* by Arthur C. Clarke
*Childhood's End* by Arthur C. Clarke
*Rendezvous with Rama* by Arthur C. Clarke
*Do Androids Dream of Electric Sheep?* by Philip K. Dick
*Among the Hidden* by Margaret Peterson Haddix
*Stranger in a Strange Land* by Robert A. Heinlein
*The Lathe of Heaven* by Ursula K. LeGuin
*The Left Hand of Darkness* by Ursula K. LeGuin
*The Stepford Wives* by Ira Levin
*Animal Farm* by George Orwell
*The Transall Saga* by Gary Paulsen
*The Duplicate* by William Sleator
*The Diamond Age* by Neal Stephenson
*Journey to the Center of the Earth* by Jules Verne
*The Time Machine* by H. G. Wells
*The War of the Worlds* by H. G. Wells

## Short Stories

*Love and Sex* by Michael Cart
*Who Am I Without Him?* by Sharon G. Flake
*Life Is Funny* by E. R. Frank
*Sixteen* by Donald R. Gallo
*The Color of Absence: Stories about Loss and Death* by James Howe
*Black Juice* by Margo Lanagan
*Friends* by Ann M. Martin and David Levithan
*Who Do You Think You Are?* by Hazel Rochman and
    Darlene Z. McCampbell
*Blue Skin of the Sea* by Graham Salisbury
*Help Wanted* by Anita Silvey
*What's in a Name* by Ellen Wittlinger

## Sports

*Roughnecks* by Thomas Cochran
*Crackbat* by John Coy
*Staying Fat for Sarah Byrnes* by Chris Crutcher
*Vision Quest* by Terry Davis
*Painting the Black* by Carl Deuker

*Runner* by Carl Deuker
*In Lane Three, Alex Archer* by Tessa Duder
*Hoop Dreams* by Ben Joravsky
*Danger Zone* by David Klass
*Travel Team* by Mike Lupica
*Gold Dust* by Chris Lynch
*Iceman* by Chris Lynch
*Slam* by Walter Dean Myers
*The Boy Who Saved Baseball* by John H. Ritter
*Taking Sides* by Gary Soto
*Iron Duke* by John Tunis
*Rookie of the Year* by John Tunis
*Farm Team* by Will Weaver
*Hard Ball* by Will Weaver

## War and Conflict

*Band of Brothers* by Stephen E. Ambrose
*Daniel Half Human and the Good Nazi* by David Chotjewitz
*In the Night on Lavale Street* by Jane Leslie Conly
*Heroes* by Robert Cormier
*The Red Badge of Courage* by Stephen Crane
*Bull Run* by Paul Fleischman
*Hear the Wind Blow* by Mary Downing Hahn
*Soldier Boys* by Dean Hughes
*Pagan's Crusade* by Catherine Jinks
*Lord of the Nutcracker Men* by Iain Lawrence
*In the Company of Men* by Nancy Mace
*A Boy at War* by Harry Mazer
*Tree Girl* by Ben Mikaelsen
*Shooter* by Walter Dean Myers
*All Quiet on the Western Front* by Erich Remarque
*Light Years* by Tammar Stein
*Making Up Megaboy* by Virginia Walters
*Machine Gunners* by Robert Westall
*Boy Kills Man* by Matt Whyman
*In Pharaoh's Army* by Tobias Wolff

# Books by Geographic Location

## United States

### ALABAMA

*The Watsons Go to Birmingham — 1963* by Christopher Paul Curtis
*Looking for Alaska* by John Green
*To Kill a Mockingbird* by Harper Lee

### ALASKA

*Touching Spirit Bear* by Ben Mikaelsen
*Winterdance* by Gary Paulsen

### AMERICAN WEST

*The Perilous Journey of the Donner Party* by Marian Calabro
*Lonesome Dove* by Larry McMurtry

### ARIZONA

*Downriver* by Will Hobbs
*Arizona Kid* by Ron Koertge
*Stargirl* by Jerry Spinelli

### ARKANSAS

*I Know Why the Caged Bird Sings* by Maya Angelou
*Summer of My German Soldier* by Bette Greene
*True Grit* by Charles Portis

## CALIFORNIA

*A Step from Heaven* by An Na
*Weetzie Bat* by Francesca Lia Block
*Kindred* by Octavia E. Butler
*The Perilous Journey of the Donner Party* by Marian Calabro
*Al Capone Does My Shirts* by Gennifer Choldenko
*Ball Don't Lie* by Matt de la Peña
*A Heartbreaking Work of Staggering Genius* by Dave Eggers
*The Spirit Catches You and You Fall Down* by Anne Fadiman
*White Oleander* by Janet Fitch
*The Kite Runner* by Khaled Hosseini
*Farewell to Manzanar* by Jeanne Wakatsuki Houston and James D. Houston
*The Adventures of Blue Avenger* by Norma Howe
*The Circuit* by Francisco Jiménez
*Parrot in the Oven: Mi Vida* by Victor Martinez
*Babylon Boys* by Jess Mowry
*When the Emperor Was Divine* by Julie Otsuka
*Buried Onions* by Gary Soto
*The Joy Luck Club* by Amy Tan
*Rats Saw God* by Rob Thomas
*Child of the Owl* by Laurence Yep
*Dragonwings* by Laurence Yep

## COLORADO

*Plainsong* by Kent Haruf

## CONNECTICUT

*I Know This Much Is True* by Wally Lamb
*The Night Country* by Stewart O'Nan
*Ah, Wilderness!* by Eugene O'Neill
*Homecoming* by Cynthia Voigt

## DISTRICT OF COLUMBIA

*Second Sight* by Gary Blackwood

## FLORIDA

*Tangerine* by Edward Bloor
*Nickel and Dimed* by Barbara Ehrenreich
*Their Eyes Were Watching God* by Zora Neale Hurston

## GEORGIA

*Cold Sassy Tree* by Olive Ann Burns
*The Last Night of Ballyhoo* by Alfred Uhry

*The Color Purple* by Alice Walker
*Jubilee* by Margaret Walker
*Like Sisters on the Homefront* by Rita Williams-Garcia

### HAWAII

*Under the Blood-Red Sky* by Graham Salisbury

### ILLINOIS

*Rules of the Road* by Joan Bauer
*Dandelion Wine* by Ray Bradbury
*The House on Mango Street* by Sandra Cisneros
*Things Not Seen* by Andrew Clements
*Getting Away with Murder* by Chris Crowe
*Say Goodnight, Gracie* by Julie Reece Deaver
*A Heartbreaking Work of Staggering Genius* by Dave Eggers
*A Raisin in the Sun* by Lorraine Hansberry
*No Promises in the Wind* by Irene Hunt
*The Devil in the White City* by Erik Larson
*A Long Way from Chicago* by Richard Peck
*The River Between Us* by Richard Peck

### INDIANA

*Running Out of Time* by Margaret Peterson Haddix
*The Teacher's Funeral* by Richard Peck

### IOWA

*Squashed* by Joan Bauer
*Shoeless Joe* by W. P. Kinsella

### KANSAS

*In Cold Blood* by Truman Capote

### KENTUCKY

*Hole in My Life* by Jack Gantos
*In Country* by Bobbie Ann Mason
*Beloved* by Toni Morrison

### LOUISIANA

*A Lesson Before Dying* by Ernest J. Gaines
*The Vampire Lestat* by Anne Rice
*A Confederacy of Dunces* by John Kennedy Toole

### MAINE

*The Long Walk* by Richard Bachman

*Nickel and Dimed* by Barbara Ehrenreich
*The Killer Angels* by Michael Shaara
*Lizzie Bright and the Buckminster Boy* by Gary D. Schmidt

### MARYLAND

*Kindred* by Octavia E. Butler
*Blood and Chocolate* by Annette Curtis Klause
*Jacob Have I Loved* by Katherine Paterson
*Homecoming* by Cynthia Voigt
*The Runner* by Cynthia Voigt

### MASSACHUSETTS

*Thirsty* by M. T. Anderson
*Running with Scissors* by Augusten Burroughs
*The Chocolate War* by Robert Cormier
*Fade* by Robert Cormier
*I Am the Cheese* by Robert Cormier
*Blackbird House* by Alice Hoffman
*The Perfect Storm* by Sebastian Junger
*The Crucible* by Arthur Miller
*Lyddie* by Katherine Paterson
*Revenge of the Whale* by Nathaniel Philbrick

### MICHIGAN

*Bud, Not Buddy* by Christopher Paul Curtis
*The Watsons Go to Birmingham — 1963* by Christopher Paul Curtis

### MINNESOTA

*Nickel and Dimed* by Barbara Ehrenreich
*The Unlikely Romance of Kate Bjorkman* by Louise Plummer

### MISSISSIPPI

*Getting Away with Murder* by Chris Crowe
*The Last Juror* by John Grisham
*Crimes of the Heart* by Beth Henley
*My Dog Skip* by Willie Morris
*Roll of Thunder, Hear My Cry* by Mildred D. Taylor

### MISSOURI

*I Know Why the Caged Bird Sings* by Maya Angelou

### MONTANA

*A Yellow Raft in Blue Water* by Michael Dorris

*A River Runs Through It and Other Stories* by Norman Maclean
*Young Men and Fire* by Norman Maclean
*Lonesome Dove* by Larry McMurtry
*Montana 1948* by Larry Watson

### NEVADA

*Bringing Down the House* by Ben Mezrich

### NEW JERSEY

*An Island Like You* by Judith Ortiz Cofer
*Cheaper by the Dozen* by Frank B. Gilbreth Jr. and
    Ernestine Gilbreth Carey
*Washington's Crossing* by David Hackett Fischer
*Born Confused* by Tanuja Desai Hidier
*The Body of Christopher Creed* by Carol Plum-Ucci
*Confessions of a Teenage Drama Queen* by Dyan Sheldon
*The Plot Against America* by Philip Roth

### NEW HAMPSHIRE

*A Separate Peace* by John Knowles
*A Prayer for Owen Meany* by John Irving
*Light on Snow* by Anita Shreve
*Our Town* by Thornton Wilder

### NEW MEXICO

*Bless Me, Ultima* by Rudolf Anaya
*The Wailing Wind* by Tony Hillerman
*Sammy and Juliana in Hollywood* by Benjamin Alier Saenz

### NEW YORK

*How the García Girls Lost Their Accents* by Julia Alvarez
*Proof* by David Auburn
*Rule of the Bone* by Russell Banks
*The Princess Diaries* by Meg Cabot
*Breakfast at Tiffany's* by Truman Capote
*The Alienist* by Caleb Carr
*The Amazing Adventures of Kavalier & Clay* by Michael Chabon
*Remember Me to Harold Square* by Paula Danziger
*A Northern Light* by Jennifer Donnelly
*My Heartbeat* by Garret Freymann-Weyr
*Hole in My Life* by Jack Gantos
*Annie on My Mind* by Nancy Garden
*My Side of the Mountain* by Jean Craighead George

*Andy Warhol* by Jan Greenberg and Sandra Jordan
*Snow in August* by Pete Hamill
*Selected Poems of Langston Hughes* by Langston Hughes
*Gentlehands* by M. E. Kerr
*Last Days of Summer* by Steve Kluger
*Rent* by Jonathan Larson
*West Side Story* by Arthur Laurents
*Rosemary's Baby* by Ira Levin
*The Contender* by Robert Lipsyte
*Angela's Ashes* by Frank McCourt
*Bad Boy* by Walter Dean Myers
*Here in Harlem* by Walter Dean Myers
*Hoops* by Walter Dean Myers
*145th Street* by Walter Dean Myers
*John Lennon* by Elizabeth Partridge
*The Bell Jar* by Sylvia Plath
*The Sherwood Ring* by Elizabeth Marie Pope
*Imani All Mine* by Connie Porter
*The Chosen* by Chaim Potok
*Skinny Legs and All* by Tom Robbins
*The Catcher in the Rye* by J. D. Salinger
*The Schwa Was Here* by Neal Shusterman
*Brighton Beach Memoirs* by Neil Simon
*Lost in Yonkers* by Neil Simon
*A Tree Grows in Brooklyn* by Betty Smith
*Maus I* by Art Spiegelman
*If You Come Softly* by Jacqueline Woodson
*Companions of the Night* by Vivian Vande Velde

NORTH CAROLINA

*The Moves Make the Man* by Bruce Brooks
*Cold Mountain* by Charles Frazier
*Ghost Riders* by Sharyn McCrumb
*Me Talk Pretty One Day* by David Sedaris
*Surviving the Applewhites* by Stephanie S. Tolan

NORTH DAKOTA

*Peace Like a River* by Leif Enger

OHIO

*Winesburg, Ohio* by Sherwood Anderson
*The House of Dies Drear* by Virginia Hamilton
*Beloved* by Toni Morrison

OKLAHOMA

*Out of the Dust* by Karen Hesse
*The Outsiders* by S. E. Hinton
*Stop the Train!* by Geraldine McCaughrean

OREGON

*Wild Life* by Molly Gloss
*One Flew Over the Cuckoo's Nest* by Ken Kesey
*Bat 6* by Virginia Euwer Wolff

PENNSYLVANIA

*Fever 1793* by Laurie Halse Anderson
*Washington's Crossing* by David Hackett Fisher
*Andy Warhol* by Jan Greenberg and Sandra Jordan
*An American Plague* by Jim Murphy
*Z for Zachariah* by Robert C. O'Brien
*The Killer Angels* by Michael Shaara
*Wrestling Sturbridge* by Rich Wallace

SOUTH CAROLINA

*The Secret Life of Bees* by Sue Monk Kidd

TENNESSEE

*Inherit the Wind* by Jerome Lawrence and Robert E. Lee

TEXAS

*When Zachary Beaver Came to Town* by Kimberly Willis Holt
*Lonesome Dove* by Larry McMurtry
*Holes* by Louis Sachar
*Rats Saw God* by Rob Thomas

UTAH

*This Boy's Life* by Tobias Wolff

VERMONT

*Phineas Gage* by John Fleischman
*The Secret History* by Donna Tartt

WASHINGTON

*Ironman* by Chris Crutcher
*On the Devil's Court* by Carl Deuker
*Snow Falling on Cedars* by David Guterson
*Is Kissing a Girl Who Smokes Like Licking an Ashtray?* by Randy Powell
*This Boy's Life* by Tobias Wolff

WEST VIRGINIA
*Rocket Boys* by Homer Hickam

WISCONSIN
*Seventeenth Summer* by Maureen Daly
*The Game of Silence* by Louise Erdrich
*The Dive from Clausen's Pier* by Ann Packer
*Blankets* by Craig Thompson

WYOMING
*Shane* by Jack Schaefer

## World

AFGHANISTAN
*The Breadwinner* by Deborah Ellis
*The Kite Runner* by Khaled Hosseini

AFRICA
*The Middle Passage* by Tom Feelings
*Chanda's Secret* by Allan Stratton

ANTARCTICA
*Endurance* by Alfred Lansing
*Shackleton's Stowaway* by Victoria McKernan

ANTIGUA
*Annie John* by Jamaica Kincaid

AUSTRALIA
*Sleeping Dogs* by Sonya Hartnett
*Letters from the Inside* by John Marsden
*Tomorrow, When the War Began* by John Marsden
*The Year of Secret Assignments* by Jaclyn Moriarty
*I Am the Messenger* by Markus Zusak

BOTSWANA
*The No. 1 Ladies' Detective Agency* by Alexander McCall Smith

CAMBODIA
*Children of the River* by Linda Crew

CANADA

*Maya Running* by Anjali Banerjee
*True Confessions of a Heartless Girl* by Martha Brooks
*Mrs. Mike* by Benedict and Nancy Freedman
*B for Buster* by Iain Lawrence
*The Lightkeeper's Daughter* by Iain Lawrence
*Life of Pi* by Yann Martel
*Acceleration* by Graham McNamee
*Hatchet* by Gary Paulsen

CHINA

*Golden Child* by David Henry Hwang
*Balzac and the Little Chinese Seamstress* by Dai Sijie

COSTA RICA

*Jurassic Park* by Michael Crichton

CZECHOSLOVAKIA

*The Amazing Adventures of Kavalier & Clay* by Michael Chabon
*The Last Mission* by Harry Mazer

DOMINICAN REPUBLIC

*How the García Girls Lost Their Accents* by Julia Alvarez
*In the Time of the Butterflies* by Julia Alvarez

EGYPT

*The Red Tent* by Anita Diamant
*Sarah* by Marek Halter

ENGLAND

*Watership Down* by Richard Adams
*Kit's Wilderness* by David Almond
*Skellig* by David Almond
*The Lost Years of Merlin* by T. A. Barron
*Tamsin* by Peter S. Beagle
*The China Garden* by Liz Berry
*The Shakespeare Stealer* by Gary Blackwood
*The Mists of Avalon* by Marion Zimmer Bradley
*A Great and Terrible Beauty* by Libba Bray
*Lucas* by Kevin Brooks
*The Da Vinci Code* by Dan Brown
*Doing It* by Melvin Burgess

*The Seeing Stone* by Kevin Crossley-Hollan
*Boy* by Roald Dahl
*The Last Apprentice* by Joseph Delaney
*The Hound of the Baskervilles* by Arthur Conan Doyle
*The Eyre Affair* by Jasper Fforde
*Flour Babies* by Ann Fine
*The Curious Incident of the Dog in the Night-Time* by Mark Haddon
*A Long Way Down* by Nick Hornby
*Brave New World* by Aldous Huxley
*Charmed Life* by Diana Wynne Jones
*The Beekeeper's Apprentice* by Laurie R. King
*B for Buster* by Iain Lawrence
*The Wreckers* by Iain Lawrence
*The Fifth Child* by Doris Lessing
*The Lion, the Witch, and the Wardrobe* by C. S. Lewis
*Atonement* by Ian McEwan
*Indigo's Star* by Hilary McKay
*Mary, Bloody Mary* by Carolyn Meyer
*Private Peaceful* by Michael Morpurgo
*1984* by George Orwell
*John Lennon* by Elizabeth Partridge
*The Golden Compass* by Philip Pullman
*The Ruby in the Smoke* by Philip Pullman
*Mortal Engines* by Philip Reeve
*Angus, Thongs and Full-Frontal Snogging* by Louise Rennison
*How I Live Now* by Meg Rosoff
*Harry Potter and the Sorcerer's Stone* by J. K. Rowling
*Longitude* by Dava Sobel
*I Capture the Castle* by Dodie Smith
*Kipling's Choice* by Geert Spillebeen
*The Crystal Cave* by Mary Stewart
*The Shining Company* by Rosemary Sutcliff
*The Tale of One Bad Rat* by Bryan Talbot
*Behind the Mask* by Jane Resh Thomas
*The Secret Diary of Adrian Mole, Aged 13¾* by Sue Townsend
*Montmorency* by Eleanor Updale
*The Once and Future King* by T. H. White
*Doomsday Book* by Connie Willis
*To Say Nothing of the Dog* by Connie Willis
*The Professor and the Madman* by Simon Winchester
*Sorcery & Cecelia or the Enchanted Chocolate Pot* by Patricia C. Wrede and
  Caroline Stevermer

## FRANCE

*The Da Vinci Code* by Dan Brown
*Under the War-Torn Sky* by L. M. Elliott
*Zazoo* by Richard Moser
*Me Talk Pretty One Day* by David Sedaris
*Kipling's Choice* by Geert Spillebeen

## GERMANY

*The Life and Death of Adolf Hitler* by James Cross Giblin
*Slaughterhouse-Five or The Children's Crusade* by Kurt Vonnegut
*Soldier X* by Don Wulffson

## GREECE

*Corelli's Mandolin* by Louis De Bernières
*Troy* by Adèle Geras

## GUAM

*Keeper of the Night* by Kimberly Willis Holt

## INDIA

*Interpreter of Maladies* by Jhumpa Lahiri
*Life of Pi* by Yann Martel
*Homeless Bird* by Gloria Whelan

## IRAN

*Persepolis* by Marjane Satrapi

## IRELAND

*Angela's Ashes* by Frank McCourt

## ISRAEL

*The Red Tent* by Anita Diamant
*Mary, Called Magdalene* by Margaret George
*Real Time* by Pnina Moed Kass
*Habibi* by Naomi Shihab Nye
*Sarah* by Marek Halter
*The Bronze Bow* by Elizabeth George Speare

## ITALY

*The Thief Lord* by Cornelia Funke
*Catch-22* by Joseph Heller

## IWO JIMA

*Flags of Our Fathers* by James Bradley

JAMAICA
*Rule of the Bone* by Russell Banks

JAPAN
*Lone Wolf and Cub* by Kazuo Koike
*Shizuko's Daughter* by Kyoko Mori

KOREA
*A Step from Heaven* by An Na
*When My Name Was Keoko* by Linda Sue Park
*So Far from the Bamboo Grove* by Yoko Kawashima Watkins

MEXICO
*The Circuit* by Francisco Jiménez
*Esperanza Rising* by Pam Muñoz Ryan

NEPAL
*Into Thin Air* by Jon Krakauer

THE NETHERLANDS
*Postcards from No Man's Land* by Aidan Chambers
*Girl with a Pearl Earring* by Tracy Chevalier
*The Diary of a Young Girl* by Anne Frank

NEW ZEALAND
*Whale Rider* by Witi Ihimeara
*The Catalogue of the Universe* by Margaret Mahy
*The Changeover* by Margaret Mahy

NORWAY
*East* by Edith Pattou

PAKISTAN
*Shabanu* by Suzanne Fisher Staples

PERU
*Touching the Void* by Joe Simpson

PHILIPPINES
*Ghost Soldiers* by Hampton Sides

POLAND
*The Man from the Other Side* by Uri Orlev
*Night* by Elie Wiesel
*Briar Rose* by Jane Yolen

**PUERTO RICO**
*An Island Like You* by Judith Ortiz Cofer
*The Meaning of Consuelo* by Judith Ortiz Cofer

**RUSSIA**
*An Innocent Soldier* by Josef Holub
*Soldier X* by Don Wulffson

**ST. CROIX**
*Hole in My Life* by Jack Gantos

**SOMALIA**
*Black Hawk Down* by Mark Bowden

**SOUTH AFRICA**
*Many Stones* by Carolyn Coman
*"Master Harold"... and the boys* by Athol Fugard
*Somehow Tenderness Survives* by Hazel Rochman

**SOUTH AMERICA**
*One Hundred Years of Solitude* by Gabriel García Márquez

**SPAIN**
*The Alchemist* by Paulo Coelho
*The Shadow of the Wind* by Carlos Ruíz Zafón

**SWITZERLAND**
*Zel* by Donna Jo Napoli

**TIBET**
*Into Thin Air* by Jon Krakauer

**TRANSYLVANIA**
*Night* by Elie Wiesel

**TURKEY**
*Forgotten Fire* by Adam Bagdasarian
*Mosque* by David Macaulay

**VIETNAM**
*Fallen Angels* by Walter Dean Myers
*The Things They Carried* by Tim O'Brien

ZAIRE

*The Poisonwood Bible* by Barbara Kingsolver

ZIMBABWE

*The Ear, the Eye and the Arm* by Nancy Farmer

# Books by Historical Time Line

1500 B.C.

*The Red Tent* by Anita Diamant
*Sarah* by Marek Halter

FIRST CENTURY

*Mary, Called Magdalene* by Margaret George
*The Bronze Bow* by Elizabeth George Speare

FIFTH–SIXTH CENTURY

*The Mists of Avalon* by Marion Zimmer Bradley
*The Crystal Cave* by Mary Stewart
*The Once and Future King* by T. H. White

SEVENTH CENTURY

*The Shining Company* by Rosemary Sutcliff

EIGHTH CENTURY

*The Sea of Trolls* by Nancy Farmer

TWELFTH CENTURY

*The Seeing Stone* by Kevin Crossley-Holland
*Catherine, Called Birdy* by Karen Cushman

THIRTEENTH CENTURY

*A Distant Mirror* by Barbara W. Tuchman
*Doomsday Book* by Connie Willis

**1500S**

*Sir Walter Ralegh* by Marc Aronson
*Mary, Bloody Mary* by Carolyn Meyer
*Mosque* by David Macaulay
*Zel* by Donna Jo Napoli
*East* by Edith Pattou
*Romeo and Juliet* by William Shakespeare
*Behind the Mask* by Jane Resh Thomas

**1600S**

*Sir Walter Ralegh* by Marc Aronson
*The Shakespeare Stealer* by Gary Blackwood
*Girl with a Pearl Earring* by Tracy Chevalier
*Under the Black Flag* by David Cordingly
*The Crucible* by Arthur Miller

**1700–1775**

*Under the Black Flag* by David Cordingly
*Longitude* by Dava Sobel

**REVOLUTIONARY WAR**

*Washington's Crossing* by David Hackett Fischer
*1776* by David McCullough
*The Sherwood Ring* by Elizabeth Marie Pope

**1780–1799**

*Fever 1793* by Laurie Halse Anderson
*Founding Brothers* by Joseph H. Ellis
*The Wreckers* by Iain Lawrence
*An American Plague* by Jim Murphy

**1800–1839**

*Undaunted Courage* by Stephen E. Ambrose
*Kindred* by Octavia E. Butler
*An Innocent Soldier* by Josef Holub
*Master and Commander* by Patrick O'Brian
*Revenge of the Whale* by Nathaniel Philbrick
*Sorcery & Cecelia or the Enchanted Chocolate Pot* by Patricia C. Wrede and
    Caroline Stevermer
*New Found Land* by Allan Wolf

**1840–1865**

*The Perilous Journey of the Donner Party* by Marian Calabor
*The Game of Silence* by Louise Erdrich

*Phineas Gage* by John Fleischman
*Good Brother, Bad Brother* by James Cross Giblin
*Running Out of Time* by Margaret Peterson Haddix
*The House of Dies Drear* by Virginia Hamilton
*Beloved* by Toni Morrison
*Lyddie* by Katherine Paterson

CIVIL WAR

*Second Sight* by Gary Blackwood
*Cold Mountain* by Charles Frazier
*Good Brother, Bad Brother* by James Cross Giblin
*Ghost Riders* by Sharyn McCrumb
*The River Between Us* by Richard Peck
*The Killer Angels* by Michael Shaara
*The Guns of the South* by Harry Turtledove

1870–1899

*A Great and Terrible Beauty* by Libba Bray
*The Alienist* by Caleb Carr
*The Hound of the Baskervilles* by Arthur Conan Doyle
*The Devil in the White City* by Erik Larson
*Stop the Train!* by Geraldine McCaughrean
*Beloved* by Toni Morrison
*True Grit* by Charles Portis
*The Ruby in the Smoke* by Philip Pullman
*Shane* by Jack Schaefer
*Montmorency* by Eleanor Updale
*Jubilee* by Margaret Walker
*The Professor and the Madman* by Simon Winchester

1900–1919

*Winesburg, Ohio* by Sherwood Anderson
*Forgotten Fire* by Adam Bagdasarian
*Cold Sassy Tree* by Olive Ann Burns
*A Northern Light* by Jennifer Donnelly
*Mrs. Mike* by Benedict and Nancy Freedman
*Cheaper by the Dozen* by Frank B. Gilbreth Jr. and
    Ernestine Gilbreth Carey
*Wild Life* by Molly Gloss
*Golden Child* by David Henry Hwang
*Endurance* by Alfred Lansing
*Shackleton's Stowaway* by Victoria McKernan
*Carver* by Marilyn Nelson

*Ah, Wilderness!* by Eugene O'Neill
*The Teacher's Funeral* by Richard Peck
*Lizzie Bright and the Buckminster Boy* by Gary D. Schmidt
*A Tree Grows in Brooklyn* by Betty Smith
*The Color Purple* by Alice Walker
*Our Town* by Thornton Wilder
*Dragonwings* by Laurence Yep

### WORLD WAR I

*Private Peaceful* by Michael Morpurgo
*Kipling's Choice* by Geert Spillebeen

### 1920–1945

*Dandelion Wine* by Ray Bradbury
*The Amazing Adventures of Kavalier & Clay* by Michael Chabon
*Al Capone Does My Shirts* by Gennifer Choldenko
*Fade* by Robert Cormier
*Bud, Not Buddy* by Christopher Paul Curtis
*Seventeenth Summer* by Maureen Daly
*Eleanor Roosevelt* by Russell Freedman
*Marian Anderson* by Russell Freedman
*A Lesson Before Dying* by Ernest J. Gaines
*The Life and Death of Adolf Hitler* by James Cross Giblin
*Out of the Dust* by Karen Hesse
*Selected Poems of Langston Hughes* by Langston Hughes
*No Promises in the Wind* by Irene Hunt
*The Circuit* by Francisco Jiménez
*The Beekeeper's Apprentice* by Laurie R. King
*Last Days of Summer* by Steve Kluger
*A Separate Peace* by John Knowles
*Inherit the Wind* by Jerome Lawrence and Robert E. Lee
*To Kill a Mockingbird* by Harper Lee
*Angela's Ashes* by Frank McCourt
*The Heart Is a Lonely Hunter* by Carson McCullers
*Atonement* by Ian McEwan
*My Dog Skip* by Willie Morris
*Bad Boy* by Walter Dean Myers
*A Long Way from Chicago* by Richard Peck
*Bell Jar* by Sylvia Plath
*The Plot Against America* by Philip Roth
*Esperanza Rising* by Pam Muñoz Ryan
*Something Permanent* by Cynthia Rylant
*Brighton Beach Memoirs* by Neil Simon

*Roll of Thunder, Hear My Cry* by Mildred Taylor
*The Last Night of Ballyhoo* by Alfred Uhry

WORLD WAR II

*Flags of Our Fathers* by James Bradley
*Corelli's Mandolin* by Louis De Bernières
*The Amazing Adventures of Kavalier & Clay* by Michael Chabon
*Postcards from No Man's Land* by Aidan Chambers
*Under a War-Torn Sky* by L. M. Elliott
*The Diary of a Young Girl* by Anne Frank
*Eleanor Roosevelt* by Russell Freedman
*The Life and Death of Adolf Hitler* by James Cross Giblin
*Summer of My German Soldier* by Bette Greene
*Catch-22* by Joseph Heller
*Farewell to Manzanar* by Jeanne Wakatsuki Houston and James D. Houston
*Gentlehands* by M. E. Kerr
*B for Buster* by Iain Lawrence
*The Last Mission* by Harry Mazer
*Atonement* by Ian McEwan
*The Man from the Other Side* by Uri Orlev
*When the Emperor Was Divine* by Julie Otsuka
*When My Name Was Keoko* by Linda Sue Park
*Jacob Have I Loved* by Katherine Paterson
*Under the Blood-Red Sun* by Graham Salisbury
*Ghost Soldiers* by Hampton Sides
*Lost in Yonkers* by Neil Simon
*Maus I* by Art Spiegelman
*Slaughterhouse-Five or The Children's Crusade* by Kurt Vonnegut
*So Far from the Bamboo Grove* by Yoko Kawashima Watkins
*Night* by Elie Wiesel
*To Say Nothing of the Dog* by Connie Willis
*Soldier X* by Don Wulffson
*Briar Rose* by Jane Yolen

1946–1959

*In Cold Blood* by Truman Capote
*The Amazing Adventures of Kavalier & Clay* by Michael Chabon
*The Meaning of Consuelo* by Judith Ortiz Cofer
*Getting Away with Murder* by Chris Crowe
*"Master Harold" . . . and the boys* by Athol Fugard
*Snow Falling on Cedars* by David Guterson
*Snow in August* by Pete Hamill
*Rocket Boys* by Homer Hickam

*The Poisonwood Bible* by Barbara Kingsolver
*Young Men and Fire* by Norman Maclean
*Here in Harlem* by Walter Dean Myers
*The Chosen* by Chaim Potok
*In the Shadow of the Wind* by Carlos Ruíz Zafón
*Montana 1948* by Larry Watson
*This Boy's Life* by Tobias Wolff
*Bat 6* by Virginia Euwer Wolff

## 1960–1979

*How the García Girls Lost Their Accents* by Julia Alvarez
*In the Time of the Butterflies* by Julia Alvarez
*Go Ask Alice* by Anonymous (Beatrice Sparks)
*Maya Running* by Anjali Banerjee
*Running with Scissors* by Augusten Burroughs
*Kindred* by Octavia E. Butler
*Children of the River* by Linda Crew
*The Watsons Go to Birmingham — 1963* by Christopher Paul Curtis
*Andy Warhol* by Jan Greenberg and Sandra Jordan
*The Last Juror* by John Grisham
*When Zachary Beaver Came to Town* by Kimberly Willis Holt
*Gentlehands* by M. E. Kerr
*The Secret Life of Bees* by Sue Monk Kidd
*The Historian* by Elizabeth Kostova
*The Fifth Child* by Doris Lessing
*Rosemary's Baby* by Ira Levin
*A Corner of the Universe* by Ann M. Martin
*In Country* by Bobbie Ann Mason
*Fallen Angels* by Walter Dean Myers
*The Things They Carried* by Tim O'Brien
*John Lennon* by Elizabeth Partridge
*Sammy and Juliana in Hollywood* by Benjamin Alier Saenz
*The Lovely Bones* by Alice Sebold
*Balzac and the Little Chinese Seamstress* by Dai Sijie
*A Confederacy of Dunces* by John Kennedy Toole
*The Runner* by Cynthia Voigt
*Child of the Owl* by Laurence Yep

## 1980–1989

*The Spirit Catches You and You Fall Down* by Anne Fadiman
*Rent* by Jonathan Larson
*The Vampire Lestat* by Anne Rice
*Persepolis* by Marjane Satrapi

*Touching the Void* by Joe Simpson
*The Secret Diary of Adrian Mole, Aged 13¾* by Sue Townsend

1990–PRESENT

*Black Hawk Down* by Mark Bowden
*Postcards from No Man's Land* by Aidan Chambers
*Nickel and Dimed* by Barbara Ehrenreich
*Running Out of Time* by Margaret Peterson Haddix
*The Kite Runner* by Khaled Hosseini
*The Perfect Storm* by Sebastian Junger
*Real Time* by Pnina Moed Kass
*Into Thin Air* by Jon Krakauer
*Fast Food Nation* by Eric Schlosser

# Recommended Audio Books

As mentioned in the Acknowledgments, Ellen Myrick, Tracy Taylor, and Jeannine Wiese helped to prepare this section.

## Ages 12–14

*The Lost Years of Merlin* by T. A. Barron (Listening Library)
*The Sisterhood of the Traveling Pants* by Ann Brashares (Listening Library)
*The Watsons Go to Birmingham — 1963* by Christopher Paul Curtis
  (Listening Library)
*Catherine, Called Birdy* by Karen Cushman (Listening Library)
*The City of Ember* by Jeanne DuPrau (Listening Library)
*Inkheart* by Cornelia Funke (Listening Library)
*When Zachary Beaver Came to Town* by Kimberly Willis Holt
  (Listening Library)
*Redwall* by Brian Jacques (Listening Library)
*The Giver* by Lois Lowry (Listening Library)
*Stop the Train!* by Geraldine McCaughrean (Full Cast Audio)
*A Year Down Yonder* by Richard Peck (Listening Library)
*The Last Book in the Universe* by Rodman Philbrick (Listening Library)
*Alanna* quartet by Tamora Pierce (Listening Library)
*Harry Potter and the Sorcerer's Stone* by J. K. Rowling (Listening Library)
*Holes* by Louis Sachar (Listening Library)
*Bartimaeus* trilogy by Jonathan Stroud (Listening Library)
*Surviving the Applewhites* by Stephanie S. Tolan (HarperAudio)

*Montmorency* by Eleanor Updale (Listening Library)
*Flipped* by Wendelin Van Draanen (Recorded Books)
*Homeless Bird* by Gloria Whelan (Listening Library)

## Ages 12–18

*Feed* by M. T. Anderson (Listening Library)
*A Great and Terrible Beauty* by Libba Bray (Listening Library)
*The House on Mango Street* by Sandra Cisneros (Random House)
*The Chocolate War* by Robert Cormier (Listening Library)
*A Northern Light* by Jennifer Donnelly (Listening Library)
*House of the Scorpion* by Nancy Farmer (Recorded Books)
*Keesha's House* by Helen Frost (Recorded Books)
*Fat Kid Rules the World* by K. L. Going (Listening Library)
*The Outsiders* by S. E. Hinton (Listening Library, Chivers)
*Brave New World* by Aldous Huxley (Audio Partners)
*The First Part Last* by Angela Johnson (Listening Library)
*The Earth, My Butt and Other Big Round Things* by Carolyn Mackler
   (Recorded Books)
*Tomorrow, When the War Began* by John Marsden (Bolinda Audio)
*Monster* by Walter Dean Myers (Listening Library)
*Sabriel* trilogy by Garth Nix (Listening Library)
*His Dark Materials* trilogy by Philip Pullman (Listening Library)
*The Ruby in the Smoke* by Philip Pullman (Listening Library)
*Romeo and Juliet* by William Shakespeare (Audio Partners)
*I Capture the Castle* by Dodie Smith (Audio Partners, BBC Audiobooks/
   Chivers, unabridged, limited availability)
*The Gospel According to Larry* by Janet Tashjian (Listening Library)
*The Lord of the Rings* by J.R.R. Tolkien (Books on Tape, Highbridge)
*The Secret Diary of Adrian Mole, Aged 13¾* by Sue Townsend (Chivers)
*Stuck in Neutral* by Terry Trueman (Recorded Books)
*Night* by Elie Wiesel (Audio Bookshelf, Recorded Books)
*Hard Love* by Ellen Wittlinger (Listening Library)

## Ages 14–18

*I Know Why the Caged Bird Sings* by Maya Angelou (Random House)
*The Handmaid's Tale* by Margaret Atwood (BBC)
*The Amazing Adventures of Kavalier & Clay* by Michael Chabon
   (Brilliance Audio)

*Girl with a Pearl Earring* by Tracy Chevalier (Highbridge, Recorded Books)

*The Red Tent* by Anita Diamant (Audio Renaissance)

*A Lesson Before Dying* by Ernest J. Gaines (Books on Tape, Random House)

*The Kite Runner* by Khaled Hosseini (Simon & Schuster)

*Good Poems* by Garrison Keillor (Highbridge)

*The Secret Life of Bees* by Sue Monk Kidd (Highbridge)

*The Historian* by Elizabeth Kostova (Time Warner)

*Into Thin Air* by Jon Krakauer (Random House, Books on Tape)

*Dragonflight, Dragonquest, White Dragon* by Anne McCaffrey (Brilliance Audio)

*Ghost Riders* by Sharyn McCrumb (Brilliance)

*1776* by David McCullough (Simon & Schuster)

*Master and Commander* by Patrick O'Brian (Random House, Books on Tape)

*When the Emperor Was Divine* by Julie Otsuka (Random House)

*Me Talk Pretty One Day* by David Sedaris (Time Warner)

*Killer Angels* by Michael Shaara (Random House, Books on Tape)

*The No. 1 Ladies' Detective Agency* by Alexander McCall Smith (Recorded Books)

*A Confederacy of Dunces* by John Kennedy Toole (Blackstone Audio)

# Index